OPPORTUNITY AND UNCERTAINTY:
LIFE COURSE EXPERIENCES OF THE CLASS OF '73

Paul Anisef, Paul Axelrod, Etta Baichman-Anisef, Carl James, and Anton Turrittin

Based on the longest-running survey of its kind in Canada, this book examines events in the lives of a generation of Ontario residents who graduated from grade twelve in 1973. The study recreates the world of the early 1970s in which these high school students faced the future. It recounts their educational and occupational experiences in the late 1970s, follows their vocational and career pathways during the subsequent decade, and searches for patterns in their personal and family lives through the late 1980s and early 1990s.

By painting a portrait of a little-known cohort, this interdisciplinary project provides a wealth of information about the links between schooling and employment in a time of economic instability and addresses the different ways in which women and men attempt to reconcile familial and occupational demands. The study employs life course theory, which explores the dynamic relationship between the individual and the social order. Structural forces such as social class, gender, ethnicity, and race played an unmistakable role in the lives of the Class of '73. So, too, did human agency. Using survey research, historical documentation, in-depth interviews, and personal biographies, the authors seek to explain one generation's emergence from adolescence into adulthood in an era characterized by both opportunity and uncertainty.

PAUL ANISEF is a professor in the Department of Sociology and Associate Director of CERIS at York University.

PAUL AXELROD is a professor in the Division of Social Science at York University.

ETTA BAICHMAN-ANISEF is currently working as a self-employed career and educational research consultant.

CARL E. JAMES is an associate professor in the Faculty of Education at York University.

ANTON H. TURRITTIN is an associate professor in the Department of Sociology at York University.

Opportunity and Uncertainty

Life Course Experiences of the Class of '73

PAUL ANISEF, PAUL AXELROD,
ETTA BAICHMAN-ANISEF, CARL JAMES, and
ANTON TURRITTIN in collaboration with
FRED ASHBURY, GOTTFRIED PAASCHE, and
ZENG LIN

UNIVERSITY OF TORONTO PRESS
Toronto Buffalo London

© University of Toronto Press Incorporated 2000
Toronto Buffalo London
Printed in Canada

ISBN 0-8020-4835-8 (cloth)
ISBN 0-8020-8364-1 (paper)

Printed on acid-free paper

Canadian Cataloguing in Publication Data

Main entry under title:

Opportunity and uncertainty : life course experiences of the class of '73

Includes bibliographical references and index.
ISBN 0-8020-4835-8 (bound)   ISBN 0-8020-8364-1 (pbk.)

1. High school graduates – Ontario – Longitudinal studies.   2. High
school graduates – Employment – Ontario – Longitudinal studies.
3. Educational surveys – Ontario.   I. Anisef, Paul, 1942–   .

LB1695.8.C3O66 2000   373.12'912'09713   C00-930834-2

University of Toronto Press acknowledges the financial assistance to its
publishing program of the Canada Council for the Arts and the Ontario Arts
Council.

This book has been published with the help of a grant from the Humanities
and Social Sciences Federation of Canada, using funds provided by the Social
Sciences and Humanities Research Council of Canada.

University of Toronto Press acknowledges the financial support for its
publishing activities of the Government of Canada through the Book Publishing Industry Development Program (BPIDP).

Contents

Foreword

In the last decades of the twentieth century, social commentary often has concentrated on the changing relationship between youth and society: catchwords like 'Generation X,' 'the post-materialistic generation,' and 'the individualistic generation' have become prominent, reflecting changing values and the pluralization of lifestyles. These characterizations of a generation, however, have tended to be misleading generalizations, in the sense of *pars pro toto* portraits.

Opportunity and Uncertainty: Life Course Experiences of the Class of '73 delivers a different message because it redirects youth research by putting it into a life-course framework. It is an important study, based on careful and sensitive analysis of the Class of 1973, and it is unique in the sense of telling the story of one cohort born in the mid-1950s. This cohort from Ontario, Canada's most prosperous province, graduated from high school in 1973. By following this group for twenty-one years, Anisef, Axelrod, Baichman-Anisef, James, and Turrittin provide an insightful narration of their transition to adult life. This rich portrait is based on longitudinal survey data and qualitative interviews. This unique combination of methods enables us to better understand the interplay of social change and life histories.

The Class of 1973 has experienced economic turbulence since the 1980s, which has resulted in growing disparities between educational level, fields of study, and actual employment experiences. However, compared to those of the Class of 1993, for example, this group's job entry and employment patterns were still more stable. For younger generations, the links between schooling and employment have become progressively discontinuous. Furthermore, unemployment, job changes, and underemployment are becoming characteristics of the work history of young adults. Anisef and colleagues document that the lives of their cohort evolved in a period of intensifying social change, but still within well-defined educational and career pathways. However, the 1990s have seen growing instability and uncertainty concerning employment and family patterns.

The study contributes to an understanding of the dramatic structural changes that have characterized the transition to the twenty-first century and places them in a cross-generational perspective. The authors rightly emphasize that the changing passages to adulthood can be better understood by looking at the experience of different cohorts. Their research documents substantial differences between cohorts. For example, as children, most of the respondents lived in two-parent families and over half of them in families with four or more children. Over a period of twenty years, three-fifths of the sample experienced upward, one-fourth downward, and less than one-third no mobility in their careers. Thus, there are remarkable differences between parents' occupational status and respondents' social-economic accomplishments at age forty. Upward mobility was very much facilitated by the government's educational policies and an expanding economy. Furthermore, further formal education often resulted in occupational enhancement and fulfilment of personal goals, especially for women. In their discussion, the authors delineate the ambivalent experiences of women who still have to balance employment and family roles.

The analysis presents clear evidence of intra-cohort diversity, which is illuminated by five biographies that document how social background, personal choice, educational resources, employment options, and economic circumstances interact over time to create specific life histories. Anisef and his co-authors introduce the concept of 'navigating transitions,' which is an apt metaphor for the ways young adults construct their own routes and cope with detours in the transition to adulthood.

In their chapter on first-generation Canadians, the authors make a strong point in showing crucial importance of education as a medium for cultural and social integration of foreigners. Their data show that men with foreign-born parents often surpassed non-immigrants in their careers. Parental expectations and personal aspirations, however, had to be met by educational opportunities. Compared to the situation of foreigners in European countries, the Canadian example is important: all respondents who expected to attend university actually did so. How was this possible? One reason was expressed by the daughter of East European immigrants who was raised on a tobacco farm with four siblings, all of whom have completed degrees: 'Hard work drove us to university.'

The study is also a contribution to the emergent life course theory. Anisef and his co-authors are shifting from models of status attainment and human capital to life course and transition theory, influenced by recent European and North American thinking about the dynamic relationship between the individual and society over time. These innovations are sensitizing the researcher to the interplay between socialization and selection processes across the life course and to the active part that the individual plays throughout. This approach is innovative because it overcomes the limitation of analyses that rely either on macro-level or on micro-level research. The results carry ample evidence for 'structured individualization,' which means that life course decisions have to be made individually in view of options that are embedded in a structure of social and gender inequality.

Finally, I would like to direct the reader's attention to the carefully crafted narration which combines data analysis and vivid accounts of transition experiences and biographical decisions of individual respondents. I am convinced that this study, so rich in statistical and qualitative data, will be read not only by researchers and policymakers, but also by educators and parents, who will find a unique portrait of the Class of 1973 that can be seen as a baseline for comparing the evolving and much more difficult life courses of the young adults of today.

Walter R. Heinz
University of Bremen, Germany

Acknowledgments

We wish to acknowledge the research assistance of the following people: Marshall Abecassis, Jennifer Anisef, Mary Bunch, Laurel McQueen, Christine Minas, and Scott Milne. Technical assistance in the assembling of statistical data was provided by Shibau Guo, Gon Li Xu, Noreen Stuckless, and the Institute for Social Research at York University. David Stones and Matthew Kudelka furnished valuable editorial assistance and Leanne Taylor prepared the index. This book would not have been completed, and probably not begun, without the research funding provided by the Social Sciences and Humanities Research Council and by the Faculty of Arts at York University. The Aid to Scholarly Publications Program of the Humanities and Social Sciences Federation of Canada, and the Division of Social Science, Faculty of Arts, and the Department of Sociology, Faculty of Arts, of York University helped fund the publication of the book. Virgil Duff and Siobhan McMenemy of the University of Toronto Press encouraged and endured us from beginning to end. Several anonymous readers offered suggestions which we believe strengthened the manuscript. Finally, we thank the members of the Class of '73 who, through surveys and interviews, have participated for many years in this study. Not only have they tolerated our intrusions, but many have invited us to seek them out in the future. We dedicate this book to them.

OPPORTUNITY AND UNCERTAINTY:
LIFE COURSE EXPERIENCES OF THE CLASS OF '73

Introducing the Class of '73

Reviewing the experiences of previous generations of adolescents can help us understand the problems and challenges facing today's generation of young people as it moves inexorably toward adulthood. This book outlines and analyses the experiences of a group of late 'baby-boomers' that was first contacted in 1973 when enrolled in grade 12 classes in different regions of Ontario. Over twenty-two years elapsed between our first survey of these respondents and our last study in 1995. We now refer to this study group affectionately as the 'Class of '73.'[1] When we contacted them again in 1995, they were 40 to 42 years of age and were approaching mid-life. Locating and returning to our respondents in 1995 has provided an opportunity for us to probe their educational and employment experiences as part of a life-long process. We have been able to chart their school-to-work transitions and their passage to adulthood as signified by marital and parenting roles.

The Class of '73 study began in 1972, when university enrolments were still growing but applications for admissions to universities had begun to decline. At the same time, enrolment projections, based on trend data, were proving increasingly inaccurate. For this reason, the Ontario Ministry of Colleges and Universities (MCU) became interested in monitoring the attitudes and behaviours of high school students with respect to their educational plans as a possible projection tool, and approached Paul Anisef to conduct a study of high school seniors. With the assistance of the Institute for Social Research (ISR) at York University, a sample survey of Ontario grade 12 students was carried out in the spring of 1973. Ninety-nine high schools across Ontario were selected to represent four types of communities: Metropolitan Toronto; other large and medium-sized urban centres; smaller cities and the urban fringe around Toronto; and small towns and rural areas. Ninety-seven secondary schools agreed to participate. Staff members of the ISR selected one or two grade 12 classrooms in each of these schools for the administration of the survey questionnaire. Researchers obtained a total of 2,555 usable questionnaire responses in what was subsequently designated Phase I of the project. It should be noted that this study of grade 12 students did not include those students who had left school before grade 12; these early school leavers may have constituted 20 to 30 per cent of the Class of '73.

The Ministry of Colleges and Universities wanted to know if trends in behaviour could be anticipated on the basis of intentions, and sponsored two follow-up studies. Phase II was a telephone survey, carried out in November 1973, which inquired about the present activities of respondents and their plans for the fall of 1974; this survey explored reasons why plans indicated in the first survey might have changed, and posed other relevant questions. This study yielded 2,156 respondents (an 84.4 per cent response rate) and showed that many of the former grade 12 students had entered the labour force, and that some had begun attending community college. The second follow-up, Phase III, was carried out in October and November of 1974, some eighteen months after the first survey. Its purpose was to compare the career aspirations indicated in the two earlier surveys with their actual realization. This phase yielded 2,163 subjects (84.7 per cent of the original phase sample).

In the 1970s, some segments of the public were expressing concern that too many highly trained young adults were being prepared for a job market in which fewer people were required, due to slower economic growth. Some even questioned the usefulness of postsecondary education in preparing young people for jobs. Since limited information on the link between education and the labour market was available at the time, further research was indicated; this led to a third follow-up study.

In the fall of 1977, Paul Anisef and two colleagues from the Department of Sociology at York University, Anton H. Turrittin and Gottfried Paasche, explored the possibility of turning the earlier study of Ontario grade 12 students into a longitudinal project. Almost five years had passed since the first phase of Anisef's original enquiry; by this time most of the respondents had completed their education and entered the labour market. It was therefore an opportune time to examine the links between education and employment outcomes for the study group.

The research team was aware that no longitudinal study of Canadian youth had been done beyond relatively quick follow-up surveys. Though studies had been conducted on the aspirations and expectations of high school students, on who goes to colleges and universities, and on the first jobs of university graduates, tracking a cohort over a fairly long period of time in a way that would capture in some detail the transition from school to work and beyond was a novel idea. Furthermore, most other panel studies of the link between education and work either focused on graduates of grade 12 or on graduates of universities, whereas the Class of '73 study had begun somewhat earlier, while students were still enrolled in grade 12. This important point still distinguishes the Class of '73 study from other Canadian panel research implemented in the 1970s and 1980s. Since equal opportunity was a major concern in postsecondary educational policy in the 1970s, the co-investigators felt that it was important to identify the extent to which certain socially significant dimensions, such as gender, socio-economic status (SES), and urban/rural origins, influenced accessibility to and participation in postsecondary schooling. The question of accessibility to postsecondary education for this group of former grade 12 students could be more fully answered if a social stratification perspective was employed. The research team also felt that there were important social science interests to be served. Social scientists have long been interested in understanding how a society's social institutions determine and influence the life chances of individuals in society. The co-investigators hoped that their work on the project's fourth phase would provide social scientists with empirical findings that could test hypotheses derived from competing sociological perspectives (e.g., functional versus conflict paradigms).

In developing Phase IV, the co-investigators retained their commitment to a survey approach. Its use in previous phases had yielded a wealth of information (e.g., social and social-psychological) and had enhanced the possibility of generalizing findings to the larger population of Ontario youth. Moreover, the relatively large number of sample respondents offered a means to evaluate rather complex relationships.

One major disadvantage of relying exclusively on a survey approach is that individuals can become lost through the process of analyzing aggregate numbers. Thus, explaining how individual respondents perceived their worlds of education and work, and how they developed strategies for arriving at decisions regarding them, required the use of nonsurvey, qualitative techniques. We therefore decided that in addition to mailing out a questionnaire, we would interview a subgroup of 100 participants, primarily from the Metropolitan Toronto area. The research team carried out unstructured interviews with these respondents, and from this subgroup selected a smaller group for further, in-depth interviews.

The research design stage of the main follow-up survey began in the summer of 1978. A one-page questionnaire was sent to parents to update names and addresses and to provide preliminary information on the education, employment, and marital status of participants. Financial support for this fourth follow-up was obtained from MCU in that year, which enabled us to trace subjects, prepare and send out questionnaires, and code and edit surveys. Class of '73 members who were contacted were provided with a newsletter that summarized some findings from Phases I–III. Information on 1,522 respondents was obtained, representing 59.6 per cent of the Phase I sample.

Intense analysis of the quantitative and qualitative Phase IV data led to the writing of *Is the Die Cast?* a report published by MCU in 1980. This report, along with conference papers and journal articles, stimulated considerable discussion in the social science and policy communities and did much to sustain interest on the part of the collaborative team in continuing the longitudinal project. The results of these studies shed considerable light on the educational and occupational pathways adopted by Ontario youth, as analysed from the perspectives of gender, socio-economic status, and region of origin.

Participants in the Phase IV study were asked to provide names of friends or relatives who would most likely know their whereabouts five years later. In the summers of 1987 and 1988, brief telephone interviews were conducted with respondents or their parents in an effort to update addresses and obtain some educational and occupational information. This effort – Phase V of the study – resulted in information on 1,129 respondents, or 44.2 per cent of the original sample. Joining our collaborative team at this time was Fredrick D. Ashbury, then a doctoral student in the sociology program at York University and now a health research and policy consultant.

The period 1989 to 1991 was devoted to the analysis of data deriving from the updating effort in 1987–88 and to an exploration of different conceptual and methodological strategies that could be employed in conducting a sixth phase of the project. It should be noted that the collaborative nature of the project also grew, and that as of 1992 four additional members had joined the project team: Paul Axelrod, a social historian, Carl E. James, a sociologist with the Faculty of Education, Zeng Lin, a doctoral candidate in sociology, all at York University, and Etta Baichman-Anisef, an MEd student at the Ontario Institute for Studies in Education.

In project team meetings, we concluded that the original concept of linking education to work ought to be broadened in Phase VI by considering multiple kinds of 'transition' as youth moved into adult status. Such movements were not always linear; there were frequently nonlinear transitions, during which respondents encountered detours and temporary dead-ends. The lives of Class of '73 members often followed intricate and complicated patterns as participants manoeuvred between school and employment. Furthermore, the participants were now around 37 years old, most were married, and a large number were raising children of their own. Discussions among the research team produced the sense that our project too had grown up and that a life course perspective would more effectively inform our future research. As a theoretical orientation, the life course perspective, stemming from the work of Elder (1985, 1991), brings together a broad range of ideas that can be used to understand the stages of life through which people pass. It conceptualizes these stages and passages in a way that accounts for the complex and unique events of peoples lives; at the same time it identifies similar experiences and patterns of development in the history of a given group.

In 1992 we received a research grant from the Social Science and Humanities Research Council (SSHRC) and began the process of again tracing participants and preparing a research design. In January 1994 we contacted all respondents whom we had been able to locate and requested their help in continuing the longitudinal project. The request to participate included a newsletter and a snapshot review of events in the lives of the Class of '73. We asked participants to co-operate at a future date in completing a mailed questionnaire and to volunteer their time in one-on-one or focus group interviews. The positive responses exceeded our expectations; approximately 160 people, of a total 1,150 who were traced and contacted, indicated their willingness to participate in individual or focus group interviews.

Six focus group interviews with a total of 44 participants were conducted in Toronto, London, and Ottawa during the winter of 1994. A survey questionnaire was designed and pretested by the ISR at York University; this employed the information from focus groups, individual interviews, and a literature review of life course and transitions studies. A final questionnaire was developed at the end of 1994 and sent to all subjects in January 1995. By our mid-August cut-off date, 788 people had replied to our request to complete the survey. This constituted 30.8 per cent of the original sample and 51.8 per cent of the participants we had been able to trace during Phase VI. In total, 55 one-on-one interviews were conducted across Canada.[2]

A loss of cases is to be expected in all longitudinal studies; thus, a significant concern is whether the respondents who are retained in later phases are still representative of the original sample. To address this issue we employed gender, socio-economic status, and regional variables, and tested the similarity of Phase VI and Phase I respondents with respect to these factors (see Appendix B for a detailed examination of representativeness). This evaluation confirmed the continuing representativeness of our 1994–95 follow-up study, with the proviso that respondents who originally attended secondary schools in rural areas of Ontario were somewhat overrepresented. Also, there was a substantial loss of low socio-economic status respondents in Metro Toronto by the last phase, in contrast with other regions. This loss, however, was balanced by the greater retention of low socio-economic status respondents from rural areas of the province.

Organization of Book

Chapter 1 begins with an overview of the life course perspective, with particular attention paid to two important themes that will be addressed throughout this book: *human agency* and *social structure*. Life course theory is posited as a means for explaining the dynamic relationship between the individual and the social order, at both macro and micro levels of analysis.

Chapter 2 describes the world of grade 12 students in 1973, identifies the social currents that affected them up to that critical stage in their life course, and describes the world they would face in the mid-1990s. It discusses reforms of the Ontario school system, the youth culture legacy of the 1960s, the changing role of women, and the labour market prospects from the perspective of the 1970s, in order to provide a context for the way young people perceived their world and how they began to plan their futures.

Chapter 3 analyses the educational trajectories of members of the Class of '73. It relates typical educational patterns to a number of key dimensions such as gender, class, geographical location, and personal educational preferences. It employs earlier works and writings to explore high school experiences such as tracking, and traces key educational choices respondents made during their senior high school years. These same sources are used to evaluate the effects that social structure and human agency had on further educational attainment to 1979. By 1995, many respondents had experienced profound changes in their careers – changes resulting from life course transitions and from transformations in the economy during the previous two decades. Conventional wisdom might predict that most members of the Class of '73 would have completed their formal schooling by 1980; yet the analysis of information collected in 1995 provides evidence that challenges this conclusion.

Chapters 4 and 5 both explore the transition from schooling to employment for members of the Class of '73; however, the questions raised and the perspectives employed are different. Chapter 4 provides an overview of the labour market situation from 1979 to 1995 and includes a discussion of changing technology and of the impact of the recessions of the early 1980s and early 1990s and economic restructuring on employment. Central to the analysis presented in this chapter is the question of how a changing economic climate transformed the employment opportunities of respondents. Particular attention is given to the topics of unemployment, part-time employment, self-employment, underemployment, and job satisfaction. Given the central role of formal education in Canadian society, we also seek to identify its influence, independent of social class, on the levels and types of employment attained by members of the Class of '73 in the early stages of their careers. We also examine job-related training between 1989 and 1994 and the role it played in helping respondents cope with the uncertainties produced by economic change in Ontario.

Chapter 5 reviews the social mobility experiences of the Class of '73. It assesses the success of respondents relative to their parents' social position. The social mobility of respondents is examined in terms of occupational change, geographical movement, socio-economic status, gender, and region of origin. Both intergenerational and intragenerational mobility are explored with respect to social structural and human agency dimensions. This chapter reinforces the point that in the employment world of the 1980s and 1990s, opportunity and uncertainty co-existed.

Chapter 6 builds on earlier analyses of the Class of '73 with reference to the effects of parents' and respondents' birthplace on educational aspirations, expectations, and activities. This research reveals that the first-generation Canadians involved in our study were more likely to expect to enrol in postsecondary education than either foreign-born or second-plus generation students. The question posed in this chapter is, How well did members of the Class of '73 with foreign-born parents do in terms of educational/occupational attainment and career mobility relative to peers with Canadian-born parents? The chapter considers the support received from parents, the extent to which schooling met needs and provided opportunities for achievement, the role played by ethnicity and race, and the impact of immigrant drive in the lives of respondents with foreign-born parents.

Chapter 7 provides some fascinating insights into the impact of family on the lives of members of the Class of '73. The chapter examines the dynamic transitions made by participants from their family of origin to their family of destination and offers insights into the relationships between respondents and their parents. Information on respondents' values and on their attitudes toward marriage, education, work, the family, and children are available from earlier surveys and from the survey conducted in 1994–95. This information, pulled from survey data and interviews, provides a basis for exploring these values and attitudes from when respondents were seniors in high school and from their formative years of development. It also offers a framework for exploring marital decisions, family formation, and life satisfaction issues from when respondents were in their mid-twenties in 1979, and again in 1994–95 when they were approximately 40 years old. Of particular importance is the analysis of the impact of children on the life trajectories of men and women. Gender relations in the management of household tasks and childrearing are also examined. Finally, the hopes and expectations that respondents have for their own children with respect to education and employment are revealed.

Chapter 8 offers a micro life course analysis of five members of the Class of '73. This is an attempt to examine, compare, and contrast interlinking trajectories, transitions, and turning points in the lives of these individuals. We argue that while it is useful to plot separate trajectories pertaining to education, careers, marriage, and childrearing, it is critical that we pick up on finer details to fully understand how the life course unfolds for different individuals. This attention to detail provides us with an opportunity to examine the individual solutions that people develop as they move through times governed by explicit and clear normative expectations, into periods characterized by greater risk and uncertainty. This qualitative rendering of life course pathways, unimpeded by tables and charts, attempts to provide a rich and nuanced view of individual lives.

Finally, in a short concluding chapter, we review the major insights revealed by the previous chapters and discuss the wider implications of this research for life course analyses of later generations of youth. We suggest that the hypothesis that contemporary youth are more subject to risk in the choices they make must remain a hypothesis until a full exploration and analysis of other, more recent cohorts of youth have been concluded.

Navigating the Life Course: School-to-Work Transitions in the 1990s

There is a widely held perception that young people in the 1990s faced a greater degree of early career instability and uncertainty than their counterparts in previous decades (Marquardt, 1998). Statistical studies support these impressions. In 1995 almost 20 per cent of Canadians aged 15 to 25 – some 400,000 – were unable to find either full-time or part-time employment (Human Resources Development Canada, 1995). Many of those who were able to find employment found themselves confined to entry-level positions because the competition from older workers for better jobs was so fierce. Since employers gave preference to experienced workers, young people's lack of seniority cost them jobs in a weak economy. This was illustrated by a significant decline in the workforce participation rate among Canadian youth in the period 1990 to 1995 (Human Resources Development Canada, 1996a: 3). Completing a secondary school diploma did not afford young people secure and rewarding employment. Even more telling was the finding that high school graduates without postsecondary education experienced labour market outcomes similar to those of high school dropouts (Levin, 1995: 16; Canadian Youth Foundation, 1995b: 1).

It is difficult to prove that youth in the 1990s faced life course transitions that were significantly more disorderly and stressful than those encountered by previous generations, especially those who experienced the Depression and the Second World War; however, it is evident that life course transitions, particularly from school to work, have changed dramatically in recent years. In the mid-1950s a young person typically left school, began full-time employment, left home, got married, and had children. Women tended to marry earlier than men and were less likely to enter or remain in the labour force. In recent decades, economic restructuring, globalization, skills upgrading at the workplace, labour-saving technology, and the shift from manufacturing jobs to employment in the public and private service sectors have profoundly affected the transition process (Heinz, 1996a).

Figures presented in Table 1.1 illustrate the dramatic nature of the structural changes. First, the participation rates of women in the Canadian labour force have altered dramatically since the early 1970s, when only a minority of women worked; by 1995 a clear majority of women were employed. Also noteworthy is the rise in part-time employment rates between the early 1980s and 1995. For both youth and women, this increase in part-time employment had important implications for the school/work transition. In fact, the number of part-time employed youth doubled in this decade to over 40 per cent, and the majority of part-time workers were female (Canadian Youth Foundation, 1995a: 15). Rather than representing a voluntary lifestyle change, this increase in part-time employment, when coupled with a significant increase in unemployment was a signal that substantially greater numbers of young Canadians were encountering transient job situations and that most were having to negotiate difficult school-to-work transitions. Furthermore, postsecondary credentials no longer ensured a smooth transition to good employment opportunities. By 1995 a greater proportion of recent graduates was experiencing significant difficulties in finding employment after completing their degrees (Trottier, Cloutier, and Laforce, 1996: 104).

Another indicator that the school-to-work transition was becoming more challenging was the polarization in earnings among Canadians working full-time. Polarization was especially pronounced among young male workers under 35, although young women also experienced it; however, the data presented in Table 1.1 indicate that the gap between women's and men's earnings has been slowly narrowing.

Questions and Issues

In the late twentieth century, the relationship between education and employment has been permanently altered by revolutionary changes in work technology, and in how work is organized, and in how it is perceived by average citizens. At one time education had fairly clear implications for jobs and careers; by the late 1990s this was no longer the case. For a significant portion of contemporary youth, the fit between educational decision-making and entry into the world of work

Table 1.1. Labour market changes in Canada, 1971 to 1995 (percentage)

		Year 1971	1976	1981	1986	1991	1995
Employed in goods-producing sector as % of total employed		37.2	35.6	33.7	30.2	27.7	27.0
Employed in goods-producing sector by gender	% female	18.8	20.2	22.2	24.0	23.9	24.1
Manufacturing & construction as % of goods-producing sector		75.0	75.8	74.8	75.0	75.0	76.2
Manufacturing & construction by gender	% female	19.8	21.0	22.8	24.4	23.7	23.9
Employed in service-producing sector as % of total employed		62.8	64.4	66.3	69.8	72.3	72.9
Employed in service-producing sector by gender	% female	44.3	46.4	49.7	51.3	53.1	53.1
Trade (wholesale/retail) as % of service-producing sector		27.6	26.9	25.8	25.6	24.4	23.4
Trade (wholesale/retail) by gender	% female	37.5	40.1	43.1	42.8	45.3	44.9
Finance, insurance, & real estate as % of service-producing sector		7.0	8.1	8.1	8.2	8.5	8.2
Finance, insurance, & real estate by gender	% female	51.3	57.7	60.9	60.0	59.8	59.2
Educational, health, & social service as % of service-producing sector		N.A.	N.A.	21.3	22.0	22.9	23.2
Educational, health, & social service by gender	% female	N.A.	N.A.	67.2	69.5	71.7	72.2
Public administration as % of service-producing sector		10.1	11.1	10.5	9.9	9.4	8.2
Public administration by gender	% female	24.7	32.2	36.5	39.7	43.4	44.0
Participation rate (%) in labour force	male	76.1	77.6	78.4	76.6	75.1	72.5
	female	36.5	45.2	51.7	55.3	58.5	57.4
Part-time employment rate (%) in labour force		13.3	12.3	13.5	15.5	16.3	18.6
Part-time employment rate (%) within gender group	male	6.4	5.8	6.3	7.8	8.8	10.6
	female	24.8	23.2	24.2	25.7	25.5	28.2
Unemployment rate (%) of population active in labour force		6.1	7.1	7.5	9.5	10.4	9.5
Unemployment rate (%) by gender group	male	7.0	6.3	7.0	9.3	10.9	9.8
	female	5.1	8.4	8.3	9.8	9.7	9.2

Unemployment rate (%), graduated high school	6.2*	8.8**	11.3	11.9	10.7	9.5
Unemployed rate (%), with university degree	5.1*	2.9**	3.2	3.8	4.8	4.5
Ratio of women's/men's earnings, full-time, full year	59.7	59.1	63.7	65.8	69.6	69.8***

Sources: Information on the ratio of women's to men's earnings is from Statistics Canada, *Earnings of Men and Women*, 1994 (13-217). Information on unemployment rates by educational level is for the month of December (except where noted) estimated for the population of Canada 15 years of age and over (except where noted), and is from relevant volumes of Statistics Canada, *The Labour Force* (71-001). All other information in the table, except for 1971, is based on relevant volumes of Statistics Canada, *Labour Force Annual Averages* (71-529), which reports annual averages based on estimates of the population of Canada 15 years and over. Data for industry groups is based on employment rather than the labour force. Goods-producing industries include agriculture; other primary industries; manufacturing; construction; and other utilities (electric power, gas, and water). Service-producing industries include the following sectors: transportation and communications; trade; finance, insurance, and real estate; service; and public administration. The service category in turn is comprised of business services; educational services; health and social services; accommodation, food, and beverage services; and other service industries. Industry data for 1971 and 1976 was calculated by moving the electric power, gas, and water utilities group to the goods-producing sector to conform to the current definition of the goods-producing sector. Except for the ratio of women's to men's earnings data, all data for 1971 are based on the December 1971 report of Statistics Canada's *The Labour Force* (71-001), which gives annual averages for 1971, with the labour force being defined as 14 years of age and over. N.A. stands for data not available.

* May 1971 data based on the educational categories grades 9–13, compared to university and other postsecondary education.

** Based on the educational categories some high school and no postsecondary education, compared to university degree.

*** Figures based on the year 1994.

was no longer well articulated. Yet at the same time, job and career uncertainty had increased the importance of making educational and career decisions – decisions which later had to be elaborated and refined as young people moved from late adolescence to adulthood.

We argue that in order to understand how social change has transformed the transitions made by adolescents in Canada as they move into adulthood, we must examine and learn from the experiences of previous generations. In our introduction we presented the Class of '73, a group of late baby-boomers who were first contacted in 1973 when they were enrolled in grade 12 classes in different regions of Ontario. In attempting to understand how a generation of Ontario residents who attended grade 12 in 1973 arrived at the educational and vocational decisions they made, we have employed an interdisciplinary, longitudinal, and life course perspective. We also use social-historical methods to recreate the world of the early 1970s – the period during which these high school students faced the future.

In 1995 we approached members of the Class of '73 again. By then they were 40 to 42 years of age and were entering mid-life, and many had over twenty years of labour market experience. They were well positioned to evaluate the school-to-employment and adolescent-to-adulthood transitions they had experienced, in addition to those they anticipated in the future and expected for their children. Their educational and work experiences and achievements augmented the information we had collected in earlier research phases, and provided us with data on the continuing challenges they faced in their working lives, as seen through their eyes.

We believe that the transitions experienced by high school and postsecondary graduates in the 1970s differed fundamentally from those of more recent graduates, especially in light of how Canada's youth labour markets have been restructured in the past decade. To illuminate the various themes, we will draw primarily on life course and school-to-employment theories, rather than on the human capital and status attainment theories we relied on in our earlier works. Human capital theory suggests that individual effort and investment in education, skills acquisition, and credentials are normally converted into employment and career prospects; the status attainment model emphasizes social origins and individual aspirations while de-emphasizing social opportunities and constraints. We have come to feel that these perspectives fail to provide an adequate framework for capturing the choices and experiences of the Class of '73: they simply do not address the forces that operate in families, in schools, and in the firms that employ the young adults who are making school-to-work transitions. Nor do they highlight sufficiently the role of personal agency in constructing and negotiating those 'ascribed' statuses that, for good or ill, are each individual's birthright. While various forms of 'capital' may arise from the reproduction of social class and other aspects of social background, this capital must be taken up and 'invested' by individuals. In this sense, the individual as an agent decides how her capital is to be employed, and 'invests' it in the context of a biographical transition. For this reason we turned to life course theory, which we explain more fully in the next section. Within this framework, transitions from schooling to employment are seen as constructed by individuals within the context of social forces, educational selection, work experiences, and employment options. Decisions made by participants are both more complex and more time dependent than is suggested by the human capital and status attainment models (Heinz, 1996a: 7). Still, issues of social inequality, class, and status attainment figure prominently in our story about the Class of '73, for the transition from schooling to employment has never been entirely smooth in the postwar period. Social scientists in Canada and other countries have spent decades studying this complex and puzzling transition (Heinz, 1999; Crysdale, King, and Mandell, 1999; Wyn, 1996; Coles, 1995; Jacobs, 1995; Lowe and Krahn, 1995; Roberts et al.,1994; Kerckhoff, 1995; Rosenbaum et al., 1990; Ferri, 1993; Jones and Wallace, 1992; Shavit and Blossfeld, 1993; Felmlee, 1988), and have found patterns involving social forces such as class and gender, schooling, values, and value changes that have remained important features of the school-to-employment transition process.

By applying life course theory to our study of the Class of '73, we will establish baseline data that will permit comparative analyses of school-to-employment and adolescence-to-adulthood transitions across the decades. Furthermore, we will explore interrelationships between self-concept, value orientations, and belief systems, and educational and employment choices.

Life Course Theories and Issues: General Assumptions

As stated earlier, this book explores the multiple entries and exits made by the Class of '73 in their transitions from schooling to employment and from adolescence to adulthood. To help us understand these transitions, we will draw from life course theory. The life course perspective provides a means of addressing two fundamental themes: *human agency/social structure*, and *stability/change*. Do individuals determine their own destinies? To what degree are they subject to circumstances beyond their own control? How, and how much, do the values, beliefs, self-evaluations, and satisfactions of individuals change? Is stability (or change) in individuals linked to human agency and social structure? And if it is, can we identify the patterns? These questions permit us to probe important sociological, historical, and psychological dimensions of the life course journey.

There is a growing literature on life transitions that supports the approach we follow in this study. Life course theory, which attempts to explain the dynamic relationship between the individual and social order, allows researchers to examine a cohort's collective experience without reifying it, and to remain attuned to individual differences without ignoring social context. More specifically, as Elder has noted, 'the life course refers to the pathways through the age-differentiated life span, to social patterns in the timing, duration, spacing, and order of events; the timing of an event may be as consequential for life experiences as whether the event occurs and the degree and type of change' (1978: 21). A key variable in life course research is *time*. Time is defined from the perspective of psychology in terms of personal or individual development; from the perspective of history in terms of social-historical changes of context and their impact on cohorts; and from the perspective of sociology in terms of institutional and social structural changes. Though time in general is of relevance to life course researchers, so is the *sequencing* of phases, stages, and events in individuals' developmental pathways (O'Rand and Krecker, 1990: 244, 258).

Heinz (1995) takes up the theme of the individual in the concept of biography and the biographical actor. Individuals independently make choices within a structure of opportunities and constraints in which they feel that they are 'constructing their individual life courses' (1995: 26). According to Mayer and Tuma (1990: 5), life course research is innovative in 'its potential for transcending long-held distinctions between micro- and macro-analyses of social life, and between theoretical schools and scientific disciplines.' While the life course paradigm is a valuable addition to our understanding of social life, it has not yet developed a methodology by which the influences of macro and micro forces can be analytically separated. The family may not determine the career choices of children; Heinz recognizes that opportunities for social mobility depend on the larger structure of social inequality (1995: 4).

Consideration of the historical context in which actors make decisions is central to life course research (Elder, 1974). Contextual factors include social, cultural, political, and economic conditions, which influence individuals' decisions to varying degrees. Once we introduce historical or social context, the concepts of 'normative life patterns' and 'normal biography'[1] seem less viable in terms of capturing the complex transitions identified by life course researchers (Heinz, 1991). According to Elder (1978: 28), normative assumptions about the life course vary with social context, which includes geographic location and community size (see also Rindfuss, 1991). Thus, in our analysis of the Class of '73, the inclusion of geographical residence in Ontario is of critical importance. Growing up in a city, as opposed to a town or rural area, may either constrain or enhance personal opportunities for individuals, and thereby influence their life pathways.

Terminology from Life Course Theory

Some of the terms encountered in life course research should be clarified at the outset. For example, the concept of transition within the life course is linked to movement *between* statuses, although social scientists often write of moving *from* one status *to* another (Thomas, 1993). That is to say, the idea of moving between statuses is conventionally thought of in terms of linear movement from one distinct status (e.g., student) to another (e.g., worker). In reality, people either move fluidly between statuses or occupy multiple statuses at the same time. Moreover, transitions are always embedded in life trajectories that determine their form and meaning (Elder, 1987). Thus, the transition from completing a university education to securing employment is inevitable for most young people entering university. However, the career trajectories of these university-educated individuals will vary widely with a host of contingencies. Coles (1995:13) cautions that when we concentrate on the analysis of trajectories, we risk de-emphasizing choice and focusing attention on the impact of structural forces 'determining' which sequence of statuses will be followed. Furthermore, within these transitions status passages link institutions and actors by defining timetables (as well as entry and exit markers) for shifts between social status configurations (Heinz, 1995). To illustrate, when an individual exits full-time education to enter a full-time position in the labour market, she changes status from student to prospective employee. Naturally, there are normative assumptions attached to this particular status passage, as employers make assumptions about young people from particular educational, gender, ethno-racial, and urban/rural backgrounds.

Some life course writers highlight for us the opportunity to examine transitions from the perspective of how an individual's life is affected by them and how the individual, in turn, copes with transitions. Thus, Schlossberg (1984) distinguishes anticipated and unanticipated transitions and their impact. Anticipated or expected transitions (an expected promotion, a planned career change) can be rehearsed or planned for, while unanticipated transitions (being fired or laid off, or leaving work due to illness) are nonscheduled events that are not predictable. The capacity of individuals to assimilate transitions depends on the characteristics of the transition (timing, duration), the characteristics of the individual (coping resources, egostrength), and the characteristics of the environment.

Bringing Structure and Agency Together

One aspect of examining school-to-work transitions is the public policy debate over how to structure institutions so as to prepare young people effectively for further education and meaningful employment (Heinz, 1991). In the developmental or life course perspective, the focus shifts to viewing the individual as an agent who constructs a personal pathway – educational, domestic, or career – within the larger context of social, cultural, and economic forces. Rudd and Evans (1998: 41) use the term 'structured individualization' to describe progress through the school-to-work phase; this is their way of accenting and displaying both individual choice and activity and structural influences. They describe this process by pointing out that 'a young person will typically be optimistic and will say that he or she *is* in control of his or her life course and that occupational success is largely based on individual effort, whilst there may be a whole mass of data and theory, developed at a national, societal or "macro" level, which suggests that many young people, especially from particular social groups or trajectories, "have only limited chances of success" (conventionally defined) in the labour market.' The apparent discrepancy between the subjective points of view expressed by individuals on the one hand, and the social and structural patterns typically revealed by large-scale surveys on the other hand, thus reflects different starting points and different methods employed by researchers in describing and understanding macro and micro dimensions in school-to-work transitions. In-depth interviews and group interviews are two methods employed in life course research to explore human agency within social structure.

Much of the recent emphasis on individualization can be traced back to the theoretical work of Beck (1992), whose notion of the 'risk' society has been applied to the uncertain and fragmented transition faced by young people. According to Beck, individualization is an aspect of the dissolution of the traditional parameters of industrial society – parameters that include class, culture, consciousness, and gender and family roles. The individual now must conceive of himself or herself as the centre of action – as the 'planning office' with respect to his or her own biography (1992: 135).

However, Lowe and Krahn (1995), working in the Canadian context, contend that agency and structure are embedded in each other, and that attempts to desegregate the relative effects of agency and structure may be less useful than efforts to determine, in a particular time and place, just how structural and institutional factors influence individual choices. School transitions and school-work transitions map the terrain on which issues of agency and structure combine to determine academic performance, post-secondary attainment, and career objectives. Furlong and Cartmel (1997:7), though agreeing that young people do face new risks and opportunities in the modern world, assert that the 'risk society is not a classless society, but a society in which the old social cleavages associated with class and gender remain intact; on an objective level, changes in the distribution of risk have been minimal.'

Our perspective on transitions within a life course framework, illustrated in Figure 1.1, posits an interplay between structural dimensions and individualized decision-making. The model displayed in this diagram illustrates that structure and agency work together to shape the life course, and intersect continuously as individuals construct their life 'scripts' in the context of conditions that are beyond their control (e.g., the state of the economy), and those that depend on personal choices (e.g., marriage, having children, seeking further education). Thus, individuals do their utmost to express personal agency, while at the same time recognizing that there is a 'system' that may well affect their horizons (Rudd and Evans, 1998: 61).

Figure 1.1. Life Course Experiences of the Class of '73

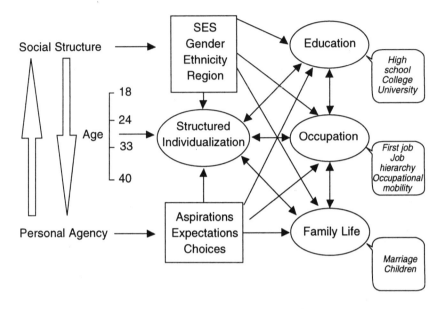

We further maintain that personal agency is always present in the transition from youth to adulthood; young people make distinctive choices about their education and career pathways at critical junctures, and at later ages they make decisions that influence employment and domestic pathways. Some individuals formulate a well-developed script of where they want to go, and express a great deal of confidence that they will reach their goals. Others, possessing a weaker locus of control, vacillate about the future or are simply not capable of expressing their future intentions. This suggests that besides factoring social and organizational structures into the analysis of life course transitions, we must also examine the critical role of personal agency – in the form of personality variations, motivations, aspirations, expectations, ambition, and so on – and its interplay with social and organizational structures. As people mature, they must deal with an increasing variety of formal organizations, including schools, postsecondary institutions, voluntary organizations, employment firms, government agencies at all levels, banks, and insurance companies. These formal organizations influence individual actions in much the same way as structural forces. Again, individuals construct personal pathways in negotiating their way through such formal organizations. With regard to the earlier adolescent and high school years, the analysis of survey findings for the Class of '73 revealed that class, ethnicity, location, and gender had a constraining effect on the lives of Class of '73 members. Our studies provided ample evidence that the educational and career ambitions of our youth cohort were developed within the constraints of these macro forces. And though the patterns revealed clearly show that structural factors strongly influence educational and occupational choices, in-depth interviews conducted in the late 1970s provided a micro perspective that underscored the diversity of transition pathways among men and women across social strata, by urban and rural location, and across ethnic minority and majority groups. It became increasingly evident to us that variations in subjective identity among members of the Class of '73 played a critical role in mediating the connection between structure and agency.

As people accumulate experiences, the interplay of structure and agency continues to affect the life course, though not always evenly. For example, our earlier publications indicate that the importance of social class and residence diminished once students entered higher education. Indeed, their occupational pathways were more strongly affected by the amount and type of education they obtained. At the same time, it is important to explore how individuals come to understand and then negotiate their ascribed characteristics (e.g., geographical residence, gender, ethnicity, social class) as they pursue their educational and occupational aspirations. In this, their efforts are strongly influenced by individual traits, including the clarity of their choices, the strength of their commitment to life goals, their locus of control, their personal priorities, and their values.

Our surveys and in-depth interviews reveal that personality, interests, family matters, and even health concerns influenced the decisions of members of the Class of '73. Structure and agency worked reflexively in the transition to adulthood, and personal choices were continuously being made and remade in the context of changing structural conditions. A discussion of capital – defined by Bourdieu as the 'set of actually usable resources and powers' and as existing in several forms (e.g., economic, cultural, social, symbolic) (1984: 114, cited in Bellamy-Andres, 1994: 122-5) – helps us better understand the constraining effects of structural forces. Bourdieu explains the unequal scholastic achievement of children of different social classes by relating academic success to the distribution of cultural capital across classes. He argues that cultural capital (e.g., tastes, perceptions, views) varies among social classes and translates into advantages in educational terms. Thus, 'high status parents can provide a familiarity with books, museums, and other "cultural events and goods" which stand their children in good stead in schools' (Looker, 1994: 164). Moreover, upper-status parents are also able to use networks of influence to ensure that their children are not treated inappropriately in schools, and they 'pull strings' later on to ease their children's transition into the world of work (Looker, 1995: 165).

The concept of capital, be it cultural or social, also helps us understand the influence of gender, residence, and ethno-racial origins. Thus, the school and employment worlds of young people are gendered, and the opportunities, experiences, and constraints encountered by young women must often be understood as distinctly different from those encountered by young men (Looker, 1994: 165). Women outperform men in school, yet this difference is not reflected in the actual attainments of youth (Looker, 1995). In this regard, some schools actually encourage the formation of distinct gender identities (Mandell and Crysdale, 1993: 33).

In our study, social class as a structural factor receives considerable attention. We are well aware, however, that social class has two important dimensions. The system of inequality as found in Ontario during the period of study did not fundamentally change, though the loss of stable, high-paid blue-collar and even white-collar jobs did represent a significant shift in one important aspect of Ontario's stratification system. At the same time, there is a dynamic dimension to social class, in the sense that individuals can change class status through time as they take advantage of educational and economic opportunities or experience various setbacks. In exploring the transition experiences, values, satisfactions, and self-evaluations of participants, it is important not to underestimate the impact of socio-economic origins during earlier stages of life course development. As members of the Class of '73 moved through the life course and made the transition to adulthood, it became increasingly important to factor in their socio-economic destinations – a topic taken up in some detail in Chapter 5. As adults, many members of the Class of '73 have had full-time occupations, earned a living, and become parents. It is therefore likely that their choices and convictions were increasingly and substantially influenced by their own achieved socio-economic status.

Similarly, there is a dynamic aspect to the normative expectations associated with gender. While gender relations in general have shown great stability over time, the choices that men and women make about their own expression of gender, and about their own gender relations, reflect an ongoing negotiated order. Kathleen Gerson (1985) examined the decisions about work, career, and motherhood made by a group of women aged 25 to 34. She looked at theories that emphasized the role of childhood socialization in forming women's lives, but found them insufficient. Structural explanations were also found wanting. The home backgrounds of the women and the expectations they voiced as young people did not allow her to predict with any degree of confidence how they would behave in adult life. As women (and men) move through the life course, they are subjected to anticipated and unanticipated life events. As Gerson points out, these factors help mute the effects of early socialization experiences; they also increase individual variations in values and decisions later in life.

Although structural inequalities based on ethnicity and race may constrain the aspirations and achievements of young Canadians, research indicates that by the third generation, many minorities have surpassed the achievements of the British-origin Canadian majority. Thus, while the structural barriers of ethnic and racial minority status may be a hurdle to overcome, they are not necessarily perceived by minorities as permanent barriers. Racial minorities cannot shed the distinguishing characteristic of colour and must contend with the yoke of racism in their quest for success; however, studies indicate that their aspirations and ambitions are not unlike those of the ethno-racial majority Canadians, and that they are prepared to meet the challenges required for success (James, 1993).

In sum, structural factors, both social and organizational, do show evidence of constraining properties, particularly when the earlier phases of individuals' life course pathways are examined. Yet as we move from the adolescent to the adult phases of the life course, it is vital that we pay close attention to how individuals, operating within the identities imparted by class, gender, residence, ethno-racial minority status, and organizational structures, construct and negotiate their future biographies. This interplay between structure and agency will emerge as an important theme of this book.

Adding in the New Social History

Previous reports and publications that have stemmed from the longitudinal research based on the Class of '73 have focused mainly on our survey data, with only limited time comparisons and with very limited reference to social and historical context. In this book, not only have we broadened our theoretical base through the life course approach to encompass structure and agency, but we have also added a significant social history dimension. Life course theory not only accounts for individual differences but also explores the influence of common elements in the lives of particular age groups. Chapter 2 traces the influence of postwar economic, social, and cultural forces on Canadian society, including the communities in which the Class of '73 youth were raised, and examines such issues as family life, changing gender roles, schooling, and youth culture. Not everyone responded in the same way to these social pressures, but all were touched by them.

Opportunity and Uncertainty

With our title *Opportunity and Uncertainty*, we have tried to capture the complexity of the Class of '73 as it made the transition from education to work and then toward middle age. Both words in our main title are meant to capture the structure and agency dimensions of social life. Regrading *opportunity*, from the perspective of the youth in our sample, the world in 1973 and in the years just following must have looked good: the economy seemed strong, and postsecondary education beckoned. Yet that opportunity was located in a social structure that differentially privileged youth depending on background factors already mentioned. At the same time, each individual was deeply concerned with making personal choices that reflected a move to independence – the hallmark of adult status. Our choice of the word *uncertainty* is meant to signify two things. *First*, the contingent nature of entry into the adult world, in which people take risks in trying out educational programs, making new friends, finding a partner (generally leading to marriage and family), and entering the world of work, where job and career paths can take one in unanticipated directions. In addition, there are decisions to be made about where to live – decisions that are strongly intertwined with decisions about employment. *Second*, the fact that the economy and culture of Ontario and Canada were changing around the members of the Class of '73 in ways that were not likely fully apparent at the time but would be revealed in hindsight.

In our next chapter we begin the story of the Class of '73 by turning to social history. Our goal is to establish the social, economic, and cultural context of Ontario in the 1970s and later decades, particularly as these contexts have affected young people and their transition from education to work.

CHAPTER TWO

Setting the Stage:
The Past and the Future

What were the key characteristics of the world facing Ontario high school students in the early 1970s? Whether they realized it or not, they were living in a period of significant social change. Born to parents whose own educational opportunities had been constrained by depression and war, young people in Canada were now completing high school and going on to college or university in unprecedented numbers. Staying longer in school meant living most of one's adolescence in the family home under the ever-watchful eye of parents or guardians. Yet at the same time, in the wake of an unprecedented social movement that erupted in the late 1960s, young people were now intent on acquiring more choice and autonomy in their lives. Women in particular were being encouraged – regretfully not by all – to pursue careers and not to give them up. Ontarians had just experienced a sustained period of material growth in which career prospects looked uniformly promising. Yet as the Class of '73 was approaching graduation, there were some unsettling economic signs suggesting that, where work prospects were concerned, the future might be less stable than the recent past.

This chapter explores these issues, outlining the social contexts within which young people both experienced their present and anticipated the immediate future. It attempts to explain how the Class of '73 understood their world and prepared to make life course choices. It focuses on the themes of family life, schooling, youth culture, and the labour market, and thereby demonstrates how life courses are influenced by history, social structure, and personal agency. And it underlines Glen Elder's contention that while individual choice matters immensely in the life course, 'choices are not made in a social vacuum' (1998: 2).

Class of '73 Roots

The typical member of the Class of '73 was born in 1955, delivered of parents whose own birthdates fell between the early 1920s and the mid-1930s. These generations came of age under very different historical conditions. The parents grew up and/or came to early adulthood during the deepest economic depression and most immense war in Canadian history. The oldest among them served as military recruits, factory workers, or community volunteers. Typically, the war was the pivotal experience of their early lives and would influence their sensibilities and values in the years ahead. Those who were too young to bear the burdens of war so directly had been exposed to the apprehension and sacrifices that came in its wake. In these strenuous times, uncertainty reigned (Granatstein and Neary, 1995; Gollub, 1991, Parts 3 and 4; McCalman, 1993).

As the Second World War ended, North Americans refocused their attention on their 'private lives,' seeking the material and emotional security that had been so difficult to sustain over much of the previous two decades (Gollub, 1991: 91). In Doug Owram's words, 'the values of marriage and family were exalted to new levels' in the fifteen years after the war (1996: 12). Canadian marriages reached a historic high in 1946 (more than 137,000), and in Ontario the birthrate peaked in 1957 at 26.8 per 1,000. Thus was the 'baby boom' generation spawned, the tail end of which included the children who would later form the Class of '73 (Granatstein and Neary, 1995: 452; Kalbach and McVey, 1979: 96; Rea, 1985: 27).

The Class of '73 students were raised in homes that valued stability and opportunity, and by parents wedded to the belief that their children's lives should be better than their own – an ambition necessarily deferred by the depression and the war. The combination of peacetime prosperity and progressive social policy seemed to make these goals attainable once again, especially in Ontario, Canada's 'wealthiest and most economically developed province' (Rea, 1985: 14). The growth of the manufacturing and service sectors, the low level of unemployment throughout the 1950s, the stimulus the government was providing to new housing construction, and the provision of family allowances and of free university tuition for postwar veterans, all contributed to the climate of optimism. Consumption levels grew steadily as householders purchased telephones, appliances, and automobiles at unprecedented rates. In Ontario, consumer spend-

ing grew most rapidly in the more prosperous south-central and ur-
banized areas of the province (Rea 1998: 84–5). A 1956 Gallup poll
reported that 79 per cent of Canadians from all social classes believed
that the 'good times' would continue (cited in Axelrod, 1982: 22).

And yet it was still difficult for Canadian families to take their
security for granted. The simmering Cold War underlined the fragility
of the social order. Lurid and sensationalist stories of Soviet political
ambitions kept North Americans on edge. In 1951, in the midst of the
Korean War, an opinion poll identified the fear of war as the major
concern of Canadians. In 1961, 42 per cent of Canadians believed that
the 'free world' could live peacefully with the Russians, while fully 48
per cent anticipated a new world war (cited in Axelrod, 1982: 24).

Throughout this period, optimism was tempered with anxiety. This
mood was reflected in family life. Parents, especially mothers, were
told by a plethora of 'experts' that their children's future depended on
the careful application of 'thoroughly modern' childrearing techniques
(Arnup, 1994: Chapter 5). Women, tens of thousands of whom had
joined the workforce during the war, were now encouraged to stay
out of the labour market and to pour their energies into meeting family demands. It was argued that the child's healthy development, the
husband's happiness, and the general well-being of society required
them to do so. Marion Hilliard, chief of obstetrics and gynaecology at
Toronto's Women's College Hospital, wrote all too typically in 1957:
'The burden of creating a happy marriage falls mainly on the wife. A
man's life is much more difficult than a woman's, full of the groaning
strain of responsibility and the lonely and often fruitless search for
pride in himself. A cheerful and contented woman at home, even one
who must often pretend gaiety, gives a man enough confidence to
believe he can lick the universe' (Hilliard, 1957). Mothers were expected to be available when their children arrived home for lunch and
after school, and to arrange for their recreational and neighbourhood
activities. The family, after all, was perceived as the main vehicle for
the 'integration of the personality and the creation of a mature adult
through affection, guidance and social interaction' (Owram, 1992: 25).

These pervasive middle-class prescriptions of the mother's domestic
role were reinforced in the popular culture by television serials that
idealized traditional images – and myths – of family life. In reality, not
all married women were full-time homemakers during the 1950s. By
1961, women constituted 27 per cent of the Canadian labour force; and
significantly, some 21 per cent of married women were employed

outside the home (Statistics Canada, 1980). Labour shortages in Ontario during the 1950s drew into the workforce a sizable minority of women – particularly working-class and immigrant mothers who were struggling to make ends meet. And farm wives (not counted in the above 'official' statistics) toiled alongside their husbands in the fields and barns. Children growing up in these homes were thus familiar with the phenomenon of the 'working mother.' Yet the ideology of 'familism' provided these women with little support and frequent reproval. Authoritative commentators claimed that women who compromised their household duties were turning out neglected and even delinquent children (Sangster, 1995; Cebotarev, 1995; Iacovetta, 1995). Most Ontario youth, including those of the Class of '73, were thus accustomed to a domestic sphere in which mothers, not fathers, were presumed to be constantly present.

Prewar gender roles were reasserted during this era, but in other respects patterns of family life literally broke new ground. Suburban living attracted a burgeoning middle class, now able to afford new homes in relatively spacious settings, assisted by government-guaranteed mortgages. In 1945 an estimated 43 per cent of Ontarians planning to buy homes expressed a preference for the suburbs. Between 1945 and 1962 the population of North York (north of the City of Toronto) grew by 914 per cent (Strong-Boag, 1995: 46).

Suburban communities were popular because they were perceived as the ideal places to raise families. As *Chatelaine* magazine explained in 1955, 'This is a land concerned with youth, for the majority of the families who buy a home in the suburbs do so to provide free growing space for their children' (Strong-Boag, 1995: 53). As one mother echoed: 'We moved to the suburbs to give [children] room to romp, where they wouldn't have to worry about street cars and ... automobiles' (Strong-Boag, 1991: 489). In this child-oriented environment, planners intended the elementary school to be the 'cultural focus,' and parent/ teacher associations achieved a conspicuous community presence (Sewell, 1993: 85; Strong-Boag, 1991: 495). The suburbs promised comfort, stability, and security; they were a new terrain where a relatively affluent part of the population was able to articulate conventional family values. In Don Mills, the model suburban community built by the developer E.P. Taylor, 32 per cent of male homeowners were executives, 24 per cent were professionals, 20 per cent were skilled technicians, and 11 per cent were salesmen (Strong-Boag, 1995: 487).

Family life thrived in other settings as well. The farm population of Ontario fell from some 694,700 to 363,600 between 1941 and 1971, but the rural *nonfarm* population, which had declined during the 1940s, grew steadily in the 1950s and 1960s to reach 995,800 by 1971 – or 13 per cent of the total population of the province (Rea, 1985: 27, 30). This meant that a significant portion of the Class of '73 grew up in small towns with a more limited range of educational and occupational options than were available in larger urban centres. The strongest population growth occurred in the six counties of Hamilton-Wentworth, Halton, Peel, York, Durham, and Metro Toronto, which held half the province's population in the 1940s but two-thirds of it by the 1960s. The Class of '73 reflected these broad residential patterns. While 43 per cent of the students lived in Metro Toronto or other large metropolitan areas, 24 per cent came from small cities, towns, and urban fringe communities, and 33 per cent from other, mainly rural areas (Anisef et al., 1980: A-10).

Immigration, mostly from Europe, accounted for a considerable portion of Ontario's population increase. Between 1941 and 1951 the net gain from international migration was 154,000; between 1951 and 1961 it was 562,000, with more than 50 per cent of immigrants to Canada settling in Ontario (Rea, 1985: 28–30). One-quarter of the Class of '73 had at least one parent born outside Canada, most likely in France, Italy, Germany, the Netherlands, or Poland.[1] Rising immigration led to greater ethnic diversity in Ontario, and this would have implications for the cultural environments within which young people came of age in the late 1960s and early 1970s.

Schooling

The educational system expanded significantly in Ontario in the 1960s and early 1970s, driven by population growth, economic demand, human capital theory, and the promise of social justice through equality of opportunity. In 1960, 1.4 million students were attending elementary and secondary school in the province; by 1970 the figure was more than 2 million. Full-time university enrolment rose from 32,100 in 1960 to 159,700 in 1975. Over the same period, 'non-university' postsecondary enrolment climbed from 16,600 to 59,600 (Rea, 1985: 104–5; Statistics Canada, 1978; Axelrod, 1982). In Ontario and in the country as a whole, advanced schooling was widely and strongly perceived as the route to a better life and a richer society. Few would have disputed Premier John Robarts' 1965 declaration that 'our true wealth resides in an educated citizenry. Our shrewdest and most profitable investment rests in the education of our people' (Axelrod, 1982: 32).

Against this 'utilitarian' background, students in the Class of '73 began elementary school in 1960 or 1961. The schools they attended had changed relatively little over the past quarter-century. Pupils were grouped in grades determined by age rather than academic ability. Classroom learning was characterized by prescribed subjects, fact-learning from standardized textbooks, and extensive testing. In public and separate schools alike, religious teaching, including Bible stories and the recitation of the Lord's Prayer, had been required since 1944, although children whose parents objected to these religious exercises could be excused from them. Strongly influenced by traditionalist educators such as Hilda Neatby, author of the popular book *So Little for the Mind* (1953), W.J. Dunlop, Minister of Education in Ontario from 1951 to 1959, stressed the role of schools in promoting the 'pioneer' virtues of hard work, civic loyalty, and Christian values (Stamp, 1982: 181, 192; Stevenson, 1970: 409–10; Fleming, 1971: 239–49).

But change was in the air. Experiments with student-centred, individualized forms of instruction were begun in a number of schools in the mid-1960s, in anticipation of systemic reforms by the end of the decade. In 1965, French was introduced into the elementary school curriculum, and by 1972, 40 per cent of anglophone elementary students were enrolled in French courses. During the 1960s, religious instruction was provoking increasing complaints because of its insensitivity to non-Christian communities. In 1969 the old program, which by then was falling into disuse, was officially eliminated following the recommendations of a commissioned study. This period also witnessed the demise of the 'one-room school house' in Ontario. Between 1965 and 1967 alone, consolidation in rural areas reduced the number of rural schools from 1,463 to 530 (Stamp, 1982: 208, 212, 219–20, 223). Thousands of students, including members of the Class of '73, were soon being bussed to large district schools that were similar in size and scope to those in urban areas.

Secondary school education, which most of the Class of '73 began in 1969, had also been swept by growth and change. The 1960s began with the introduction of the 'Reorganized [Robarts] Plan,' which created three streams in Ontario high schools: Arts and Science; Science,

Technology, and Trades; and Business and Commerce. These programs were offered in either five-year or four-year courses of study, and students hoping to attend university usually enrolled in the five-year Arts and Science stream. The technology and business programs, for which the federal government provided generous funding, had been intended to train workers for a growing industrial and service economy. The system was soon criticized for failing to equip graduates with usable work skills and for channelling less advantaged students into nonacademic streams, thereby perpetuating social disparities in the province (Stamp, 1982: 205–6; Rea, 1985: 112; Curtis et al., 1992: 87–92; Gidney, 1999: 63–66).

The community college system was created in 1966 to offer extended training for high school leavers without jobs who were either not interested in university or not qualified to enter it. By 1973, twenty-two such institutions were operating, as were fifteen universities. For Ontario families, the realization was growing that a young person's career prospects depended on the acquisition of some form of postsecondary education. Between 1961 and 1971, the proportion of Canadians aged 15 to 19 who were attending school full-time had risen from just under 60 per cent to more than 70 per cent (Baker, 1989: 8).

Befitting the spirit of social reform that marked the era, Ontario schools were further transformed at the end of the 1960s. The Report of the Royal Commission on the Aims and Objectives of Education (the Hall-Dennis Report of 1968) embraced a 'progressive' educational philosophy that stressed holistic learning, freedom of choice, and a 'humane,' noncompetitive classroom environment. This led to significant changes in both elementary and secondary schooling (Stamp, 1982: 217–20). In 1969 the Robarts Plan was replaced by a 'credit system' that based students' promotion through high school on the successful completion of individual courses rather than on passing an entire grade. Subjects were now grouped in four broad areas: communications, social sciences, pure and applied sciences, and arts. As long as students selected a minimum of three courses from each field, they had complete freedom of choice. They needed 27 credits to earn a grade 12 diploma and 33 to graduate from grade 13. Provincial departmental examinations for grade 13 students had ended in 1968. Schools would now set their own graduation examinations in a more flexible, less standardized curricular setting. If they were drawn to more radical educational philosophies, students could attend publicly funded alternative schools, such as Everdale, Seed, and C School in Metropolitan Toronto, where the teaching was more innovative and even less structured. In planning their futures, students – including those in the Class of '73 – now had more choice but also greater responsibility. For example, by opting out of high school language or mathematics courses, they might be limiting their postsecondary educational program options.

The reformed school system, though it was more responsive to the interests of individual students, did not end the streaming of students by socio-economic strata. Instead of the two-, four-, and five-year streams, subjects were now grouped into advanced, general, basic, and modified categories. University enrollees came almost entirely from the advanced (arts and science) stream. Students from the general and basic streams (i.e., the business and vocational programs) either registered in community college or attempted to enter the work force directly after leaving school. A Toronto survey published in 1970 found that children from working-class families were ten times more likely to enrol in the city's vocational secondary schools than were those from middle- and upper-class backgrounds. Furthermore, children of unemployed parents and of parents on welfare were significantly overrepresented in the vocational stream (Wright, 1970). As our 1980 study on the Class of '73 reported, 70 to 80 per cent of students from higher socio-economic strata had enrolled in high school academic programs leading to the possibility of university attendance; and rural students were significantly less likely than their urban counterparts to enter the academic high school stream. Community colleges drew a higher proportion of students from lower socio-economic strata than did universities (Anisef et al., 1980: 109-13).

The reforms flowing from the Hall-Dennis Report were greeted enthusiastically at first, but they soon aroused wide public concern. Conservative sceptics were joined in the early 1970s by some disillusioned liberals, such as the editors of the *Toronto Star*, and by frustrated teachers, who claimed that the credit system 'simply [wasn't] working' (Stamp, 1982: 246; Toronto Star, 1973a, 1973b, 1973e; Manzer, 1994: 159). Detractors charged that students in the new system were bewildered by the choices before them, that they were less literate than graduates of the previous decade, and that teachers were overburdened by the rapidity and scope of the recent changes. Partly in response to the mounting pressure, in 1974 the Ministry of Education introduced six compulsory high school credits: four in English and two in Canadian Studies. Additional requirements were announced in

1976 (Stamp, 1982: 246; Wilson, 1982: 203–4). Since the Class of '73 graduated before these new regulations were imposed, our study group completed high school in an era of unprecedented curricular flexibility (Royal Commission on Learning, 1994: 20–1).

The educational environment was further disturbed by sudden concern over the costs of schooling. In 1970, after a decade of expansion, the government imposed budget ceilings on Ontario school boards.[2] Consequently, teacher militancy grew and labour relations deteriorated. On 18 December 1973, halfway through the graduating year for Class of '73 members who had proceeded to grade 13, Ontario high school teachers walked off the job in defiance of proposed provincial legislation imposing compulsory arbitration. Some 30,000 teachers and their supporters gathered at Queen's Park for the largest protest in Ontario history. The immediate crisis passed, but labour actions erupted the following year, and in 1975 nearly 9,000 high school teachers in Metropolitan Toronto went on strike for two months (Stamp, 1982: 243–4; Gidney, 1999: 117–22). By the mid-1970s the climate of harmony and optimism had yielded to one of tension and concern.[3] Chapter 3 discusses the responses of individuals to these challenges.

The Class of '73 had run up against a fickle public mood and a changing educational environment. Reformers, reflecting the optimism of the late 1960s, had sought to liberate students, trusting them to make sensible academic choices. But critics were already questioning the liberalized system and the competence of its users. Furthermore, despite pretensions to social equality, it was clear that in less advantaged neighbourhoods, and in small towns and rural areas, a form of socio-economic streaming was continuing to narrow educational pathways. It was by no means impossible for individuals to surmount these structural barriers; even so, good students in poorer communities were less likely to attend university than those from middle-class neighbourhoods of large cities. The Class of '73 approached the end of high school at a time of shifting public priorities. To young people and their families, advanced education clearly mattered, but specific routes were being selected in a world that included both abundant choice and growing uncertainty.

Family Ties: Gender, Parents, Peers

While the Class of '73 was progressing through high school toward graduation, the traditional place of women was being seriously questioned. Gender roles stressing the appropriateness of domestic life for women and of careers for men were promoted widely in the two decades following the Second World War. School textbooks during the 1960s continued to 'cast the adult female characters predominantly as housewives/mothers while male adult characters appeared in a wide variety of roles' (Pierson, 1995: 163). A 1973 study of 9,000 grade 12 Ontario students confirmed that class and gender still influenced educational aspirations. Students from more affluent families were more inclined to pursue university; and at virtually all class levels, males had higher aspirations for university than did females. Girls from families with the least social status were the most inclined to leave school early for the work force in order to take up traditionally 'female' occupations (Porter et al., 1982: Ch. 5).

At the same time, the feminist movement, which challenged the discriminatory treatment of women in the work force, in politics, in education, and within the family, had become a prominent presence in Canadian society. In its 1970 report, the Royal Commission on the Status of Women documented the conditions facing men and women and recommended legal and social changes to foster gender equality (Prentice et al., 1988: Chs. 13, 14). Important social changes were signalled by a series of developments: divorce laws had been liberalized in 1968; women constituted 45 per cent of university students in 1976, compared with 38.5 per cent in 1961; women's studies courses were now part of university curricula; and the labour force participation of women had reached 37 per cent by 1971 (Baker, 1989: 176). Magazine and newspaper articles highlighted the accomplishments of professional women and debated – crudely at times – the merits of feminism itself (*Toronto Star*, 1973g; Cornell, 1973; *Maclean's*, 1975). While feminist writers were encouraging women to pursue their rights vigilantly, a psychiatrist denounced the movement and labelled its promoters 'libchicks' who were blind to the problems of men (Rich, 1971: 34; Greenglass, 1973: 55; Thompson, 1971: 7).

As reflected in popular surveys, young women held mixed views on the subject of women's liberation. In a 1971 *Chatelaine* article, the 'under 21s' were found to favour women's independence (and greater autonomy for youth in general), broad choice of occupations, and equal pay for equal work. Yet those who expressed specific vocational ambitions generally selected traditional 'women's' fields such as the social services, nursing, and teaching. No respondents were in a great hurry to get married and have children, though most felt they would eventually. Some young women sympathized with the goals of feminism but also believed that feminists were impractical. Attitudes were at times contradictory. As one 19-year-old put it: 'I'm a believer in the [feminist] movement ... [but] ... I grew up playing with bride cutouts: how can I possibly accept the idea of a having a career and not getting married?' (Rockett, 1971: 40). Interviews with members of the Class of '73 conducted in 1979 reflected both an awareness of women's changing roles and the persistence of traditional thinking. Janice, an ambitious, self-confident woman with a BEd, had 'always wanted to be a teacher,' and in 1979 was working part-time while searching for such a position. She expected eventually to get married but to remain childless: 'I don't think it's fair to work and have children.' She believed in 'equality in the work force' but she was not a 'woman's libber ... I like guys to open doors and I want to get dressed like a woman.' With respect to her career prospects and social life, she was unmistakably optimistic about the future (Anisef et al., 1980: 305–10).

A mother of two (in 1979), Rose lived on the outskirts of a small, eastern Ontario town. She worked part-time as a bookkeeper in her father's company and was married to a manufacturing plant worker. Rose had found school difficult; she took commercial subjects and left after grade 12. Transferring to a 'huge high school district' had been a major transition for Rose, a shy person with low self-confidence. What she enjoyed most in school was theatre class, and in her last year she directed the school play. Yet she never considered pursuing this interest academically, nor did her high school commercial program allow for such a route. She was not satisfied being a housewife and longed for other outlets, but at the time she had no specific plans. Her husband helped a great deal with the children and the housework, which she appreciated, and aware of her dissatisfaction, he encouraged her to pursue new interests.

Rose's experience highlights the link between gender and self-esteem, a dynamic that in the academic literature has been found to affect adolescent perceptions and expectations. Teenage girls in the early 1970s had lower self-esteem than teenage boys, and females with the highest educational and occupational aspirations were likely to have the least self-esteem. Even as girls' ambitions grew, fear of failure lurked in the background (Bush et al., 1977–8; Orenstein, 1994; Gilligan, 1982). Furthermore, teenage women were far more inclined than men to take marriage and children into account in anticipating their vocations and careers. A study of Hamilton youth born in 1957 found that in 1975, their parents were still 'more likely to say they preferred and expected a university education for their sons than for their daughters' (Looker, 1994: 173).[4] Confronted with such social conditioning, young women continued to structure their expectations in accordance with a gender-specific social script (Wand, 1977; Looker, 1993).

As these studies and individual experiences illustrate, the Class of '73 grew to maturity in an era when the ideal of gender equality competed for legitimacy with traditional values regarding women's place in the family, in the community, and in the workplace. Women were pursuing postsecondary education in increasing numbers, yet in the 1970s they were concentrated in programs that led to professions and vocations offering lower status and incomes than those dominated by men. A survey of 1976 graduates of Canadian universities two years after graduation found that men earned on average $2,000 more per year than women (Clark and Zsigmond, 1981: 11, 59–70; Anisef et al., 1980: 216). Thus, even while horizons were opening for women in the 1970s, patterns of gender inequality persisted.

In the early 1970s, the demand for choice, autonomy, and equality – goals that had already infused the feminist movement – spread from the world of youth onto the wider social landscape. A decade before, groups of young people in North America and elsewhere had joined activists of older generations to protest the nuclear arms race, which was threatening the world's peace and stability. This movement spread to envelop other issues. Convinced that Western liberal democracies were failing to realize their fundamental ideals, youthful critics confronted conventional values and entrenched authority. Racism, poverty, inadequate schooling, and particularly the Vietnam War were the major objects of their political agitation. Inspired by the example of the Free Speech Movement at the Berkeley Campus of the University of California in 1964, university students organized frequent demonstrations demanding an end to educational paternalism and military research on campuses. They sought a greater role in governing their institutions and more access to higher education for disadvantaged people. While the Ontario student movement lacked the intensity and occasional violence of the movement in the United States, all universities – and many high schools – were challenged in some way by this campaign for political and educational change.[5]

As the Vietnam War wound down, the student movement dissipated. By the time the Class of '73 was completing high school, the spirit of activism was less conspicuous in schools and universities. To some degree the Ontario school system had already sated its appetite for educational reform. And as we have seen, students moving through the school system at this time felt the impact of this pedagogical change. Perhaps even more visible – and enduring – was the effect on Ontario youth of 'countercultural' beliefs and practices emanating from the turbulent world of the late 1960s.

In their quest for autonomy and freedom from traditional social restraints, baby boom youth had virtually transformed sexual standards and normalized the practice of premarital sex. Even so, by the early 1970s young women were still more inclined than young men to remain virgins until marriage. Furthermore, rural youth were more traditional in their attitudes toward sexual activity than those in urban centres (Hobart, 1974). The birth control pill had reduced dramatically the fear of unwanted pregnancy and had provided women with greater control over their sexual lives. Teenage pregnancy in Canada (age 15 to 19) fell from 33.7 per 1,000 in 1971 to 26.4 per 1,000 in 1976 (Nett, 1986: 186). Comparing results from 1968 to 1977, Hobart found a significant increase in the proportion of English-Canadian youth, male and female, who believed that sexual intercourse was acceptable for those who were in love or engaged (Hobart, 1979: 46).

Homosexuality was being discussed more openly, but young people who were gay still had not achieved equality of treatment or a sense of personal security within their peer groups or communities (Ramu, 1979: 177). Alex, who was aware of his gay orientation, was 'terrified socially' in his Toronto high school and felt unable to confide in his friends, teachers, or parents: the atmosphere was simply too threatening. Similarly, Rebecca struggled with her sexual orientation at the age of 16. When she was 22, after being a practising bisexual for several years, she fully acknowledged her lesbian identity. Her parents were very supportive when her health deteriorated as a result of her experiments with drugs, yet she never spoke to her parents about her sexual orientation. By that time the law in Canada no longer criminalized homosexual relations; even so, in the early 1970s gay youth could well testify to the painfully slow growth of social tolerance for this 'alternative' lifestyle.

Change was more evident in another social sphere. Growing divorce rates notwithstanding, marriage still mattered to young people, and most intended eventually to 'tie the knot.' But different living arrangements – particularly cohabitation by unmarried couples – became more acceptable in the 1970s (Hobart, 1972). By 1981 nearly half of Canadians polled approved of common law arrangements (twice the percentage from a decade earlier). In the same year, 30 per cent of cohabiting Canadian couples aged 15 to 24 were unmarried (Nett, 1986: 192; Demers, 1986: 26; Wilson, 1990). Though not necessarily typical of other parents with children in the Class of '73, the attitude of Shannon's father was one indication of how times had changed. When she entered university, he advised her to leave home, live with her boyfriend, and for the time being avoid marriage. 'I think young people today ... jump too soon into marriage,' he said, 'and it might be better to [move in together] to see how it goes.'

Parents would likely have shown less equanimity regarding a different manifestation of youth subculture: the consumption of hallucinogenic drugs. Drug use, which was often linked (often through media caricatures) with the 'hippie' culture of the late 1960s, rose significantly in Toronto high schools between 1968 and 1970. With the exception of marijuana, alcohol, and glue consumption, which continued to increase, overall drug use stabilized in city schools in 1972 (Smart and Fejer, 1974). The 1973 report of a national commission on the 'nonmedical' use of drugs inspired calls, finally unheeded, for the legalization of marijuana and hashish (LeDain, 1973). The law aside, drugs were accessible to the Class of '73 and were commonly if not universally used. A number of interviewees described the peer pressure associated with this 'illicit' recreational activity. One woman, 16 at the time, lost her brother to heroin addiction. Another was 'heavily involved' in drug use but gave it up at age 17. Whether they indulged frequently, occasionally, or not at all, young people lived in a social world in which drugs were an acknowledged and available commodity.

As the above cases suggest, in the most extreme instances drug use could play a role in the lives *and* deaths of disaffected youth. Suicide rates among young people tripled between 1960 and 1980. In 1981 the suicide rate for males 15 to 24 was 12.7 per 100,000, up from 3.7 per 100,000 in 1971; for females it rose from 3.1 per 100,000 to 3.8 during that decade (Baker, 1989: 9). Researchers have surmised that the pressures of 'mass' society, the changing family structure, and the particular alienation of native youth (for whom the suicide rate was highest), all contributed to this disturbing trend, which was especially severe in the mid to late 1970s (Coté and Allahar, 1994: 58–61).

Less tragically, peer culture for the Class of '73 included the important diversions of music and travel, both of which were popularized through sophisticated systems of technology and communication. The icons of 1960s rock – Bob Dylan, the Beatles, the Rolling Stones – continued to rouse the enthusiasm of youth, as did superstars of the 1970s such as David Bowie, Abba, Stevie Wonder, and Carole King. Television, movies, and the record industry spread American-dominated popular culture around the globe, which itself was increasingly traversed by Canadian youth.

Taking advantage of affordable air travel, student rail discounts, and youth hostels, young travellers headed across North America or overseas for extended vacations and missions of self-discovery (*Toronto Star*, 1973f). Following the completion of her BA, Rachel travelled to Israel to work on a kibbutz before attending graduate school. Paul, who was undoubtedly more affluent than the average student in his year, took several summer trips to Europe while completing his university education. Unhappy at home, Kate felt resourceful and independent after travelling and working in Germany. 'Finally,' she recalled, 'I broke into my own.' For many young adventurers, such trips were a rite of passage.

The collective life course of the Class of '73 signalled elements of social change. Yet at the same time, there were signs of generational stability and continuity. Young people were spending less leisure time with their families than in the past; even so, children and their parents still had to negotiate the excitement, the challenges, and the periodic tensions of the passage through adolescence. Some observers, drawing from traditional social/psychological theory, assumed that turbulence in adolescence and strife between the generations were inevitable, particularly in the wake of the conspicuous 1960s example (Feuer, 1969). Later studies, however, cast doubt on these claims, finding instead a greater degree of shared values and co-operation between youth and their parents than was implied by media portraits (Douvan and Adelson, 1966; Coleman and Hendry, 1990: 84–90; Ishwaran, 1979a). Such research found that conflict between adolescents and parents erupted commonly around 'day-to-day' concerns, but that 'outright rejection or rebellion' by young people was rare (Coleman and Hendry, 1990: 89).

A timely Ontario investigation lent support to this thesis (Kallen and Kelner, 1976). Designed to explore the supposed 'generation gap,' it sampled the views and behaviours of secondary school and university students in Toronto in 1970–71. They were found to be more liberal than their parents regarding sexuality and drug use, yet they favoured monogamous marriage, they valued the opinions of their parents, and they believed Canada to be a 'democratic' and 'flexible' society. Their peer groups served as vehicles for experimenting with alternative lifestyles and allowed for the cultivation of relationships outside family scrutiny, but this did not lead to a rejection of parental links or authority. These and other youth certainly valued their autonomy, and 'modern' parents were advised to be communicative rather than authoritarian in addressing family problems. But their children were far from revolutionary.[6] Indeed, by the mid-1970s journalists were reporting that pragmatism and individualism, more than rebelliousness and iconoclasm, characterized the mood of young people in Canada.[7]

Postwar Ontario included a growing proportion of immigrant families, whose children were particularly exposed to the competing forces of tradition and change. Their strong desire to make their way in Canadian society was revealed in a study assessing the 'educational plans' of the Class of '73. Both 'foreign born' and 'mixed' students (those born in Canada whose fathers were not) had higher educational aspirations than 'Canadian born' children of the same academic year (Anisef, 1975b; Porter et al., 1982: 82–3). Differences by ethnicity and social class notwithstanding, most 'new Canadians' believed in encouraging their children to pursue advanced education.

At the same time, immigrant parents were concerned that the forces of cultural assimilation might erode their children's commitment to their particular ethnic community. Consequently, children were encouraged and even pressured to date (and later, to marry) within their own ethnic and/or religious community (Peters, 1984). In some cases, young women were subjected to especially severe restrictions on their social activities (Simmons and Turner, 1976; Ishwaran, 1976). While a trend toward greater cultural assimilation, including 'interfaith' marriage, was identifiable, traditional patterns of behaviour continued into the 1970s. Nearly 80 per cent of all Canadians who married in 1972 selected mates of their own faith, and most ethnic groups showed 'a high to moderately high' degree of ethnic endogamy, with rates 'ranging from 52 to 93 per cent' (Ramu, 1979: 182; see also Moon, 1979; Chimbos, 1980; Sturino, 1980). As G.N. Ramu observed in 1979, notwithstanding 'the magnitude of changes taking place in other aspects of social life ... race, religion and ethnicity continue[d] to exercise a dominate influence in mate-choice and take precedence over other considerations' (1979: 182).

Though gradually becoming more ethnically and racially diverse, Ontario in the 1970s could still be inhospitable to those outside the culturally dominant groups. A study of West Indians in Toronto found deep concerns about both the experience of discrimination and the heavy concentration of black high school students in vocational as opposed to academic programs. 'Parents perceived [the latter] as a direct attempt by the school system to prevent blacks from achieving high educational levels' (Ashworth, 1975: 162–7; see also Head, 1984).

Some members of the Class of '73 distinctly recalled being culturally marginalized. Kate, who was of German/Catholic background and who lived in a small 'Protestant/Canadian' community, was painfully conscious of her 'minority status.' Carl arrived in Canada from Portugal at the age of 7. His family settled in a predominantly Italian area. Periodically branded an 'immigrant,' a term he hated, he behaved rebelliously in school, something he partially attributes to his sense of 'second class' citizenship.

For some youth, the experience of exclusion served to strengthen cultural identity. Dom, the son of a garbage collector in Hamilton, was of Italian descent 'and proud of it.' His father died when he was in grade 10. He then worked part-time with his mother at a laundromat and finally left school in grade 12. He was determined to maintain his family and community ties, and today his children identify themselves as 'Italian.' Rachel, raised in a nonreligious Jewish family, undertook a voyage of spiritual self-discovery while in university and became an orthodox Jew along with her future husband. Later in this book we will discuss at length how the forces of ethnicity, religion, and race affected the lives of youth coming of age in the 1970s.

Prospects for Employment

As the Class of '73 approached high school graduation, they were compelled – normally in concert with their families – to make some important decisions about the future. Would they apply to college or university, and if so for what programs? If their formal schooling was ending, where would they look for work? More than ever, preparation for the world of work – either through additional schooling or direct entry – mattered in these young people's lives.

Given Canada's recent economic performance, they had good reason to be hopeful. In 1970, Ontario was Canada's 'industrial heartland' and had the country's lowest unemployment rate. Those with jobs had higher real incomes and better working conditions than any previous generation (Rea, 1985: 241–2). Owing to the impressive expansion of the past decade, there was a wider than ever array of educational training options for both women and men. Yet at the very time personal choices were being weighed, economic conditions were changing. Ontario's unemployment rate rose to 6 per cent in 1975, at the time higher than that of three other provinces (Rea, 1985: 254). More seriously, the national unemployment rate for those 15 to 24 was rising steadily. In 1977 it reached 14.5 per cent, which was more than twice the rate (5.8 per cent) for those over 25 (Statistics Canada, 1978b: 51; Denton et al., 1981: 20).[8] (A decade earlier the comparable unemployment rates for these age groups had been 6.1 and 2.8 percent, respectively).

Furthermore, young people with the least education were the most likely to be unemployed. During the years 1974 to 1977, 15 to 24 year olds with only an elementary education faced an average unemployment rate of 23.2 per cent. For secondary school graduates the rate was 13.5 per cent; for college certificate or diploma holders it was 6.3 per cent; and for university graduates it was 5.4 per cent (Denton et al., 1981: 54).

A nationwide survey covering 45 per cent of the 97,000 students who graduated from colleges and universities in 1976 found that two years after graduation, 8.2 per cent of university degree holders and 6.7 per cent of college grads were unemployed. However, more than one-third of university degree holders were 'underemployed,' and only 42 per cent of university graduates believed that their jobs were directly related to their educational qualifications. Some 65 per cent of college graduates held this view (Clark and Zsigmond, 1981: 7, 59–70, 128–31). Other studies indicated that the problem of underemployment tended to diminish the longer one was in the work force (Anisef and Axelrod, 1993). Still, the statistics contained a sobering message: educational institutions were producing graduates at a faster rate than the economy could absorb them, and employment prospects were especially grim for those with no postsecondary education.

Policymakers in the mid-1970s found themselves confronted with inflation, unemployment, and rising government debt. This previously unheard-of combination created labour market volatility in the public and private sectors. The goods-producing sector in Ontario had been declining in importance since the Second World War, and new opportunities were to be found primarily in service-related activities, a significant proportion of which were funded by government (Rea, 1985: 7–8). Concerns about the levels of public spending constrained growth in the government sector as well; thus, students leaving high schools, colleges, and universities in the mid to late 1970s encountered a particularly uncertain job market.

College and university graduates in business, computer science, engineering, and health fared better than those in the arts, the humanities, and the social sciences. The teaching profession no longer absorbed a significant proportion of degree holders the way it had in the 1950s and 1960s. In 1971, 63.3 per cent of Ontario graduates from teacher colleges were able to find work in Ontario. By 1976–77, that figure had fallen to 43.3 per cent, reflecting a national trend (Jackson, 1977).

High school graduates and their parents who paid attention to media stories and economists' lectures were receiving a mixed message. On the one hand, there were alarming reports questioning the value of an advanced education. The 'rate of return' was falling. There would be 'one job for every two graduates.' PhDs were driving taxis (Gwyn, 1973; *Toronto Star*, 1973c; Dodge, 1972; Berg, 1970). So why pursue higher learning? On the other hand, these same studies documented that employers were using educational credentials to screen recruits. Thus, during periods of labour surpluses the job seekers with the most education, whatever the positions, were the most employable. As a noted economist observed: 'Education doesn't make you more productive. It just helps convince your boss you're worth more' (Ostry, 1972). This was a powerful argument for staying in school and pursuing a postsecondary diploma or degree; and most Ontario families, including those from the Class of '73, continued to heed the call (Axelrod, 1982; Anisef et al., 1980).[9] In later chapters we will follow the trail of this cohort as it negotiated its way through the world of work.

Conclusions

Unlike the previous generation, the Class of '73 was born in an era of relative prosperity. Despite insecurities arising from the Cold War, children were raised (predominantly by mothers) in a spirit of expectancy and optimism. Increasingly, schooling was perceived as the bridge to the good life – a message reinforced by bountiful public funding. Idealized middle-class standards, promoted in the media and sustained by 'experts,' informed childrearing practices, teaching methods, gender relations, and suburban living.

Social consensus was eroded in the mid to late 1960s by a variety of critics, including youth, women, and school reformers, who argued that true individuality and social equality had yet to be achieved in Ontario and elsewhere. To a limited degree, a reformed educational system reflected these concerns and touched the lives of students in the Class of '73. Youth culture stressed the virtues of choice and autonomy. Following precedents set in the late 1960s, young people adopted more liberal modes of social interaction. However, there is little evidence that they were repudiating the practical concerns of their parents. In a sea of social change, at a time when even revolutionary rhetoric was being espoused, some core values endured. As their parents hoped, young people pursued postsecondary education in unparalleled numbers, and they looked forward to useful and rewarding vocations. The unexpected economic downturn of the 1970s loomed as a possible impediment to this goal.

These historical forces moulded the environment in which the Class of '73 experienced childhood, schooling, and adolescence. But our analysis also reveals that within this context, experiences were far from identical. The structures of economic life, social relations, and cultural origin produced different life course paths. Rural and working-class youth were likely to attain less education than their middle-class, urban counterparts. Young women enjoyed a wider range of educational and occupational options than had their mothers, but the notion of domestic 'responsibility' continued to exert a strong pull on their thinking. Youth whose families had recently arrived in Canada, and others whose racial, religious, or ethnic background was outside the social mainstream, faced unique challenges at home, at school, and in their peer group or workplace.

Gender, social origin, and cultural background are useful predictors of young people's values and behaviour, but these social categories by no means explain *all* perceptions and choices. Psychological traits, interests and tastes, family trauma, and health issues all affect the life course in unforeseen ways. In the pages that follow we continue to consider the range of structural and agentic factors that shaped our respondents' experiences as they moved from early adulthood to middle age.

CHAPTER THREE

Educational Pathways

Education is a formative experience for Canadians, as school experiences occupy a significant proportion of the life course. Schooling is also a collective experience, especially at the primary and secondary levels. Classrooms not only develop our skills, knowledge, and intellectual capacities, but also expose us to the wider culture and its value orientations, albeit in competition with other socializing agents such as families, mass media, and religion.

As children become adolescents and enter secondary school, educational routines change. They must now move between classrooms according to timetables, with each classroom being specifically subject-oriented. Schooling becomes explicitly competitive, and students are sorted into levels and courses according to their presumed interests and abilities. This process is widely recognized and is labelled as 'streaming' or 'tracking.'

The secondary school years are marked by an awareness among youth that adulthood is not far off and that they will soon be challenged to secure their place in society through employment. Members of the Class of '73 undoubtedly had some work experience even while in high school, through part-time and summer jobs. But in the first half of the 1970s, employment meant finding an occupation, not just odd jobs, and embarking on a valued career. This challenge probably held different meanings for our various respondents and was informed by differences in social class, race, ethnicity, gender, and region. However, what particularly distinguished Class of '73 members was their level of education, which influenced how they approached adulthood and employment.

In the 1970s, Ontario's educational system was linked to the world of employment through three main pathways. The first involved moving from high school directly into the labour market. Before the reforms to Ontario's educational system in the 1960s, this pathway was quite common, and vocational high schools (in contrast to the collegiates) provided specific types of vocational training for many young people. Entry into jobs after grade 12 was still common in the early 1970s, though graduation from specific vocational courses in high school was on the decline. A second main pathway was to continue one's education for a few years at a community college. The community college system had been introduced by the provincial government to provide a much fuller range of vocational training than was offered by the vocational high schools. The third main pathway was to continue on to university. Once bastions of élite professional training, by the 1970s universities were viewed as the initial providers of general postsecondary education, although they still served as gateways to various important professions. In an era when university credentials acted as a screening device in the labour market, students poured into universities. In the 1960s employers were less concerned with a graduate's specific degree than with the evident economic value of a general university education. Higher education was considered a worthy, negotiable commodity in the work force (Axelrod, 1982).

These three pathways formed an institutionalized structure of opportunity, which had been established to produce the human capital needed by the economy. However, there were some young people who might have graduated as part of the Class of '73 but whose lives did not coincide with this structure, and these chose to drop out of high school before grade 12. Also, while some students entered postsecondary education immediately following high school graduation, others took time out to work and travel. Among those who expected to attend a community college, many found employment after high school and stayed in their jobs. In sum, while there were clearly three main pathways or transitions between education and work, many individuals adopted variations on these themes.

While formal education is largely concentrated in the early years, it does not necessarily end with graduation from a community college or university. Many members of the Class of '73 engaged in occupation-related training at their places of work. Others returned to community college and university for a few courses, or to complete degrees, or to obtain new degrees, certificates, or diplomas. Their motivation to do so ranged from simple curiosity to a desire to pursue an entirely new career direction.

In this chapter we attempt to reveal the combined influence of structure and agency on the formative high school years and beyond. We focus on the critical high school years when the Class of '73 was formulating educational and career options that would do much to establish future life scripts. For some, the future was clear, guided as it was by their constructed career goals, which seemed achievable given their social and economic backgrounds. For others, ambivalence and indecision were key features, particularly during their adolescence, and this required them to negotiate structural barriers over which they had limited control. Formal education is highly institutional in character, and this easily leads to structural interpretations linking typical educational pathways to key aspects of people's lives such as class, gender, ethnicity, and geographic location. Nevertheless, our more fine-grained biographical material shows an underlying human agency – a diversity of actual paths, entrances, and exits as Class of '73 members tried various educational programs, experimenting with subjects, majors, and certificates, perhaps changing educational levels and institutions, and punctuating their educational experiences with periods of employment, travel, family formation, and/or being parents. Though structural factors help us understand the educational pathways followed by the Class of '73, it is the individuals' own actions, based on their distinctive perceptions and motivations, that have shaped their educational and vocational decision making. As the world around them changed, they themselves changed. Some members of the Class of '73 altered their personal outlooks, which resulted in a rethinking of occupational goals, which perhaps required a return to advanced forms of learning. The significance of this will be considered in Chapter 5.

Because of the highly structured nature of formal education, and the great amount of aggregate information we have about Class of '73 members' educational attainments, this chapter emphasizes the structural side of the structure/agency coin. Particularly significant here is the extent to which the organizational features of schooling (e.g., high school program, postsecondary fields of study) channelled the transition from high school to postsecondary education. Joel Spring (1976) has described the educational system as the 'sorting machine' for society, since its students move on to adult labour force positions that are highly associated with particular levels of educational attainment. By focusing on educational attainment, we begin to address a key social issue: the extent to which education reinforces class structure and social inequality or, by contrast, provides a means by which individuals can transcend their social background. We will address these questions in Chapter 5.

The Critical Juncture Years, 1973–1974[1]

Three Pathways to Jobs and Education

The Critical Juncture study, as Paul Anisef's original project was known, had its roots in the Ontario government's concern about future enrolment in postsecondary education. The province had just gone through a major expansion of provincial universities and had also created *de novo* a community college system. The factors driving this expansion were described in the previous chapter: a dramatic increase in the number of young people, an increase in the proportion of young people completing high school, and an increase in the number of young people (especially young women) who wanted postsecondary education. All of this educational change took place in a period of strong economic growth. Originally, the Anisef study proposed to examine whether background factors, attitudes, and aspirations could be used to predict the flow of young people into different forms of higher education and the labour market. A provincewide questionnaire study of grade 12 students was selected as the data-gathering tool. The initial survey was undertaken in the spring of 1973; two follow-up telephone surveys were conducted in the fall of 1973 and the fall of 1974.

By the fall of 1974, as Table 3.1 shows, almost two-fifths of former secondary students were in the labour force full-time, almost half were continuing their education (with almost twice as many attending university as a community college), and the remainder were involved in other activities. The pattern emerging at this point in the lives of the Class of '73 reflected the institutional articulation of education and the labour market at the time. An examination of the data generated up to the fall of 1974 shows two main paths as youth moved from secondary education into the labour market. The first was a transition directly into the labour market from high school; the second ultimately led to the labour market, but through grade 13, a university education, and related forms of professional training. As we shall see, these two routes led to different kinds of employment and income opportunities and to different social class status: the first led to working-class and lower-middle-class jobs and social status; the second led to upper-middle-class status and associated white-collar and professional occupations.

Table 3.1. Work or educational activity expected for Fall 1994 in Spring 1973 vs. activity executed in fall 1974 (percentage)

Work and educational plans for Fall 1974			Activity executed in Fall 1974					
Plans for Fall 1974	(n)	%	Work full-time	Attending college	Attending university	Part-time study	Other activity	Total
Work full-time	426	22.2	79.8	4.2	1.4	0.9	13.6	100.0
Attending college	450	23.5	31.1	42.9	10.7	2.4	12.9	100.0
Attending university	673	35.1	10.8	9.2	68.9	1.8	9.2	100.0
Part-time study	97	5.1	48.5	14.4	15.5	4.1	17.5	100.0
Other activity	271	14.1	48.7	9.6	19.2	1.8	20.7	100.0
Total number	1,917	100.0	38.2	16.3	30.5	1.9	13.1	100.0

Both paths were significantly gendered: men and women received different kinds of education, especially at postsecondary levels.

There was also a third pathway, which was really two variant paths within the first main path. One of these was not captured by our research: as we have already indicated, the Critical Juncture study did not include those who left high school before grade 12.[2] The other variant path was entry into the labour market through community college and related private vocational schools. This route focused on vocationally oriented educational programs leading to trades and white-collar occupations, including some semiprofessional occupations. Typically, the courses taken were of one or two years' duration and occasionally of three years. For example, a significant semiprofessional occupation acquired through community colleges in Ontario in the early 1970s was nursing, which was taken up mainly by women.

We can obtain a sense of the number of youth in the emerging pathways in 1974 by estimating the number of the one group that was missing from the Class of '73 – those who dropped out before completing grade 12. The size of this group is difficult to estimate. Crysdale and MacKay (1994) began studying less privileged 'Eastside' Toronto youth in 1969, with follow-up interviews in 1972, 1974, and 1978. They noted that 'the overall provincial rate of drop-outs has been one-third for over a decade' (p. 9). But their Eastside youth had a 63 per cent dropout rate – a rate estimated to be two-and-a-half times higher than in suburban areas, indicating a great deal of variation in dropout rates among schools. Tanner, Krahn, and Hartnagel (1995: Ch. 1) report that in the 1980s there was a widespread belief that Canada's high school dropout rate averaged 30 per cent. They mention, however, that Statistics Canada's *School Leavers Survey* found a different result: in a telephone survey of 9,460 youth done between April and June of 1991, Statistics Canada found that about one in four young people had dropped out of high school at some point. However, many returned to complete their high school diplomas, resulting in a figure of about 18 per cent for those failing to complete high school – a figure much below the accepted 30 per cent (Gilbert et al., 1993).

If we assume conservatively that 20 per cent of the Class of '73 left school before grade 12, then the percentages shown in Table 3.1 would have to be altered significantly if we added early school leavers to our data. Let us assume that these early school leavers went to work full-time and were still working in 1974; if we hypothetically included this group in the table, the fall of 1974 proportions would show half the sample in the labour force, 13 per cent attending a community college, almost 25 per cent attending university, 1.4 per cent in part-time studies, and 10 per cent engaged in some other activity. This would considerably reduce the proportions shown as going on to postsecondary education.

By the fall of 1974, one-third of respondents who had opted for the world of work had already held two or more full-time jobs since leaving high school. About one-fifth of those attending a community college stated that they had held one or more jobs since leaving high school, but this was the case for only one-tenth of university enrollees. Three-quarters of those in part-time studies, and half of those in the 'other activity' group, had held one or more jobs since leaving high school. By the fall of 1974, about 7 per cent of the Class of '73 were married (four times as many women as men). Furthermore, nine out of ten married people reported their fall activity in 1974 as being in the labour force.

A critical element of adult status is full-time employment. Respondents in the Critical Juncture study who entered the world of work after grade 12 appear to have been successful in obtaining full-time employment, thus moving into full adult status rather quickly. Overall, unemployment was low for this group (5 per cent), especially compared to the labour market experiences of young people in the 1990s. Some in this group continued to pursue completion of high school; others enrolled in apprenticeships or trade or business schools. Those who decided to pursue postsecondary education put off entry into the world of work – and thus full adult status – by a few more years.

Predicting Who Goes to Work, College, or University

Can expectations predict the transition from high school to work or higher education? The Critical Juncture study showed that intentions stated at the end of grade 12 corresponded fairly well with activity in the fall of 1974. As Table 3.1 shows, grade 12 youth tended to be overly optimistic about continuing their education, but not by a great deal, at least in the aggregate. Compared to their 1973 intentions, 16 per cent more respondents were employed by the fall of 1974. But the aggregate numbers disguise a much larger shift of individual behaviour. In fact, 45 per cent of respondents were not doing what they thought they might be doing as reported in 1973. The aggregate data understated change over time because the changing of one's mind can work in both directions, and this mix of changes did not show up in the aggregate. Thus, some young people aspired to further education but actually went to work; others who had indicated a desire to go to work actually enrolled at a community college, and a few were even attending university by the fall of 1974.

How were educational choices related to the characteristics of individuals? The Critical Juncture study attempted to sort out some of these linkages by examining parents' educational expectations, respondents' grades in school, peer group educational plans, self-concept of academic ability, and parental encouragement with respect to respondents' educational outcomes. The respondents' pursuit of working, or going to a community college, or attending university, correlated strongly with parents' perceived expectations. Higher marks in high school were more likely to be associated with attending university or a community college than with working full-time. Similarly, perceived ability to graduate from a university or community college was associated with attending such institutions. High school students who later entered university had received stronger encouragement to pursue postsecondary studies than did those who did not attend. Findings from the Phase IV (1979) study showed that parental encouragement to pursue further education after high school was highest among university enrollees, next highest among those going on to community college, and lowest for those working full-time.

Like other studies, this one confirmed that it was middle and upper class students from large urban and suburban communities who were most likely to attend university. The need to leave home and pay residence costs could well have deterred the less affluent from pursuing postsecondary education (Porter et al., 1973). But interviews suggest that factors other than mere affordability could affect post-high school educational decisions: personal agency and a desire to succeed played an important role in some decisions to pursue postsecondary studies. Consider Walter, who lived in a middle-class neighbourhood of suburban Toronto. A 'loner' with few friends, an average student whose memories of high school were not fond, he nevertheless always knew he would attend university. He grew up in a professional family (as opposed to a blue-collar one), and 'there was never any decisions to be made as to whether you would pursue postsecondary education or university. It was more a function of when you would go.' For Walter, this expectation was so internalized that it required little discussion with his parents. 'It was an assumption I had made for myself,' he commented. In his life, university attendance was an important stepping stone in a natural progression of events.

In contrast, Max grew up on a farm in western Ontario. His parents wanted him to get an education, though for them this meant completing secondary school, which he did manage to do. However, he was in those years a teenage rebel and a poor student. Max spent five years after high school driving trucks before enrolling in a three-year diploma program in journalism at a community college; from there, he went on to complete a BA in political science at a university. It was at university that Max discovered he enjoyed learning. In 1995 he was working for the provincial government, after spending some years as a freelance journalist. In describing his family background and his educational pathway, Max told us:

> I grew up on a farm that's been in my family since 1821. That's all my family had ever done is farm. Neither one of my parents finished high school and so it's not surprising that was their goal for the kids. I tried to quit. I wanted to go work in the factory. They said, If you do we'll kill you before you get to the factory. All their emphasis was on finishing high school. There was no emphasis on postsecondary. No one else had experienced it, so it was do as you want. And also, growing up on the farm you never had time to do anything else. You came home from school, you worked. You didn't do all the things kids are exposed to today. The decision to go to school or college and to university came after being out in the working world. It may be that kids who grew up in the city were exposed to college and university. They probably had more exposure to college and university.

When we contacted Ada in 1979, she was completing her four-year university degree on a part-time basis and seriously considering a career in journalism. Her parents pushed her to do well in school, and she internalized the drive to succeed:

> I wanted to attain the award. Marks were important. I was a borderline case. I think that my final average came out to 79.8 per cent and my English teacher ended up boosting my mark in English so I would get the Ontario Scholarship. I wanted it. I wanted that acknowledgment. I had worked really hard for it. But I think by then the pattern was set. I knew I was going to go on and I think just getting the award gave me the extra boost. You're somebody. You can make it.

Though Ada's parents, Italian working-class immigrants, prodded her to excel academically in high school, they never actively encouraged her to pursue postsecondary studies. Rather, they clung to Old World ideals and told Ada, 'You're the girl and if you choose not to get on, it's okay because you can get married and have babies and sit at home.' This attitude caused Ada to rebel, embrace the women's liberation movement, and strive to have it all – a good career as a journalist, a happy love life, marriage, and the opportunity to travel and meet interesting people.

High school students rarely identified the specific vocations or careers they wanted to pursue, but as the sociological literature suggests, the range of options ahead was at least generally determined before they graduated. Students in the advanced stream were more likely to have been raised in homes that stressed the rewards and prestige of a university education. Those in basic and general programs were not perceived as academically equipped to thrive at university, nor did they view themselves that way. Notably, they did not necessarily see themselves as educationally or socially deprived. If they found satisfying employment out of high school or college, and if their achievements met their aspirations, then they were pleased with their choices. Like others in their year, whatever their social backgrounds, circumstances, and special challenges, they largely took responsibility for the diverse paths they followed.

This was especially true for those whose experiences went against the grain of the general sociological patterns described above. Many students did not do what might have been expected, given their class and family backgrounds. For example, given his background, Tim, from Pickering, would not have been the most likely candidate to attend university and obtain a teaching degree. His parents were Irish immigrants who had been raised on farms. They shared the attitude that 'as soon as you could contribute [to the family income] you quit school.' Tim left high school after grade 12 and worked in a variety of unskilled jobs for a few years. A trip to Europe aroused his latent intellectual curiosity. He began reading more, developed new interests, enrolled in university, and obtained an English degree. One of his first professional jobs was as a teacher in Nigeria.

Jeremy, on the other hand, was expected by his parents, who were both professionals, to follow their occupational examples. He recalled being 'programmed to become a dentist.' He enrolled in premedical school for two years, but dropped out when he realized he had no interest in dentistry. He then took a community college course in electronic technology and worked for five years servicing computers – a career in which he also eventually lost interest. So he took another two-year course, this time in audio technology, and found a job at a film company, where he soon became the technical director. At the age of 31, he had finally found fulfilling work. As these cases illustrate, one's class origin was a strong but by no means all-powerful predictor of educational and employment outcomes.

What is the significance of this evidence? First, social class and geographic region affected the amount and level of education that students received. When Anisef employed a statistical technique called discriminant analysis, he was able to correctly classify 64 per cent of Phase III respondents in terms of the five activity outcomes shown in Table 3.1. Second, parental expectations and individual motivation may have promoted educational and occupational aspirations in a way that helped many students surmount social barriers. Indeed, irrespective of parental views, members of the Class of '73 at times forged occupational pathways independently and unpredictably.

Is the Die Cast? The Class of '73 Follow-up Study of 1979

When we returned to the Class of '73 in 1979 (Phase IV), we found most members at yet another significant transition point in their lives. Those who had pursued postsecondary education had completed their education and entered the labour force. The exceptions were mainly those pursuing professional training following a university degree.

Many had married or would soon marry; and married women in each of the main pathways faced or would soon face decisions about combining childrearing with continuing employment (a theme to be taken up in Chapter 7). Returning to the Class of '73 also gave us an opportunity to add some important information about the background of respondents. The Critical Juncture study did not focus explicitly on the role of gender, socio-economic status, and geographic area of residence with respect to educational choices.[3] However, we were able in the 1979 survey to create measures of socio-economic status and region of origin in Ontario based on Phase I data, as well as to ask retrospectively about 'track' in high school. Unless otherwise noted, the remainder of this chapter (whether the 1979 or a later study phase is considered) concentrates on the 788 members of the Class of '73 whom we successfully studied through to 1995.[4]

Demographic Overview and Educational Attainment by 1979

A snapshot picture of the Class of '73 in 1979 shows that at the average age of 24, one-third of the men and almost half of the women were married. Sixty per cent of the university graduates had attended university for four years, and about 30 per cent had attended for three years. The vast majority (close to 90 per cent) began their university studies in 1975. Half of those obtaining a community college certificate or diploma attended two years, one-fifth for one year, and one-quarter for three years; most had started their studies in 1974 or 1975. By 1979, the vast majority of men (89 per cent) and women (81 per cent) were in the labour force, with the unemployment rate for men being 4.8 per cent and for women 7.9 per cent. Close to one-fifth of men and women were still students, either part- or full-time, and half combined being a student with part- or full-time work. Although nearly 50 per cent of the women reported being married in 1979, only one-fifth of married women indicated that they were homemakers and not in the paid labour force.

The Phase IV report, *Is the Die Cast?* (Anisef, Paasche, and Turrittin, 1980), showed that by 1979, nearly three-quarters of the respondents still lived in the general region of the high school they had attended in 1973; the remainder had moved elsewhere in Ontario. Only about 3.6 per cent had left Ontario by 1979. While only about one-quarter of the men living in rural areas had chosen to leave their home community by 1979, two-fifths of the women living in similar rural areas had

Table 3.2. Educational attainment by 1979 and by 1995 (percentages)

Educational attainment	(n)	1979 Male (381)	1979 Female (407)	1979 Total (788)	1995 Male (381)	1995 Female (407)	1995 Total (788)
Attending graduate or professional school*		4.5	5.2	4.8			
University degree		21.5	23.1	22.3			
Other professional degree (LLB, CA, MD, DDS)					2.9	1.7	2.3
University graduate degree (MA, MBA, PhD)					4.7	6.6	5.7
University degree					19.7	19.7	19.7
University degree and college diploma or certificate		0.3	1.2	0.8	3.1	5.7	4.4
University degree and some college courses		1.3	0.2	0.8	1.8	1.5	1.6
Some university courses		6.8	3.4	5.1	4.2	1.5	2.8
College diploma or certificate		15.7	22.6	19.3	22.0	25.3	23.7
College diploma/certificate and some university courses		2.6	2.7	2.7	6.6	4.7	5.6
Some college courses		7.3	5.2	6.2	7.1	3.9	5.5
Some university and some college courses		3.4	1.0	2.2	1.6	2.0	1.8
No postsecondary courses		36.5	35.4	35.9	26.2	27.5	26.9
Total		48.4	51.6	100.0	48.4	51.6	100.0

* Most Class of '73 members in this category had obtained university degrees and were continuing postgraduate or professional education at the time of the Phase IV survey in the summer of 1979.

elected to move. This indicates that rural women in the sample were early on highly geographically mobile compared to women and men residing in the other study regions.

Table 3.2 shows in detail the educational attainment of the Class of '73 as of 1979. To simplify this information, the reader is asked to consider three kinds of enrolments: university only, community college only, and enrolment in both types of postsecondary institutions. These categories include individuals with and without degrees, but exclude individuals with no postsecondary educational experience. Of the 64 per cent of respondents with postsecondary education, about 50 per cent had enrolled in university; about 40 per cent had enrolled in community colleges; and 10 per cent had been enrolled in both types of postsecondary institutions. The small size of this latter group bears testimony to the Ontario government's intention (in contrast to some other provinces) to have community colleges comprise a separate educational stream, rather than serve as transfer institutions to universities. It should be noted that this group was diverse, with almost two-fifths having a college diploma and some university experience, almost one-third having some university and some college, and the remaining one-quarter split between university graduates with college diplomas and university graduates with only some community college experience.

The Class of '73 data for 1979 reveal that the educational or work pathways begun by the end of 1974 were largely followed through 1979. Of those who were working full-time in the fall of 1974, 78 per cent had not undertaken any postsecondary education by 1979; 3.7 per cent had a record of university enrolment; and 17.2 per cent had a record of community college enrolment. Of those attending a community college in the fall of 1974, almost 85 per cent had achieved a college diploma or certificate by 1979, and 3.5 per cent had obtained a university degree. Of the small group that reported some other activity in fall of 1974, 13.8 per cent had obtained a university degree by 1979, 19.5 per cent a college diploma or certificate, and 46 per cent no postsecondary education.[5] It is important to point out that, of the one-third of the Class of '73 who indicated they had only a high school education as of 1979, many had elected to pursue other forms of learning after high school. For example, 37.4 per cent attended short courses, 13.8 per cent pursued apprenticeships, 11.6 per cent participated in some other kind of adult training, and 4.1 per cent attended a private vocational school in the six years following grade 12.

The Influence of Gender, Class, and Region

From the vantagepoint of 1979, by which time most of the Class of '73 had completed their formal education and had entered the labour force, one can clearly see the impact of social background and other factors on educational attainment. With respect to gender, the good news was that women's participation in postsecondary education was now on par with that of men. As indicated in Table 3.2, as many women as men had completed university, and as many women as men had opted not to pursue a postsecondary education. In an assessment of gender differences between 1975 and 1989 with regard to parents' preferences for their teenagers after high school, Looker (1994: 178) reported that in the early period, parents preferred and expected a university education for their sons rather than for their daughters. By 1989 this pattern had reversed: parents preferred and expected their daughters more often than their sons to attend university.

There was a major gender difference with regard to attending community college: a greater proportion of women from the Class of '73 graduated from a college (26.5 per cent, compared to 18.6 per cent for men). This can be attributed in part to many women enrolling in nursing programs, which in the 1970s in Ontario were offered at community colleges. In assessing the status of Ontario women in postsecondary education at this time, Aylward (1983: 27) wrote:

> The majority of full-time female students were concentrated in areas dominated by women. Over 75% of women in post-secondary education were clustered in the social science, humanities, arts and health and education fields ... More women are, however, entering the traditionally-defined male subject areas. In 1976, the engineering field, for example, [comprised] 7.8% of female undergraduates which increased to 10.7% in 1981.

As indicated in Table 3.3, socio-economic status was significantly related to educational attainment in 1979. University graduates and those enrolled in graduate and professional studies were disproportionately drawn from the highest socio-economic quartile and were drawn least often from the lowest socio-economic quartile. Those who had gone no further than a high school education were disproportionately located in the lowest socio-economic quartile and were drawn least often from the highest socio-economic quartile. In contrast, community college graduates were drawn roughly equally from all socio-economic groups, which attests to the success of the colleges in fulfilling their mandate to foster equality of educational opportunity.

The findings reported here are consistent with those reported in other studies conducted in the same time period. Thus, Breton's (1972: 138–9) national study of high school students revealed a relationship between socio-economic status (SES) and educational aspirations: among those who intended to finish high school, 12 per cent more students from a high SES background planned to attend postsecondary school than those from a low SES background. The difference between high and low SES groups in postsecondary plans for boys varied from 9 to 26 per cent, and, for girls, from 3 to 18 per cent, depending on the

Table 3.3. Educational attainment in 1979 by socio-economic status (percentage)

Parental socio-economic status (1973)	(n)	High school only	Educational attainment by 1979			
			Some college/ university	College graduate	University degree	Total
Low SES	213	52.1	9.9	22.5	15.5	100.0
Medium low SES	183	38.8	12.6	27.3	21.3	100.0
Medium high SES	189	37.6	14.3	23.8	24.3	100.0
High SES	203	14.8	17.2	14.8	53.2	100.0
Total	788	35.9	13.5	22.0	28.7	100.0

province of residence, showing the independent effect of region across Canada. Pavalko and Bishop (1968) in a survey of 899 grade 12 students in six high schools in Thunder Bay, Ontario, found that the proportion of students with college plans increased with socio-economic status: 52 per cent of high SES students planned to attend college, as compared with 34.9 per cent of low SES students. Using complex regression models, Gilbert and McRoberts (1977) employed the Survey of Ontario Students Aspirations (1970) data to ascertain the relative importance of class background to students' educational plans. They concluded that it is not so much SES itself as it is 'the avenues through which it operates ... Our overall interpretive framework and one that appears to be supported by the data is that schools serve to perpetuate existing inequalities rather than to enhance equality of opportunity' (44–5).

University graduates were drawn disproportionately from Metro Toronto, as Table 3.4 indicates; college graduates and those with no postsecondary education more frequently came from rural areas and small towns. A higher proportion of rural and small town youth did not complete a postsecondary education; this was related in part to the fact that a disproportionate number of lower-SES youth were located in these regions of Ontario.[6] Not surprisingly, youth from the smaller cities and from rural areas and small towns more frequently had to leave home to attend a university or community college. This affected their decisions to pursue postsecondary studies.

In the fall of 1973 we asked our high school sample whether they anticipated living at home while pursing a postsecondary education. More than three-quarters of respondents living in small towns and rural areas and planning to attend a community college indicated that

Table 3.4. Educational attainment in 1979 by urban/rural region (percentage)

High school region of residence (1973)	(n)	Educational attainment by 1979				
		High school only	Some college/ university	College graduate	University degree	Total
Metro Toronto	129	25.6	17.8	14.0	42.6	100.0
Other large urban areas	147	29.3	17.0	20.4	33.3	100.0
Smaller cities and Metro urban fringe	191	31.4	13.1	20.9	34.6	100.0
Rural areas and small towns	321	45.8	10.3	26.5	17.4	100.0
Total	788	35.9	13.5	22.0	28.7	100.0

they thought they would not remain at home, and over nine in ten planning on a university education thought similarly. In contrast, only 12.8 per cent of Metro Toronto residents planning on college thought they would have to leave home, while more than one-third of those planning on university thought they would have to make such a move. The anticipations mirrored the practice: in 1979, close to three-quarters of the Class of '73 from small towns and rural areas who became college graduates reported that they had had to leave their home town or city to attend school; so did nine-tenths of those who obtained a university degree. In contrast, 16.7 per cent of Metro Toronto residents who graduated from college reported leaving town, though more than 40 per cent of those who obtained a university degree left town. In the 1970s the socio-economic characteristics of rural areas, and their distance from postsecondary institutions, posed a double-hardship to students seeking access to higher education. In general, the Class of '73 findings show that the proportion of young people with postsecondary education in 1979 varied strongly within the province, ranging from 74.4 per cent in Metro Toronto to 54.2 per cent in small towns and rural areas. As Looker (1993: 64) indicates, the very characteristics that make rural areas attractive to youth (e.g., a close-knit community, strong family ties) also make it difficult for youth to leave. The bonds set up are difficult to break, yet most rural youth see themselves as having to do precisely this in order to improve their economic lives.

Kelly, whose family was poor, grew up in a small rural community in eastern Ontario where only in the rarest cases did students go on to university. For the better students from her peer group, attending a community college, which still required moving away from home, was an increasingly common step. Kelly was aware that there were few job options for those with only a high school diploma, particularly in her small community. She was also determined not to become a 'farmer's wife' – a role she perceived as burdensome and limiting. She was advised by a teacher and encouraged by her parents to go into nursing, a choice she never regretted. Vocational as opposed to academic education that might lead quickly to employment was Kelly's preferred pathway. University attendance lay outside the normal life course expectations of her siblings, her neighbours, and her classmates. Kelly's resolve to abandon farming life was itself a significant and increasingly common generational transition for youth in rural Ontario, and a college education was perceived as an important stepping stone along this path.

The high educational attainment of women must be interpreted in relation to the striking gender differences in the majors and programs selected by members of the Class of '73 who attended university or community college. We assume that gender differences existed in secondary school with respect to course selections, but we cannot confirm this, as we did not seek out this information in the early phases of our research. However, in 1979, we did obtain information on majors and programs (data summarized in Table 3.5). The top half of Table 3.5 shows that at university, men clearly predominated in physical science and mathematics, in applied science (especially engineering), and in business, economics, and commerce majors. Women predominated in the arts, the fine arts, and the humanities and performing arts, and predominated somewhat in the social sciences.

The lower half of Table 3.5 indicates that with respect to community college, men predominated in programs in business management and commerce, in primary industries, electronics, and electrical technologies, and in engineering and related technologies. In comparison, women predominated in secretarial arts and science, community services, teaching and social welfare, and nursing, and in medical and dental technologies programs. Clearly, for community college graduates, the gender imbalance in terms of specific vocationally oriented programs would lead to future employment in gender-segregated occupations. Nursing and secretarial services were typical choices for women; engineering, mechanical, metal, and construction trades were typical choices for men. Even for university graduates, the gender concentrations in specific majors would lead to a future concentration

Table 3.5. Last field of study while attending university or community college by gender, 1979 (percentage)

Major field at university reported by university graduates (1979)	(n)	Male (105)	Female (121)	Total (226)
Agricultural and biological science		10.5	8.3	9.3
Health professions		1.0	5.0	3.1
Arts, fine arts, humanities, performing arts		5.7	16.5	11.5
Physical sciences and mathematics		10.5	3.3	6.6
Applied science (architecture, engineering)		17.1	1.7	8.8
Education, physical education, and social work		6.7	12.4	9.7
Business, economics, and commerce		20.0	9.9	14.6
Social science		24.8	36.4	31.0
Other studies		3.8	3.3	3.5
No answer		0.0	3.3	1.8
Total		100.0	100.0	100.0

Programs reported by community college graduates (1979)	(n)	(62)	(100)	(162)
University transfer and arts and science		1.6	1.0	1.2
Secretarial arts and science		1.6	16.0	10.5
Business management and commerce		19.4	8.0	12.3
Fine, applied, and performing arts		1.6	6.0	4.3
Communications		4.8	2.0	3.1
Community services, teaching, and social welfare		8.1	14.0	11.7
Nursing (leading to R.N. only)		0.0	34.0	21.0
Data processing		1.6	1.0	1.2
Primary industries		11.3	1.0	4.9
Medical and dental technologies		0.0	9.0	5.6
Electronics and electrical technologies		16.1	0.0	6.2
Engineering and related technologies		24.2	• 0.0	9.3
Other programs		9.7	8.0	8.6
Total		100.0	100.0	100.0

Note: Top panel is based on last field of study reported by Class of '73 members who attained a university degree by 1979; bottom panel is based on last field of study of Class of '73 members who attained only a community college diploma or certificate by 1979; table excludes individuals who did not have, or did not complete, any postsecondary university or community college education.

of graduates in gender-specific occupations. For example, Max told us that several male friends who returned to school followed this trend: 'A couple of the guys went back to school with me, one went from being a mechanic to an engineer. One went into civil engineering at college and he's with Ontario Hydro. They tended to stick with some sort of technical area when they went to college or university.'

The 1996 Census figures indicated that more women than men in their twenties had a postsecondary degree; even so, gender differences with respect to fields of study had not altered significantly. Thus, women made up two-thirds of the graduates with degrees in the arts, the humanities, and the social sciences, while men comprised two-thirds of the graduates in mathematics and the physical sciences and four-fifths of the engineering graduates (Carey, 1998: A3). In spite of the enrolment gains made by women in recent years, an assessment by Anisef et al. twenty years ago still seems pertinent: 'Proportionately more women, in spite of generally superior academic performances, are tracked into vocationally-oriented [community colleges] where they primarily train in female dominated programs for placement in sex-segregated occupations. The situation of women in universities is no different' (Anisef, Paasche, and Turrittin, 1980: 12).

Parental and Peer Group Influences on Educational Attainment

Anisef and Okihiro (1982) analysed Phase IV data from the Class of '73 survey and found that parental influence had a clear and significant impact on the educational attainments of their offspring. At all academic performance levels and at all socio-economic levels, the expectations of the parents did much to influence the future educational plans of the children. Thus, 'low socio-economic status males with high marks in high school, and who were exposed to parents with high educational expectations, were 28 per cent more likely to enrol in higher education than peers whose parents had low educational expectations' (Anisef and Okihiro, 1982: 81). This also held for low socio-economic level women, though to a lesser extent. Earlier research reveals similar findings. Williams (1972) analyzed longitudinal data from the Carnegie data bank on students across Canada entering grade 9 in 1959–60 and found that parental influence had the greatest impact on students' aspirations; teacher and peer expectations ranked second and third respectively. At the grade 9 level, the impact of parental influence was similar for boys and girls, but this did not continue from grade 10 to grade 12; during these years, peers and teachers gained influence with respect to girls, while for boys parental influence increased. He concluded that 'the matter of a boy's educational future has a greater saliency for parents, who go beyond the visible evidence of capabilities in forming their expectations of him' (126). In the later *Survey of Ontario Students Aspirations* study conducted by Porter, Porter, and Blishen (1973: 117), the authors concluded that as much as class, sex determines a young person's expectations. Thus, for lower-class girls there is a double-jeopardy.

In commenting on his parents' influence on his educational plans, John had this to say during a 1979 interview: 'My dad influenced me a lot. Well not really influenced, but he told me he would pay the shot. I wanted to go to university ... not like my brothers. My older brother who quit grade 10 is working.' John, with the encouragement of his father and his own self-professed ambition to succeed, did go on to complete a three-year university degree. When we last spoke with him in 1979, he was enrolled in a chartered accountancy course. It is important to note that John grew up in a working-class, nonuniversity culture, yet, despite this always wanted to go to university. His father, who worked in a construction company, continued to encourage and support his educational goals well into John's 20s.

Carl spoke about his parents' expectations with respect to his future career plans and how they influenced his academic performance:

> In the third term I really worked again. I really liked school life, the whole atmosphere. My parents pushed school. They would say, 'We left Portugal for you.' My mother was a teacher and I wanted to be a teacher.

Though Carl did well in grade 13 and worked diligently to improve his grades, two universities declined his application, while a third offered him acceptance into a general program. He decided to register in a community college program instead, but subsequently dropped out and took a skilled job on the production line of a major manufacturing company. At the time of the last interview with Carl in 1979, he was in the process of rediscovering his Portuguese identity. He claimed that 'there is an advantage to being an immigrant, in that it leads to trying harder, and provides an added sense of identity.'

Many teenage youth readily acknowledge not only the importance of academic achievement in their lives, but the significance of forming strong social bonds and of getting along with their peers in school. Pavalko and Bishop (1968), in their survey of grade 12 high school students in Thunder Bay, Ontario, found that a strong relationship existed between the future educational plans of high school students and those of close friends. Those whose friends planned on going to college (55.7 per cent) were themselves more likely to attend, in comparison with those whose friends did not have such plans (27.4 per cent). The effect of friends' plans persisted across all levels of socio-economic status for boys, but persisted only among girls of high socio-economic status.

In 1979 we asked our respondents whether they felt they had been part of the leading crowd in their high schools. Less than one-third considered themselves popular enough to answer affirmatively. While neither grades nor gender related to this perception, the social capital built by class membership did affect perceptions: a significantly greater proportion of upper socio-economic status respondents recalled themselves being part of the leading crowd in their high school. When asked how they wanted to be remembered, almost one-third mentioned 'as a brilliant student,' and fewer than one-fifth wanted to be remembered as 'most popular.' Not surprisingly, those choosing 'brilliant student' were themselves academically superior and disproportionately obtained postsecondary degrees. The choice of other images such as 'outstanding athlete' and 'leader in activities' was found to relate to gender, class, and region of residence. By way of illustration, rural students were more likely than urban students to choose 'outstanding athlete,' and women were more likely than men to want to be remembered as a 'brilliant student.'

Shannon, who grew up in a small town in southern Ontario where her father was the local barber, described the impact of peer pressure in a 'one-high school town' with a strong drug subculture. She began experimenting with drugs in grade 11 and spent most of that year in a 'purple haze.' By grade 12 she was totally disillusioned with the drug scene. Several of her friends had died in car accidents or drug overdoses, and she realized she had to get out of that environment as soon as possible. Consequently, in spite of obtaining high academic grades, she elected to attend a community college after completing grade 12 instead of completing grade 13 and going on to university. She later transferred to a university, completed a BSc, and after a variety of jobs entered chiropractic practice in her late twenties. She described her experiences in high school as follows:

Oh yes, it was pressure ... I just thought my brain was going to be fried and I wanted to leave. The influence was a very difficult thing to fight. In order to be accepted you did what the others did, and in order to fight it

I felt I had to leave ... High school was awful. I grew up in a very small town and not too many people were interesting. I was always in the top of my class. You get ostracized that way because you're bright and you're a girl ... I was kind of a chameleon. I hung out with different groups. I could talk with any group and blend in any way. I was more of a loner blending in with different groups. I recognized that the only way out for me was going to school. And so I worked hard at developing my intellect.

Shannon was born in a rural setting to a large family with a modest income, but she knew herself to be bright and with strong potential. In her formative high school years, she was set on developing her intellect and future professional status. Thus, in spite of a highly unstable personal life, she endured. She left her rural community and by the time of the 1995 interview had managed to fulfil some of her personal ambitions.

Jason, who attended an academic program at a Toronto high school and went on to complete an engineering degree and become a systems analyst, recalled his high school experiences in a much more positive way:

We had sort of a little clique, people who were interested in computer science. And because I went to the enriched math curriculum, usually most of the people in that class were all into engineering. We took the three basic maths and they had to be scheduled around the same one enriched math class all the way through. So I went through high school with a specific group of friends. Most of them I still talk to on a day-to-day basis ... I look back to the school with very fond memories.

Jason's positive memories and comfort level with engineering were consistent with his background. The son of an engineer and an only child, Jason emigrated from Hungary when he was in his early teens. He had a strong interest in computers and engineering, as did a number of his friends in high school, who wound up enrolling at the same university. For Jason, structure and agency came together. His parents played a very active role in his life, providing him with sufficient cultural capital that, combined with his strong interest in computers and strong social and academic bonds with like-minded friends, he was able and eager to pursue an industrial engineering degree at the University of Toronto.

Streaming and Tracking: High School Experience in Retrospect[7]

The late 1960s and the decade of the 1970s saw a series of studies that examined the relationships between educational and occupational aspirations and social background. Raymond Breton (1970, 1972) gathered data on 145,817 students in 360 Canadian secondary schools and found that students from higher socio-economic backgrounds were more likely to be in academic nonterminal programs compared with students from lower socio-economic backgrounds, who were more likely to be in terminal programs and less likely to continue their education after leaving high school. The *Survey of Ontario Students Aspirations* (SOSA), which included approximately 9,000 Ontario high school students and 3,000 of their parents, initiated by Bernard Blishen and John Porter in the fall of 1970 (with follow-up in 1973 and 1976), offered findings that were of relevance to the four and five year programs entered by members of the Class of '73 (Porter, Porter, and Blishen, 1982). On the surface it appeared that the allocation of students to programs was based on universalistic criteria because the likelihood of being in five-year (academic) programs was strongly related to high aspirations and good marks; however, the researchers found that as early as grade 8, social class had a strong effect on aspirations and grades, and thus did much to influence ultimate placement in five-year programs (312).

Using data from the SOSA study – in particular data on course selection – Gilbert and McRoberts (1977) examined the effect of school stratification on the educational plans of secondary school students from grades 8, 10, and 12. Generally, their analysis revealed that the higher the socio-economic status of a student, the greater his or her chances of being in the university preparatory course. Approximately 6 in 10 working-class but over 7 in 10 upper middle-class students were enrolled in this course. In addition, the higher the socio-economic status of students already in the university preparatory course, the greater were their expectations regarding entering university: 6 in 10 of upper-class, nearly 5 in 10 of middle-class, and just over 3 in 10 working-class students expected to enter university. Fewer females than males in the preparatory course planned to enrol in university, and more females of lower socio-economic status expected to enter other forms of postsecondary education. As Crysdale and McKay (1994: 30–31) indicated, tracking or streaming is a sorting mechanism that takes place when students are 13 and 14 years old and serves to steer most children of the working class into applied programs and most middle-class students into academic programs, where the ethos of advanced courses challenges and encourages achievement.

While the educational reforms of 1969 allowed students greater flexibility in choosing programs and courses, in the 1979 survey most Class of '73 members were able to identify their high school program as one of four types: academic, commercial, technical, or vocational. Six in ten of the male participants reported that they had been in the academic stream, one in three reported being in the technical/vocational stream, and only 5 per cent were in a commercial program. Three-quarters of the women were in the academic stream, almost one-quarter reported being in a commercial program, and only 1 per cent indicated that they were in the technical/vocational stream. The commercial and technical/vocational tracks were clearly sex segregated, and students with lower grade averages were inclined to these tracks. Most students on these tracks proceeded directly into the labour market after high school. In addition, high school program selection was strongly related to socio-economic status and region of origin: proportionately more respondents from higher socio-economic background and from urban areas selected academic programs. More recent research findings show that working-class children continue to predominate in the 'lower' secondary school streams, while children of professionals and more privileged families are placed in academic streams and schools (Curtis, Livingstone, and Smaller, 1992).

As reported in 1979, nearly 70 per cent of Class of '73 members indicated that they were in academic programs; the remainder were equally divided between commercial and vocational/technical programs. Over 90 per cent of high socio-economic students and almost 50 per cent of low socio-economic students had chosen academic placements by grade 12. A larger proportion of females (76.2 per cent) than males (61.4 per cent) enrolled in academic programs; also, males dominated the vocational/technical programs and females displayed a similar near-monopoly with regard to commercial programs.

Students enrolled in academic programs had a significantly greater 'lock' on obtaining very good grades in high school than peers in other programs (especially the vocational and technical programs). As Penny, who graduated from a four-year high school program, explained: 'The five-year kids got the high marks.' By Phase IV of our study, the consequences of high school sorting had become clear: almost 40 per cent of students in academic programs graduated from university, but less than 6 per cent of students in commercial and vocational/technical programs did so. However, community college proved a viable option for those in the nonacademic programs: nearly 16 per cent of commercial and 20 per cent of technical/vocational high school students obtained college certificates.

The high school track chosen paid out occupational dividends for the Class of '73, as evidenced in the occupational prestige scores of those who were 'currently working' in 1979. Members of the Class of '73 from the academic track enjoyed relatively more job prestige than those who had chosen other programs of study in high school. In addition, the starting salaries of those entering the labour market from the academic and technical/vocational tracks were substantially higher than for those in commercial programs. To a large extent this latter finding can be attributed to the overwhelming number of women in commercial programs and to the tendency for women to earn lower salaries than men. That the track chosen in high school has a strong impact on future careers is supported by the analysis of Raymond Breton (1972: 247), who reported that there is 'a 35.8 per cent difference in the likelihood of expressing a preference for a high status occupation between those in the academic-university preparatory program and those in the terminal technical.'

Usefulness of Education

In recent years the value of a Canadian education has been strongly questioned, and there have been claims that few Canadians find the performance of our Canadian education system acceptable (Gallagher, 1995: 1). But the student protests of the 1960s, and pressures to make education more responsive to changing times in the 1970s, indicate that concerns about the quality of education preoccupied earlier generations of Canadians as well.

During interviews conducted in 1979 and 1994–95, we asked respondents to comment on their educational experiences and to indicate whether their education had been useful to them both in general terms and in relation to their current employment. We were thus able to obtain a more nuanced view of respondents' pathways.

From the Perspective of 1979

In 1979 we asked members of the Class of '73 to consider their most recent educational experience and to indicate its usefulness both at a general level (e.g., whether it helped them to appreciate ideas and to

Table 3.6. Assessment of general usefulness of most recent educational experience by educational attainment, 1979 (percentage)

Usefulness of recent educational experience		Level of usefulness of education			
		Very or frequent- ly useful	Occa- sionally useful	Rarely or not at all useful	Total
	(n)	High school only			
a) Developed my basic appreciation of ideas	262	47.0	40.8	12.2	100.0
b) Increased my ability to think clearly	264	61.4	27.3	11.3	100.0
c) Increased my leadership ability	263	27.8	34.6	37.7	100.0
d) Learned to evaluate my life goals in light of own opportunities and abilities	263	38.0	34.6	27.4	100.0
e) Developed my social and interpersonal skills	262	36.6	37.0	26.3	100.0
	(n)	College graduate			
a) Developed my basic appreciation of ideas	170	62.9	29.4	7.6	100.0
b) Increased my ability to think clearly	171	68.4	22.8	8.8	100.0
c) Increased my leadership ability	169	50.9	29.6	19.6	100.0
d) Learned to evaluate my life goals in light of own opportunities and abilities	170	61.8	25.9	12.4	100.0
e) Developed my social and interpersonal skills	171	50.3	38.6	11.1	100.0
	(n)	University graduate			
a) Developed my basic appreciation of ideas	225	80.0	18.7	1.3	100.0
b) Increased my ability to think clearly	225	81.8	14.7	3.6	100.0
c) Increased my leadership ability	224	50.0	35.7	14.3	100.0
d) Learned to evaluate my life goals in light of own opportunities and abilities	224	64.2	21.0	14.7	100.0
e) Developed my social and interpersonal skills	224	65.2	26.8	8.0	100.0

Question: Looking back at your most recent educational experience (be it high school, private vocational school, college, university, etc.) please indicate the extent to which it has been useful in each of the following ways.

think clearly) and in terms of their current employment (e.g., whether it helped them develop a career choice and provided job knowledge, skills, and techniques). We show some of the results of these questions in Tables 3.6 and 3.7.

Roughly one-third of respondents whose highest level of education in 1979 was high school evaluated their schooling experience as very or frequently useful at a general level. Members of the Class of '73

Table 3.7. Assessment of job-related usefulness of most recent educational experience by educational attainment, 1979 (percentage)

Job usefulness of recent educational experience		Level of usefulness of education			
		Very or fre-quently useful	Occas-sionally useful	Rarely or not at all useful	Total
	(n)	High school only			
a) Helped me decide on a career	266	32.0	18.4	49.6	100.0
b) Provided the knowledge, skills, and techniques that are directly applicable to my present job	211*	41.7	29.4	28.9	100.0
c) Increased my chances of finding a good job	208*	43.8	26.4	29.8	100.0
	(n)	College graduate			
a) Helped me decide on a career	170	63.6	16.5	20.0	100.0
b) Provided the knowledge, skills, and techniques that are directly applicable to my present job	149*	67.8	17.4	14.8	100.0
c) Increased my chances of finding a good job	149*	65.8	18.8	15.5	100.0
	(n)	University graduate			
a) Helped me decide on a career	225	56.9	17.3	25.8	100.0
b) Provided the knowledge, skills, and techniques that are directly applicable to my present job	145*	51.1	24.1	24.9	100.0
c) Increased my chances of finding a good job	144*	59.7	25.0	15.3	100.0

Question: Looking back at your most recent educational experience (be it high school, private vocational school, college, university, etc.) please indicate the extent to which it has been useful in each of the following ways.
* Answered only if respondent was currently employed in 1979.

who had only completed high school gave a fairly high evaluation to education's usefulness 'in promoting the appreciation of ideas' and 'for increasing one's ability to think clearly.' By comparison, 50 to 60 per cent of community college and university graduates said that their most recent educational experience was generally useful. Like their high-school-only counterparts, university graduates especially strongly believed that education was useful for the appreciation of ideas and for developing clear thinking.

With regard to job-related usefulness, half of the high-school-only respondents found high school not to have been of much use in helping decide on a career. Almost one-third of these respondents also believed that their education was not useful in providing knowledge and skills directly applicable to their present occupations, and that it did not increase their chances of finding a good job. However, at least six in ten community college graduates mentioned that their education helped them decide on a career, built knowledge and skills applicable to their present employment, and increased their chances of finding a good job. Close to 60 per cent of university graduates found that their education helped them decide on a career, and increased their chances of finding a good job, though only half thought that their education provided them with knowledge and skills applicable to their present employment.

Interviews with members of the Class of '73 suggest that as high school students, they understood how important school was to their future. Yet they were only dimly aware of the broad debates about educational and economic policy that affected school life. Their perceptions and concerns were more visceral and individualistic. These adolescents were grappling with questions of identity, self-esteem, peer associations, and parental relations, and judged high school in highly personal terms. Their views and experiences varied in ways that reflected the diversity of their backgrounds, personalities, and family life.

The most positive high school memories were held by respondents who had close friends, supportive teachers, and reasonable encouragement from their parents. These factors, more than any others, informed recollections of their high school years. John, who attended a small high school in a middle-class Toronto neighbourhood, recalled high school as the 'best five years of my life.' The highlight of his experience was being named 'athlete of the year' – an achievement that enhanced his confidence and sense of accomplishment. Shannon, on the other hand, detested the high school she attended in a small town in southwestern Ontario. She felt unchallenged and isolated, and grew disillusioned, and floundered educationally until she eventually entered university. For her, high school interfered with rather than facilitated her personal growth.

The credit system was a source of both challenge and frustration for students. The opportunity to study new high school subjects such as anthropology and law was appreciated by many. Others, however, believed that too many courses were impractical and that students were ill-informed about the specific requirements of the work world. Their attitudes on this question may well have been influenced by their employment situations at the time of the interview. When we interviewed him in 1979, Ray had completed a BCom degree and was working unhappily in an accountancy firm. He expressed the view that both high school and university training had been 'a waste of time.' As we note below, more than a decade later his memories had evolved.

From the Perspective of 1995

Approximately two-thirds of participants shared the view that their formal education had improved their communication and reasoning skills. Less than 10 per cent claimed that education had no discernible impact. Fewer than two-thirds of respondents, though still a majority, concurred that education had made their lives more meaningful, though a large minority (28.6 per cent) neither agreed nor disagreed with this statement. When these views regarding education were examined in relation to the highest level of education participants had attained by 1995 (Table 3.8), we found generally that those with advanced degrees were significantly more likely to attribute improved communication and reasoning skills to their education; they were also more likely to feel that their lives were more meaningful as a consequence of their educational experiences.

Those members of the Class of '73 who did not pursue a university degree expressed regret at not doing so, noting that opportunities might have been more plentiful if they had. As Matt noted:

I don't have a university degree and I wish I had one. It would be an achievement. It's something to say you have, it's well looked upon by society, to find a job also ... If I had it to do again, I would do university. And my two children will.

Duncan echoed the same sentiment:

I think I might have had an easier time over the long run had I had a degree. I have had to demonstrate through my skills and commitment,

Table 3.8. Assessment of education by educational attainment in 1995
(percentage)

General views on education		Strong-ly agree	Some-what agree	Neither agree nor dis- agree	Some-what dis- agree	Strong-ly dis-agree	Total
My education has:	(n)			High School only			
a) Improved communication skills	208	11.5	34.1	44.2	7.2	2.9	100.0
b) Improved reasoning skills	208	9.6	36.5	41.8	6.7	5.3	100.0
c) Improved career prospects	206	9.2	30.6	38.8	13.1	8.3	100.0
d) Made life more meaningful	207	10.1	27.1	43.5	13.5	5.8	100.0
e) Been useful in finding a job	206	8.7	36.4	32.5	12.1	10.2	100.0
				College graduate			
My education has:	(n)						
a) Improved communication skills	230	28.7	43.0	22.2	4.3	1.7	100.0
b) Improved reasoning skills	230	25.7	45.7	24.3	3.0	1.3	100.0
c) Improved career prospects	230	37.4	36.5	18.7	5.7	1.7	100.0
d) Made life more meaningful	230	27.8	36.5	25.7	7.4	2.6	100.0
e) Been useful in finding a job	230	37.4	37.8	15.7	7.4	1.7	100.0
				University graduate			
My education has:	(n)						
a) Improved communication skills	265	42.3	42.3	10.6	2.6	2.3	100.0
b) Improved reasoning skills	265	41.1	41.9	11.3	4.2	1.5	100.0
c) Improved career prospects	265	46.8	33.2	12.1	4.9	3.0	100.0
d) Made life more meaningful	265	38.1	36.6	17.4	4.5	3.4	100.0
e) Been useful in finding a job	263	39.9	35.0	15.2	7.6	2.3	100.0

Question: We'd now like to ask you about your view of education more generally. Please indicate how strongly you disagree or agree with the following statement.

my ability to do the job, in order to gain acceptance and also advancement. I've had to work a lot harder. It's paid off ... it's also a demonstration that you don't need the degree. But it would be easier.

It is important to consider that respondents' views of the value and relevance of their education could well have been influenced by their employment status at the time. John had this to say in 1979:

I think about my university experience and sometimes wonder was it worth it, when you consider there were no jobs afterwards ... I wonder about the courses in university and the ridiculous selection they give you ... It's for the birds. I may have set my goals too high in high school, but my guidance teacher said that you got your brains, so do it. Like I said, sometimes I wonder was it worth it, but I've got the degree and that is something that no one can take away from me. But now I wonder, what good is it?

Ray, who in 1979 stated that both high school and university training had been 'a waste of time' was interviewed again in 1995. In the interval he had become a successful self-employed businessman, and he remembered his high school years far more positively. 'Probably the best time of my life,' he declared. Indeed, he told us that his favourite course in university had been 'one of the least useful' – medieval history.

It is interesting to note that hard work in school was not necessarily viewed as a strategy for ensuring a good job (Table 3.9). Nearly one-quarter of respondents disagreed with the statement that if someone has worked hard in school, they are entitled to 'a good job,' and 30 per cent neither agreed nor disagreed. This may suggest that the Class of '73 did not see effort alone as a route to good jobs: performance and merit may also have played an important part in optimizing career mobility. Yet nearly two-thirds of respondents agreed somewhat or strongly that their education had been useful in helping them find a job, though a minority – 14.8 per cent – disagreed somewhat or strongly with this assessment. It is important to note that on this point there was significant variation among participants by degree level. Half of those with lower levels of education (high school only or community college) believed that hard work in school should pay off in a good job, whereas only two-fifths of university graduates took this position. In contrast, only 45.1 per cent of the high-school-only Class of '73 members felt that their education had helped them find a job, while three-quarters of college and university graduates believed that their education had produced that result. Though a relatively large number of participants believed that it was important that their job be related to their field of study or specialization (44.1 per cent), a larger proportion (56 per cent) were indifferent to or disagreed with this notion. Those with advanced degrees were substantially more predisposed to believe it was important that their work be related to their field of study or specialization. Respondents were somewhat more hesitant to support the notion that

Table 3.9. Further assessment of education by educational attainment in 1995 (percentages)

Views on education and employment		Strong-ly agree	Some-what agree	Neither agree nor dis-agree	Some-what dis-agree	Strong-ly dis-agree	Total
	(n)		High School only (n = 206)				
a) Those who worked hard in school are entitled to a good job	207	13.0	40.1	26.6	12.6	7.7	100.0
b) It is important that my job be related to my field studied	203	7.9	25.6	43.3	15.3	7.9	100.0
c) Everyone has the right to the kind of job prepared for by their education and training	206	14.1	35.9	23.8	14.6	11.7	100.0
d) These days, people require higher levels of education than than they did in the past	206	54.4	29.1	9.7	4.4	2.4	100.0
	(n)		College graduate (n = 230)				
a) Those who worked hard in school are entitled to a good job	230	15.2	36.5	30.4	11.7	6.1	100.0
b) It is important that my job be related to my field of study	230	26.5	31.3	28.3	9.6	4.3	100.0
c) Everyone has the right to the kind of job prepared for by their education and training	229	17.5	31.9	23.6	14.8	12.2	100.0
d) These days, people require higher levels of education than they did in the past	230	58.7	26.5	8.7	4.3	1.7	100.0
	(n)		University graduate (n = 263)				
a) Those who worked hard in school are entitled to a good job	262	8.4	30.5	29.0	20.6	11.5	100.0
b) It is important that my job be related to my field of study	263	21.3	25.5	27.8	16.0	9.5	100.0
c) Everyone has the right to the kind of job prepared for by their education and training	262	9.5	19.8	21.0	26.3	23.3	100.0
d) These days, people require higher levels of education than they did in the past	263	44.1	35.4	11.8	5.7	3.0	100.0

Question: We'd now like to ask you about your view of education more generally. Please indicate how strongly you disagree or agree with the following statement.

everyone has the right to the kind of job for which education and training has prepared them: 35.8 per cent disagreed, and 23.2 per cent were neutral, while 40.9 per cent agreed with this proposition. Participants with university degrees were less supportive of this proposition than were college graduates and those with only a high school education.

Can Educational Attainment Be Predicted? Evidence from the 1979 Data

In the 1975 Critical Juncture study there was one factor, not used in the report's statistical analysis, that was tied very strongly to future educational activity. This factor can be termed '(1973) level of educational expectation.' In multiple regression analyses not shown here, this variable proved to be the most significant factor influencing not only actual educational activity in the fall of 1974 but also completed level of education as of the 1979 Phase IV survey.[8] It would be deceptively easy to conclude that embarking on any one of the three main pathways through education into the labour market is simply a matter of attitude – of wishing for a particular educational and occupational future. However, level of educational expectation on the part of members of the Class of '73, expressed at the end of grade 12 in the Phase I survey, was itself the product of a complex combination of social forces and individual determination. The list of contributing factors is substantial, and we have already discussed some of these in this chapter. They include background factors such as socio-economic status, gender, and region of origin; program in high school; peer group educational goals; and parental educational expectations; as well as other relevant factors such as high school grades, family and nonfamily academic encouragement, self-concept of academic ability, and occupational expectations.[9]

While the element of human agency was visible in participants' decisions at the end of grade 12 to pursue particular education/work pathways, structural factors were still at work in shaping those decisions. This is illustrated by our data from 1979, as shown in Table 3.10, in which we have tabulated educational attainment as of 1979 by socio-economic background and level of educational expectation as voiced in the spring of 1973 by respondents. The table shows the interaction of personal decision-making and SES on subsequent attainments. Of

Table 3.10. Effects of socio-economic status by plans for 1974 category by educational attainment as of 1979 (percentages)

Socio-econmic status 1973	(n)	Educational attainment in 1979				
		High school only	Some college/ university	College graduate	University degree	Total
Panel I		Expected to go to work in Spring 1973				
Low SES	75	86.7	4.0	6.7	2.7	100.0
Medium low SES	40	80.0	5.0	12.5	2.5	100.0
Medium high SES	37	89.2	8.1	2.7	0.0	100.0
High SES	17	64.7	5.9	17.6	11.8	100.0
Total	169	83.4	5.3	8.3	3.0	100.0
Panel II		Expected to go to college in Spring 1973				
Low SES	65	32.3	9.2	46.2	12.3	100.0
Medium low SES	59	30.5	11.9	52.5	5.1	100.0
Medium high SES	49	22.4	18.4	51.0	8.2	100.0
High SES	33	15.2	21.2	39.4	24.2	100.0
Total	206	26.7	14.1	48.1	11.2	100.0
Panel III		Expected to go to university in Spring 1973				
Low SES	34	2.9	20.6	17.6	58.8	100.0
Medium low SES	50	8.0	20.0	12.0	60.0	100.0
Medium high SES	70	14.3	14.3	18.6	52.9	100.0
High SES	110	2.7	16.4	5.5	75.5	100.0
Total	264	6.8	17.0	11.7	64.4	100.0

those who had completed only a high school education by 1979 and who in the spring of 1973 had indicated that they intended to enter the labour force directly after high school, 83.4 per cent had gone only as far as high school by 1979. In contrast, of those who indicated a preference to enrol in university, 64.4 per cent had obtained a university degree by 1979. Those indicating a preference for community college fell somewhere in the middle: 48.1 per cent had graduated from a community college by 1979. Still, SES played an influential role in the actual outcomes. High socio-economic status was especially powerful in moving youth toward university degrees, even though original expectations voiced in 1973 were to go to work or to attend a community college. Similarly, low socio-economic status acted to diminish attendance at university. The level of educational expectation least affected by SES was attending community college.

Conclusions

A review of the educational pathways chosen by members of the Class of '73 after they left high school leads to a number of important insights regarding the impact of social forces and agency in the lives of Canadians. It also underscores the importance of education over the long term from the subjective standpoint of the participants. The findings reported from phases conducted in 1973 and 1979 clearly document the importance of social background forces such as class, gender, and region in shaping educational preferences and decisions taken in the high school years. When deciding on their high school programs and future educational goals, participants were strongly influenced by class structures, gender considerations, and the opportunities available in their region of residence. In general, there appears to be a strong reciprocal association between social background and educational pathways taken: social privilege increases the likelihood of gaining higher educational credentials and (as will be seen in the next chapter and in Chapter 5) achieving later employment and occupational success. This finding continues to receive support in more recent studies. Additionally, though the participation of women in postsecondary education has increased significantly since the late 1970s, gender segregation patterns at secondary and postsecondary levels continue to be troublesome (Wotherspoon, 1998: 163–166, 179). Though attitudes toward schooling tended to be more favourable in rural than in urban areas, recent data document continuing inequalities in rural areas with respect to educational opportunity and results (Wotherspoon, 1998: 187).

Once members of the Class of '73 had developed their personal educational expectations, these did serve to mediate the influence of social background on subsequent educational choices, particularly as they began their careers and assumed new responsibilities and challenges (e.g., marital and parental status). The impact of structural factors in sustaining educational advantage should not be minimized; however, our analysis illustrates the important role also played by personal agency in the critical high school and postsecondary years. Working-class origins may influence future success in the sense that, as Bellamy-Andres (1994: 122) notes, 'the culture that is transmitted and rewarded by the educational system reflects the culture of the dominant class'; even so, some working-class participants were able to overcome the lack of cultural capital, complete grade 13, and move on to a university or community college education. Similarly, a significant number of women were able to surmount gender obstacles. Many of these women were from rural areas, and a high proportion chose to leave their community to improve their educational and career opportunities.

Participants in the study had positive feelings about the role that education had played in improving their communication and reasoning skills. The following two chapters will investigate more closely the outcomes of education in terms of employment and career mobility.

There is one more set of educational experiences still to consider. Most Class of '73 members had completed their education by 1978, with some continuing to pursue professional studies for a few additional years. In our 1995 survey, however, we asked about further formal education since 1978–79. A surprisingly high proportion of Class of '73 members reported taking up some kind of additional formal education during the sixteen years following 1979. We will examine this phenomenon in Chapter 5.

CHAPTER FOUR

The World of Employment

The employment world encountered by young people in Canada has changed greatly over the past fifty years (Driver, 1985). In the immediate postwar period, employment was experienced mainly in terms of either a 'steady state' career concept, which required a lifelong commitment to a specific field, with little actual job movement (e.g., doctors, clergy), or a 'linear' career concept, which was associated with climbing a career ladder through promotion. More recently, a third concept, that of the 'spiral' career, has become more predominant in the corporate world. This career track is associated with occupational flexibility; movement is predominantly horizontal, and there is less occupational change through promotion. A fourth concept, the 'transitory' career model, captures the erratic and constant job movement (e.g., contract work) of youth and others who comprise the part-time work force (Venne, 1996: 47). The spiral and transitory career concepts are more descriptive of the employment experiences of young people in the 1980s and 1990s.

This chapter, and the following one on social mobility, explore the transition from schooling to employment for the Class of '73, a cohort presumed to have generally experienced steady state or linear career paths. How the changing economy affected their employment opportunities, and how our participants navigated their way through an increasingly unpredictable environment, are the central themes in the discussion that follows. Though the majority of study participants have experienced employment pathways that have been steady state or linear, a significant minority have encountered uncertainty, not unlike the employment experience of young people in the 1980s and 1990s.

Furthermore, in 1995 members of the Class of '73 were in their late thirties or early forties and most had at least one child; the majority had at least two children who ranged in age from infants to high school students. In other words, most of the men and women in this study were fully engaged in parenting. We therefore found it especially pertinent to examine the impact of parenthood on the employment and career paths of our cohort. This is especially relevant to the women in our study, since most of the responsibility of childrearing has rested on their shoulders. While women in contemporary Canada have more choices than previous generations with respect to education, occupation, marriage, and motherhood, their employment opportunities and conditions are still constrained by the availability of childcare and by household demands (Wilson, 1991: 34). Thus, the impact of gender as a social force on working life merits continuing attention.

We are also guided in this chapter by scholars who have begun to explore the 'interplay between the actions of individuals and the constraints exerted on them by social structures' (Krahn and Lowe, 1993: 3). Using both 'macro' (social structural) and 'micro' (individual agency) analysis, Krahn and Lowe illustrate how Canadian employees have prospered from, adapted to, or confronted the enormous changes in the labour market. This approach accounts for the broad social forces that shape the parameters of working life; at the same time, it humanizes the analysis by giving voice to individual experience. We draw from survey and interview data spanning two decades (1973–4 to 1994–5), to offer insights into the opportunities and uncertainties that have faced Canadians in both prosperous and recessionary times.

Specifically, we explore the following questions: What were the consequences of an individual's formal educational achievements for her or his chances of employment success and movement up the career ladder? How did these trajectories vary by key social factors (e.g., socio-economic status, gender, geographic location)? How have economic and labour market restructuring transformed employment and occupational opportunities for the Class of '73? What role has formal, on-the-job training played in this process? What has been the impact of unemployment, part-time employment, and self-employment on the career transitions of this generation? And finally, what effect does bearing and raising children have on men and women with regard to employment experiences and career trajectories?

Given our interest in exploring the links between schooling and employment, we sought from the outset to obtain complete employment and occupational information on our subjects through successive phases, and for discrete years from 1974 to 1994–95. While we were prevented by limited resources from coding all occupational information in these years, we were able to explore the transitions from schooling to employment for the years 1974, 1979, 1987–88, and 1994–95. In addition, we have detailed information on the first full-time occupations obtained by Class of '73 members and the year in which this employment was obtained. First full-time employment was strongly influenced by level of education sought. Thus, for those electing to move directly into full-time work after high school, the first full-time job was usually secured in 1974 while those going on to various kinds of postsecondary education obviously found full-time employment at a later date.

In analyzing the transitions from schooling to employment, we sought a categorization system that made intuitive sense and that also conveyed the hierarchical nature of occupations in Canadian society. The concept of hierarchy is especially important for answering questions about social and career mobility – questions taken up in detail in Chapter 5. For this reason, we grouped occupational titles of respondents[1] in such a way as to yield a ranking of occupations from the highest (self-employed professionals) to the lowest (farm labourers) in terms of years of schooling and income.[2] In exploring the combined impact of social structural factors and personal decision-making on the occupational pathways of the Class of '73, we focused in particular on gender. Specifically, we used the accounts of respondents to analyse the impact of gender – especially in terms of parenthood – on the employment and career trajectories of men and women.

Entering the Labour Market: The Early Years

In this section we explore initial labour market experiences. In the fall of 1974, at the point that grade 13 graduates would have started university or community college, 51.3 per cent of the Class of '73 members who responded to our telephone survey were attending a university or community college full- or part-time. Of those not attending postsecondary education in the fall of 1974, 81 per cent were working either full-time or part-time (in fact, three-quarters were employed full-time). The remaining 19 per cent indicated a number of statuses such as taking grade 13, doing an apprenticeship or manpower training, attending business school, or being a homemaker. For this small group, unemployment was about 10 per cent. Of those attending a postsecondary school, very few were employed full-time (2 per cent) but 26 per cent were employed part-time.

Asking respondents in 1979 retrospectively to describe their first full-time occupation revealed that the modal year of reported first full-time job was consistent with the main patterns of educational attainment. Thus, most members of the Class of '73 who did not continue with postsecondary education obtained their first full-time jobs in 1973 (54.5 per cent) and 1974 (27.4 per cent). Those who obtained community college diplomas and certificates began their first full-time jobs in the four-year period from 1974 to 1977. About 50 per cent of those who obtained university degrees found full-time jobs in 1978, with smaller percentages entering the labour force in the years 1977 and 1979 (16.9 per cent and 16.3 per cent respectively).

For high school, college, and university graduates, entering the labour market during the 1970s was at once an exciting and a sobering experience. Optimistic and ambitious, impatient and apprehensive, the Class of '73 exuded the range of emotions associated with their stage of personal development. They were forging their identities and seeking independence and paid employment – preferably in a rewarding full-time job, which was an essential ingredient in the formula for success.

These goals were easier to articulate than to achieve. The increasing levels of youth unemployment and the distressing challenge of under-employment in the late 1970s (discussed in Chapter 2) had a direct effect on the experiences of members of the Class of '73. Many individuals moved directly into the jobs for which they had been prepared. Cheryl trained as an X-ray technician and obtained a hospital position immediately on graduation. Gary, who had always aspired to a career in engineering, was offered a number of jobs at the conclusion of his studies. He settled on a position with an oil company in Calgary. Similarly, Nancy's veterinary degree allowed her to select from several full-time employment options.

But these fortunate experiences were far from universal. As shown in Table 4.1, those attempting to enter the labour market directly from high school encountered limited occupational prospects and opportunities. Over 50 per cent of those employed in 1974 (and not enrolled in school) were working in unskilled positions, with some 35 per cent holding skilled jobs; few had any higher-status occupations. Even young people of high socio-economic status (SES) background were largely confined to unskilled or skilled work if they left high school directly for the job market.[3] This suggests that for those in the high-school-only category, educational attainment more than social class origin affected their initial employment situations. In 1974 there were only small differences in the proportion of males and females working in skilled and unskilled jobs; however, the types of occupations in which they were employed differed sharply by gender. These gender differences were related to the particular high school programs chosen (see Chapter 3) and to the gendered nature of the labour market encountered by the Class of '73. This movement by participants into male and female segments of the labour market would have major long-term effects on respondents' employment and career prospects.

The experiences of Carl, Andrew, and Alice illustrate the pattern of employment faced by those with only a high school education. After dropping out of community college, Carl got a 'great job' in a large company as a 'mail boy' and was promoted to the inventory department. He left this post when he declined an invitation to work for the company in a different city. By 1979 he was employed on the production line of an automobile manufacturer, a position he characterized as 'dead end.' Another youth, Andrew, left school after grade 12, went to a Manpower Centre, and the 'next day' got a job as a truck driver. Later he was hired as an expediter for a radio manufacturer, but after three months he was laid off. He started work at Bell Canada and in 1979 had been there for three years. His entry-level position was once a 'good job' but had become 'repetitious ... and boring.' He was hoping to move into management.

On graduating from grade 12, Alice applied for entry into several nursing schools, but without success. So she took a factory job. While working full-time she was accepted into a nursing program, but she chose to continue at the factory. After two years she left to begin working in the retail industry. She took time out to have a child and to recover from an illness. In 1980 she returned to work, but was soon laid off and was without work for several months. Juggling family and childrearing commitments, she was later employed in a variety of retail positions.

A particularly interesting pattern was revealed by the first full-time jobs held by respondents in 1979, as indicated in the bottom portion of Table 4.1. Men entered high-level management or professional positions much more frequently than women; in contrast, women became middle managers and semiprofessionals more frequently than men. This finding is consistent with earlier differences in academic programs selected in post-secondary education (e.g., very few women

Table 4.1. Occupations in 1974 and first full-time job by gender, socio-economic status, region of origin, and educational attainment (percentage)

	Occupation category					
	High-level management/ professional	Mid-management/semi-professional technical	Skilled workers	Unskilled workers	Agricultural	Total
Occupation in 1974 for respondents not enrolled in postsecondary education and working full- or part-time						
	(*n*)					
Gender						
Male	152	2.0	5.9	34.2	52.0	5.9	100.0
Female	135	2.2	3.7	34.8	57.0	2.2	100.0
Socio-economic status 1973						
High	55	3.6	9.1	38.2	47.3	1.8	100.0
Middle	113	2.7	4.4	33.6	55.8	3.5	100.0
Low	119	0.8	3.4	34.2	55.8	5.8	100.0
Region of origin						
Toronto and other cities	144	1.4	6.9	29.9	59.7	2.1	100.0
Rural areas and small towns	143	2.8	2.8	39.2	49.0	6.3	100.0
First full-time occupation for all members of Class of '73 (1974–79)*						
Gender						
Male	326	9.8	14.1	29.8	40.5	5.8	100.0
Female	349	5.2	20.6	30.4	43.6	0.3	100.0
Socio-economic status 1973						
High	203	9.9	19.7	30.0	38.9	1.5	100.0
Middle	239	7.5	19.7	28.5	41.8	2.5	100.0
Low	233	5.3	13.3	31.8	45.1	4.7	100.0

Region of origin						
Toronto and other cities	384	8.7	19.0	29.4	41.9	1.0	100.0
Rural areas and small towns	291	5.8	15.5	30.9	42.3	5.5	100.0
Educational attainment by 1979						
High school	264	2.3	3.8	34.5	54.5	4.9	100.0
Some college/university	88	1.1	14.8	26.1	55.7	2.3	100.0
College	168	4.8	35.7	30.4	28.6	0.6	100.0
University	155	22.6	22.6	24.5	27.7	2.6	100.0

* The modal years for respondents starting their first full-time occupation were, respectively, 1973 for those designated as having high school only, 1975 for those who took some college and university courses, 1976 for college graduates, and 1978 for those completing a university degree.

chose to major in business administration) and with the gendered nature of the job market.

The higher the SES background, the more likely respondents were to begin with a high-management/professional occupation; those from a low-SES background were more likely to start in the unskilled worker category or in agriculture. As we indicated in Chapter 3, educational attainment was closely linked to class origins, and in turn, educational attainment was a key factor influencing early occupational selection.

Area of residence was also influential. Those from larger cities had an advantage with regard to entering high-level management and professional jobs. At the beginning of their careers, young people located in cities clearly had economic advantages over those living elsewhere. However, Table 4.1 also indicates that education had the power to overcome other background factors: high school and some postsecondary education were strongly associated with skilled and unskilled first jobs, and community college diplomas and certificates and university graduation with management, professional, and semi-professional and technical first jobs.

Early Employment Patterns to 1979

In 1979 we returned to the Class of '73 members to obtain information on educational and occupational trajectories. That year, 79.5 per cent of the Class of '73 were in the labour force; of that group, 5.5 per cent were unemployed. Fewer than 5 per cent were working part-time. In addition, 15.1 per cent were still full- or part-time students. Almost half the women in our sample were married, as were about one-third of the men. About one-fifth of the married women were neither students nor in the labour force. These gender differences may be largely explained by childrearing responsibilities. Of particular significance was that early on, there were divergences in men's and women's employment and career trajectories.

The top portion of Table 4.2 shows the occupations of Class of '73 members in 1979 using fairly general occupational categories (at least one-third of respondents held jobs in 1979 that were also their first full-time jobs). The table displays these occupations by our main social background variables: gender; socio-economic status of parents; region of province when attending high school; and educational attainment.

Those who had completed college or university enjoyed greater occupational opportunities; however, those opportunities were less certain than in the past. Table 4.2 indicates that in 1979, 31.8 per cent of men and 34.2 per cent of women were in the high or middle management, or professional and semiprofessional, or technical occupational categories, while 64.5 per cent of men and 64.6 per cent of women were in the skilled and unskilled worker categories.[4] Respondents from larger cities were more likely to be employed in upper occupational categories. As we indicated earlier, economic and occupational opportunities in urban settings tend to be greater than in rural communities. These differences likely affected Class of '73 members' occupational aspirations and expectations.

Those from middle and upper classes were more likely to have attained higher occupational positions than those from lower socio-economic backgrounds, though the link between class and occupation in 1979 was weak. High and middle socio-economic background was associated with 1979 occupations in high-level management and professional occupations, with middle management, and with semi-professional/technical occupations; low socio-economic status was associated with unskilled work. It should be noted that the relationship between socio-economic background and occupational attainment at an early career stage is influenced by timing considerations: higher proportions of working-class persons enter the labour force directly after high school graduation; middle-class persons are more likely to delay entry into the labour force in order to pursue postsecondary education.

The top portion of Table 4.2 demonstrates that education exerted a strong influence on occupational outcomes in 1979. Early in their careers, university graduates overwhelmingly dominated the upper management and professional occupations. The middle management, semi-professional, and technical occupations had heavy concentrations of community college and university graduates; skilled and unskilled workers were drawn from high-school-only or community college backgrounds.

Whatever one's educational attainment, the journey to rewarding employment was not necessarily smooth or rapid in the period immediately following graduation. It was fairly common for graduates to work part-time and to be underemployed or unemployed before attaining more fulfilling and lucrative occupations (Anisef et al., 1996).

Bill, who obtained a college diploma in marketing administration in 1977, secured part-time employment at a grocery store and simultaneously sent out hundreds of résumés. He recalled 'going through interviews where you were one of 300 [applicants] and it got down to

Table 4.2. Occupations in 1979 and 1995 by gender, socio-economic status, region of origin, and educational attainment (percentage)

	(n)	High-level management/ professional	Mid-management/semi-professional technical	Skilled workers	Unskilled workers	Agricultural	Total
			Occupation in 1979				
Gender							
Male	352	10.5	21.3	40.1	24.4	3.7	100.0
Female	325	10.2	24.0	35.7	28.9	1.2	100.0
Socio-economic status 1973							
High	223	14.3	28.3	34.5	22.0	0.9	100.0
Middle	229	8.3	24.0	40.2	24.5	3.1	100.0
Low	225	8.4	15.6	39.1	33.3	3.6	100.0
Region of origin							
Toronto and other cities	393	11.2	26.2	35.6	26.5	0.5	100.0
Rural areas and small towns	284	9.2	17.6	41.2	26.8	5.3	100.0
Educational attainment by 1979							
High school	250	2.4	8.4	45.6	39.2	4.4	100.0
Some college/university	86	1.2	17.4	47.7	32.6	1.2	100.0
College	155	5.2	39.4	35.5	18.1	1.9	100.0
University	186	29.6	30.1	25.3	14.0	1.1	100.0

Occupation in 1995 (respondents reporting employment and/or self-employment in 1995)

Gender							
Male	347	26.1	33.4	30.5	11.8	2.6	100.0
Female	329	21.6	36.2	18.8	23.1	0.3	100.0
Socio-economic status 1973							
High	229	31.4	39.3	19.2	8.7	1.3	100.0
Middle	226	18.1	38.1	27.9	14.6	1.3	100.0
Low	221	14.9	26.7	27.6	29.0	1.8	100.0
Region of origin							
Toronto and other cities	396	26.5	36.9	23.0	13.4	0.3	100.0
Rural areas and small towns	280	14.6	31.8	27.5	22.9	3.2	100.0
Educational attainment by 1995							
High school	175	5.1	25.7	36.6	29.7	2.9	100.0
Some college/university	67	11.9	35.8	38.8	11.9	1.5	100.0
College	203	10.8	41.9	28.6	18.2	0.5	100.0
University	231	46.3	35.1	8.7	8.7	1.3	100.0

maybe 20 to 30 people. I kept coming in second or third or fourth.' Finally, he was hired in the accounting area by a dairy food company, a position that allowed him to get his 'foot in the door.' John obtained a BA in economics but secured employment as a stock clerk full-time and at a beer store part-time. Craving an interesting, challenging, and 'steady' job, he declared himself to be 'pretty satisfied with my life, but not my job situation.'

Trained teachers, who had been heavily in demand a decade earlier, often searched with futility for full-time positions. Failing to find one in Ontario after graduating in 1977, Angela took a secretarial course at a community college. Janice, whose specialty was physical education, described herself in 1979 as an 'unemployed teacher.' She had worked at five part-time jobs, including waitressing. But she remained optimistic that a teaching position would materialize. Eventually one did.

Such early struggles in the labour market soured some respondents on the practical advantages of an advanced education, but most, like Angela the aspiring physical education teacher, did not despair: they perceived their difficulties finding good work as temporary rather than permanent. After finishing an administrative studies degree at the University of Western Ontario, Jennifer worked in secretarial jobs, for which she was 'overqualified.' But she was set on paid employment and took 'the first thing [she] could get.' After a year she was hired by a bank, where she was able to apply her university training and eventually moved into a managerial position. Ada, intent on going into journalism, worked at a brokerage firm while honing her writing skills. 'My career is very important to me,' she asserted in 1979. 'I will not stand for ... a career which is [less than] entirely stimulating to me, that fulfils my creative and intellectual needs.' For the Class of '73, the future was uncertain but far from hopeless.

Employment Patterns to 1995

The lower panel of Table 4.2 shows the occupational distributions of Class of '73 members in the 1995 survey, cross-tabulated by the background variables of gender, parental socio-economic status, region of province when attending high school, and educational attainment by 1995. With the passage of time, members of the Class of '73 had the opportunity to advance in their careers, and this occupational movement is clearly indicated in our data. Background variables definitely influenced career advancement. If we take into account only general occupational categories, it appears that gender had little impact on occupations in 1995. But in fact, gender was highly significant in terms of the segments of the labour market where men and women actually found employment. Still, while the proportions of men and women in the highest two occupational categories were similar, in the skilled worker category there were larger numbers of men, and in the unskilled worker category there were larger numbers of women.

Growing up in a large city was associated with obtaining a high-level management or a professional occupation; growing up in a smaller city or a town or rural area was associated with unskilled work. This pattern was evident at each stage of the life course of members of the Class of '73, and confirms that region has a powerful impact on occupational expectations and on entry into occupations.

The long-term effects of education are indisputable, as can be seen in the lower portion of Table 4.2. By 1995 almost half of university graduates were in high-level management or professional positions. Middle management, semiprofessional, and technical occupations drew heavily from all educational backgrounds, including Class of '73 members with only high school. Very few university graduates were found in either skilled or unskilled employment; these kinds of occupations drew heavily from persons with community college or high school only education.

In the next chapter we examine career and social mobility in greater detail; however, a sense of the career movement experienced by the Class of '73 can be formed by comparing the occupational distributions over three of our surveys. Table 4.3 shows reported first full-time jobs in the period 1973–79, as well as jobs held in 1979, 1987–88, and 1995. This table allows us to compare men's and women's occupations in more detail, using nine rather than five occupational groupings. Also, in Table 4.4 we examine these occupational groupings in 1979 and 1995 by the three main educational levels: high school only; community college degree or certificate; and graduation from university.[5]

Comparing first jobs with occupations in 1979 (Table 4.3) reveals the beginnings of career movements through time as the Class of '73 started to shift to higher-status, better-paid work. For example, women shifted out of lower white-collar work and increased their proportions in upper white-collar and semiprofessional/technical employment. For men, the proportion in lower blue-collar jobs declined and the proportions in upper blue-collar and in middle management increased.

Table 4.3. Distributions of respondents' first-time occupations, occupations in 1979, 1988, and 1995, and their fathers' occupations at age 55 (percentage)

	Father's job at age 55		First-time job (1973–79)		Occupation in 1979		Occupation in 1987–88		Occupation in 1995*	
	Male (n=322)	Female (n=349)	Male (n=326)	Female (n=349)	Male (n=300)	Female (n=264)	Male (n=333)	Female (n=281)	Male (n=347)	Female (n=329)
Occupation										
High-level management	6.2	7.4	1.5	0.6	1.0	0.4	3.0	0.7	6.1	4.9
Professional	9.3	12.6	8.3	4.6	8.3	6.4	14.4	18.5	15.6	16.7
Mid-management	9.6	10.6	2.8	1.4	5.7	1.9	13.5	7.5	19.3	13.4
Semiprofessional/technical	4.3	4.3	11.3	19.2	15.0	24.6	13.2	23.5	14.1	22.8
Upper white collar	7.1	8.3	10.7	28.9	12.7	38.6	8.1	22.1	9.8	17.6
Upper blue collar	24.2	23.2	19.0	1.4	28.7	1.1	24.0	1.8	20.7	1.2
Lower white collar	6.8	5.2	11.7	38.4	7.3	23.5	8.7	20.6	3.5	18.8
Lower blue collar	22.0	17.8	28.8	5.2	17.0	3.0	10.5	4.3	8.4	4.3
Agriculture	10.2	10.6	5.9	0.3	4.3	0.4	4.5	1.1	2.6	0.3
Total	100.0	100.0	100.0	100.0	100.0	100.0	100.0	100.0	100.0	100.0

* Only respondents who reported being employed and/or self-employed in 1995.

Table 4.4. Occupations in 1979 and 1995 by educational attainment and gender (percentage)*

	(n)	High level manage-ment	Profes-sional	Mid-manage-ment	Semi profe-sional/ technical	Upper white collar	Upper blue collar	Lower white collar	Lower blue collar	Agri-culture	Total
Educational attainment, 1979											
High school only Male	126	0.8	2.4	4.0	4.0	6.3	43.7	6.3	26.2	6.4	100.0
Female	91	0.0	1.1	2.2	7.7	44.0	2.2	37.4	4.4	1.1	100.0
College certificate or diploma Male	62	1.6	3.2	4.8	29.0	17.7	22.6	6.5	9.7	4.8	100.0
Female	83	1.2	3.6	1.2	43.4	33.7	0.0	16.9	0.0	0.0	100.0
University degree Male	66	1.5	30.3	10.6	21.2	22.7	4.5	1.5	4.5	3.0	100.0
Female	67	0.0	17.9	3.0	29.9	25.4	1.5	16.4	6.0	0.0	100.0
Educational attainment, 1995											
High school only Male	88	1.1	1.1	11.4	11.4	8.0	35.2	6.8	19.3	5.7	100.0
Female	87	3.4	4.6	11.5	17.2	28.7	1.1	23.0	10.3	0.0	100.0
College certificate or diploma Male	98	3.1	7.1	16.3	20.4	11.2	29.6	4.1	7.1	1.0	100.0
Female	105	6.7	4.8	11.4	35.2	16.2	1.0	21.0	3.8	0.0	100.0
University degree Male	118	11.0	38.1	25.4	10.2	9.3	1.7	1.7	0.8	1.6	100.0
Female	113	5.3	38.1	14.2	20.4	4.4	1.8	14.2	0.9	0.9	100.0

* Only respondents who reported being employed and/or self-employed in 1995 are included in the 1995 occupational data.

With respect to 1979 occupations, as with first jobs, there were important differences in occupational distribution by educational achievement. By 1979, few men with only secondary education had moved into managerial, professional, or semiprofessional/technical occupations, but the proportion of men in the upper blue-collar ranks had increased by 50 per cent, with a corresponding decline at the lower blue-collar level. However, women with only secondary education somewhat increased their proportion in the upper white-collar category, with a corresponding decrease in the lower white-collar sector.

Male community college graduates increased their presence in the semiprofessional/technical, upper white-collar, and upper blue-collar categories between first job and 1979 occupation, while the distribution of female community college graduates did not change. Male university graduates started to increase their presence at the semiprofessional/technical and middle management levels, and female university graduates began leaving lower white-collar positions and increasing their presence in the semiprofessional/technical category.

These findings support an earlier analysis in which we compared the occupational status attained by university graduates with that attained by community college graduates. It is useful to summarize the conclusions of this analysis:

> Because community college education results in occupations with higher prestige scores compared to parents' occupations, students graduating from community colleges may well perceive that they have attained social mobility as a result of their education. Still, our data strongly suggest that universities and colleges are, in fact, doing the jobs that are generally agreed they are mandated by society to do. Universities prepare youth for high status occupations in the managerial, professional and white-collar sectors of the occupational structure. The major component of such an education is a general education with only a few programs being fairly job specific (engineering at the undergraduate level and professional education after university education). By contrast, the CAAT system is designed for specific occupational training with only some general education. (Anisef, Ashbury, and Turrittin, 1992: 78)

Table 4.3, which compares occupations in 1979 and 1987–88, reveals a major increase in the number of male and female professionals over this time interval. This increase is not a trend; rather, it reflects the fact that in 1979 those pursuing professional education were still in school;

by 1980 or 1981 they had completed their education and entered professional occupations. A comparison of the two points in time shows
several trends: a small increase in men at the high-level management
level; an increase in persons occupying middle management positions;
a decrease in upper white-collar occupations; and decreases in both
blue-collar categories for men. The trends established between 1979
and 1987–88 continued into 1995. The proportion of men and women
at both levels of management rose; however, decreases occurred in
upper and lower white-collar employment for women and in upper
and lower blue-collar jobs and in lower white-collar jobs for men.

The impact of education continued to be played out in our 1995
data (Table 4.4). Men with university degrees strengthened their hold
on high-level management positions, from 1.5 per cent in 1979 to 11
per cent in 1995. Similarly, their proportion in the professions increased
from 30.3 per cent to 38.1 per cent. Among university graduates, we
found twice as many men as women in upper management positions,
though twice as many female as male community college graduates
held upper management positions. Equal proportions of men and
women were found in the professions (almost all respondents in the
professional category were university graduates). Men and women
university graduates substantially increased their profiles in middle
management positions from 1979 to 1995, with men more than doubling and women more than tripling their proportion. Male and female community college graduates also substantially increased their
presence in middle management.

A comparison between 1979 and 1995 (Table 4.4) shows significant
declines of university and college graduates, both men and women, in
the occupational sectors of semiprofessional/technical work and upper and lower white-collar and upper and lower blue-collar work, as
well as in agriculture. The only exception was a small increase over
time of college-educated women in lower white-collar and blue-collar
work.

While Class of '73 men and women with high school only were not
found in higher-level occupations in either 1979 or 1995, by 1995 substantial percentages had made their way into middle management
and semiprofessional/technical occupations. As with the other educational groups, by 1995 even high-school-only men and women had left
lower white-collar and blue-collar occupations and agriculture (women
were never present in agriculture at any educational level). The exceptions were high-school-only men, whose proportions remained steady

(though small) in both upper and lower white-collar work; and women, who increased their presence somewhat in lower blue-collar work between 1979 and 1995.

These findings support the notion that cumulative employment experiences provided entry into high-level management for university graduates and, similarly, that job experience allowed people with more limited education to enter middle management positions. Thus, access to management positions appears to be significantly age-related, as well as gender-related; and high-level management positions are reserved for people with university and professional backgrounds.

The Social and Economic Context of Employment

Having faced the challenge of underemployment at the end of the 1970s, the Class of '73, along with older Canadians, confronted in 1981 and 1982 the deepest economic recession since the Great Depression of the 1930s. According to David K. Foot and Jeanne C. Li, this coincided with 'the movement of an unusually large cohort of youth through the secondary school system' (cited in Krahn, 1996: 11). In those years, the average annual employment level in the country declined 3.3 per cent – the first such decrease recorded since 1958, when employment levels declined by 0.4 per cent (Moloney, 1986). Between 1981 and 1984 some one million workers in Canada lost full-time jobs and were not recalled. Plant closures were the largest single cause of job losses. Those in the 20-to-34 age group, which included the Class of '73 cohort, were the most likely to be laid off. Younger employees – those with one to three years of job tenure – were more vulnerable still. Significantly, 'the likelihood of permanent lay-off was not strongly associated with educational attainment. More highly educated employees (those with post-secondary education) were just as likely to experience job loss as the less educated' (Picot and Wannell, 1987: n.p.; also Johnson and Reitz, 1981). The construction, mining, and manufacturing industries were the most severely affected; also, reflecting a pattern that would continue throughout the decade, employment in the goods-producing sector declined relative to the services sector. Job prospects also grew dimmer in the public sector, in which the proportion of total employment in the country declined from 7.2 per cent to 5.9 per cent between 1976 and 1986 (Gower, 1987). And between 1975 and 1986, the proportion of part-time workers in the labour force rose from 10.6 per cent to 15.6 per cent. More than half the increase in part-time work was accounted for by a single industry, 'business and personal services' (Levesque, 1987).

Ontario certainly felt the 1980s recession, but not as deeply as other provinces. The decline in employment levels of 2.5 per cent in 1981 and 1982 was below the national average, and Ontario's economic recovery through to 1985 was, with Quebec's, the strongest in the country. Indeed, there were 5.5 per cent more Ontarians employed in 1985 than in 1981. As Moloney stated, 'this growth in total employment was accomplished not only through strong growth in the service-producing sector, but also through a better than average recovery in the goods-producing sector, in which employment was only 2.5 per cent lower in 1985 than in 1981' (1986: n.p).

The period 1985 to 1994 was characterized by severe fluctuations in the business cycle and by structural changes in the Canadian economy. Stock market prices peaked and then crashed in the fall of 1987. Similarly, the real estate market crested at the end of the decade before dipping abruptly. By mid-1980s standards, it would remain relatively soft for the next several years. Trade liberalization 'in response to a changing global economy' was marked by North American free trade agreements (Krahn, 1996: 11). These changes were accompanied by accelerated 'downsizing' by private corporations and by governments (including Ontario's), which took steps to reduce their work forces and annual deficits during the early 1990s. Employment conditions were also affected by a later recession that gripped the country between 1990 and 1992. Instability and unpredictability were the economic order of the day.

The unemployment rate in Canada rose from 7.1 per cent in January 1990 to 10.6 per cent in January 1991. In January 1994, despite the supposed end of the recession, it remained at 11.4 per cent. By the end of the year, unemployment had fallen to 10.4 per cent, although for Canadian youth it had risen, reaching 18.9 per cent for those 15 to 19 years old, and 15.4 per cent for those 20 to 24. In August 1995 the unemployment rate in Ontario was slightly below the national average, stalling at 9.3 per cent (Krahn, 1996).

A Statistics Canada study compared the impact on future employment prospects of the 1981–82 and 1990–91 recessions. It found that the duration of unemployment in both periods was about 19.6 weeks. Yet it went on to say that 'what distinguishes the recent recession from that of a decade ago is the fact that the chances of leaving unemployment during the first two months of unemployment appear to be better, but the chances of leaving at three months and longer are worse: unemployment has become more polarized. This finding is attributed to a long-standing structural change that occurred in the aftermath of the 1981–82 recession, and that was not reversed by the recovery and expansion of the 1980s' (Corak, 1993: n.p). In Ontario, those 'permanently laid-off ... suffered a 107 per cent increase in the duration of unemployment between 1988 and 1992. This [was] due to a very large decline in the probability of leaving unemployment during the first month of unemployment' (1993, abstract).

An important characteristic of the changing labour market over the years was the continuing shift toward part-time employment, which grew from some 12 per cent of employed Canadians in the late 1970s to about 17 per cent in 1992. In 1993, part-time jobs constituted 24 per cent of all jobs in Canada. Of particular significance was the rise in involuntary part-time labour. In 1975, only 11 per cent of part-time workers claimed to be 'involuntarily' employed in that capacity – that is, unable to find full-time jobs. By 1993 the figure had risen to 35 per cent. However, this increase was almost entirely accounted for by young employees and would thus have been less of a phenomenon (though not an absent one) among (older) workers in the Class of '73 (Krahn: 1996).[6]

Negotiating the Boom and Bust of the 1980s and 1990s

Unemployment and Underemployment

How did these economic currents affect employment opportunities among the Class of '73? A significant proportion of respondents – some 42 per cent – reported being unemployed at some point between 1978 and 1994, though this included women who had taken time out to have children. As Table 4.5 indicates, those in unskilled occupations were the most likely to have experienced unemployment over this period. The university educated and those in professional and managerial occupations were the least likely to have experienced unemployment. Still, fully 33.6 per cent of those in the highest occupational category had been unemployed. Since leaving high school, members of the Class of '73 had held an average of four full-time jobs (of at least 30 hours per week), with men averaging 4.5 jobs and women 3.4. In 1995, 74.6 per cent of the Class of '73 was employed; 15.6 per cent was self-employed, and 9.8 per cent was not working. There was a significant gender difference regarding employment status, with 6.1 per cent of men but 13.3 per cent of women indicating that they were not employed in 1994–95. About half of the men who were not employed were actively engaged in looking for work at this time, whereas only about one-fifth of the nonemployed women were looking for work.

For a significant minority of the Class of '73, the challenge of underemployment – the mismatch between education and work – continued. That being said, for the majority of university-educated respondents, underemployment diminished with time (see Anisef, Ashbury, Bischoping, and Lin, 1996). Eleven years after finishing their education, approximately two-thirds of employed university graduates held jobs commensurate with their academic qualifications, while 35 per cent were evidently underemployed. Between 1979 and 1988 the number of respondents reporting a match between education and employment increased by 20 per cent. In addition, the skill/job mismatch varied across fields of study, with 37.5 per cent of social science graduates still underemployed in 1988 but only 19.2 per cent of applied science graduates similarly mismatched (Anisef, Ashbury, Bishoping and Lin, 1996: 163). This result is similar to the findings of surveys conducted by the Department of Secretary of State (1978, 1984, 1988).

In recent decades there has been increasing tension between those proponents of higher education who endorse the pursuit of education for its own sake and those who argue that universities need to be of increased utility to their graduates, particularly in supplying the skills required to locate good jobs (Anisef and Axelrod, 1999). In the 1995 survey we asked respondents with respect to their current or most recent full-time job, 'How related is/was the field of study of your most recent degree or diploma in terms of specific skills you learned (e.g., lab techniques, translating, computer programming, design)?' Some 62.1 per cent of respondents ($n = 754$) replied that their jobs were 'very related' or 'somewhat related' to the skills they had learned; 37.9 per cent said 'not very related' or 'not related at all.' In terms of general skills (writing ability, solving technical or mechanical problems, thinking analytically), respondents were more positive: 82 per cent said 'very related or somewhat related'; only 18 per cent who said 'not very related' or 'not at all related.' Study participants were also asked to assess the truth of the following statement: 'the job matches my educational background and training.' Here, 55.6 per cent answered 'very true' or 'true,' 21.5 per cent reported 'some-

Table 4.5. Employment status, job-related training, and job satisfaction by gender, educational attainment, and occupation in 1995 (percentage)

| | Unemployed anytime during 1978–94[1] | | Employment status[2] | | | |
	n	Yes	n	Employed	Self-employed	Not employed[3]
Gender						
Male	347	34.3	378	76.7	17.2	6.1
Female	327	42.5	406	76.8	9.9	13.3
Educational attainment 1995						
High school	172	31.4	210	75.8	12.9	11.4
Some college/ university	67	44.8	79	67.1	21.5	11.4
College graduate	200	45.0	230	80.4	11.3	8.3
University degree	235	35.7	265	77.4	13.2	9.4
Occupation 1995						
High-level management/ professional	143	33.6	158	82.3	10.1	7.6
Mid-management/ semiprofessional/ technical	219	36.1	247	80.9	14.2	4.9
Skilled workers	163	38.7	194	73.2	13.4	13.4
Unskilled workers	111	48.6	133	75.2	12.8	12.0
Agriculture	10	10.0	11	36.4	54.5	9.1

1 Only respondents who reported being employed and/or self-employed in 1995.
2 The employed category includes a small proportion of respondents who indicated that they were both employed and self-employed (under 4.0 per cent in all subcategories except for the 1995 subcategory occupation agriculture, where the proportion was 9.1 per cent).
3 The 1995 occupations reported for this group are the respondent's most recent full-time job.
Note: Section 8 of the 1995 survey asked about job-related training activities 'which have a structured plan and objective designed to develop or upgrade knowledge or a skill.' In Section 5 of the survey, respondents were asked about their current full-time job or, if not employed, their most recent full-time job.

| Received training[1] | | | Job satisfaction[1] | | | | |
n	Yes	n	Very dis-satisfied	Some-what dis-satisfied	Neither satisfied nor dis-satisfied	Some-what satisfied	Very satisfied
335	70.4	353	13.3	11.9	6.5	36.3	32.0
322	67.7	337	11.3	14.2	5.3	33.5	35.6
164	57.9	179	10.6	12.8	7.8	34.1	34.6
67	62.7	70	11.4	12.9	7.1	42.9	25.7
197	73.1	205	14.6	12.2	6.8	34.6	31.7
229	75.5	236	11.9	14.0	3.4	33.5	37.3
139	79.1	146	12.3	13.7	4.1	29.5	40.4
223	78.0	233	12.4	11.2	4.7	33.9	37.8
155	59.4	168	13.1	16.7	5.4	36.3	28.6
107	57.9	117	11.1	11.1	10.3	42.7	24.8
8	62.5	10	10.0	10.0	20.0	40.0	20.0

what true,' and 22.9 per cent responded 'not very true' or 'not true at all' ($n = 573$).

Navigating the economic waves of boom and bust was a preoccupation for the Class of '73. Those who found employment in the public sector soon after graduation – posts that were increasingly difficult to obtain – managed relatively well. Like Frank, who obtained a teaching job in 1979, they tended to remain in these occupations throughout the 1980s and early 1990s. Those working in the private sector, including some with professional degrees, were likely to change jobs more frequently and to experience periods of involuntary unemployment. Gary, the engineer who had several options to choose from on graduation, was laid off from his position in Calgary after four years. He moved to

Vancouver and found a job with B.C. Hydro and had been working there for twelve years when we interviewed him in 1995. Martin, also an engineer, moved from northeastern to southwestern Ontario when the company he was working for closed its Canadian operation. After a commuting stint to Montreal, he found a 'secure' job with Ontario Hydro. Alice, who as we noted earlier had been laid off in 1980, worked in a variety of retail sales jobs over the next decade. In 1995 she was employed as a sales clerk in a pharmacy. She believed her job was vulnerable because the organization had recently been sold to a larger corporation, and she was prepared to move to a different city in order to stay employed.

George, a mechanic, was laid off during the recession of the early 1980s. Eventually he found a job with an auto manufacturer where he remained for ten years. When the automotive dealer for whom George worked went bankrupt in the early 1990s, his job disappeared. 'It was a strange feeling ... There [was] no reason to get up and I have never been like that.' Eventually he became a self-employed mechanic, working out of a farm he bought in eastern Ontario.

Personal and financial factors led Sheila to a small community in eastern Ontario, where in 1995 she was working as a bank clerk. Together, she and her husband were running their own television and VCR repair and rental company. For a time they had five employees but by 1995, 'in this economic climate,' they were down to only one employee. 'Everything in this economy is touch and go,' she noted. 'It's a roller coaster ride [and] we just manage to hang on. I thought everything at this point in our life would just move along so much smoother. You'd be certain to have a job and you worked all those years to get to that point. But nothing was guaranteed.' Fearing the prospects of job loss at the bank, where layoffs had already occurred, she and her husband derived greater pleasure and personal rewards from their family and community life.

Part-Time Work and Self-Employment

We noted earlier that by 1995, members of the Class of '73 have held an average of four full-time jobs. This figure was derived from a question asking how many full-time jobs respondents had held since leaving high school. We also asked respondents to present their job history by filling in a job history table with twelve possible job entries. Respondents indicated the dates of jobs, the kind of occupation and industry, whether it was full- or part-time (less than 30 hours per week), and whether it was self-employment. If we take the last job reported in the job table, cross-classified by a question about current employment (the choices were employed, self-employed, not employed), we can get some sense of the current level of part-time employment of Class of '73 members. Seventy-five per cent of all respondents reported being currently employed, and of these, 16.5 per cent reported their last job in the job history table as being part-time employment. Seven per cent of men reported being employed part-time; for women the figure was 25.3 per cent. These figures were almost identical to national part-time employment rates for 1991: 16.5 per cent of the labour force was employed part-time which included a 25.5 per cent part-time rate for women compared to 8.8 per cent for men (Krahn and Lowe, 1993: 93). Women clearly worked part-time at a far higher rate than men.

We do not have complete information on the reasons for part-time employment. The few who did provide us with their main reasons for part-time work indicated that this employment fit well with their lifestyles, or suited the demands of homemaking, or enabled them to contribute financially to the family, or was the only alternative to a suitable full-time job, or was necessary to pay for education. According to Krahn and Lowe, the number of 'involuntary' part-time workers increased in Canada from 11 per cent in 1975 to 28 per cent in 1991 (Krahn and Lowe, 1993: 94).

Levels of self-employment are shown in Table 4.5. Men were more than 1.5 times more likely than women to be self-employed. Self-employment constituted about 15 per cent of any educational or occupational group, except for those in the agricultural category: three-fifths of this group mentioned that they were self-employed. Of those who indicated that they were self-employed, many mentioned that they had been so for ten years, and about 60 per cent stated that they were incorporated. Just over one-third of self-employed respondents employed no other persons; another one-third employed an additional one to four persons; the remainder employed a range of persons, with five respondents reporting employing 150 or more individuals.

Job-Related Training

Job-related training is an increasingly common feature of the working world. Of the respondents who replied to the 1995 survey, 65.5 per cent received job-related training at least once between 1989 and 1994; 34.5 per cent had no such experience. The number of those receiving such training increased significantly between 1989 and 1994. While 32.1 per cent of participants obtained job-related training in 1989, 43.7 per cent did so in 1994. The respondents' most recent job-related training took up an average of 17.4 hours per week and lasted 5.9 weeks. An eight-hour training session was the most frequent session length reported. Almost half of job-related training was completed within a week's time, and three-quarters within six weeks. One-third of respondents who reported receiving job-related training indicated that this training was required, and one-fifth said it was recommended though not required by their employer; almost two-fifths decided on their own to take such training. Some 38 per cent were trained on the job site (mainly during working hours); 55.2 per cent were trained away from the job site (mainly during daytime); 6.8 per cent had some combination of training sites and times of day. Regarding financial support, 69 per cent of the training was funded by employers, 7.1 per cent by government, 15 per cent by the employees themselves, and 9 per cent by other sources or some combination of sources.

The reasons reported for taking job-related training included the following: to upgrade or improve job skills; to meet requirements of the employer or of government regulations; and to improve the chances of promotion. Some respondents viewed the training as a means for creating or improving job opportunities or for effecting career changes.

Many of the job-related courses involved computer training; others involved sales or customer relations training; still others involved improving job performance and proficiency. When asked how much their most recent job-related training helped them meet their job-related objectives, 44.7 per cent of respondents reported 'a lot'; 37.2 per cent said 'some'; 15 per cent said 'a little'; and 3.1 per cent reported 'not at all.' On the whole, 79.5 per cent of trainees received assistance from their employers, and 20.5 per cent did not. Referring to Table 4.5, there was little gender difference related to job-related training. Levels of job-related training were somewhat higher for the higher educational groups.

Rewards and Stresses of Working Life

Through the 1980s and early 1990s, members of the Class of '73 made their way in the world of employment, a world in which opportunity and uncertainty coexisted. When they looked back over the period from the perspective of 1995, the majority of respondents – 66 per cent – declared themselves satisfied or very satisfied with the way things had turned out with respect to 'work or career.' Some 22 per cent were neither satisfied nor dissatisfied; almost 12 per cent were dissatisfied or very dissatisfied. In contrast, more than 85 per cent were very satisfied or satisfied with their 'family life,' with 5.7 per cent being dissatisfied or very dissatisfied. Some 83 per cent were similarly content with their 'personal life,' and slightly fewer than five per cent expressed dissatisfaction. Thus, in 1995 most respondents were positive about or at least reconciled to the reality of their working lives. But employment was far from their chief source of fulfilment. Given the economic vagaries of the previous two decades, this attitude was understandable.

Without question, economic factors beyond the control of individuals affected the working lives of the Class of '73. Throughout the 1980s and early 1990s, inflation, recession, free trade, corporate downsizing, and public-sector deficit cutting all affected the availability and conditions of employment. So too did gender, type of education, and social background. But personal choice also accounted for the unique directions taken by individuals. However daunting the social and economic pressures, the men and women of the Class of '73 seemed determined to preserve their autonomy and to direct the course of their working lives, even at the expense of some material comforts. How successful was the Class of '73 in achieving its occupational goals? How did its members describe the rewards and stresses of contemporary working life?

Our 1995 survey found that on the whole, respondents viewed their occupations more positively than not, though as we noted earlier, they derived even more fulfilment from their personal and family lives. Some 56 per cent of those working full-time expressed satisfaction with their pay, and an additional 28 per cent were somewhat satisfied. A slightly smaller proportion were happy with their benefits package. Respondents were also asked whether their level of pay was appropriate given their 'education, training, and experience.' Here, a significant minority felt insufficiently rewarded: while some 55 per cent believed they were earning the 'right amount,' 41 per cent felt that they were earning less than they deserved (some three per cent felt that they were earning *more* than they deserved).[7]

Overall, the respondents appeared to enjoy their work, with women enjoying a slight edge in job satisfaction. By 1995, however, job satisfaction, as reported in Table 4.5, bore no clear relationship to educational attainment. Still, those respondents who held high-level management/professional positions and middle management/semiprofessional jobs were more likely to express strong satisfaction than respondents who held skilled or unskilled jobs.

Somewhat more than 60 per cent believed that their work offered opportunities for 'exercising leadership,' and an additional 20 per cent felt that this was 'somewhat true.'[8] On another questionnaire item, only about 12 per cent of employees thought that they lacked 'freedom to decide how to do my work.' And nearly 74 per cent of respondents disagreed with the statement that their 'job is boring.' As indicated earlier, some 56 per cent believed that their job 'matches my educational background and training,' and another 21 per cent felt that this was 'somewhat true.' Were respondents able to 'use their abilities' on the job? It would appear so: just under 79 per cent of respondents believed this to be 'very true' or 'true,' and an additional 16 per cent said this was somewhat true. Half the respondents agreed that their 'job allows for personal growth and development,' while another 29 per cent considered this to be somewhat true. Half the respondents disagreed with the statement that the 'work is routine and predictable,' while 22 per cent agreed and 27 per cent somewhat agreed.

Interviewees described – often in considerable detail – the conditions that both enriched and diminished the quality of their working experiences. The joys of autonomy, diversity of tasks, flexibility, and creativity were highlighted by many people in a variety of occupations. When one or more of these were absent, respondents often made changes, including voluntarily leaving their positions, in order to improve the quality of their work and their lives.

Ray, a chartered accountant, gave up a high-paying but 'boring' job with a large firm to start his own company. This was a risky venture in the mid-1980s, given the fluctuations in the economy, but with the assistance of his wife, who helped with the books, he succeeded. He came to realize that accountants are employable in both good and bad economic times, and that to some degree the profession is 'recession-proof.' Now self-employed, he cherishes the control he has over the hours and terms of his work.

While working as an occupational therapist, Jessica ran a small catering service at the hospital where she was employed. Entrepreneurial ambitions led her and her husband into the real estate market, in which they worked successfully during the housing boom of the mid-1980s. In one three-week period they sold eleven houses. Her husband did the marketing while she worked closely with clients, a facet of her job with close parallels to her work in occupational therapy: in both fields she was required to 'hold [the client's] hand' and provide emotional support under stressful circumstances. She cut back on her real estate activities to raise her children. Her husband continued in the real estate business full-time while she worked with him 'in the background.'

After obtaining a BA, Tim taught English in Africa in the early 1980s. When he returned to Canada he found an interesting job as a human rights worker for a provincial agency. Four years later, he gave up this position in order to obtain his teaching degree, which he hoped would lead to the vocation that most attracted him. But in the early 1990s there were few openings for teachers, and by 1995 he had worked only as a supply teacher.

Our survey shows that many women left paid employment, either temporarily or permanently, to raise children. Some 81.5 per cent of the women who were not employed in 1994–95 identified family responsibilities, including pregnancy, and problems arranging childcare, as reasons for being out of the labour force in 1994–95. Employed women frequently described the challenges of reconciling family and occupational demands, and those who managed this successfully were the most fulfilled. Others wrestled with the problem on a daily basis.

Stephanie enjoyed her work as a music teacher, which took her many years to find. But in 1995 she was experiencing stress. She was the mother of three children, and her teaching job required her to offer programs at two schools, and she felt 'burned out' by the competing demands of work and family. Having regularly banked a portion of her salary, she was preparing to take a year off from her job, though she remained 'passionate' about her career. In contrast, Judy achieved the kind of balance that Stephanie had long sought. Her job as a cafeteria administrator took her out of the house by 5:30 a.m., which allowed her to be home every afternoon when her children return from school. At first her husband reluctantly looked after the children when he lost his job and was unemployed for six months. He eventually obtained full-time employment again, and by then was enthusiastically caring for the children in the early morning.

Heather, who earned a college diploma as a forestry technician, was one of twelve women enrolled in a class of several hundred. Following her graduation, she found employment in unrelated areas. She then left the labour force for ten years in order to raise her children. By 1994 she had taken up a part-time position as a forestry technician in Northern Ontario – a job she found interesting and respectful of her desire for autonomy.

Other factors besides the contest between family and occupational demands contributed to the stresses of contemporary working life. Kelly and Anna both enjoyed their jobs in the nursing profession, but because of cutbacks in health care were confined, to their dismay, to part-time work. As a single mother, Anna especially was struggling to make ends meet.

Even when financial strain was not a major concern, the sheer drudgery of work was sometimes disconcerting. A high school graduate who received no encouragement to pursue postsecondary education, Kate left home and travelled in Europe in her late adolescence. When she returned to Canada, she found secretarial work in the 'freight-forwarding' business, a field she has worked in ever since. At the time of her interview she was intensely dissatisfied with the repetitive and unchallenging nature of her job and with the company's failure to modernize. It had yet to install computers, and she was spending much of her time typing. She often thought of returning to school but hadn't yet done so.

Chuck, an editor of a small town newspaper, aspired to the managing editor's position. Given the relatively young age of the current incumbent, he did not expect such a promotion, and he felt 'stuck' in his current role.

Ron was a tool maker. After a series of recession-induced job changes, he had been working for an automobile manufacturer for ten years. He lamented the technological changes that had overtaken his craft. 'Computer-controlled machines' were now determining a large part of the production process. He still enjoyed teaching apprentices, but believed that his true skills were unappreciated and becoming increasingly obsolete.

Cliff, a residential worker for the physically and mentally challenged, was growing more cynical on the job. He was more interested in the world of art, and had initially entered social work because his girlfriend was in the profession. He found his work physically and emotionally exhausting, and his supervisors often identified performance problems. As he said, 'nobody pats you on the back for doing a good job ... People burn out very quickly.' In 1994 his position was threatened by cutbacks in government funding. He had already witnessed long-term employees retaining employment only by being assigned to lower-status positions in which they had no interest or background. He anticipated facing similar circumstances in the near future.

The combined effects of social structure and personal agency – of economic challenge and personality – are poignantly illustrated in the life experiences of the Class of '73. Many faced both opportunity and uncertainty in the 1980s and early 1990s. Personal histories, circumstances, priorities, and choices, as well as the vagaries of the economy, gave different shape to their respective life courses.

Employment, Careers, and Gender

Both survey data and interviews indicated the pervasive importance of gender in the occupational histories of our respondents. Men and women are subject to the same social and economic forces but tend to experience them quite differently. In particular, childbirth and childrearing affect women's career pathways in distinctive ways.

Most members of the Class of '73 were married sometime in their twenties, and almost all of them had children by 1995. The timing of the latest phase of our study placed many of these people on the other side of their childbearing years. We are therefore in a good position to examine the consequences of childbearing on the employment and occupational history of these individuals and their families.

It has been said that both 'work and family are "greedy institutions" (Coser, 1974) that make simultaneous demands on ... emotional energy, physical strength and intellect. Family life shapes the nature of people's work experience, just as employment affects families' (Crouter, 1984). The interviews provided ample evidence of this assertion. Marriage itself has consequences for the employment and career of each partner, but that is only the beginning.

Among those we interviewed, the woman who married and had a first child in her early twenties was an exception. The majority, even if they married in their early twenties, waited a number of years before having the first child. Some married in their late twenties or thirties and either had children right away or waited a few more years. Among the women we interviewed, the predominant pattern was to work full-time for a number of years prior to having the first child. This pattern held even among women who married much earlier.

One of the consequences of marriage that had a much greater impact on women than on men related to geographical mobility. Some respondents were working in occupations in which relocation was common (e.g., construction and mining); in other situations the decision to relocate was based on employment prospects or career options. A number of women mentioned that they had moved because of their spouses; however, none of the men we interviewed mentioned moving because of their wives. This indicates that our respondents gave priority to the employment and career opportunities of the male partner. The reasons behind decisions to move may have varied among individual families, but they were generally based on men having greater earning potential than women, as well as on ingrained notions of gender-appropriate behaviour.

A few men among those we interviewed made decisions about their location that resulted in more restricted employment opportunities, but that benefited their families in other ways. For example, in spite of the difficulties inherent in earning a living in farming, Ben elected to remain on his farm rather than move to the city. He believed that for him and his family, the quality of life on the farm far exceeded that of a more urban setting, and he was fully prepared to sacrifice monetary gains to preserve his family's lifestyle.

Only rarely were the careers of men negatively affected by marriage and children. Women were much more likely to see their careers harmed by marriage and particularly children. There has been a tendency for women to enter gender-specific occupations that offer lower pay. Also, women have faced discrimination with respect to career advancement because of the possibility that they might have children. And when they do have children, they have had to deal with the conflicting demands of childrearing and employment. To explore these effects in more detail, we now look at findings from our 1995 interviews with women.

Many women, after taking time off during pregnancy and for the first months of childrearing, continued to work full-time while raising their children. In effect, they moved into the 'second shift' (Hochschild, 1990), or the 'double ghetto' (Armstrong and Armstrong, 1984). Many were in occupations such as nursing and teaching, which allowed them to stay for long periods in one particular niche. Sandra was in a traditional women's occupation (nursing) and had worked continuously. Jennifer also worked steadily, as an administrator in a financial institution; however, she felt that the responsibilities of caring for her two children had cost her promotions. Stephanie, a teacher, reported that while her job provided her with flexibility with respect to her childcare responsibilities, she had had to give up her ambition to become a principal. Sheila moved with her family to another city when her husband was relocated by his employer, and settled for a less demanding job so that she could care for her children.

These examples suggest that even when they worked continuously, women often found that having and raising children affected the types of jobs they found, their responsibilities on the job, and the incomes they received. A few women did not have children, and all of them worked. Janice was doing exactly what she wanted to do – teaching. Suzanne reached the top of her profession in journalism. Freda was in administration. Kate worked in a small company, and believed that because of her gender she had never been promoted. The absence of children did not eliminate the possibility of gender discrimination on the job, but women who did not have children were evidently better able to achieve their career goals than those who did.

Among those we interviewed, only women with childrearing responsibilities were employed part-time in 1995, and all had previously worked full-time. But the situations varied. Heather had worked full-time before having children. She had taken ten years off work to raise her children and had recently begun a part-time job as a means of working her way back into full-time employment. Kelly, a nurse, had switched to part-time work in order to care for her children, but when she later sought full-time employment because of financial needs, she could not find such a position. Nancy was in a profession in which the movement between part-time and full-time work was quite smooth. In fact, some fields, such as technical and scientific ones, seem to lend themselves to part-time employment. For example, Cheryl, a technician, was able to find part-time work in her occupation, in spite of numerous moves arising from her husband's career. On the other hand, Rachel, having worked full-time in a professional field, switched to part-time employment after having her third child, knowing full well that this would effectively end her career. Clearly, part-time work always has an impact on income and occupational prospects. Beyond this, the significance for employment and careers depends largely on the particular situation and context. It should be noted that in 1995, part-time employment in the Class of '73 was predominantly limited to women.

All of the men we interviewed were employed, and only a small group of women, almost all with childrearing responsibilities, were not working. Among the interviewees, Ann was the only one who had never worked, this despite having completed a community college diploma. Her spouse worked in a field in which frequent relocation was a requirement, and this was partly why she did not seek some form of employment. In 1995 she was single again and struggling to enter the workforce.

Among the others, leaving the labour force seems to have been the result of a mix of unanticipated events. Terry, who had been well established in her occupation, found herself married to a man with an occupation in which relocation was common, and which provided an adequate income to support a family. Laura wanted to work part-time but found that opportunities for part-time positions in her field had dried-up. For Angela the situation was more complex: she had a university degree, but a lack of suitable positions in her field when she graduated forced her to take a series of secretarial jobs, which she disliked. When her husband found a new job in another city, and when she gave birth to her first child, she dropped out of the labour force.

It is interesting that no men gave up their jobs in order to take care of their children; only women took this step. It will be interesting to see how these women manage their lives once their children leave home. At what level will they re-enter the work force? What kind of training will they choose or be forced to take?

This analysis has demonstrated that gender has a strong effect on employment and career trajectories, specifically with regard to marriage and childrearing responsibilities. We have focused on the women simply because the effects are so much more dramatic. But for men, too, marriage and family have consequences for careers. Given the various constraints, men and women make the choices that benefit their families. Women are more often found in occupations and careers with lower earning potential, and in situations where they are expected to take primary responsibility for childrearing, so it is they who have made the necessary compromises in the work place.

Conclusions

What conclusions can be drawn from this account of the employment experiences of the Class of '73? Merely having a job fulfilled virtually no one. Even earning a good income was insufficiently rewarding if the job lacked challenge or prospects for advancement. Positions without flexibility or humane conditions also earned the subjects' disdain. In contrast, the respondents valued work in fields for which they felt equipped. Employment that provided relative security, improved status, significant autonomy, and a flexible schedule elicited much enthusiasm.

As our survey showed, in 1994–95 the majority – though not an overwhelming one – expressed satisfaction with the state of their employment. Interviews, however, indicated a marked level of anxiety about the impact of corporate downsizing and government funding cutbacks. Income mattered to our subjects – as the survey pointed out, a significant minority felt undercompensated in light of their qualifications – but this theme was not often emphasized in interviews. Some interviewees expressed appreciation for the standard of living their incomes provided; others had sacrificed money for a preferred way of life. Living in the country, spending more time with one's family, and being one's own boss instead of an employee, explained these choices for men and women alike. Not surprisingly, the matter of family income was stressed with greater urgency in circumstances where financial pressures were particularly severe.

For most women, experiences of employment were different from those of men. Shifts in the economic climate affected both sexes, but these effects were filtered through the lens of gender. In their daily lives, men and women adapted to the realities they faced and acted accordingly. But women continued to occupy traditionally 'female' occupations, even in light of structural changes in the economy. Hughes (1998: 26) reports that between 1971 and 1991 the proportion of women in either nontraditional or intermediate occupations rose from 14.2 per cent to 20 per cent, leaving 80 per cent of the female labour force within traditional occupations. Few women were able to keep pace with the career advancement and income accumulation of men while simultaneously raising children.

Having faced a number of challenges in the 1980s, arising largely from an economy in flux, members of the Class of '73 had for the most part made great strides in achieving their goals and improving their occupational status. By 1995 they were faring far better than young people entering the labour force for the first time. But the sources of uncertainty remained, and the security of those with jobs – even good ones – could by no means be guaranteed. In the next chapter we examine in greater detail the social and occupational mobility of members of the Class of '73.

CHAPTER FIVE

Social, Career, and Geographic Mobility

In a society that promotes the myth of individual success, there is bound to be some curiosity about how people have progressed with their lives, particularly with respect to their jobs and careers. In this chapter we focus on the occupational pathways taken by members of the Class of '73, noting how their attainments in 1995 compared with those of their fathers.[1] Social mobility refers to the shifts by individuals or groups from one status position to another within a system of social stratification. Sociologists argue that all societies are stratified, meaning that social positions are differentially structured in terms of access to power, wealth, and prestige. Metaphorically speaking, stratification can be conceived as a series of ladders of linked social positions. These ladders allow social mobility – up, down, and even across ladders – with social change altering the system as a whole over time.

In the tradition of stratification research, we focus on status attainment, that is, on the stages in the process by which children are distributed in a continuous status hierarchy, given fathers' positions in the same hierarchy (Ganzeboom, Treiman, and Ultee, 1991). Kerckhoff (1995) argues that we need to understand the role of institutional arrangements (e.g., schools, work organizations) in shaping status attainment processes. The function of institutional arrangements was discussed in Chapter 3 when we considered the role of the educational system as a 'sorting machine' moving students into hierarchically arranged employment positions, which are themselves highly correlated with levels of educational attainment. In discussing social mobility, our emphasis here is on the structural side of the structure/agency duality. This is the case because the labour market itself is so highly structured as a system of social inequality. Nevertheless, we do not neglect the agency dimension, because we are able to address the question of the resources that individuals employ in order to alter their socio-economic position.

For individuals and groups, the notion of social mobility is problematic in at least three respects. *First*, one must compete for, find, and hold one's place in the stratification system. This aspect of stratification, which highlights the role of personal agency, manifests itself most commonly in terms of establishing a career. *Second*, as social structure changes, the ladders are altered and rearranged, some disappearing altogether, and this changes the bases for competition. This invites comparison between present and past generations – what is called 'intergenerational mobility.' *Third*, people want to provide for their own progeny, so they seek to make the process of social mobility more secure and predictable for them. This suggests that the process contains elements of risk when moving up or down, or when changing ladders of mobility. These risks can be minimized by drawing on family resources and by building institutional forms that are favourable to mobility (e.g., accessible higher education) through political and community action (Matras, 1984: 8; Beck, 1992: 94; Heinz, 1991: 11).

One of the key dimensions of the life course is geographic movement at different stages in one's biography. Simply put, most adults move away from the places where they grew up. Such moves are often related to employment and reflect push and pull factors, such as moving away from an economically depressed community, or moving to another area while following job progression, or (as is often the case for women) moving with the spouse whose work has been relocated. In this way geography is linked to social mobility. Moves can also be made for noneconomic reasons; for example, a couple may decide to move (or stay) because they wish to be close to a particular set of parents. For the Class of '73, we have conceived of geographic mobility in terms of two categories: stayers and movers.

Social Structure, Personal Agency, and Mobility

Members of the Class of '73 exhibited the influences of both personal agency and social structure as they moved through the life course. For example, the decision to leave a small town because a stable, well-paying job in one's field is not available is both a comment on the state of the local economy (structure) and on how an individual makes a decision that changes his or her situation (personal agency). Because the Class of '73 project captured information about its members at only a few discrete points in time, there were fairly large gaps between follow-up inquiries in the final stages of the project. We relied on aggregate data about different segments of the Class of '73 to demonstrate the effects of structural forces; we relied on interviews to reveal how people present decisions they have made as turning points that have changed their life situations substantially.

Before turning to the Class of '73 data focusing on social and geographical mobility, it is worthwhile to briefly take stock of our main findings so far. During the 1960s, Ontario's educational system was transformed from a strongly class-based system to a more mobility-oriented system; the educational system was extended and diversified, and young people – especially young women – responded by attaining more education. Class of '73 members were early beneficiaries of the new era of educational opportunity. Even so, socio-economic status and region of origin within Ontario had a substantial impact on the educational expectations of members of the Class of '73. For those young people who decided to pursue postsecondary education, a large range of new (and expanded old) white-collar professions and semiprofessions had opened up career alternatives. (Admittedly, this expansion that was just then coming to a close.) While the Class of '73 women participated equally with men in taking advantage of the new educational opportunities in Ontario, gender differences in the selection of programs and majors, and in jobs sought after completing their education, resulted in persistent gender differences in employment. Then as women married, they had to organize their lives around the dual role of homemaker/mother and employed income earner – a theme we will examine in detail in Chapter 7.

In the previous chapter on employment, we indicated how schooling was related to first jobs, to how these jobs were related to various background factors such as gender, socio-economic status, and region of origin within Ontario, and to how job patterns have altered for the Class of '73 since the 1970s. In this chapter we make further comparisons in order to understand the process of mobility. Comparing the occupation of a Class of '73 member to the occupation of his or her father enables us to assess *intergenerational mobility* – that is, to consider individual movements between generations in terms of changing socio-economic status. Comparing first full-time jobs to occupations at later points in time (*intragenerational mobility*) provides us with information about career changes and adds another dimension to our understanding of changes in socio-economic status. At first glance, these changes appear to be the result of personal agency – accumulated decisions made by individuals. However, as we have already argued, the process is much more complex than a simple notion of individual wills at work. With respect to economic success, many personal career decisions are also the result of significant structural shifts in the Canadian economy. Our exploration of mobility ought to be able to demonstrate this duality of structure and personal agency for the Class of '73. We shall also explore the continuing role of background factors in the mobility process.

Intergenerational Social Mobility

The intergenerational social mobility of the Class of '73 can be looked at from two different angles. We can take a broad view in terms of the three levels of socio-economic status (SES) by comparing parents' socio-economic status as reported in 1973 to a respondent's own SES in 1995, or we can take a somewhat more specific focus by comparing the occupation of a respondent's father at age 55 to the same respondent's own occupation in 1995.[2]

A sense of overall social mobility can be obtained by examining social class mobility for the Class of '73, as shown in Table 5.1. Respondents from the lower and upper socio-economic status groups were more likely than middle-class respondents to maintain their class position. Thus, 48.1 per cent of lower, 37.3 per cent of middle, and 51.3 per cent of upper SES respondents had maintained their class position by the time of the Phase VI survey (1995). A second important observation is that lower-SES respondents were somewhat more likely to move into upper-SES positions (22.1 per cent) than upper-SES respondents were to move into lower-SES positions (15.6 per cent) – an indication of general net upward mobility for Class of '73 members. Third, it was middle-SES respondents who were most likely to experience intergenerational change: 36.1 per cent moved down and 26.6 per cent moved up the social class ladder.

Whatever the class of origin of our respondents, as children or as parents they frequently expressed mobility aspirations. Ron, a toolmaker with two young children who grew up on a farm, responded this way when asked about his hopes for his children: 'I have the same feelings most fathers do. As my father said to me when I was young ... I'd like to see you better than me, and I'd like to see them

Table 5.1. Socio-economic mobility for all respondents by region of residence in 1973 and geographical mobility status (percentage)

1973 Socio-economic status (SES) (family of origin)		(n)	1995 Family socio-economic status (SES)			
			High SES	Middle SES	Low SES	Total
High SES						
All respondents		263	51.3	33.1	15.6	100.0
1973 region of	Metro Toronto	77	64.9	24.7	10.4	100.0
residence	Other large cities	60	43.3	40.0	16.7	100.0
	Smaller cities/ Metro fringe	58	50.0	32.8	17.2	100.0
	Small towns/ rural areas	68	44.1	36.8	19.1	100.0
Geographic	Stayer	133	48.9	33.8	17.3	100.0
mobility status	Mover	130	53.8	32.3	13.8	100.0
Middle SES						
All respondents		263	26.6	37.3	36.1	100.0
1973 region of	Metro Toronto	34	29.4	32.4	38.2	100.0
residence	Other large cities	52	36.5	42.3	21.2	100.0
	Smaller cities/ Metro fringe	70	34.3	37.1	28.6	100.0
	Small towns/ rural areas	107	15.9	36.4	47.7	100.0
Geographic	Stayer	148	22.3	35.1	42.6	100.0
mobility status	Mover	115	32.2	40.0	27.8	100.0
Lower SES						
All respondents		262	22.1	29.8	48.1	100.0
1973 region of	Metro Toronto	18	44.4	33.3	22.2	100.0
residence	Other large cities	35	37.1	31.4	31.4	100.0
	Smaller cities/ Metro fringe	63	28.6	31.7	39.7	100.0
	Small towns/ rural areas	146	13.0	28.1	58.9	100.0
Geographic	Stayer	165	18.8	25.5	55.8	100.0
mobility status	Mover	97	27.8	37.1	35.1	100.0

better than myself ... You can't pick and choose what they do, but you can make suggestions and give guidelines.'

We can get a sense of what lies behind socio-economic mobility by examining how some of the components of SES have changed over time. Table 5.2 reveals the changes in the separate factors that went into creating the two composite SES measures in Table 5.1. Starting at the middle of the table, it is clear that Class of '73 members markedly increased their levels of education relative to their parents. As reported by their children in 1973, high-SES parents had a leading edge compared to the other parental SES groups. While 46 per cent of high-SES fathers held university degrees, hardly any parents in the medium or low SES groups attended or graduated from university. In 1995, three-quarters of the Class of '73 members in the high-SES group (1995 definition) held university degrees compared to only one-quarter in the medium-SES group. Though there was a marked increase in the level of education attained by members of the Class of '73, those from a low-SES background tended to have completed high school only, although one-quarter of this group had obtained college diplomas or certificates by 1995.

As the bottom left area of Table 5.2 demonstrates, high socio-economic status for parents was associated with fathers and mothers holding management, professional, and semiprofessional occupations in 1973, whereas medium and low parental socio-economic status was associated with largely blue-collar employment. Interestingly enough, the majority of mothers in high and medium socio-economic groups were employed in 1973 as clerical and sales workers, though this was the case for only one-quarter of the low-SES mothers. Seventy per cent of low-SES mothers who were employed in 1973 held blue-collar jobs. The occupational distribution of members of the Class of '73 in 1995 is quite different from that of their parents. As indicated in the bottom right portion of Table 5.2, in 1995 significant proportions of Class of '73 members and their spouses in the high and medium SES groups held management, professional, or semiprofessional occupations, while one-quarter of respondents in the low-SES group held such jobs. Only one-fifth to one-third of Class of '73 members in the medium or low-SES categories held clerical and sales jobs.[3] The decline of blue-collar work in the Ontario economy between 1973 and 1995 is indicated by the fact that roughly half as many low-SES respondents held blue-collar jobs in 1995 compared to their fathers in 1973.

Having more education and higher-status occupations than their parents likely gave members of the Class of '73 a strong sense that they had improved their lot in life, as well as a strong sense of personal agency; that being said, social structural factors also contributed to their upward mobility. For the Class of '73, getting ahead was also a function of the Ontario government's heavy investment in higher education, beginning in the 1960s. In addition, the occupational shifts

Table 5.2. Socio-economic status index components comparing parents in 1973 with children (and spouses) in 1995 (percentage)

Parents 1973 (respondents in grade 12, Phase I) Socio-economic status Category 1973	High SES	Medium SES	Low SES
Parents' total income 1973			
$7,000 or less	0.5	9.8	33.9
$7,001–10,000	8.4	27.8	37.5
$10,001–16,000	29.3	50.2	26.2
$16,001 or more	61.8	12.2	2.4
Average ($)	17,147	11,783	8,619
(n)	191	205	168
Parents' level of completed education			
Fathers			
Elementary or less	2.5	22.0	75.5
Some secondary schooling	8.8	42.3	21.2
Completed secondary	23.3	26.1	2.9
Some university or college	19.6	8.3	0.4
University degree(s)	45.8	1.2	0.0
(n)	240	241	241
Mothers			
Elementary or less	2.6	9.1	59.8
Some secondary schooling	15.2	37.6	33.2
Completed secondary	40.4	40.9	6.6
Some university/college	24.8	10.7	0.4
University degree(s)	17.0	1.7	0.0
(n)	230	242	244
Parents' occupation 1973			
Management, professional,			
semiprofessional Father	69.6	13.1	1.7
Mother	42.5	18.7	5.3
Clerical, sales Father	13.4	19.3	9.3
Mother	54.0	65.3	25.2
Other Father	17.0	67.6	89.0
Mother	3.5	16.1	69.5
(n) Father	253	244	237
Mother	200	193	151
Average Father's			
Blishen score occupation 1973	58.4	39.6	33.6

Children 1995 (respondents in Phase VI) Socio-economic status Category 1973		High SES	Medium SES	Low SES
Household income 1994				
Under $30,000		0.8	7.5	22.3
$30,000–49,999		6.7	18.3	30.7
$50,000–69,999		13.8	34.1	27.1
$70,000 or more		78.7	40.1	19.9
Average ($)		87,293	65,893	48,536
(*n*)		254	252	251
1995 respondent's/spouse's level of completed education				
Respondent's				
High school only		1.9	16.0	63.0
College diploma		19.8	43.3	24.8
Some college/university		3.0	16.0	11.1
University degree		55.1	21.3	0.8
Postgraduate or professional degree		20.2	3.4	0.4
(*n*)		263	263	262
Spouse's				
High school only		3.8	42.3	78.4
College diploma		30.5	39.7	20.7
University degree		45.3	14.3	1.0
Postgraduate degree		10.2	2.1	0.0
Professional degree		10.2	1.6	0.0
(*n*)		236	189	208
1995 respondent's/spouse's occupation				
Management, professional, semiprofessional	Respondent	77.5	59.9	21.5
	Spouse	81.2	46.6	17.2
Clerical, sales	Respondent	13.0	23.0	34.4
	Spouse	12.1	23.6	32.2
Other	Respondent	9.5	17.1	44.1
	Spouse	6.8	29.9	50.6
(*n*)	Respondent	262	257	256
	Spouse	207	174	180
Average Blishen score	Respondent's occupation 1995	58.5	50.8	41.4

caused by an expanding and changing Ontario economy resulted in the creation of new job opportunities at the upper end of the occupational hierarchy.

The third and final factor in SES is income. Assuming that grade 12 children reported their parents' income accurately, it appears that educational and job improvements between generations since 1973 have also brought economic benefits.[4] To read the data for incomes accurately, however, we must allow for inflation, which was especially high during the 1980s. Between 1973 and 1994, Statistics Canada's consumer price index increased by a factor of 3.63. Thus, in 1994 dollars the parental household incomes shown in Table 5.2 for 1973 would therefore be $62,244, $42,772, and $31,287 respectively for the high, medium, and low 1973 SES groups. A comparison of these figures with the household income data shown in Table 5.2 for members of the Class of '73 indicates that respondents' household income in 1994 was 40 per cent higher than their parents' income in 1973 for the high-SES group, and about 55 per cent higher for the medium and low SES groups. It should be stressed that these increases in earnings between respondents and their parents, as reported in Table 5.2, are likely a reflection of the increases in educational levels on average across generations and of the higher-status jobs that are obtained with higher education, rather than of increases in real wages for occupations over the relevant decades. Another factor favouring an income advantage for respondents over their parents is the greater frequency of two-earner families among Class of '73 members.[5]

The last line of Table 5.2 reveals the combined effects of educational and occupational change as reflected in average occupational Blishen scores. High-SES fathers in 1973 and high-SES respondents in 1995 had virtually identical average occupational Blishen scores of 58. Medium-SES children in 1995 had an average Blishen score of 51 compared to 40 for medium-SES fathers in 1973. Low-SES respondents had an average Blishen score of 41 in 1995 compared to 34 for low-SES fathers in 1973.

As Table 5.2 demonstrates, by 1995 those members of the Class of '73 who remained in the same socio-economic category as their parents still experienced improvement in terms of the three components of status: education, occupation, and income. Shifts up or down in terms of respondents' socio-economic levels category were associated with further significant increases or decreases in average amounts of education, occupation, and income.

Occupational Mobility

A more detailed understanding of social mobility can be obtained by examining our occupational data for the Class of '73. We highlight two kinds of occupational mobility: intergenerational occupational mobility, assessed by comparing the father's occupation with the son's or daughter's occupation; and intragenerational career mobility, assessed by comparing the occupations of the sons and daughters themselves over time. For this purpose we employed a modified Porter-Pineo-McRoberts scale of occupational categories.[6]

Intergenerational Occupational Mobility

With regard to intergenerational mobility, in the Phase VI survey of 1995 we asked respondents to report their father's occupation when he was 55 years of age so that we could compare the father's occupation with the respondent's current full-time employment in 1995.[7] First we examine intergenerational occupational mobility by gender (see Table 5.3).[8]

As indicated by the percentage row totals at the bottom of the table, the overall occupational attainments of men and women by 1995 were roughly similar, though higher proportions of women were found in the professional, semiprofessional, and white-collar categories, and men were more frequently found in high and middle management, blue-collar, and agricultural occupations. It is interesting to note that 'occupational inheritance' was higher among men than among women (20.2 per cent compared with 15.5 per cent). Occupational inheritance was most common for professional and middle management categories and, for men, within the upper blue-collar category. In addition, compared to their fathers, men were somewhat more likely than women to move up the occupational ladder (58.7 per cent versus 52.9 per cent), while women were substantially more likely than men to move down the occupational hierarchy (31.6 per cent compared to 21.1 per cent).[9]

The gross mobility pattern for women differs somewhat from that for men. Few women chose to enter blue-collar or agricultural occupations. For women whose fathers were employed in upper-status occupations, 61.7 per cent also entered occupations in this sector, whereas the percentage for men remaining in upper-status occupations was 72.0 per cent.[10] In the case of women whose fathers were employed in

Table 5.3. Intergenerational mobility: From fathers' occupation to respondents' occupation in 1995 (percentage)

Father's occupation at age 55	Gender	%	(n)	Occupation in 1995* High level management	Professional	Middle management
High-level	Male	6.3	20	**20.0**	15.0	20.0
management	Female	7.7	25	**12.0**	28.0	8.0
Professional	Male	9.1	29	10.3	**24.1**	17.2
	Female	13.0	42	7.1	**26.2**	9.5
Middle	Male	9.5	30	16.7	23.3	**33.3**
management	Female	10.5	34	0.0	23.5	**23.5**
Semi-professional/	Male	4.4	14	14.3	21.4	14.3
technical	Female	4.3	14	0.0	7.1	14.3
Upper white-	Male	6.9	22	0.0	22.7	9.1
collar	Female	8.7	28	0.0	21.4	7.1
Upper blue-	Male	24.3	77	1.3	14.3	20.8
collar	Female	22.6	73	2.7	13.7	12.3
Lower white-	Male	6.9	22	9.1	13.6	13.6
collar	Female	5.3	17	0.0	11.8	23.5
Lower blue-	Male	22.4	71	2.8	11.3	15.5
collar	Female	17.6	57	7.0	3.5	8.8
Agriculture	Male	10.1	32	9.4	3.1	9.4
	Female	10.2	33	6.1	36.4	6.1
Total	Male	100.0	317	6.9	15.1	17.7
	Female	100.0	323	4.3	18.3	11.8

* If not employed full-time in 1995, respondent reported most recent full-time job; see endnote 7 for explanation.

the lower occupational status sector, 48.6 per cent moved into the upper occupational status sector, while 51.4 per cent remained in the lower occupational status sector; for men, the percentages were very similar – 49.5 and 50.5 per cent respectively. Almost all respondents whose fathers were in agriculture did not enter farming; those who did were largely the sons of farmers.

These patterns of intergenerational occupational mobility are consistent with the socio-economic mobility described in the previous section. Taking the Class of '73 as a whole, and based on the nine-category system shown in Table 5.3, overall upward mobility was 57.0 per cent, and overall downward mobility was 26.4 per cent, and 16.6

Semi profes- sional/ technical	Upper white- collar	Upper blue- collar	Lower white- collar	Lower blue- collar	Agri- culture	Total
20.0	15.0	0.0	0.0	5.0	5.0	100.0
8.0	24.0	4.0	16.0	0.0	0.0	100.0
13.8	10.3	10.3	6.9	6.9	0.0	100.0
23.8	11.9	0.0	19.0	2.4	0.0	100.0
10.0	3.3	6.7	0.0	6.7	0.0	100.0
20.6	8.8	0.0	11.8	11.8	0.0	100.0
7.1	21.4	14.3	0.0	7.1	0.0	100.0
21.4	35.7	0.0	14.3	7.1	0.0	100.0
27.3	18.2	13.6	0.0	9.1	0.0	100.0
17.9	21.4	0.0	28.6	3.6	0.0	100.0
14.3	9.1	27.3	3.9	9.1	0.0	100.0
23.3	20.5	4.1	19.2	4.1	0.0	100.0
9.1	13.6	22.7	4.5	13.6	0.0	100.0
17.6	29.4	0.0	17.6	0.0	0.0	100.0
16.9	8.5	28.2	5.6	11.3	0.0	100.0
24.6	28.1	0.0	22.8	5.3	0.0	100.0
3.1	0.0	40.6	3.1	6.3	25.0	100.0
21.2	9.1	3.0	6.1	6.1	6.1	100.0
13.9	9.5	21.8	3.5	8.8	2.8	100.0
21.1	19.8	1.5	18.0	4.6	0.6	100.0

per cent of respondents were in the same occupational category as their fathers. The Class of '73 women in particular have made great strides occupationally. Among women whose mothers were employed at age 55, 57.1 per cent were employed in upper or lower white-collar occupational sectors; only 29.2 per cent of their mothers had been in management, professional, or semiprofessional and technical positions. By 1995 the Class of '73 women were employed in a diversity of occupations, and were even outshining the men in the professional and semiprofessional categories. By 1995, 52.9′ per cent of the Class of '73 women held upper-status occupations. However, as shown in the previous chapter, a high proportion of women were still employed in job categories that are traditionally dominated by women. The Class of '73 men held a greater diversity of occupations than women. In addition to being employed in upper-status occupational categories, many men held blue-collar jobs. By comparing fathers and sons in the blue-collar work categories, one can get a sense of their upward mobility: 46.7 per cent of fathers held blue-collar work at age 55; the proportion of sons in blue-collar work was 30.6 per cent, with an especially sharp decline in lower blue-collar employment.

Kurt, a dentist, experienced significant upward career mobility compared to his parents, who immigrated to Canada from Germany after the Second World War. His father worked as a miner and his mother was a florist. While a student in university, Kurt held a variety of summer jobs to help pay for his education, ranging from working in the mines with his father to driving a delivery truck. His parents were very strict and had high expectations of their son in terms of performance in school. He did not disappoint them. He received his BSc and DDS and has worked as a dentist since 1981. Kurt succeeded in his work, earning a high income that allowed him to provide a comfortable lifestyle for his wife, a former dental hygienist, and his three children. He told us that in spite of working very hard, he was quite satisfied with his life and particularly enjoyed the lifestyle his income provided and the time he was able to spend with his family.

Another dimension of intergenerational occupational mobility is occupational inheritance, which can take a number of different forms. Normally it refers to the handing down, so to speak, of an occupation from one generation to the next. An illustration of this pathway was offered by Gary, who at the time of his interview was employed as an engineer. When queried about his choice of professions, Gary replied: 'I suppose it's the family profession. My grandfather's an engineer, my uncle's an engineer, my father's an engineer. Three of my brothers are engineers. So, it was almost, without ever being said, it was expected of me, and I suppose that's the way we all grew up.' Our interviews revealed some variations on this theme. For example, Sam's mother was a cook in a restaurant, and he and his brother started working with her when they were quite young. Since that time he has done almost every job in the hotel and restaurant service industry. He has 'moved up the ladder' and was running his father-in-law's hotel when we interviewed him in 1995. Debbie, whose father was in the police force, described her decision to enter the military as follows: 'My father was very liberal with me all along. I was the appointed "son," I guess. I was out with him on the range, firing the rifles, hauling wood. I did everything with him. So he was very pleased when I joined the military because I was following in his footsteps.'

A question often posed of mobility tables is this: What do they reveal about the openness of the class structure of a given society? Relative to European industrial societies, Canada, Australia, and the United States have somewhat greater 'social fluidity,' with greater upward mobility and less occupational inheritance.[11] Because our intergenerational mobility data are limited to a narrow age cohort and to only Ontario, they cannot indicate definitively the state of social fluidity in Canadian society. Still, the mobility proportions referred to earlier in this chapter can be compared to a national survey of employed adult Canadians undertaken in 1973 (McRoberts, 1985: 77). This survey compared sons (aged 25 to 64) with fathers and found 77.2 per cent upward and downward mobility, compared to 83.4 per cent for the Class of '73. Moreover, the national survey found 22.7 per cent occupational inheritance, compared to 16.6 per cent for the Class of '73. These comparisons suggest that Class of '73 members have been somewhat more mobile than was reflected in the occupational mobility patterns of the 1973 national survey.

Some of the mobility between generations is due to changes in the economy, as when blue-collar occupations decline over time, balanced by an increase in white-collar occupations, forcing shifts to white-collar jobs for younger generations. Employing the nine-category occupational scheme of Table 5.3, we estimated minimal structural mobility (i.e., mobility due to changes in occupational distributions between generations) for the Class of '73 to be 28.9 per cent out of the 83.4 per cent total mobility ($N = 640$). For the national survey of employed adults in 1973, the proportion of mobility due to structural change was 21.8 per cent (McRoberts, 1985: 77).

The overall mobility patterns of the Class of '73 can be summarized as follows. Members of the Class of '73 experienced levels of intergenerational occupational mobility that somewhat exceeded levels reported for all Canadians. This was to be expected, given that the national sample included older Canadians (born prior to 1955), who had not had the advantages of higher levels of education with which to secure higher-paying jobs and higher social status. In terms of the components of social mobility, mobility generated by a changing economy (28.9 per cent) had an impact roughly equal to mobility generated by downward movement between generations (26.4 per cent).

To conclude, the elevated mobility levels for the Class of '73 were due on the one hand to occupational shifts (a social structural factor), and on the other hand to increased overall movement (an indication of greater personal agency).

Intragenerational Career Mobility

Our data on career mobility is derived from the last three of the six phases of our longitudinal research, and provides occupational data at four points in time. By 1979, most respondents had completed their formal education, and we obtained information on their first full-time jobs and on the full-time jobs they held at the time of the survey. Stratification research regards first full-time job as significant in terms of career because certain initial or entry-level jobs may be steps on job ladders; also, some ladders have significant future payoff in terms of status and earning power, while others present more limited economic opportunities (Blau and Duncan, 1967: 48–58). We obtained information on current occupation again in 1987–88. In the 1995 survey we asked for job history information, including occupations held during 1995. These four points in time provided a dynamic picture of career mobility. While we obtained current job information in 1979, 1987–88, and 1995, first full-time jobs (as reported in 1979) actually ranged over a period of years from 1973 to 1979, since full-time entry into occupations was delayed for many who were continuing their education.

In the preceding chapter we presented considerable occupational and career information. In this section of the mobility chapter, we shall refer to some of these data and supplement them with further data, focusing especially on occupational paths from first full-time jobs to occupations held in 1995. There is a significant methodological difference between the career information presented in Chapter 4 and the career data we are about to review. In our chapter on employment, the career data were based on various points in time and we examined how distributions of occupations changed at various points in time. However, the people in the job categories were not necessarily the same from point to point. In the next set of tables we compare first full-time jobs to 1995 occupations in a cross-tabulation whereby specific individuals are traced from first full-time job category to occupational category in 1995. We refer to this form of tracking as *intragenerational mobility*.

In reviewing some of the early career data presented in Chapter 4, it is useful to refer back to Table 4.3. This table indicates that in 1979 there did not appear to be much of a shift between a person's first full-time job, which in our survey could have commenced at any time between 1973 and 1979, and his or her 'current job' reported for 1979. However, the percentage of men in the middle managerial and semi-professional/technical categories rose somewhat. Also, there was a large increase in upper blue-collar employment and decreases in lower white- and blue-collar work. The pattern was the same for women except that women were largely absent from blue-collar occupations of all kinds. The proportion of women in the upper white-collar category increased between first full-time and 1979 job. Thus, the data show that within a relatively brief period, respondents had made moves to leave the two lower-prestige occupational categories for occupational groups one or two rungs up the hierarchy.

Moving through time, and again referring to Table 4.3, we see that there was an increase in high-level managerial occupations between 1987–88 and 1995, suggesting movement into managerial positions as a function of accumulated experience in the labour market. The numbers in the professional category increased between 1979 and 1987–88, which is a consequence of respondents' additional educational attainment after 1979. Male middle managers had increased in numbers by 1987–88 and continued to increase to 1995, whereas for women in this category, the increase took place only between 1987–88 and 1995. There were corresponding declines over time in all other occupational categories – in particular, marked declines for women in the upper and lower white-collar categories, and for men in the lower blue-collar and agriculture categories. These changes in distributions at different points in time would have resulted from a wide variety of patterns of occupational change for men and women, and may also reflect the influence of educational attainment. Thus, in 1995 almost all individuals in the professional category were university graduates, though by 1995 middle management and semiprofessional and technical occupations had been attained by a significant proportion of respondents with only a high school diploma or community college education.

Table 4.3 reveals a number of intra-occupational shifts that provide insights for life course researchers interested in understanding employment transitions within particular occupational clusters. When we examine high-level management occupations, it is apparent that the major increases occurred between 1987–88 and 1995, for men and women alike. In 1987–88 only 0.7 per cent of women were employed in high-level management jobs. By 1995 this proportion had grown to 4.9 per cent – more than a six-fold increase. For men the increase was from 3.0 per cent to 6.1 per cent. In contrast, substantial increases in the proportion of respondents in professional and middle management occupations occurred over a longer period of time and at earlier ages. By way of illustration, by 1979, 1.9 per cent of women and 5.7 per cent of men had found full-time jobs as middle managers. By 1987–88, these proportions had grown substantially, to 7.5 per cent and 13.5 per cent respectively. The ranks of middle managers also increased from 1987–88 to 1995, with 13.4 per cent of women and 19.3 per cent of men occupying such positions by 1995. This analysis suggests that the speed with which one moves up the occupational hierarchy depends on age-graded norms for entry and exit in an occupation. Movement into executive corporate positions is more likely to be related to age than movement into middle management positions.

Returning to our mobility data, career mobility and intragenerational occupational mobility can be looked at in terms of the number of rungs typically negotiated by people as they clamber up the ladder of success. Table 5.4 of this chapter provides information in this regard. The data in the table are based on underlying tables using the nine occupational categories of the revised Pineo-Porter-McRoberts occupational scale. The data in the table represent four points in time, each point a comparison with each respondent's present occupational category in 1995. Thus, the first column of Table 5.4 summarizes information that comes from cross-tabulating respondents' first full-time job occupational categories with these same respondents' 1995 occupational categories. The second column compares 1979 occupation with 1995 occupation, while the third column represents the 1988–95 comparison. Column four of the table is the intergenerational comparison of respondents' fathers at age 55 compared to sons' or daughters' 1995 occupations. The data in the table summarize broadly the types of movement that can be logically shown in a table with occupational cross-tabulations.

Table 5.4 demonstrates that short-range occupational mobility occurred more frequently than long-range mobility, measuring movement as steps indicated by the number of categories an individual shifted from the origin category to the destination category. Whether moving up or down the occupational ladder, the majority of respon-

Table 5.4. Step patterns of occupational mobility: Career mobility compared with intergenerational occupational mobility (percentage)

	First full-time job vs. occupation 1995 ($n=642$)		Occupation 1979 vs. occupation 1995 ($n=541$)		Occupation 1988 vs. occupation 1995 ($n=591$)		Father at age 55 vs. occupation 1995 ($n=640$)	
Moving direction	Up	Down	Up	Down	Up	Down	Up	Down
Total percent	54.5	15.7	42.1	16.6	29.4	13.6	56.9	26.3
Moving range								
6 or more	3.4	0.5	1.9	0.2	0.8	0.4	6.4	1.5
5 steps	5.6	0.8	3.9	0.9	2.6	1.1	5.0	2.6
4 steps	8.4	0.5	6.8	0.7	4.0	1.1	8.9	2.8
3 steps	10.9	3.1	9.6	3.5	7.3	1.6	12.3	3.3
2 steps	16.7	5.8	12.2	7.4	9.3	6.1	11.2	6.9
1 step	9.5	5.1	7.8	3.9	5.3	3.4	13.1	9.3
No mobility	29.8		41.2		48.9		16.5	

dents experienced no more than three steps during their occupational careers. As respondents spent more time in the labour market, they also experienced increased upward mobility (54.5 per cent from their first full-time job to a job in 1995; 42.1 per cent from a job in 1979 to a job in 1995; and 29.4 per cent from a job in 1988 to a job in 1995). Fewer respondents experienced downward mobility over the course of the study (15.7 per cent from their first full-time job to current job in 1995; 16.6 per cent from their job in 1979 to their job in 1995; and 13.6 per cent from their job in 1987–88 to their job in 1995).

One among many respondents who experienced upward career mobility is Jeremy, who at the time of our interview was employed as the technical music director of a large film distribution company. Oddly enough, he began his education in dentistry. Jeremy believed that he had been 'programmed' to be a dentist at an early age by his parents, a civil engineer and a teacher. His marks in high school were sufficiently high to gain him admission to pre-med, though he deliberately missed getting on the honour roll in order to annoy his mother. He attended university for two years and then dropped out because he felt he could not tolerate waking up every morning and going to work just to look in other people's mouths. After returning home, he worked for a year at odd jobs in construction and factory work and collected unemployment insurance. He then entered community college to complete a three-year program in electronic technology. At the time, the government was offering incentives to attend technical programs, and he believed that graduating from this program would guarantee him employment. After graduation he worked for five years servicing computers, but he was dissatisfied with this type of employment. Jeremy subsequently completed a two-year course in audio engineering, which he financed through student loans and a scholarship and by working part-time. Immediately after completing the program, through contacts he had made at school, he found work servicing and repairing audio equipment. Shortly thereafter, he and his brother started their own business installing equipment in studios. One year later he was offered a position by his present employer, a former client who needed Jeremy to help his company set up audio equipment. He became the supervisor of the unit after several months and eventually worked his way up to his present position as technical music director when his company was bought out by a large film distribution firm.

Rick, on the other hand, had a bumpy career path characterized mainly by downward mobility. He started with high aspirations, beginning his postsecondary training at college in an automotive technician program. He learned many of his technical skills from his father, who was an automotive teacher at a local high school. After graduating, he worked as a manager in a lumberyard. He was forced to leave this job when the company collapsed during the recession of the early 1980s. He returned to school with the intention of becoming an archaeologist, and attained a BA in religious studies and an MA in languages and archaeology. He then attended teacher's college and got a short-term contract with the Separate School Board. When his contract ran out, he worked for a building supply company, subsequently leaving for the Middle East to participate in an archaeological expedition. When he returned to Canada, he was accepted into a PhD program, but he had to withdraw for financial reasons. He had applied to this program a number of times. When we interviewed Rick in 1995, he was working part-time at a lumberyard. He seemed embittered by the path his life had taken and confided in us that his educational and employment 'ups and downs' have been an 'emotional roller coaster' for his wife. He believed that she blamed him for his inability to continue his education or to secure a job in his field of study. Rick, in turn, blamed external structures – the economy, the educational system, and especially immigrants. He felt that his failings could not possibly be his own responsibility, but had to be that of others.

In summary, at each successive point in time in our data collection, Class of '73 members altered their occupational and career mobility. By 1995, 56.9 per cent of respondents had experienced upward mobility, and 26.3 per cent downward mobility. However, this movement up or down was largely within three adjacent occupational categories, though in comparison to their fathers, 8.9 per cent had made shifts of four steps. Career mobility ultimately produced significant intragenerational occupational mobility for Class of '73 members, with upward movement about twice as frequent as downward movement.

We wished to tease out the effects of structural forces (i.e., gender, family of origin, residence) and the effects of leaving home. To this end, we developed a series of tables to compare first full-time occupation to occupation in 1995 employing a structural factor as an intervening variable. Instead of the nine Pineo-Porter-McRoberts occupational categories used in previous tables, we employed five in order to reduce the impact of small numbers. The results are shown in Tables 5.5 through 5.7.

Table 5.5 shows the impact of gender in relationship to career mobility. The left-hand side of the table shows the five categories of first full-time job. The cells to the right of each category indicate the mobility destinations of young adults as they moved to their 1995 occupations. Gender is reported within each of these first-job categories. Focusing on youth who started out as high-level managers and professionals, we found that more men than women began their careers at this occupational level (9.8 per cent versus 4.6 per cent). While 60 per cent of women and men who started off at this level remained in high-level manager/professional positions, women overall achieved more occupational success than men because they obtained more middle management positions compared to men. Table 5.5 illustrates a pattern of upward mobility for both genders over time, with men having somewhat more upward career mobility than women. The reader should interpret the table carefully, given low cell frequencies.

The effects of SES on career mobility by occupational category are shown in Table 5.6. It is interesting to note that both high and low SES youth started out with roughly similar occupational distributions in terms of first jobs. However, they ended up with significantly different job distributions by 1995, differences that favoured individuals from the high-SES group in terms of occupations in the managerial and professional categories. The rows in Table 5.6 indicate the workings of the SES bias at every occupational level. Among those whose first job was in the skilled category (white and blue collar), respon-

Table 5.5. Gender and occupational mobility from first full-time occupation to occupation in 1995 (percentage)

First full-time occupation	Gender	%	(n)	Occupation in 1995*					
				High-level management/professional	Middle management/semiprofessional/technical	Skilled workers	Unskilled workers	Agriculture	Total
High-level management/professional	Male	9.8	31	61.3	19.4	12.9	6.5	0.0	100.0
	Female	4.6	15	60.0	26.7	0.0	13.3	0.0	100.0
Middle management/semiprofessional/technical	Male	14.2	45	20.0	55.6	17.8	4.4	2.2	100.0
	Female	20.6	67	13.4	59.7	7.5	17.9	1.5	100.0
Skilled workers	Male	30.0	95	15.8	29.5	41.1	12.6	1.1	100.0
	Female	30.5	99	14.1	32.3	31.3	22.2	0.0	100.0
Unskilled workers	Male	40.4	128	10.2	32.8	34.4	21.9	0.8	100.0
	Female	44.0	143	16.8	25.9	24.5	32.2	0.7	100.0
Agriculture	Male	5.7	18	11.1	16.7	33.3	5.6	33.3	100.0
	Female	0.3	1	0.0	0.0	100.0	0.0	0.0	100.0
Total	Male	100	317	18.3	32.8	31.9	14.2	2.8	100.0
	Female	100	325	17.2	34.8	22.2	25.2	0.6	100.0

* If not employed full-time in 1995, respondent reported most recent full-time job; see endnote 7 for explanation.

Table 5.6. Socio-economic status of family of origin and occupational mobility from first full-time occupation to occupation in 1995 (percentage)

First full-time occupation	Socio-economic status of family of origin	%	(n)	Occupation in 1995*					
				High-level management/professional	Middle management/semiprofessional/technical	Skilled workers	Unskilled workers	Agriculture	Total
High level management/professional	Upper half	6.8	21	76.2	19.0	0.0	4.8	0.0	100.0
	Lower half	7.5	25	48.0	24.0	16.0	12.0	0.0	100.0
Middle management/semiprofessional/technical	Upper half	20.8	64	21.9	60.9	7.8	7.8	1.6	100.0
	Lower half	14.3	48	8.3	54.2	16.7	18.8	2.1	100.0
Skilled workers	Upper half	30.0	92	19.6	35.9	31.5	13.0	0.0	100.0
	Lower half	30.4	102	10.8	26.5	40.2	21.6	1.0	100.0
Unskilled workers	Upper half	40.1	123	15.4	33.3	30.9	19.5	0.8	100.0
	Lower half	44.2	148	12.2	25.7	27.7	33.8	0.7	100.0
Agriculture	Upper half	2.3	7	14.3	28.6	14.3	0.0	42.9	100.0
	Lower half	3.6	12	8.3	8.3	50.0	8.3	25.0	100.0
Total	Upper half	100.0	307	22.1	38.8	23.8	13.7	1.6	100.0
	Lower half	100.0	335	13.7	29.3	29.9	25.4	1.8	100.0

* If not employed full-time in 1995, respondent reported most recent full-time job; see endnote 7 for explanation.

dents of lower-SES origin remained skilled or were downwardly mobile into unskilled work by 1995, whereas those of higher-SES background stayed less often in the skilled category and tended to move up to the middle management/semiprofessional/technical and high-management/professional categories. This table suggests that SES origins have long-term effects that are much less prominent with reference to respondents' first full-time jobs.

In Table 5.7 we sorted 1973 region of origin into urban and nonurban areas and found that region of origin had a modest effect on first jobs, with city origins favouring entry jobs in the two higher-status occupational categories. Rural origins were strongly linked to the small number of respondents starting out as farmers. By 1995 the occupational distributions of participants from cities and rural areas differed substantially: even higher percentages of those with city origins had ended up in occupations in the two higher-status occupational categories. Focusing on youth who started out in unskilled first jobs (white and blue collar), Table 5.7 indicates that as of 1995, those with city backgrounds were upwardly mobile into the managerial and professional ranks, while those with rural origins were either upwardly mobile into skilled occupations (white and blue collar) or remained in the unskilled occupational category.

Geographic Mobility: Movers and Stayers

Geographical location or residence as a social force has received only limited research attention, and its effects are not particularly well documented (Looker, 1995). Our study examines geographic mobility and the impact of geographical forces on social mobility. Some Class of '73 members experienced the pace of urban life in Toronto; others grew up in a small town, or on a farm, or in a rural, nonfarm environment. Though the major trend has been toward urbanization, the actual number of persons living in rural areas has not declined. In fact, the rural, nonfarm population in Ontario increased from 2.7 million in 1956 to 5 million in 1986 (Biggs and Bollman, 1994).

Mobility studies that compare rural and urban populations of youth have found differences in values, attitudes, motivations, and socioeconomic status. For some, growing up in a rural setting leaves lasting impressions of the importance of family, mutual aid, co-operation, hard work, and community involvement (Fuller, 1998). Jones found that young people from remote rural areas in Scotland who migrated

Table 5.7. Urban/rural origin and occupational mobility from first full-time occupation to occupation in 1995 (percentage)

First full-time occupation	Region of origin	%	(n)	Occupation in 1995*					
				High-level management/professional	Middle management/semiprofessional/technical	Skilled workers	Unskilled workers	Agriculture	Total
High-level management/professional	Urban	8.5	31	67.7	22.6	3.2	6.5	0.0	100.0
	Rural	5.4	15	46.7	20.0	20.0	13.3	0.0	100.0
Middle management/semiprofessional/technical	Urban	18.7	68	19.1	57.4	14.7	8.8	0.0	100.0
	Rural	15.8	44	11.4	59.1	6.8	18.2	4.5	100.0
Skilled workers	Urban	29.8	108	21.3	32.4	32.4	13.9	0.0	100.0
	Rural	30.8	86	7.0	29.1	40.7	22.1	1.2	100.0
Unskilled workers	Urban	41.9	152	15.1	32.2	26.3	25.7	0.7	100.0
	Rural	42.7	119	11.8	25.2	32.8	29.4	0.8	100.0
Agriculture	Urban	1.1	4	25.0	25.0	50.0	0.0	0.0	100.0
	Rural	5.4	15	6.7	13.3	33.3	6.7	40.0	100.0
Total	Urban	100.0	363	22.3	36.1	24.2	17.1	0.3	100.0
	Rural	100.0	279	11.8	30.8	30.5	23.3	3.6	100.0

Note: Urban consists of Metro Toronto, other large cities, and small cities and the Metro suburban fringe. The rural category in this table refers to rural areas and small towns.
* If not employed full-time in 1995, respondent reported most recent full-time job; see endnote 7 for explanation.

to towns by the age of 19 were more likely to miss their families than other types of youth, and least likely to have left home because they did not get along with their parents (1995: 43). As Looker (1995) indicated in her study of Hamilton, Halifax, and rural Nova Scotia youth, the decision to pursue higher education or to access larger labour markets resulted in rural youth leaving their area and moving into urban centres. Research on internal migration patterns showed that migrants tended to be young adults with above-average education and high socio-economic status. Furthermore, they moved short distances – generally from smaller rural areas to larger urban areas (Shulman and Drass, 1979).

Jones (1995) provided a framework for connecting geographical mobility with a life course perspective. She emphasized that the first 'leaving home' event for young adults is part of the transition to independent living. Furthermore, leaving the parental home needs to be understood in historical context. For more recent generations of young people, returning to the parental home has not necessarily signalled continued dependence; rather, it may be part of an increasingly common process for making the transition to adulthood during periods of economic hard times. In contrast, members of the Class of '73 grew up in a time of greater economic certainty and opportunity than experienced by later generations. For our respondents, leaving the parental home may have been more of a life marker – one that more clearly designated the beginnings of full independence.

People make independent choices within a structure of opportunities and constraints and believe that they are 'constructing their individual life courses' (Heinz, 1995: 26). This study recognizes that young adults who decide to leave their home community in order to enhance their personal opportunities may also be responding to structural forces such as socio-economic origin.

The choices made by some members of the Class of '73 are illustrated by the following comments (Anisef, Ashbury, James, and Paasche, 1994):

> Some people left because they viewed their home community environment as confining and felt they needed to break away from their family. One said, 'I wanted to get out ... [My home town] was a little Peyton Place ... Everybody knew me as little Joe - my father.' Another said, 'Beautiful downtown Beamsville was about 4,000 people when I lived there ... I was really desperate to move out of there ... you don't really

know what you might have been like if you had grown up in a city instead of a small town.'

However, some preferred small town or country life. Brad grew up on a farm. After finding employment on a tobacco farm after Grade 12, he decided to leave because he was not earning enough money. He had aspirations of becoming an electrical engineer, but decided against this career option because of his love of the outdoors. A number of rural respondents in our study believed that a city job, for all the security it offered, would not provide the lifestyle they desired. Though Brad had struggled (and worked as a mailman to support his farm), he was clearly committed to a farming lifestyle.

Region of origin strongly influences educational and economic opportunity. We defined four regions of origin based on where a member of the Class of '73 attended high school: Metro Toronto, other large Ontario cities, smaller cities and the Metro Toronto fringe, and small towns and rural areas. Parents' socio-economic status in 1973 was strongly associated with region. For example, 59.7 per cent of respondents living in Metro Toronto while attending high school were from the high-SES category, compared to 25.9 per cent of those living in rural areas and small towns; the proportions in the low-SES category for these regions were 14.0 per cent versus 55.7 per cent respectively. These socio-economic differences reflected regional differences in economic opportunity. For instance, in 1973 in Metro Toronto, 47.2 per cent of fathers of respondents worked in the administrative, professional, and semiprofessional sectors, and 33.6 per cent worked in the service, farming, and blue-collar sectors; in contrast, in rural areas and small towns the respective percentages were 16.7 per cent and 69.6 per cent. As a consequence of being geographically distant from postsecondary institutions, 77.0 per cent of small town and rural respondents had to leave home to attend a community college or university, compared to 34.4 per cent of respondents living in Metro Toronto.

As Table 5.1 shows, region of origin has a substantial effect on career success, independent of socio-economic status. For instance, while 77.7 per cent of lower-SES Toronto respondents succeeded in moving up to the middle and high SES categories by 1995, only 41.1 per cent of lower-SES small town and rural respondents made this transition. Conversely, upper SES respondents who spent their high school years in Toronto were less likely to experience downward mobility (35.1 per cent) than were their small town and rural counter-parts (55.9 per cent). About one-third of respondents from Toronto and from small town/rural areas with middle-SES origins maintained their SES position over the course of the study. However, a higher proportion of small town and rural respondents (47.7 per cent) experi-enced downward mobility than Toronto respondents (38.2 per cent). Respondents with lower-SES backgrounds who came from small town and rural areas showed the lowest levels of upward mobility: 58.9 per cent of small town/rural area members from the lower-SES category were still in that category as of 1995.

Part of the success myth is the notion that people have to be pre-pared to go to where there is opportunity. We attempted to assess the role of geographic mobility with respect to socio-economic status by developing an indicator of geographic movement. Respondents were designated as stayers if they remained in the immediate vicinity of their high school; they were designated as movers if they were resid-ing elsewhere by 1995. Our stayer/mover concept is sociological and is not based on distance. Thus, we considered the Greater Toronto Area to be one large urban centre stretching from Burlington to Pickering. A Class of '73 member who went to high school in Burlington but moved to Pickering was counted as a stayer even though the distance moved was greater than in the case of someone moving from St. Mary's to London (St. Mary's is a small city close to London). We categorized stayers and movers on a case-by-case basis by con-sidering the relationship between high school location and current 1995 address.

We were aware that if our data showed a relationship between improved economic circumstances and geographical mobility, no firm cause-and-effect conclusion would be warranted. We did not ask re-spondents *why* they had moved away from or stayed in the area where they attended secondary school. There are many reasons to move or not to move, and we were very much aware that any relationship our data might show between geographic mobility and economic advan-tage would likely result in a low correlation, and that any interpreta-tion of the data would be tentative.

Our distinction between stayers and movers appears to have some utility. Table 5.1 includes the geographic mobility variable as an inter-vening variable between the socio-economic status of respondents' family of origin and their own socio-economic status in 1995. The table shows that in 1995, being a mover was associated with shifts upward into the high and middle SES categories, and that being a stayer was associated more often with downward mobility into the low-SES category or, in the case of respondents with low SES origins, with remaining in the low-SES category. However, the picture regarding geographic mobility is more complex than this table indicates.

First, while geographical mobility is often viewed as a feature of modern life, the majority of Class of '73 members have been stayers – that is, they have tended to live in the same general area where they attended secondary school. However, there are some regional differences. Six in ten urban origin respondents were stayers, but only slightly over half (52.3 per cent) of rural and small town respondents. We mentioned earlier that respondents from small towns and rural areas started out with limited economic opportunities, and that high proportions of their parents were in low-SES occupations in the service, farming, and blue-collar sectors. Did being a mover lead to economic opportunity? Were movers from the three urban regions also motivated by a desire to improve their economic opportunities?

Before answering these two questions, we wondered whether being a resident in a rural area in 1995 was still associated with limited opportunity. Indeed it was. In the Phase VI survey (1995), we asked respondents to characterize where they were living in 1960 and where they were living at the time of the survey in terms of five categories: rural area, small town, city, suburb of a major city, and major city (500,000-plus residents). Separating the rural and small town respondents from the urban dwellers, we found almost the same distribution of socio-economic status between those living in rural areas and small towns in 1995 and those living in rural areas and small towns in 1960. The situation was the same for 1995 and 1960 urban dwellers. However, for rural and small town residents, there has been a dramatic shift in the *composition* of occupations since 1960.

Using the 1973 Phase I survey information for father's occupation, 36.0 per cent of respondents who reported living in urban regions in 1960 indicated that their fathers had occupations in the administrative, professional, and semiprofessional sector; 16.4 per cent reported fathers in clerical and sales occupations; and 47.6 per cent reported fathers in the service, farming, and blue-collar sectors. For respondents who reported living in small towns and rural areas in 1960, 21.6 per cent reported fathers in administrative, professional, and semiprofessional occupations; 11.6 per cent in clerical and sales; and 66.8 per cent in service, farming, and blue-collar work. By 1995 a shift toward higher-status occupations was evident for both urban and rural respondents, with 58.5 per cent of urban respondents in the administrative, professional, and semiprofessional sector, 25.6 per cent in clerical and sales, and only 15.8 per cent in the service, farming, and blue-collar sectors. Also by 1995, the occupational composition in small towns and rural areas was 47.2 per cent in the administrative, professional, and semiprofessional sector, 21.0 per cent in clerical and sales, and 31.8 per cent in the service, farming, and blue-collar sectors. Thus, the composition of respondents from small towns and rural areas had evolved over the last several decades; a greater proportion of respondents were in higher-status occupations, though they had not by any means caught up with respondents in urban areas. Moreover, a greater proportion of rural and small town dwellers earned lower incomes and had less education.

Returning to the question of whether being a mover provided benefits, we decided to explore this relationship by holding constant both family of origin SES and region of origin; region was assigned two categories: respondents from small towns and rural areas, and respondents from all other larger and smaller cities and Metro Toronto and its suburbs (see Table 5.8). As our focus was on mobility, we developed two separate measures of occupational mobility. The first was a measure of intergenerational occupational mobility, which we conceived as the difference between the respondent's 1995 occupation Blishen score and the father's occupation Blishen score at age 55. A positive difference would indicate upward mobility; a negative difference would indicate downward mobility (a very small or zero value would signal occupational inheritance). The second measure was career mobility. For each Class of '73 member, we calculated the difference in Blishen scores between the respondent's 1995 occupation and his or her first full-time job. A positive difference would indicate a higher-status occupation relative to first full-time job.

With respect to intergenerational occupational mobility, for virtually all the SES/region combinations being a mover improved the average Blishen score difference, though not greatly. The exception was for high-SES members from urban areas, for whom geographic mobility had almost no impact on intergenerational occupational mobility in terms of Blishen scores. (The negative average Blishen values for the urban high-status group reflect the fact that at the extreme, only downward mobility is possible if there is any mobility.) Similar findings were made for the impact of being a mover on career mobility.

Table 5.8. Occupational mobility by geographic mobility status based on Blishen scores for occupations (percentage)

		Blishen score difference between father's occupation at age 55 and respondent's 1995 occupation (intergenerational mobility)*					
Region 1973	Geographic mobility	High SES 1973 mean	(n)	Medium SES 1973 mean	(n)	Low SES 1973 mean	(n)
Urban	Stayers	−5.7	86	7.0	67	11.9	70
	Movers	−6.5	72	8.5	47	17.8	28
Rural/small town	Stayers	−6.3	24	6.9	47	7.0	58
	Movers	−4.5	32	10.8	40	10.7	41

		Blishen score difference between respondent's first full-time job (1973–1979) and current occupation 1995 (career mobility)*					
Region 1973	Geographic mobility	High SES 1973 mean	(n)	Medium SES 1973 mean	(n)	Low SES 1973 mean	(n)
Urban	Stayers	5.0	69	6.3	75	3.3	72
	Movers	4.8	62	3.3	50	7.4	27
Rural/small town	Stayers	4.9	26	4.1	52	1.7	70
	Movers	6.9	30	4.5	43	3.5	49

		Blishen scores for current occupation 1995 (current occupation baseline)*					
Region 1973	Geographic mobility	High SES 1973 mean	(n)	Medium SES 1973 mean	(n)	Low SES 1973 mean	(n)
Urban	Stayers	55.2	97	51.3	82	49.4	79
	Movers	54.0	84	52.7	59	53.5	33
Rural/small town	Stayers	47.9	27	46.5	55	42.1	76
	Movers	54.6	37	49.4	45	46.8	56

Note: Urban consists of Metro Toronto, other large cities, and small cities and the Metro suburban fringe. The rural category in this table refers to rural areas and small towns.
* If not employed full-time in 1995, respondent reported most recent full-time job; see endnote 7 for explanation.

At the bottom of Table 5.8 we show the average Blishen scores for current occupations by SES, region, and stayer/mover status. These data do not reflect occupational mobility, but only achieved occupational status by the time of the 1995 survey. The data show that stayer/mover status had little impact on respondents of urban origin; however, for those from the small town and rural origins, being a mover had benefits. It should be noted that the differences between stayers and movers shown in Table 5.8 need to be interpreted with caution, as the differences are small; while the differences do suggest there are benefits to being a mover, due to small cell frequencies, statistical significance between stayers and movers could not be established.[12]

A good example of the transition from a rural to an urban environment having a positive impact on intergenerational career mobility is the experience of Sean. One of eight children, Sean grew up on a dairy farm in rural Ontario. As a child, he thought he would follow in his father's footsteps and become a dairy farmer. He performed well in high school and was the only one in his family to attend college. His parents were very supportive of his decision to obtain a diploma in business administration and accounting, and offered him financial support in addition to his student loans. While attending college in Ottawa, he determined that he really enjoyed the opportunities a large city had to offer. Nonetheless, after graduating he returned to his rural community and worked in a factory, soon quitting because he hated shift work. He then left for Ottawa to work in a consulting firm. Two years later he entered an administrative training program with a large insurance firm, encouraged by his girlfriend's father, who was an insurance agent. He successfully completed the program and was employed by the company in a number of positions that required him to move around the country. In 1985 the company opened a regional head office in Vancouver and asked him to work there hiring trainees. He became deeply attached to the city, and when the company asked him to move again, he changed jobs in order to remain in Vancouver. When we caught up with Sean in 1995, he was employed as a manager in an insurance company. He also mentioned the possibility of eventually starting a new business, possibly a wine-making shop, with his wife.

At this point it is worthwhile to summarize some of the salient differences between stayers and movers. As we mentioned earlier in this chapter, the Class of '73 faced a range of structural constraints in growing up in the 1960s. Factors such as class of origin played an important role in shaping their educational and occupational expectations. A higher proportion of stayers were of lower socio-economic origin than movers (37.0 versus 28.4 per cent, using three levels of SES), with 29.8 per cent of stayers being of high SES origin and 38.0 per cent of movers having high SES background. Conversely, among those of lower SES origin, where being a stayer was the common pattern (63.0 versus 50.6 per cent for the high SES group), still somewhat more than one-third elected to leave home and moving, as we have seen, served to enhance their social mobility. Within the urban origin regions, there were statistically significant differences in stayer–mover proportions by SES level. Thus, while half of high-SES urban members of the Class of '73 were movers, less than one-third of low-SES urban respondents were movers. The smaller variations in proportions of stayers and movers by SES in the small town and rural region were not statistically significant. For most regions, gender was not related to being a stayer or mover, except for small towns and rural areas, where 57.5 per cent of women and 42.5 per cent of men were movers.

In our 1979 survey, members of the Class of '73 were asked to describe themselves using a series of adjectives known as a semantic differential. Movers were significantly more likely than stayers to describe themselves as 'important,' 'effective,' and 'interesting.' By way of illustration, 56 per cent of movers but 42 per cent of stayers characterized themselves as 'effective' (marking 1 or 2 on the 7-point scale). Moreover, movers, at the point that they attended Grade 12, were more likely than stayers to have assessed positively their academic ability to graduate from university (67.8 per cent) than were stayers (57.6 per cent).

Instead of examining geographic mobility in relation to the socio-economic status of family of origin, we considered staying and moving from respondents' achieved socio-economic status in 1995 (i.e., class of destination). When we examined the class of destination of respondents with respect to their geographic location, we found that over six in ten of lower-SES respondents who lived in small towns and rural areas during their high school years remained at home (or returned there). In contrast, two-thirds of small town and rural respondents who achieved high-SES destinations chose to move to more urban settings, or to major cities such as Toronto. It appears that among members of the Class of '73, choosing to leave home in late adolescence figured significantly in the shaping of personal biographies.

A further examination of the class of destination in 1995 reveals that 39.2 per cent of movers and 28.9 per cent of stayers were classified as high SES (using the three SES categories). In contrast, 39.9 per cent of stayers but only 24.6 per cent of movers were classified as low SES. Movers were significantly more likely than stayers to have acquired a university degree (42.7 per cent versus 26.9 per cent), and stayers were more likely than movers to have attained only a high school education (33.0 per cent versus 19.0 per cent).

Further Formal Education to 1994

Further formal education is of significance in this section because of the strong role that education in general has played with regard to social mobility in the postwar decades. We had documented the role of education in the life course trajectories of members of the Class of '73; now we wondered whether education later in life contributed to their social mobility.

Presuming a conventional educational trajectory for most participants in our study, the respondents would have completed their formal education by the summer of 1978, except for a minority who stayed on to pursue professional certification (e.g., a graduate degree or a medical or law degree). By returning to our respondents in 1995, we were able to look at patterns of further formal education since our last major survey in 1979. We asked respondents to indicate whether they had had further formal education since 1978–79. If the reply was 'yes,' we asked them to complete an educational history table to indicate the following: the years of their educational experiences, names of schools, whether their studies were part-time or full-time, the areas of study, and the degrees, diplomas, or certificates received. This educational history covered a possible seventeen academic years between 1978 and 1994.

We divided the respondents into four groups with respect to further formal education. The first group consisted of those who reported no further formal education from 1979 to 1994. The second group consisted of respondents who continued their education but whose attainment did not constitute a significant upgrade. Respondents in groups three and four experienced a significant educational upgrade: a college certificate and a university degree, respectively.

A large proportion of our sample (45.9 per cent) reported that they had attained further formal education after 1979. Unfortunately, we did not ask respondents to indicate the purpose of each listed further education experience. So while we were able to show basic patterns of further formal education for the Class of '73, we were not able to determine whether the reasons to get further education were work-related, or for career advancement, or for personal interest and satisfaction. When we tried to predict further formal education using a regression model, we found that the only predictor variable that surfaced as important was previous educational attainment. This finding suggests that personal agency was the key factor in decisions to undertake further education after 1979. Only one group that had pursued further formal education after 1979 could be considered in a different light. This group included individuals who in 1979 were completing their professional training through graduate or other professional degrees. We are confident that the pursuit of further education by members of this group reflected the implementation of a career plan already set in their minds some time before our 1979 Phase IV survey.

The kinds of further formal education listed by respondents in 1995 ranged widely from people taking some college or university courses, whether they had previous degrees or not, to people taking a second community college diploma or even a second university degree, to people continuing on from university to pursue graduate degrees, teaching certificates, or professional degrees (e.g., law, accounting). Two-thirds of the 362 respondents who indicated further formal education after 1979 did not significantly upgrade their educational qualifications; of the remainder who did significantly upgrade, 11.6 per cent obtained a university degree and 21.3 per cent obtained or added a college certificate or diploma. The largest single category of respondents (some fifty individuals) making an educational upgrade comprised those with high school only in 1979 who obtained community college certificates or diplomas by 1995.

The four groups were examined in terms of gender and socio-economic background. With respect to gender, the four groups were evenly split, except that more men obtained college certificates, the reason being that more men than women with high school only returned after 1979 to obtain a college certificate or diploma. Respondents in the group continuing their education with no significant upgrade were similar to those completing university degrees with respect to socioeconomic backgrounds – that is, both groups were disproportionately from the highest socio-economic level. In addition, they were more frequently from academic tracks in high school than those who obtained a college certificate or who had no further formal education after high school. Parental educational expectations were relatively high for all groups (expectation of university in 50 to 60 per cent of the cases), except for the 'no further formal education' group (university expected in 34 per cent of the cases). Level of occupational expecta-

tions was lower for those who obtained a community college certificate than for the other groups – a finding consistent with the origins of
this group, most of whom did not go on to postsecondary education
between 1973 and 1979.

Though we investigated the further educational acquisition of each
of the four groups, the patterns were too intricate and detailed to
present succinctly here. Some results, however, are worth highlight-
ing. Of the 362 members of the Class of '73 with further formal education, 140 held university degrees or were continuing in graduate or
professional schools in 1979; among this 140 there were somewhat
more women (56.0 per cent) than men (44.0 per cent). Four patterns
emerge from this group. *First,* close to half this group (47.9 per cent)
pursued further professional education – professional training such as
master's, law, and medical degrees and teaching certificates. These
degrees were pursued early and were largely completed by 1985,
though a few individuals began their advanced degrees after 1985 –
for example, going back to university to become teachers. A *second*
group (17.1 per cent) attended community college, some completing
certificates and diplomas. A *third* small group of seven (5.0 per cent)
even took a second university degree. The *fourth* group, 18.6 per cent,
was very diverse in terms of further education, attending community
college or university or other private institutions. However, many did
not complete certificates or degrees (six started master's degrees). Professional studies in the first pattern were clearly work related. For the
other patterns, the courses and programs chosen suggest educational
choices related to work, but also that personal interest and personal
development strongly influenced respondents' decisions to pursue further formal education. By 1979, 201 respondents had attended community college; 152 had obtained a CAAT diploma or certificate (some
more than one); and another 49 had taken some community college
courses. Of these respondents, 89 reported further formal education
beyond 1979. By 1995, 57 in this group had obtained one or more
further college certificates; six had taken more college courses; 16 had
taken some university courses; six had obtained a university degree
(and sometimes another college certificate as well); and four had completed additional graduate degrees. The courses and certificate selections of this group of 89 indicate the vocational nature of their further
education. The preponderance of women (61.8 per cent) in this further
education group suggests that many women are comfortable in

returning to community college for further education. Women espe-cially have utilized the community college system to obtain further credentials in the health field, especially nursing. The high enrolment in part-time community college studies suggests that college courses and programs are especially accessible to adults who are employed full-time and/or are full-time homemakers. For some respondents, enrolment in further community college courses and certificates pro-grams has been spread over the eighteen-year reporting period; this suggests that these courses and programs have been taken to fit indi-vidual needs and personal timetables.

Community college opened doors for those respondents (especially men) who had been away from education for at least six years after completing high school. As the titles of the programs they pursued indicate, this further formal education was strongly work related. For this group, community college made sense. Their entrance to univer-sity was hampered by low high school grades and the lack of a grade 13 diploma. Community colleges offered courses and programs that were linked to provincially recognized trades. They offered upgrading in terms of extending one's skill base. They provided courses that added skills that were not essential but that complemented a particu-lar skills specialization (e.g., computer courses). And finally, they of-fered courses that people could take for the sake of personal interest and development. Moreover, community colleges tend to be receptive to mature students, and offer courses and programs that are perceived as accessible, as personally valuable, and/or as occupationally valu-able either for a current occupation or in terms of making a job or career change.

One final further education group that should be noted includes members of the Class of '73 who had not gone beyond high school by 1979 (283 individuals), but by 1995 reported further formal education (83 individuals). In this latter group, 46 obtained a college certificate or diploma, 4 obtained a university degree, 4 obtained both a univer-sity degree and a college certificate, 8 had some community college, 7 had some university, 2 combined some university with some commu-nity college, and 11 took short courses at a university, community college, or high school that did not appear to be part of a certificate or degree. Of the 83 respondents who pursued further formal education, 51.8 per cent were men and 48.2 per cent were women; and of the 50 who received community college certificates, 60 per cent were men and 40 per cent were women – a reversal of the pattern up to 1979. Our data suggest that the further formal education of this group was spread fairly evenly over the eighteen-year reporting period.

Aaron is an example of someone who dropped out of high school in grade 12 and returned several years later to complete his studies. A bright, articulate young man, he began his high school education at a traditional school but found the experience boring and uninspiring. At a teacher's suggestion, he enrolled in an alternative secondary school, which he much preferred to his former high school. When Aaron was 17, his parents moved to the United States, but he refused to move with them. He was forced to work at several menial jobs to support himself and found himself barely attending classes. After living in this unstable environment for several months, he dropped out of school in the middle of grade 12. Until he was 23, Aaron worked in the retail trade and as a general carpenter, but the desire to secure better employment motivated him to enrol at university as a mature student. His parents' earlier expectations that he pursue postsecondary education also influenced his decision. While enrolled in a master's program in economics, he taught economics and worked with mainframe computers at his school. After graduating, he worked for his graduate supervisors on a three-year part-time contract, during which time he accepted a position as an economist with a utility company. He later switched to a more established utility company, where he developed the company budget. In our interview with Aaron in 1995, he told us he had been employed with this company for nine years, during which he had held a number of different jobs. Each position called on him to use different skills, and consequently he found his work interesting and satisfying.

We said earlier that our 1995 survey did not explore motivations to continue education. Nevertheless, as our short review indicates, further formal education was very often job related. This conclusion is supported by t-tests on means between those Class of '73 members who obtained further formal education and those who did not. Intergenerational mobility differences were not statistically significant between the two groups. However, with regard to career mobility, the differences between the groups were statistically significant, there being a three-point Blishen score career mobility difference in favour of those Class of '73 members obtaining further formal education (6.10 versus 3.09). The average Blishen score for occupations in 1995 was 53.3 for those having further formal education, in contrast to 48.1 for

Table 5.9. Reported 1994 personal income by 1979 educational attainment and further formal education status

	Average category means for personal income reported for 1994[i]			
	Further formal education after 1979			
Educational attainment 1979	Yes	(n)	No	(n)
University graduates	$49,926	101	$54,315	73
CAAT graduates	36,859	78	41,536	83
Some university/CAAT	44,605	57	51,750	40
High school only	39,608*	83	32,961*	179
Graduate and professional degrees 1995[ii]	68,864	33		

* Only the average category means for the 'high school only' group differ statistically by further formal education status (p < .05).
i. Question 86 in the 1995 survey asked respondents to indicate their personal income from all sources. The data coding is based on the mean of each of the response categories provided. The first response category was 'no income,' which was coded zero; the second category was income under $5,000, which was coded $2,500; the third category was income from $5,000 to $9,999 and was thus coded as $7,500; and so on. The top category 16, income of $100,000 or more, was coded $105,000.
ii. For clarity, this category includes only those individuals who had a university background and who, in 1979, reported that they were continuing in graduate school or were taking professional education. Personal income in 1995 represents income likely obtained from occupations based on that successful graduate and professional training. Thus, in the last category of this table, most individuals finished graduate and professional education prior to 1985. In effect, this group is treated as not having further formal education beyond 1979. In the other categories above, there are other individuals who obtained graduate or professional degrees through further formal education that was not a continuation of their education through 1979.

those with no further formal education – a difference of over 5 points (a statistically significant group difference).

There is, however, one other indicator of relevance that we can employ, and that is the economic payoff of further formal education. Table 5.9 tabulates average category means for personal income reported for 1994 by further formal education status and level of educational attainment in 1979. A predictable finding is that those respondents who continued graduate and professional education in 1979 drew very high personal incomes, likely as a result of their high-level professional and managerial occupations. Of course, the table also shows that greater personal income is also generally associated with greater levels of educational attainment. Surprisingly, however, an income payoff for further formal education was only indicated for the group that did not have postsecondary education up to 1979 and that subsequently chose to pursue education; all other groups taking further education suffered an income *loss*. We speculate that some university and college graduates may have received a rocky start in the labour market, and then sought to correct this through more education, and thereby suffered income penalties due to an uneven career line. It appears that for the high-school-only group (as of 1979), further formal education provided a higher income job payoff, relative to those who did not pursue educational upgrading. This suggests that the labour market has been significantly divided to the disadvantage of individuals with no postsecondary credentials.

Earlier, we noted some of the background differences among further formal education groups. We can assess to some extent the role of further formal education by looking at some of the correlates of additional education, employing the simple dichotomy of either having or not having further education. Using this dichotomy, further formal education is not associated with parental socio-economic status, community of origin, or gender. While just over three-quarters of the Class of '73 were employed in 1995, those with further formal education tended to be less often self-employed compared with those with no further formal education (9.9 per cent compared with 16.3 per cent out of 751 cases). Those with further formal education appear to have had more jobs since high school than those without further formal education (4.36 versus 3.33 full-time jobs since leaving high school). Regarding the five areas of life satisfaction assessed in our 1995 survey, only on 'work or a career' and on 'education' did the two groups show some modest difference; those with further formal education were somewhat less satisfied with their work, but somewhat more satisfied with their education, compared with those with no further formal education. Further formal education, however, helps with respect to socio-economic mobility. Further formal education was associated with higher current socio-economic status, and no further formal education with lower current socio-economic status. For each parental level of socio-economic status, further formal education tends to advance current socio-economic status.

To sum up this section, further formal education patterns were complex for the Class of '73. Yet having such education offered advantages, not only for personal development but for occupational careers as well. The advantages were especially strong for women with a community college background who pursued further community college education, and for men with high school only as of 1979 who decided to seek formal education through community college. As we have shown in the previous chapter and in this chapter, educational attainment had its greatest impact on employment and on social and occupational mobility.

Conclusions

This chapter presents the view that our understanding of the school-to-employment transitions of younger generations can be expanded by looking back at the pathways taken by previous generations. While adopting the main premises of life course theory – that is, that individuals construct their transitions from school to employment within the context of social origin and other social dimensions – we posit that it is useful to adopt the language, and to employ the techniques, that allow us to identify patterns of social, intergenerational occupational, and intragenerational occupational mobility. In applying these techniques we have replicated gender and social class findings typically found in North American stratification and mobility studies.

Members of the Class of '73 had good reason to be hopeful about their future prospects as they moved into their high school years. In 1970, Ontario had the country's lowest unemployment rate; and as cited earlier, those with jobs had higher real incomes and better working conditions than any previous generation (Rea, 1985). However, conditions were changing in Ontario, and by 1975 the unemployment rate had risen to 6 per cent – higher than that of three other provinces, though low by today's conditions (Rea, 1985). Though our data analysis of social mobility focused exclusively on full-time employment, in the previous chapter we showed that an increased minority of respondents had turned to part-time work and self-employment. Furthermore, a greater proportion of women than men experienced periods of unemployment in the period 1978–94.

Our findings also indicate that the middle class was particularly vulnerable to change, with over 60 per cent moving up or down the ladder of success with respect to intergenerational mobility. Yet a minority of respondents from more humble origins took advantage of economic opportunities and moved into upper socio-economic positions. Furthermore, it is important to note the gender differences that favour greater occupational inheritance among men, and the tendency for the gross mobility patterns of women to be quite distinct from those of men. It is also clear that the impact of geographical location and of decisions to leave home should be taken into account when examining intergenerational mobility patterns. Living in a city fosters upward mobility, and the location one moves to influences intergenerational mobility. Thus, for respondents with lower socio-economic origins, relocation generally served to increase socio-economic status. A subsequent analysis of those who remained in one location, or chose to move, revealed structural and psychological correlates. For example, compared to movers, stayers were more likely to be drawn from lower socio-economic origins, were less likely to assess positively their academic ability to graduate from university, and were less likely to assess themselves as effective, important, or interesting.

Our analysis of career mobility for respondents who held full-time jobs revealed that the Class of '73 moved up the occupational hierarchy; the proportion of unskilled, agricultural, and skilled workers steadily decreased as they moved to Phase VI. Less than one-third experienced no occupational mobility from first full-time job to full-time occupation held in 1995. Movement up or down was incremental, however, and most respondents had experienced no more than three steps or shifts by 1995. Both men and women experienced upward career mobility, though the pattern seemed somewhat stronger for men. It is also important to note that the impact of socio-economic origins proved more prominent in the long run, favouring those of higher socio-economic origins. Residence and geographical mobility also proved to be of some importance in understanding career mobility patterns. Respondents with a city background experienced greater career occupational mobility than rural respondents, and movers were more likely than stayers to benefit from leaving their community by mid-career.

In examining the Class of '73, we have been struck both by the complexity of life course transition entries and exits made by respondents, and by the degree of uncertainty respondents expressed at various phases of the project. However, given that we can expect even more frequent nonconventional pathways among the emerging younger generations, life course researchers wishing to employ conventional social, occupational, and career mobility theories will likely encounter methodological or practical difficulties. For example, between 1975 and 1994 the part-time employment rate for women 15 to 24 more than doubled, from 22 to 48 per cent (Krahn, 1996: 16), making the use of full-time occupations to measure social mobility problematic. These measurement problems need to be thought through carefully, if useful and valid comparisons across generations are to be made in the future.

CHAPTER SIX

The Experiences of First-Generation Canadians

The upward trend in non-British European immigration to Canada began in the 1950s and continued well into the 1970s. During this period immigration to Canada increased dramatically from a low of 73,912 in 1950 to a high of 222,876 in 1967. By 1971 that number had dropped to 125,000 (Richmond and Kalbach, 1980). The steady increase in the number of immigrants to Canada up to 1967 was fuelled by the strongly held belief that immigrants were crucial to the economic growth of the country. In 1967 the federal government dispensed with the preferential categories based on nationality; it also expanded the number of source countries from which immigrants were recruited and introduced a 'point system' for selecting independent immigrants. Independent immigrants (and in a similar way, those nominated by close relatives) were thereafter selected on the basis of training, education, and skills as opposed to ethnic origin and nationality.

By the early 1970s an increasing number of high school students had parents who were foreign-born. These families of ethnic, racial, linguistic, and religious minority Canadians had to contend with a society that was struggling with a rapid increase in diversity. Their children grew up in a social environment that was often significantly different from that of their country of origin and was sometimes inhospitable to them because of their 'difference' (Porter, 1965; Ashworth, 1975; Head, 1975; Ramcharan, 1975; Jansen, 1981; Special Committee on Visible Minorities, 1984).

Some members of the Class of '73 were either born outside Canada or had one or both parents who were born outside Canada. In fact, 149 of the respondents surveyed in 1995 (18.9 per cent) indicated that they had two parents who were foreign-born.[1] These foreign-born parents

Table 6.1. Birthplace of both parents born outside Canada (percentage)

Country of birth	Father's birthplace		Mother's birthplace	
	Number	Per cent	Number	Per cent
Italy	24	16.1	24	16.1
British Isles	30	20.1	32	21.5
Western Europe	46	30.9	49	32.9
Eastern Europe	36	24.2	33	22.1
Asia	7	4.7	7	4.7
Caribbean	3	2.0	2	1.3
Other	3	2.0	2	1.3
Total	149	100.0	149	100.0

(Table 6.1) came largely from Italy, the British Isles, Western Europe (viz. Germany, Greece, France, Belgium, the Netherlands, Denmark), and Eastern Europe (viz. Hungary, Poland, Russia).[2] Fifty respondents from this group were foreign-born (33.8 per cent); less than 5 per cent were racial minorities.

This chapter outlines and reviews the experiences, aspirations and expectations of the members of the Class of '73 with foreign-born parents.[3] We examine not only their experiences as first or second generation Canadians, but also the roles that ethnicity and race played in their lives and in their perceptions of opportunity.[4] While immigrant background, race, and ethnicity are central to our discussion, we remain conscious of the complex interrelationships between these socially constructed factors and others such as social class, gender, and region (or area of residence). As we have seen in the preceding chapters, these latter factors have had an impact on how members of the Class of '73 have organized their lives into particular sequences of actions and reactions in order to participate effectively in Canadian society. In examining the lives of immigrant respondents, we also learn about how their aspirations, choices, and opportunities enabled them to attain occupational and social statuses that were different from those of their parents.[5]

Earlier analysis of the effects of birthplace on the Class of '73's educational and occupational aspirations, expectations, and activities revealed that first-generation Canadians were more likely to expect to enrol in postsecondary education than foreign-born and second-plus generation students. At the same time, foreign-born students were more likely to continue with part-time studies or to enrol in trade schools or apprenticeship programs (Anisef, 1975b). Chisholm (1999) argues that the public education system provides important 'transitional services' to marginalized groups such as immigrants and people at the lower end of the socio-economic ladder. It enables them to obtain the education necessary to meet their occupational aspirations; it also provides a means by which they can become aware of the opportunity structures, acquire social and cultural capital, develop social and occupational networks, and become acculturated. The services and opportunities provided by schools were particularly significant to the children of foreign-born parents who came to Canada in the 1960s and 1970s. In the early years these families tended to reside in small, ethnically homogeneous communities in cities (Dreidger, 1996). Lacking some of the necessary cultural capital, they were inclined to rely on educational institutions to help them negotiate the social and educational structures that would enable them to achieve their goals in Canada.

Given the particular issues and special situations that children of foreign-born parents face in a new society, we asked this question: How well did respondents do in terms of their educational and occupational attainment relative to the children of Canadian-born parents, and relative to their own parents? In exploring this question, we examine the support they received from their parents; the extent to which their schooling met their needs and provided opportunities for achievement; and their educational and occupational attainments. We look first at the role played by ethnicity and race in their lives.

Our examination is premised on the idea that the experiences of these respondents, and their educational and occupational outcomes, were influenced not only by the social structures related to their status as first-generation Canadians, but also by how they understood their situation, constructed aspirations, and made choices in order to achieve their aspirations. Ethnocentrism, xenophobia, anti-Semitism, and racism could have operated to limit the opportunities and outcomes of these members of the Class of '73 (Henry et al., 1995); however, the personal choices they made in terms of their education, occupation, and family life for the most part enabled them to respond to conditions in ways that have facilitated their participation in Canadian society, and made it possible for them to achieve their goals.

Constructing Identities, Negotiating Differences

For the children of foreign-born parents – particularly those of ethnic minorities – ethnicity tended to operate as a way of identifying their 'difference.' It was often used to explain particular behaviours and habits; at the same time, it provided a source of support for members of the ethnic group. One respondent, Tim, who was of Irish-born parents, said that his Irish roots were important to him and that he learned at an early age to differentiate himself from people with an English background. He felt that he was 'emotionally demonstrative ... and happy-go-lucky,' like a stereotypical Irish person. Dom proudly mentioned that while he was born here, he remained Italian and his children identified themselves as Italian. He pointed out that he belonged to a group of hard-working Europeans 'that build a lot of Canadian institutions.' As Aboud (1981: 54) concluded from his research, these attempts to identify themselves in ethnic terms indicate that ethnicity is an important 'psychological' reference for students, who generally regard it 'as a characteristic internal to themselves, comparable to their beliefs and emotions.'

The tendency of first and second generation Canadians to identify themselves in ethnic terms may have been related to whether they grew up in heterogeneous communities (as opposed to homogeneous ones) (Akoodie, 1984; Aboud, 1981; McGuire et al., 1978; Berry et al., 1977). Residing in heterogeneous neighbourhoods contributed to the tensions and conflicts that respondents experienced as they attempted to construct their identities while dealing with their differences. Jessica, whose parents immigrated to Canada from Eastern Europe, reported that she grew up feeling 'very different' and bearing 'the brunt of European parents.' There were 'very few Jewish kids' in the neighbourhood in which she was raised. This contributed to the conflicts she had with her parents, particularly her father, whom she described as 'very old country,' and who insisted that his daughters date only Jewish men. Jessica's experience was not unique; like many children of immigrants or ethnic minority parents, she was caught between the 'old world' values of her parents and the values and expectations of the host society or dominant cultural group.

Individuals identified religion as a significant feature in their parents' lives, particularly as they struggled to maintain their ethnic identities and values and to pass them on to their children. Many of the respondents, as they reflected on their adolescent years, mentioned the significance of the church and synagogue in their parents' and their own lives. By going to a Roman Catholic church and attending Catholic schools, Tim and Dom had their cultural values re-enforced. For Anna it was the Mennonite church, and for Jessica it was 'Hebrew school every three days and Sundays.' Many of these respondents came to connect the church or synagogue and religious schooling not only with their parents' cultural identity but also with their own. They saw religious institutions as having played a very important role in their parents' lives as they struggled to adjust to Canadian society, and these institutions seem to have helped their parents and themselves to realize educational, occupational, economic, and social goals. Many of these first-generation Canadians also perceived these institutions as significant for instilling ethnic pride in their own children.

The career and occupational aspirations and choices of individuals were related, in varying degrees, to ethnic and immigrant backgrounds. Many individuals learned about particular jobs and career possibilities through their parents' aspirations for them, and through their knowledge of and exposure to their parents' work. For instance, Kelly's work on her Belgian parents' farm, and Ray's work in his Italian family's business, exposed both to specific skills that helped point them in particular occupational directions. Furthermore, it is likely that some of these ethnic minority group members entered particular occupations or careers in order to reinforce ethnic identities. This in turn helped them deal with the contradictions, tensions, and conflicts they experienced in their acculturation processes – particularly prejudice, racism, and discrimination (Haas and Shaffir, 1978; James, 1990).

Ethnic identity is also related to individuals' positive or negative experiences with respect to ethnicity and race, and to their perceptions of what it takes to participate effectively in the larger society and to realize their social and economic goals. This was evident in our interview with Jason, who throughout the interview session referred to himself only as Hungarian. It was only at the end of the interview, when he was asked about the private school his child attended, that he indicated he was Jewish. Jason's attempt to keep this information private was likely related to how his family had experienced that identity.

The cases of Freda and Frank are also instructive. It was not possible for them to keep their South Asian ethnic identity private, but it was evident that they had distanced themselves from their ethnic roots. Freda, who left India with her parents at age 12, and Frank, who left

Pakistan with his parents at age 3, stated that their ethnic identity was not significant to them. They rejected the 'visible minority' label, which suggests that they believed that acknowledging racism and discrimination would likely raise barriers to their achievement (Henry and Ginzberg, 1985; James, 1990).

These children of foreign-born parents did not passively accept the consequences of their status as first-generation Canadians. Some, like Tim and Dom, seemed content to identify with what might be considered stereotypical constructions of their ethnic group; others, like Jessica and Jason, struggled with the problems raised by their ethnic identification. However, on the basis of their understanding of their situation in society, they all negotiated and established their occupational and career possibilities.

The Role of Parents

Members of the Class of '73 with foreign-born parents reported that their parents significantly influenced their educational and occupational aspirations. Often, their parents' aspirations were related to a desire for social and economic advancement, for themselves as well as their children. A Survey Research Centre study (1979) showed that immigrant parents often were ambitious and independent and worked hard to provide their children with opportunities for success.[6] According to Brice (1982: 127), 'even if they are not well educated, they come to hope, and sometimes expect that their children and their grandchildren will achieve more than they do.' Anna's Russian immigrant parents hoped that their children would accomplish the goals they had been unable to achieve. Anna's father's dream had been to be a bookkeeper or accountant, but after coming to Canada he worked in the furniture business as a cabinetmaker. Her mother helped with the household income by cleaning people's homes. It was her mother, Anna recalled, who encouraged her and her siblings to get an education so that they would not have to do the kind of work their parents did.

Many parents believed that high educational attainment would enable their children to take advantage of occupational opportunities, to achieve economic and social success, and to participate effectively in society. Angela's German-born parents strongly valued education and encouraged her to attend university. Her experiences were similar to those of Jessica, whose parents were of Eastern European origin, and

Susan, whose parents were British-born professionals. All grew up with the strongly impressed understanding that economic and social success could best be achieved through a postsecondary education. Cynthia's Polish-born parents, who had 'very little education,' both used to say to her, 'I don't want my children to end up working in a factory.'

Pamela, of South Asian origin, is another respondent whose parents encouraged her to go to university; however, she indicated that the factor of race influenced her own aspirations and those her parents held for her. Indeed, studies show that racial, ethnic, and linguistic minority parents, and immigrant parents, tend to perceive education not only as a means of accessing occupational and career opportunities, but also as a means of dealing with the ethnic and racial discrimination that might operate as barriers to their children's success (Lam, 1994; Dei et al., 1995; Cheng et al., 1993; James, 1990; Brathwaite, 1989; Calliste, 1982; Larter et al., 1982; Anisef, 1975b; Head, 1975, Ramcharan, 1975).[7] Generally, foreign-born parents perceived that educational institutions, particularly postsecondary institutions, would provide their children with the necessary cultural capital – the values, knowledge, and skills – that would enable them to succeed on merit.

Furthermore, as found by Richmond and Kalbach (1980), Herberg (1982), Anisef (1975b), and Danziger (1978), the birthplaces of immigrant parents have a major influence on their children's educational and occupational aspirations, motivations, and attainments. Richmond and Kalbach (1980: 260) found that foreign-born parents, particularly those born in Eastern and Central Europe, were more likely than Canadian-born parents 'to ensure that their children were in full-time school attendance' for a longer period of time, often until age 18. Parents born in Britain, Northern and Western Europe, Asia, and Southern Europe (in that order) were less likely to do the same. However, equally significant were parents' education and occupation,[8] and where they lived. These factors, and to some extent the gender of their children, influenced what parents viewed as models of success for their children.

Kate's family, of German origin, is one example. She grew up on a farm in a small town in southwestern Ontario with three sisters and a brother. She stated that her father was her greatest influence, but he never encouraged her to complete grade 13. Instead, her parents were more concerned with her 'developmentally delayed' brother and his education. Kelly, whose parents were of Belgian origin, grew up on a tobacco farm with her ten siblings. Only her third sister went to grade 13, but she'd had to fight to get that far because her 'father did not see the importance of education,' particularly for the girls, whom her parents expected to get married. By the mid-1990s all of her brothers except one were farmers, and Kelly, who was married to a carpenter, had graduated from a community college and become a nurse.

Tim grew up in a suburban area of Metropolitan Toronto with his Irish-born parents and six siblings. His father, a factory worker, and mother, a homemaker, did not encourage the children to pursue postsecondary education. Rather, according to Tim, 'they had the idea that when you finish school you get a job.' Tim did what was expected of a working-class male. After completing high school he worked for about four years as a land surveyor with the government until he was laid off. After being unemployed for about six months, he returned to school and completed a BA in English. He then became a high school teacher.

The parents of these members of the Class of '73 held educational and occupational aspirations for their children that likely corresponded to generational differences (Kruger, 1998), to the cultural values of their country of origin, and to their ambitions as new Canadians. These factors helped determine how parents understood what was possible for themselves and for their children, given the social and economic conditions of the family and society. Thus, some parents encouraged some of their children – in many cases the male children – to attain high levels of education, while others preferred their children to complete high school and 'get a job.' Evidently, social class, gender, and race helped structure parents' understandings of the extent to which their aspirations for their children were achievable. Thus, working-class parents such as John's were unlikely to think of postsecondary education as a possibility. And Kelly, being female and working class, received limited support from her parents. On the other hand, the desire to see their children work at 'better jobs' than they had, and the understanding that this would probably require a high level of education, prompted some parents to encourage their children accordingly. Education, then – particularly for racial minority parents like Pamela's – was perceived as the instrument that would remove barriers to achievement.

Immigrant parents, like other parents of the Class of '73, influenced their children and constructed educational and occupational paths for them. However, equally significant were the choices their children made with respect to their *own* aspirations. At times, without encouragement from their parents and irrespective of their views, respondents made choices that enabled them to attain their goals.

Schooling and Preparing for the Future

Jason, who immigrated to Canada from Hungary with his parents at 14, found high school to be a very positive factor in his life. However, his educational experiences were exceptional; many research findings show that immigrant students – particularly those of ethnic and racial minority backgrounds – tend to be in lower-level educational programs, which blocks them from high educational attainment (Herberg, 1982; D'Oyley and Silverman, 1976; Head, 1975; Ashworth, 1975; Ramcharan, 1975; Wright, 1971; Deosaran, 1976).[9] The older students were at the time of arrival, the more likely they were to be in special education classes (Wright, 1971; Deosaran, 1976; Deosaran, Wright, and Kane, 1976). Studies conducted by the Toronto Board of Education found that the occupation of parents and the age at which immigrant students arrived in Canada were critical factors in the educational placement of all immigrant students, particularly non-English-speaking students.

Jason's father, an engineer who had immigrated to pursue a postdoctoral fellowship in Canada, was able to support his son throughout the adjustment process. And Jason's interest in computers and achievements in mathematics helped him assemble a network of individuals who were quite helpful to him. Jason recalled the 'little clique' of friends who together with him took computer science and enriched math courses all the way through high school. The school did not offer computer science, but by grade 11 his math teacher, who 'had a lot of contacts at the University of Toronto,' managed to get his group access to computers at the university. Jason's accomplishments were quite remarkable, given that in grade 9 he spoke 'virtually no English [and] passing the year, especially in English, was a challenge. I did get 50 per cent in English at the end of grade 9 ... Anything that was language oriented was extremely difficult because I didn't speak English.'[10] At the time of our interview, Jason looked back at his schooling 'with fond memories,' pointing out that after high school he went to the University of Toronto, where he and all his friends pursued degrees in engineering. His years at university were also fulfilling. 'It was a lot of work, but it was enjoyable.'

Unlike Jason, who viewed schooling as a very positive experience that opened up many opportunities, Pamela believed that her schooling did not prepare her 'for the future.' She was particularly critical of her high school guidance counsellor, who discouraged her from pursuing her interest in mathematics. Instead, Pamela was advised to take psychology at university because the tests she was given showed that she was 'good with people.' Following the advice of her guidance counsellor, she majored in psychology at university – a subject area she disliked and regrets taking. Pamela believes that the advice she received was related to gender and expressed annoyance that the counsellor did not at that time encourage her to become a psychiatrist or to pursue some other math-related career.

For some Class of '73 members, sports provided a lifeline in high school; sports maintained their interest in school, gained them peer support, and obtained scholarships for them to pursue postsecondary education. Ray and Sam, both of Italian-born parents, are good examples. In 1979, when we first interviewed Ray, he told us that football and basketball had occupied most of his after-school time. He felt that 'most high school was a waste of time. The five years could be condensed into two years.' When we interviewed him again in 1995, Ray, who since that time had become a chartered accountant, was looking back on his high school years much more positively. He described his high school experiences as 'probably the best time of my life, academically, socially, and athletically.' Sam completed high school and obtained a sports scholarship at an American university. He gave up the scholarship after a semester, but still managed to graduate from university with an MBA. Dom, also of Italian-born parents, played sports in high school, but unlike Ray and Sam he did not pursue postsecondary studies. Even though he had gained acceptance from his peers through his involvement in sports, he dropped out of high school before completing grade 12.

For students like Ray, Sam, and Dom, sports seemed to have been a forum 'for the expression of their individuality and uniqueness' and the means by which they were able to gain some recognition at the schools they attended (Karp et al., 1991: 212). Sports operated as a cultural resource, whereby they were able to learn the norms and values of Canadian society. It also provided an emotional benefit, in that it helped them relieve their tensions and stresses.

While at school, Jason, Pamela, Ray, and Sam made choices that enabled them to cope with their limitations and plan for the future.

Table 6.2. Expectations in 1973 compared with activities in 1974 by parents' birthplace (percentage)

	Parents' birthplace	
	In Canada	Outside Canada
Expectations in Spring 1973 for		
Fall 1974	(n = 509)	(n = 125)
Work full-time	27.3	23.2
Attend community college	32.6	31.2
Attend university	40.1	45.6
Total	100.0	100.0
Activities reported in Fall 1974	(n = 586)	(n = 139)
Working full-time	37.0	34.5
Attending community college	16.4	12.9
Attending university	33.3	42.4
Part-time study	1.0	0.7
Other activity	12.3	9.4
Total	100.0	100.0

And seemingly conscious of their families' expectations in terms of their willingness to provide opportunities, respondents like Jason, Pamela, Ray, and Sam utilized schooling for what it was able to provide them.

Expectations and Attainment: The Educational Route

As the top part of Table 6.2 indicates, in 1973, when respondents were asked about their plans for the fall of 1974, 45.6 per cent of students with foreign-born parents expected to attend university compared to 40.1 per cent of those with Canadian-born parents. A similar number of both groups expected to attend community college, but more children of Canadian-born parents expected to go directly into the work force after high school.

While there was only a small difference in the expectations of both groups of students to participate in postsecondary education, we can observe a trend on the part of students of foreign-born parents. They tended to believe that education was important if they were to realize their life goals in Canada. Indeed, where our study directly explored the educational and occupational aspirations of students with immigrant backgrounds – particularly members of racial and ethnic minority groups – we found that they tended to have high aspirations (Dei et al., 1995; Lam, 1994; James, 1990; Calliste, 1982; Larter et al., 1982; Richmond and Kalbach, 1980).

We have already discussed the significant role that many foreign-born parents played in encouraging their children to attend university. Sonia, whose parents were of Eastern European origin and who eventually obtained a master's degree in library science, best articulated what we heard from many members of the Class of '73: that despite their 'humble beginnings,' they managed to successfully complete their postsecondary education.

> Why I went to university? I can't remember my parents saying this, but somehow we knew – all of us [and] there were five children in our family – that we were going to university. Somehow this was instilled in us ... Actually, all of my brothers and sisters have completed degrees ... I come from a tobacco farm, work is very labour intensive – you work from seven a.m. to seven p.m. hoeing tobacco. One hour for lunch and 90 degree heat. I can remember hoeing tobacco and I had blisters on my hands and they were bleeding, and I'm going, 'There's an easier way to earn a living.' It was hard work. None of us wanted to go back to it ... It also gave us an option. If we wanted to go back there was the farm, but our parents gave us an option ... We had to unload the fertilizer trucks after school. Hard work drove us to university.

As students, respondents differed in their perceptions of a community college education. Some, like Ray, did not consider a community college education because they felt that university had higher status. Others, like Brian and Dom, went to Ryerson Polytechnic University (then 'Institute') or a community college because they did not believe they could succeed at university, or they believed that a 'practical education' would provide them with a competitive edge when it came to getting a job. Others opted for community college because of the affordable cost and relatively short period of study. For example, Kelly, who, as we pointed out earlier was from a poor immigrant farming background, was encouraged by her guidance counsellor to attend college. She recalled that, while her parents were willing to pay for her college education, they would not have paid for her university education because 'it would have taken too long.'

When members of the Class of '73 were first asked about the occupations they expected to obtain once they left high school, occupations in the areas of health and medicine, teaching, the natural sciences and engineering, the clerical field, and the social sciences were most often mentioned (see Table 6.4). Many of these occupations required at least a high school diploma and, in a significant number of cases, a university degree. The high career aspirations of the members of the Class of '73 seemed in keeping with the findings of Burstein et al. (1975) and Friendly et al. (1979), who found that the majority of young Canadians tend to have high career aspirations. Masemann (1975) noted that immigrant students perceived a clear link between school training and their subsequent employment. They were aware that their parents held menial jobs and were determined to obtain better employment.

Many members of the Class of '73 indicated that a postsecondary education was critical to achieving their career aspirations and goals; it is worthwhile, therefore, to explore how many went on to postsecondary education after completing high school. In our follow-up study in 1974, as the lower portion of Table 6.2 shows, 50 per cent of the respondents with Canadian-born parents, compared to 55.3 per cent of those with foreign-born parents, were attending university or community college. Respondents with foreign-born parents seemed to favour university over community college more than those with Canadian-born parents. In fact, as the table shows, a greater proportion of children of foreign-born parents were in university (42.4 per cent versus 33.3 per cent). And while 16.4 per cent of this latter group attended community college, 37.0 per cent went on to work full-time.

When we compared respondents' expectations in 1973 with their activities in 1974 (Table 6.2), we noticed that there was a difference between 3 and 18 per cent in what respondents said they would do after high school and what they eventually did one year later. About 10 per cent more of the respondents found full-time work, while only about 50 per cent of those who expected to attend community colleges actually did so. There were smaller differences in the proportions who expected to attend university and did so. About half the respondents with Canadian-born parents and a little more than half those with foreign-born parents were engaged in postsecondary education in the fall of 1974. This likely reflects the employment situation of the 1970s – the accessibility of universities and colleges, and the emphasis placed on postsecondary education as requirement for many jobs (see Chapters 2 and 5).

It is interesting that among children of foreign-born parents, almost all who expected to attend university actually did so. This highlights a

Table 6.3. Educational attainment by parents' birthplace (percentage)

Parents' birthplace	n	No post-secondary education	Some college/ university	College diploma/ certificate	University degree	Total
Educational attainment						
1979						
In Canada	632	36.6	13.8	22.2	27.5	100.0
Outside Canada	149	32.2	12.1	21.5	34.2	100.0
1995						
In Canada	632	27.8	10.8	28.8	32.6	100.0
Outside Canada	149	23.5	7.4	29.5	39.6	100.0

point made earlier, that the value and importance of a university education were clearly beacons for respondents, particularly those of foreign-born parents. It may also be that those who eventually attended university were in the academic or postsecondary education stream in high school and were encouraged by teachers and their parents to obtain a university education. We have already mentioned that while many respondents viewed a community college education as less valuable than a university education, for some it was a viable alternative. That more respondents than expected went to work full-time may be a reflection of peer influence, academic performance in high school, and lack of financial and parental support. Some students, like Dale, resisted their parents' pressure and decided not to attend university. The child of Western European-born parents, Dale said he did not attend university, contrary to the expectations of his parents and his high school biology teacher, because he 'just wanted to get out of the house.'

Some students elected to participate in apprenticeship programs when they completed high school. They expected that this would result in them establishing their own businesses. Geoff, who grew up in a small town in western Ontario, told us: 'I was out of high school for two days and I got a job in an autobody shop; and now I've got my own shop ... I didn't like going to university or anything like that. I didn't have the money for it either. I wanted to be an auto mechanic and I ended up in an autobody repair shop instead ... So, I apprenticed for four years and got my licence.'

In 1979 and 1995 we again asked members of the Class of '73 to indicate their level of educational attainment. Table 6.3 reveals the continuing pursuit of post secondary education over time. Children of foreign-born parents were much more likely than those of Canadian-born parents to hold a university degree. The increase in the number of respondents, specifically those with foreign-born parents, who returned to college and university after 1979 may be an indication of their strong reliance on education as a 'safety net' or 'back-up system' (James, 1990). For example, after graduating from grade 13, Dale went to work at a hydro company, where he completed two years of training and four years of apprenticeship. He eventually worked his way up to the position of supervisor in the training department. Dale decided to pursue a university degree through correspondence because of the importance his employer seemed to place on such credentials: 'The letters after your name are very important. You must have a degree.' Dale's position on the need for further education seemed to support the finding of Friendly et al. (1979) that young people in the 1970s believed that their greatest obstacle to job advancement lay in their lack of education.

Many children of foreign-born parents followed through with their educational plans and received their postsecondary degrees. This is likely a reflection not only of their own aspirations, and of their own readings of their social contexts, but also of their desire to please their parents and to demonstrate that they were worthy of the goals their parents set for them. This is what Danziger found in his research on lower-class Italian immigrant boys in Toronto. He pointed out that parental expectations often tended to operate as 'a counter-balance to the inability of these foreign-born parents to provide their children with all the cognitive skills needed to succeed in the new society' (Danziger, 1978: 156). Furthermore, it is possible that the high educational and occupational expectations these foreign-born Canadians and their children held demonstrated that despite low socio-economic status, they 'are less entrenched in their class positions and are more highly motivated, more achievement and more upwardly mobile than working class Anglo-Canadians' (Calliste, 1982: 15).

Employment and Occupational Achievements

After several years of educational preparation, the Class of '73 generally achieved their occupational goals through a combination of their desire to enter particular occupations and their recognition that specific types and levels of education were prerequisites for achieving

Table 6.4. Occupational aspirations in 1973 and occupational achievement by 1979, by parents' birthplace (percentage)

	Aspiration 1973		Occupation 1979	
	Parents' birthplace		Parents' birthplace	
		Outside		Outside
	In Canada	Canada	In Canada	Canada
Occupation	(n = 561)	(n = 139)	(n = 450)	(n = 106)
Managerial, administrative	6.6	5.0	4.7	9.4
Natural sciences, engineering	12.5	15.1	6.9	10.4
Social sciences and related	9.6	7.2	3.6	1.9
Teaching and related occupations	15.3	15.8	3.6	0.9
Medicine and health	16.6	12.9	7.6	10.4
Artistic, literary, and recreational	8.0	8.6	4.0	2.8
Clerical and related occupations	10.7	12.2	30.7	30.2
Sales occupations	1.6	4.3	6.0	6.6
Service occupations	4.5	5.8	3.8	2.8
Farming, horticulture	3.7	4.3	3.3	0.9
Machining and related	0.7	0.7	3.3	2.8
Product fabricating, assembling	3.6	2.9	7.1	10.4
Construction trades	3.2	0.7	6.2	6.6
Transport equipment operating	1.6	2.2	2.7	1.9
Other occupations	1.9	2.1	6.6	1.8
Total	100.0	100.0	100.0	100.0

those ambitions. Specifically, Table 6.4 shows that there was no significant difference between the occupational aspirations of the children of Canadian-born and foreign-born parents. They seemed to expect to achieve – and many did achieve within their early years of work – the occupations to which they aspired. Still, as can be seen in a comparison of 1973 aspirations with 1979 occupations, early career jobs often did not measure up to our students' glorious hopes as expressed in the latter years of high school. Clearly, more students desired managerial and professional occupations in grade 12 than had actually achieved those occupations in 1979.[11] Table 6.4 also shows some differences based on birthplace: the sons and daughters of foreign-born parents began to make greater headway in managerial, science and engineering, and medical occupations compared to Canadian-born youth.

Respondents' 1973 occupational aspirations were likely influenced by their perception of the possibilities in Canadian society, given not only their educational attainments and their parents' financial resources and support, but also their hard work, dedication, and willingness to do what was necessary to get the job. For example, Frank, after graduating from the University of Western Ontario with a degree in teaching, 'applied to forty places as far away as Yukon' in order to get a teaching job. Fortunately, he found one in his home community of Metropolitan Toronto. Tim, who graduated from university with a BA in English, went to Nigeria to work as a teacher; and Ray and Sam, after completing their postsecondary education, went into their families' businesses.

Between 1974 and 1979, when the majority of respondents obtained their first full-time jobs, most of their employment fell into the categories of skilled and unskilled work (see Table 6.5).[12] Still, there was some difference between the starting jobs of young people with Canadian-born parents and the starting jobs of those with foreign-born parents. In both groups, the majority started out modestly in the skilled or unskilled occupational categories; however, the children of foreign-born parents less often began working in the unskilled worker category and more often began at the managerial and professional levels. This difference persisted as the respondents continued on their life course. By 1995 there were significantly fewer sons and daughters of foreign-born parents in unskilled and skilled work, and significantly more in the middle management/semiprofessional and high-level management/professional categories (roughly 5 percentage points difference for each of the four occupational categories); the reverse was true for those employed in skilled and unskilled worker positions.

Comparisons of first occupations and occupations in 1995 suggest there was job betterment for everyone over time, though even more so for the children of foreign-born parents. Changes in occupational positions from unskilled to skilled, and from skilled to managerial or professional, may also have reflected the further education and apprenticeship training that many respondents attained, particularly those with foreign-born parents. It seems that with parental support and through their education, hard work, determination, and 'optimism' (Friendly et al., 1979; James, 1990), many of the respondents managed in the long term to attain the occupations to which they aspired (see Burnstein et al., 1975). Jessica is one example. On leaving high school, she went to university and obtained her qualification in occupational therapy. After working at this for four years, she established a real estate business with her husband. Commenting on her love for the job and how hard they worked, she said that in the first seven months

Table 6.5. Full-time employment in 1974, 1979, and 1995 by parents' birthplace (percentage)

| Year of employment | Parent's birth place | n | Occupation level | | | | | |
			High-level management/ semipro- fessional	Middle management/ semipro- fessional	Skilled workers	Unskilled workers	Agriculture	Total
1974–79	(First full-time job)							
	In Canada	545	6.1	17.2	30.3	43.5	2.9	100.0
	Outside Canada	123	12.2	19.5	30.1	35.0	3.3	100.0
1979	(current job)							
	In Canada	542	9.4	22.0	39.1	26.6	3.0	100.0
	Outside Canada	129	14.0	25.6	34.1	25.6	0.8	100.0
1995	(current/most recent)							
	In Canada	600	20.2	32.3	27.2	18.7	1.7	100.0
	Outside Canada	139	25.2	38.1	22.3	13.7	0.7	100.0

they did not take a day off: 'At two a.m. everyone is sleeping, and we are making money. It took two months of stress, dividing up and taking on different responsibilities ... Once we had sorted that out, everything was fine.'

We have already mentioned that individuals like Kelly, Ray, and Jason were supported by their teachers and counsellors in preparing not only for their future educational paths, but also for what turned out to be the careers they attained. Here, the counsellors and teachers used their 'gatekeeping roles' (Rosenbaum, 1999) to help these students: first, to understand the 'mainstream culture' with which they had to be conversant in order to realize their occupational goals; and second, to gain career focus and become part of an employment network. Recall that for Kelly the career focus was nursing, and for Jason it was engineering. The role played by these school personnel was in keeping with Rosenbaum's contention that 'mainstream' teachers can play an instrumental role in assisting ethnic, linguistic, and racial minority students in their school-to-work transitions. Apprenticeship programs served to place some members of the Class of '73 in employment networks through which they were able to secure skills and employment. As a result of such a program, Geoff became a mechanic and Dom a painter. It is likely that the gendered structure of society and the nature of the advice they received led them to aspire to and eventually attain these occupations.

According to Mortimer and Johnson (1999), part-time jobs provide students with the skills and discipline that later enable them to be successful in employment. Examples are Dom, who worked with his mother in the laundromat business; Ray, who worked with his father in the construction business; and Sonia, Kate, and Kelly, who worked on their parents' farms. They all talked about the impetus these experiences provided in helping them seek occupations that were similar to or better than those of their parents. However, it is worth noting that daughters were not as likely to benefit from some of the part-time job activities as sons. This is related to the fact that females tended to engage in unpaid work in the household.

There is little evidence in our data to suggest that being children of foreign-born parents posed any kind of a handicap for members of the Class of '73.[13] The parents' lack of cultural capital and finances, and of the social networks necessary to access particular areas of employment, seemed not to have affected their employment and the types of jobs they attained compared to their peers with Canadian-born parents. It is possible, as Sonia, Cynthia, Tim, and others suggested, that the social position of their parents inspired them to construct a situation where through their hard work they would be able to attain their occupational goals. Furthermore, contrary to the findings of Kalin (1981), Billingsley and Muszynski (1985), and Henry and Ginzberg (1985), ethnic and linguistic background did not seem to produce discriminatory experiences with regard to respondents' access to and participation in jobs – particularly skilled, management, and professional jobs. None of the respondents told us that their backgrounds had a negative influence on their job search or work experiences. Interestingly, Frank's situation as a South Asian may be an exception to this. According to Frank, he had the necessary qualifications to become a school principal. He had been a department head, a principal of summer school for seven years, and a vice principal for one year, and had 'glowing' evaluations. He also had an MSc. Yet these qualifications were not sufficient to get him the jobs for which he applied. He did not believe that race had prevented him from acquiring any of the administrative positions for which he had applied with his school board. He reasoned that 'appointments aren't made on merit ... I don't think I've been blocked because of my skin colour. I think I've been blocked by a woman and because her point of view [on] math wasn't mine.' It is possible that Frank and other racial and ethnic minority members of the Class of '73 chose not to construct themselves socially in racial or ethnic terms, as a means to avoid the limiting consequences of race and ethnicity.

Given their parents' expectations, their educational attainment, their work ethic, and their occupational opportunities (particularly through family help), coupled with their construction of self, it is understandable that respondents with foreign-born parents would have less difficulty with unemployment. In fact, when asked about their employment history during the period 1978 to 1994, 62.2 per cent of the respondents with foreign-born parents compared to 57.0 per cent of those with Canadian-born parents reported that they had not experienced unemployment. Evidently, there was little difference between the two groups of Canadians. In fact, a 1970s study conducted by Burnstein et al. (1975) on the work ethic showed that young Canadians had a strong willingness to work. They believed that work was very important to their attainment of success in life, and in spite of some difficulties they had experienced in accessing work, they said that they would rather work than be unemployed and receive unemployment benefits (Burnstein et al., 1975: 37–42). It is possible that for young Canadians with immigrant backgrounds, their commitment to work was also related to their immigrant pride. Dom, for example, expressed pride in the fact that when his immigrant parents arrived in Canada, they did not rely on the government for support like today's immigrants, who 'come here, don't do anything, and are given the royal treatment, and expect to work at white-collar jobs.'

As discussed in earlier chapters, the communities in which members of the Class of '73 grew up, and their willingness to relocate, also helped determine their educational and occupational outcomes. Foreign-born families tended to live in urban areas rather than in rural areas and small towns. In fact, in 1973, 45.1 per cent of respondents with Canadian-born parents, but only 23.5 per cent of respondents with foreign-born parents, resided in small towns and rural areas; the corresponding figures for 1995 were 35.6 per cent and 24.8 per cent. In 1973, 13.3 per cent of respondents with Canadian-born parents and 28.9 per cent of respondents with foreign-born parents resided in Metropolitan Toronto; in 1995 the figures were 20.7 per cent and 39.6 per cent respectively.[14] These differences are understandable, since it was in the large cities that foreign-born Canadians in particular were likely to find jobs, and that they could live close to family members and friends, from whom they could receive support as they adjusted to a new society. Jason's family is a good example. Most of his father's 'very best friends from Hungary were living in Toronto,' so that is why his family settled there. 'They could have a class reunion here and have more people attend than if they had it in Budapest.' Jason went on to say that most of his closest friends were also Hungarians, who were the children of his parents' friends.

According to the data, there was a shift in patterns of residence for the Class of '73 toward Metropolitan Toronto and away from rural areas and small towns. Respondents with foreign-born parents veered from this general pattern; they shifted toward Metro Toronto in even greater numbers, but instead of moving out of rural/small town areas, where they were not widely present in 1973, they tended to move away from smaller cities. Respondents with foreign-born parents were 1.2 times more likely than those with Canadian-born parents to stay in the areas in which they grew up. Specifically, 54.0 per cent of respondents with Canadian-born parents compared to 66.4 per cent with foreign-born parents did not change their area of residence between 1973 and 1995. That the children of foreign-born parents tended to be 'stayers' rather than 'movers' (see Chapter 5) may be explained by their reliance on the economic, social, and cultural support of their parents, other family members, and friends. Or it may simply be that they were more able to live and work in urban settings. In any case, being 'stayers' appears to have helped them maintain close family ties, which in some cases led them to the occupational and business endeavours that they pursued. For example, Ray, the accountant of Italian-born parents, worked as a labourer with his father while attending the University of Toronto, and lived with his parents until he got married. He eventually went into business in Toronto with his brother.

Dom grew up in Niagara Falls. After leaving school in grade 12, he worked with his Italian-born mother in a laundromat. Later, he worked for two years at a construction company before attending college, where he received training as a house painter. He eventually obtained a job through his uncle at an electrical company. He left his mother's home when he was 27 (his father died when he was about 16 years old) to marry a woman he met in his uncle's bar 'from the other side' – Niagara Falls, New York. Like Dom, Sam grew up in Niagara Falls and still resides there. On graduating from high school, he received a hockey scholarship to the University of Springfield in the United States. Sam became homesick at university and returned home after his first semester. Later he transferred to the University of Buffalo. In 1995, Sam was managing his father-in-law's hotel in Niagara Falls. He recalled getting his start in the service industry through his mother, with whom he worked in a restaurant when he 'was quite young.' During university, he continued to work part-time in hotels and restaurants. At one of those jobs, he met his wife. For individuals like Dom and Sam, the environment in which they grew up provided opportunities and exposure that proved invaluable for them in realizing their occupational goals.

The Influence of Foreign-Born Parents

The data show that members of the Class of '73 with foreign-born parents tended to do as well as or, in many cases, even better than members with Canadian-born parents. They held similarly high educational and occupational aspirations and expectations, and in most cases proceeded to fulfil their aspirations. They were more likely to obtain postsecondary education and eventually attain somewhat higher

Table 6.6. Comparison of intergenerational socio-economic status by parents'
birthplace (parents in 1973 and respondents in 1995) (percentage)

Parents' birthplace	n	High	Mid-high	Mid-low	Low	Total
		Socio-economic status				
		Parental socio-economic status in 1973				
In Canada	632	27.5	24.7	24.1	23.7	100.0
Outside Canada	149	18.8	22.1	20.1	38.9	100.0
		Respondents' socio-economic status in 1995				
In Canada	632	23.7	25.2	25.3	25.8	100.0
Outside Canada	149	30.9	24.8	23.5	20.8	100.0

levels of occupational status. Hence, it is no surprise that respondents with foreign-born parents tended to have higher incomes. Specifically, our data indicate that in 1994 the median personal income of the children with Canadian-born parents was between $35,000 and $39,999, whereas for children of foreign-born parents the median income was $40,000 to $49,999.[15]

How well did the members of the Class of '73 with foreign-born parents do relative to their parents? Generally, we expected almost all members of the Class of '73 to meet or exceed their parents in terms of educational attainment because of the general rise in educational attainment levels in Canada from the 1950s through the 1960s and into the 1970s, which would likely translate into better jobs and incomes. Our data indeed show intergenerational mobility to be a reality for Class of '73 members. Specifically, in comparing the socio-economic status distributions of the Class of '73 for two points in time, 1973 and 1995 (see Table 6.6),[16] we observed that the children of foreign-born parents began with a socio-economic status disadvantage in 1973, but ended in 1995 better off than their peers with Canadian-born parents.

It is also possible to compare the socio-economic status of parents in 1973 with their children's SES in 1995 – a strategy similar to the mobility comparisons made in Chapter 5. When we do this, we find that for the Canadian-born parents group, 35.6 per cent of children were in the same SES category in 1995 as that of their parents in 1973 (using the four SES categories of high, medium high, medium low, and low); 29.0 per cent had moved into a higher SES category; and 35.4 per cent had moved into a lower SES category. For the foreign-born parents group, 28.9 per cent of children were in the same SES category in 1995 as that of their parents in 1973; 47.7 per cent had moved into a higher SES category; and 23.5 per cent had moved into a lower SES category. These results show a remarkable degree of upward economic mobility for children with foreign-born parents compared to children with Canadian-born parents. Such economic success was especially strong for children with foreign-born parents who were in the lowest SES category in 1973: half this group had arrived in the two highest SES categories by 1995, whereas only one-quarter with children of Canadian-born low-SES parents had moved into the two highest SES categories by 1995.

One useful way to establish upward occupational mobility is to examine the attainment and retention of high-status occupations across generations. We compared respondents' occupations in 1995 with those of their fathers at age 55. This crude measure of intergenerational occupational mobility reveals that children with foreign-born parents were more mobile than their fathers and their peers with Canadian-born parents. Some 43.1 per cent of children with Canadian-born parents whose fathers were unskilled workers were upwardly mobile,[17] but 55.1 per cent of children with foreign-born parents whose fathers were unskilled workers were upwardly mobile. While 47.8 per cent of children with Canadian-born parents whose fathers were skilled workers were upwardly mobile, 68.4 per cent of children with foreign-born parents whose fathers were skilled workers were upwardly mobile. This shows that the children with foreign-born parents of working class background were able to move into white-collar ranks.

Not surprisingly, when we compared the 1995 occupations of male and female respondents with foreign-born parents to the occupations of male and female respondents with Canadian-born parents, as in Table 6.7, we found that male respondents with foreign-born parents tended to do better in terms of professional employment, and tended not to be found in blue-collar jobs. On the other hand, female respondents with foreign-born parents were not much different from their peers with Canadian-born parents, except that they had a somewhat greater presence in the semiprofessional/technical job category. This supports our earlier point: gender operated to influence the extent to which daughters (compared to sons) were encouraged to pursue postsecondary education and professional careers. As Table 6.8 shows, the sons of foreign-born parents (55.7 per cent) were especially encouraged to obtain university education, relative to the sons of Cana-

Table 6.7. Occupational status in 1995 by gender and parents' birthplace (percentage)

| | | | | | | Occupational status in 1995 | | | | | | |
Gender	Parents' birthplace	n	High-level management	Professional	Middle management	Semi-professional/technical	Upper white collar	Upper blue collar	Lower white collar	Lower blue collar	Agricultural	Total
Male	In Canada	294	6.5	12.9	18.0	13.6	9.2	23.8	4.1	9.2	2.7	100.0
	Outside Canada	72	6.9	22.2	20.8	16.7	8.3	15.3	4.2	4.2	1.4	100.0
Female	In Canada	306	4.6	16.3	12.4	20.6	20.3	1.3	19.0	4.9	0.7	100.0
	Outside Canada	67	3.0	17.9	13.4	25.4	19.4	1.5	17.9	1.5	0.0	100.0

Table 6.8. Educational expectations of parents and educational attainment of respondents by gender and parents' birthplace (percentage)

			Highest educational level expected by parents (1974)				
Gender	Parents' birthplace	n	University degree or higher	Community college	High school or less	Other	Total
Male	In Canada	231	44.6	23.8	29.9	1.7	100.0
	Outside Canada	61	55.7	14.8	24.6	4.9	100.0
Female	In Canada	273	40.3	27.1	27.1	5.5	100.0
	Outside Canada	59	40.7	25.4	28.8	5.1	100.0

			Educational level acquired by respondents (1995)				
Gender	Parents' birthplace	n	University degree or higher	College diploma/ certificate	Some college/ university	High school	Total
Male	In Canada	302	31.1	26.5	13.6	28.8	100.0
	Outside Canada	74	37.8	35.1	10.8	16.2	100.0
Female	In Canada	330	33.9	30.9	8.2	27.0	100.0
	Outside Canada	75	41.3	24.0	4.0	30.7	100.0

dian-born parents (44.6 per cent). Consequently, by 1995 the sons of foreign-born parents had achieved substantially more education than the sons of Canadian-born parents at the community college and university levels. Expectations for daughters of foreign-born parents were virtually the same as for the daughters of Canadian-born parents. Respondents reported in 1974 that 40 per cent of parents wanted their daughters to obtain a university degree. While daughters of Canadian-born parents received less university education than reported parental expectations, they more frequently attained a community college education than reported parental expectations. But daughters of foreign-born parents exceeded parental expectations with respect to university education while obtaining community college education in the same proportion as parental expectations.

The differences in the occupational attainment of the children were a reflection of the gender socialization that the parents brought from the 'old country,' but they were also a product of how opportunities

Table 6.9. Employment status in 1995 by gender and parents' birthplace (percentage)

| | | | | | Employment status in 1995 | | | | |
Gender	Parents' birth place	n	Em- ployed	Self- em- ployed	Employed and self em- ployed	Not em- ployed	Likely unem- ployed	Other	Total
Male	In Canada	300	74.7	17.7	1.3	0.3	5.7	0.3	100.0
	Outside Canada	74	75.7	16.2	2.7	0.0	2.7	2.7	100.0
Female	In Canada	329	73.3	9.1	2.4	9.7	4.3	1.2	100.0
	Outside Canada	75	77.3	12.0	4.0	4.0	2.7	0.0	100.0

for men and women were structured in Canada. This could account for the fact that while they all came from immigrant labourer backgrounds, Kelly and Anna became nurses, Kurt became a dentist, and Dom was employed in 1995 as a maintenance worker with an electrical company.

Gender also played a role in how members of the Class of '73 participated in the work force (see Table 6.9). Overall, slightly more than 13.4 per cent of respondents were self-employed. However, men were generally more likely than women to be self-employed. Also, the daughters of foreign-born parents were more likely to be self-employed than the daughters of Canadian-born parents (12.0 per cent compared to 9.1 per cent). Overall, women were half as likely to be unemployed. However, while 14.9 per cent of women with Canadian-born parents were not employed, only 6.7 per cent of women with foreign-born parents fell into that category (most likely being homemakers).

A good example is Jessica, who in 1995 was running a successful real estate business with her husband. In her interview she recalled how she quit her first job as an occupational therapist to set up her 'baking business ... selling muffins and apple strudel' to restaurants. After working with her husband for a real estate company for some years, the two of them left to set up their own firm. That business allowed Jessica to work with her husband. In their first seventeen months they did not take a day off. This exhausted them, but 'it was fun, fun, fun. We were able to buy fancy clothes and dress up.' Her immigrant parents, though initially sceptical of her entrepreneurial endeavours, were later supportive because 'they saw we were making money and were a success from the start.' Self-employment was a means by which respondents ensured that they remained employed; possibly, it was also a mark of success, for both of them and their parents, that they were in control of their own economic situation.

Conclusions

In this chapter we explored the question of how well members of the Class of '73 with foreign-born parents have done in terms of their educational and occupational attainment relative to their peers with Canadian-born parents and to their own parents. With reference to our sample of 149 respondents, our findings show that like their peers with Canadian-born parents, respondents with foreign-born parents tended to hold high occupational aspirations and expectations, which often necessitated the acquisition of high levels of education. Many members of the Class of '73 pursued postsecondary education. This helped situate them to achieve the careers to which they aspired. That there were no significant differences in aspirations and expectations between respondents with foreign-born parents and those with Canadian-born parents suggests that differences based merely on being children of foreign-born parents did not operate as barriers to educational and occupational attainment. Nor did their social situation seem to play a negative or limiting role in their perceptions of their possibilities in Canadian society. Perhaps the 'immigrant drive' or 'minority determination' operated to influence the high aspirations and expectations of respondents with foreign-born parents.

A higher percentage of those with foreign-born parents went on to postsecondary education – in most cases university rather than community college. This likely enabled them to achieve high-status occupations and to earn the salaries they did. This connection between high level of education and high occupational achievement, strongly instilled by their parents, seems to have fuelled respondents' belief in the importance of education as a means of achieving success in Canadian society. This is consistent with a number of research findings, which have shown that immigrant parents tend to believe that education makes occupational success possible. However, while education was generally encouraged, there were different expectations for sons relative to daughters: sons were more likely to be encouraged to get a postsecondary education and were more likely to be financially assisted in doing so.

Schooling seemed to have played an especially significant role in the lives of respondents with foreign-born parents. It provided them with the cultural capital and opportunities for social networking. Besides attending classes, they also participated in extracurricular activities such as computer clubs and sports teams. Through these activities they were able to learn the subtleties of the culture, and to establish important links with educational institutions and significant others that helped them take advantage of educational opportunities.

In contrast to their counterparts with Canadian-born parents, who were more likely to move from urban to rural areas, respondents with foreign-born parents tended to move between urban areas. This is likely a reflection of the cultural, social, and economic realities that newcomers to a country experience. It is in the metropolis that they are likely to find work and to connect with members of their own ethnic communities. Respondents with foreign-born parents used these familial and social connections to obtain job training and eventually to attain their occupational goals.

While there were many similarities between the men and women who participated in this study, there were also some notable gender differences both within and among groups. Specifically, while for the most part both women and men held high educational and occupational aspirations and expectations, their particular aspirations and eventual achievements were influenced by gender. Some of this had to do with the sex role socialization they received not only through society and schooling, but also from their parents. Some women of foreign-born parents reported that while their parents expected them to complete high school, they were not encouraged to pursue post-secondary studies. Nevertheless, many did and managed to attain occupations commensurate with their education. Also significant is that women with foreign-born parents, compared to their counterparts with Canadian-born parents, were much less likely to be unemployed, and were twice as likely to be self-employed.

Generally, members of the Class of '73 with foreign-born parents did very well occupationally, socially, and economically compared to their parents. Although more likely to come from working-class family backgrounds than to their counterparts with Canadian-born parents, the children of foreign-born parents were more likely to take advantage of the educational and occupational opportunities available to them. The school system provided them with educational possibilities; but it was the strong support of their parents – as observed in their hard work in Canada and in the decision to immigrate in the first place – that enabled them to attain their own goals and aspirations, as well as to meet those of their parents. Furthermore, their educational, occupational, and social achievements attest to the accurate readings they and their parents made of structural conditions in Canada, the realism of the aspirations they constructed, and the wisdom of the numerous choices they made in negotiating these conditions. In sum, their attainments reflect the active roles they played over the years in constructing their lives within the changing structural conditions of Canada.

CHAPTER SEVEN

Family Life

During the early 1970s, members of the Class of '73 were in the process of differentiating and separating themselves from their families of origin, yet they were still dependent on their families in important respects. It was a time of transition, the experience of which was mediated by the positions of individual families in social, economic, and geographical space. As King and Elder (1995) note, a central principle of the life course perspective is that of 'linked lives,' through which the values and experiences of different generations are melded in important ways. Thus, the social, economic, and cultural capital that parents of the Class of '73 were able to provide influenced respondents' educational and career choices. Unquestionably, each family's social class, region, ethnicity, race, and gender affected each son's or daughter's life course. Yet these youth, like those in every era, were not mere 'instruments of their families' – or society's – designs. They sought, as well, to play a significant role in shaping their own futures. As we have seen, children from similar family backgrounds often followed strikingly different educational and career paths. Moreover, the Class of '73 lived through, and contributed to, radical changes in how family 'norms' were constructed, as the mainly nuclear-family structure of the 1950s and 1960s (see Chapter 2) gave way to the diverse contemporary arrangements, which by the 1990s included common law, double-income, blended, single-parent, and same-sex parent families (Baker, 1996). As we have suggested throughout this book, both structure and agency mattered in the process through which individuals from the Class of '73 negotiated their way from adolescence to adulthood.

Drawing from survey data collected in three different periods, this chapter examines the dynamic transitions participants made as they moved from their family of origin to their family of destination. The data collected in 1973 and 1979 offer insights into the relationships between parents and children, though in hindsight, during the 1970s we would have asked additional questions designed to elicit richer responses on the dynamics of family life. Using 1995 data, we explore respondents' actual experiences in terms of the intersection between family life, education, and career trajectories, and examine gender relations as they relate to management of the household. In 1995 we also asked respondents how satisfied they were with the course their lives had taken. Finally, as the new millennium approached, we explored the hopes and expectations they possess for their own children.

Family Life in Social Context

As we noted in Chapter 2, the generation that includes the Class of '73 came of age during a period of significant social change. School reforms, the rise of feminism, the unprecedented participation of women in postsecondary education and in the labour force, and the liberalization of divorce laws helped reshape the environment in which family life was conducted. The conventional nuclear family by no means disappeared, but it was augmented throughout the 1980s and 1990s by alternative family forms barely conceivable a generation earlier. For example, the number of couples living common law in Canada nearly doubled to 726,000 between 1981 and 1991, representing in the latter year 12 per cent of the adult population and 23 per cent of those 30 to 54 (La Novara, 1993: 10; Hobart, 1996: 155). Fertility rates dropped, and many women delayed having their first child until their thirties in order to complete their schooling and begin their careers. Indeed, 58.2 per cent of women were in the labour force in 1991 compared to 51.7 per cent in 1981. Single-parent families, mostly headed by women, increased from 11 to 20 per cent of the population between 1961 and 1991. Blended families, which included at least one spouse previously married, constituted 12.3 per cent of families in 1967 and 32.3 per cent in 1991. The divorce rate rose from 6.4 per 100,000 in 1921 to 355.1 in 1987 before leveling off at 280 per 100,000 in 1991 (Baker, 1996).

If family life has changed, so too have the interpretations employed to explain it. Functionalist sociology, which dominated the field in the 1950s and early 1960s, both described and prescribed the 'normal' nuclear family. Premarital sex, homosexuality, divorce, working mothers, and other unconventional practices were considered 'deviant' and bound to impede the effective rearing of children and adolescents (Baker, 1996; Luxton, 1996). Critics, largely emerging from the feminist movement, questioned the ideological and empirical basis of such research. Functionalist family experts were found to be insensitive to class, cultural, and ethnic variations in family life. They justified excluding women from academic and labour force sectors dominated by men, and either denied or demeaned the existence of same-sex relationships. In contrast, scholarly research emerging over the past two decades has sought to explore the changing dynamics of family life, and to expose the impediments to achieving social and gender equality (Mandell and Duffy, 1988). Research topics now include (among many others) the impact of political and economic changes on family life (political economy), power relations within the family (including domestic abuse), gender role socialization in schooling and the family, the unique challenges facing ethnic and visible minorities, and the experience of gay youth and adults. The growing complexity of family experience is also addressed by the life course approach, which studies 'the synchronization of individual transitions with collective family behavior, as well as ... the cumulative effect of earlier transitions on subsequent ones' (Rajulton and Ravanera, 1995: 115).

The characteristics of both the academic literature and the (post) modern family arise from similar roots, which are too complex to explore in detail here. A number of factors, however, have unmistakably affected the way family life is both lived and understood. Canadians are less likely than in the past to defer to the conservative authority of religious institutions and government, and women are now more likely to challenge men's once unquestioned role as 'head of the household' (Adams, 1998). As symbolized by statutes such as the Charter of Rights and Freedoms, and as reflected in federal policies on multiculturalism, both individual and collective (community) rights now comprise an important part of social policy campaigns and agendas. As Baker (1996: 26) notes, the rising incidence of divorce can be explained not only by more liberal laws, but also by 'growing individualism, including the idea that people deserve happier personal relationships.' Also, the typical family now has fewer children, and most women now work outside the home; these factors make divorce more feasible than in the past. Usually with less drastic results than divorce, men and women grapple with the competing demands of employment, economic uncertainty, and childrearing, and with the desire for personal fulfilment. As they entered middle age in the 1990s, members of the Class of '73 conducted family life on a social stage remarkably different from that of their childhoods. Yet as we shall see, not everything had changed, especially with respect to the role of women in the family. And the institution of the family itself, though reformed and redefined, remained a cherished and enduring part of the Canadian landscape.

Family Experiences: The Early Years

In 1973 the vast majority (93.5 per cent) of respondents lived in two-parent families, and most had grown up with at least one other sibling (97.2 per cent). Indeed, slightly over half (53.9 per cent) of the cohort were raised in families with four or more children. Socio-economic status (SES) appears to have been a factor in family size: low-SES respondents were more likely to report that their families had five or more children. We also found a significant relationship between community of origin and family size: respondents from small towns and rural areas were much more likely to report having four or more siblings. One-third of the respondents were first-born children.

Parental encouragement can be an important factor in how offspring identify and plan their life goals. Most members of the Class of '73 reported receiving at least some encouragement from their parents to continue their education after high school. The encouragement that respondents received from their mothers (79.7 per cent) slightly edged out the encouragement they received from their fathers (75.7 per cent). Perhaps not surprisingly, socio-economic status appears to have influenced our cohort's perceptions of parental encouragement. Low-SES respondents (32.3 per cent) were significantly less likely to report that they had been encouraged 'very much' by their mothers, compared to medium-low SES (40.4 per cent), medium-high SES (43.9 per cent), and high SES (43.7 per cent) respondents. The story was the same when we related SES to the level of encouragement respondents felt they had received from their fathers: only 29.3 per cent of low-SES respondents reported that they had been encouraged 'very much' by their fathers, in contrast to medium-low SES (34.1 per cent), medium-high SES (45.2 per cent), and high SES (53.5 per cent) respondents. It is interesting to note that high-SES respondents perceived that they received more encouragement from their fathers than from their mothers.

No significant relationship was found between perceived levels of encouragement (from either parent) and the gender of respondents. It might have been expected that male offspring were more likely to receive encouragement from their parents to pursue their life goals, yet we found no such distinction in our analyses of the survey data. In the interviews, the importance of parental support came through clearly. Sally's comments on her decision to pursue postsecondary education confirm that the women in our study appeared to have received as much encouragement from their parents as did the men – albeit in regard to typically 'female' occupations, such as nursing and library science: 'Neither of my parents went to university, but they really encouraged me to go, and paid for all six years of my university, including residence. I felt really very lucky for their supporting me. And that was typical of my peer group. Certainly all the close friends I had from my small town had a similar kind of experience. In large part, we are what we are today because of the support our parents gave us.'

Parents did not seem to play a significant role in respondents' decision-making processes with respect to their future life choices; however, parents may have been included in the sources of advice and information on which many in the cohort based their decisions. Typically, parental advice was not indicated as the most important reason, or even as another important reason, for going to a college or to university. Grade 12 students bound for community college were more likely to mention 'the kind of program' they could take at a college, and also that college cost less than going to a university. But while most university-bound students indicated that a university education was needed for the types of jobs they wanted, and that they preferred the kinds of programs that universities offered, one-quarter of the respondents did add in 1973 that parental advice to go to university was an additional factor. Coleman and Hendry (1990: 110) have noted that while young people are influenced by their peers throughout high school, 'parents are valued for their nurturance and counsel.' While parental influence with respect to further education and occupations may not alone have determined the course taken by respondents, parental advice undoubtedly mattered in families with good levels of communication between parents and children. As one respondent explained in the 1970s, 'I ask dad to help me make decisions and I consult with my friends. Then I make the decision on my own, and I'm willing to take the consequences' (Anisef, Paasche, and Turrittin, 1980: 313).

Whether or not grade 12 students took their parents' views into account on the importance of further education, they were aware that they would need family help in financing postsecondary education. When asked in the spring of 1973 about potential sources of funding for further education, 43.4 per cent of respondents indicated that their parents were the most important source, and 24.1 per cent said that parents were the second most important source. Next most important sources were savings from summer work (22.0 per cent), followed by government loans and grants (15.5 per cent) and personal savings (11.5 per cent). Not surprisingly, respondents from high-SES backgrounds were significantly more likely to report that their parents were the most important source of financial support. Women (49.1 per cent) were somewhat more likely than men (37.2 per cent) to report that their parents were their most important financial source. We also noted a significant relationship between community of origin and financial support. Respondents in Metropolitan Toronto (40.0 per cent), and small town and rural area respondents (38.9 per cent), reported a similar dependence on their parents as their most important source of financial support for further education. But in Metro Toronto, only 5.0 per cent listed government grants and loans as their most important source, whereas respondents from small town and rural areas listed this source in 29.1 per cent of cases. Summer job savings were the most important source for 28.8 per cent of Metro Toronto respondents and for 15.3 per cent of small town and rural respondents. These differences may be attributed to differences in occupational structures and economic opportunities between rural and urban areas. As was indicated in Chapter 4, parents living in rural areas had fewer financial resources to support their children's higher education, and faced higher costs to send their children to distant universities. As a consequence, substantially fewer respondents living in rural areas and small towns relied on their parents to finance their postsecondary education.

The financial dependency on parents for further education that had been anticipated in the grade 12 survey was borne out by the results of the fall 1974 follow-up survey. When respondents were asked about their actual major source of funding for their first or second year of schooling, over one-third (36.8 per cent) indicated that their parents were their main source of financial support – down somewhat from expectations in Phase I. Savings from work were the most important source mentioned in 38.7 per cent of cases – a substantial increase over Phase I – while 12.0 per cent reported government loans and grants as the most important source of funding. Women were still much more dependent on family support than men. Also, SES and community of origin continued to affect the pattern of funding sources. High-SES respondents were twice as dependent on parents for financial support, relative to respondents from the low-SES category (52.3 per cent versus 23.9 per cent), with respondents from the latter category relying much more heavily on government loans and grants (26.7 per cent versus 1.5 per cent for the high-SES group). One-third of both SES groups relied on savings from work. With regard to major sources of educational funding, there were significant differences between Metro Toronto residents and those from small towns and rural areas: reliance on parents was 43.5 versus 36.6 per cent respectively; reliance on government loans and grants was 2.9 versus 24.1 per cent respectively; and reliance on savings from work was 40.6 versus 29.5 per cent respectively. Family ties, at least with respect to material support, remained important to members of the Class of '73 as they pursued higher education.

When we asked respondents to rate their personal values in 1973 (Table 7.2), 56.5 per cent said that family (husband or wife, and children) was 'very important.' However, taking into account their age in the life course, it is not surprising that respondents placed an even higher value on 'developing friendships,' with over 71.2 per cent rating friendships as 'very important.' Women were somewhat more likely than men to attach importance to family. It should also be noted that urban living did not appear to diminish the importance attached to family. In fact, we found that those from Metropolitan Toronto were significantly *more* likely to report that family was important to them. We did not identify any differences in attitudes toward family that could be attributed to the SES of origin of our respondents.

In our Phase III survey in the fall of 1974, a small proportion of the sample (6.5 per cent) reported that they were now married. The vast majority of these respondents were women (Table 7.1). While we did not detect any differences attributable to residence, there was a weak

Table 7.1. Marital status in 1974, 1979, 1987–88, and 1995 (percentage)

Marital status	1974: Phase III		1979: Phase IV		1987/88: Phase V		1995: Phase VI	
	Male ($n = 354$)	Female ($n = 381$)	Male ($n = 375$)	Female ($n = 400$)	Male ($n = 342$)	Female ($n = 376$)	Male ($n = 381$)	Female ($n = 407$)
Single	97.5	89.5	52.0	38.8	17.8	14.6	8.1	8.1
Married	2.5	10.2	34.7	46.8	78.1	78.2	75.9	78.6
Living with partner or companion			4.5	5.3	1.5	1.9	8.1	4.7
Engaged			8.0	6.8	0.0	0.3		
Separated	0.0	0.3	0.5	1.5	2.3	1.6	3.7	3.4
Divorced			0.3	1.0	0.3	2.4	3.9	4.7
Widowed					0.0	1.1	0.3	0.5
Total	100.0	100.0	100.0	100.0	100.0	100.0	100.0	100.0

Table 7.2. Personal values in 1973, 1979, and 1995 (percentage)

	1973: Phase I			1979: Phase IV			1995: Phase VI		
	(n)	Very important	Somewhat important	(n)	Very important	Somewhat important	(n)	Very important	Somewhat important
Personal values									
1. Developing friendships	(782)	71.2	21.9	(769)	54.9	31.3	(787)	44.1	42.9
2. Involvement in work or a career	(782)	47.2	39.8	(769)	39.0	38.6	(784)	40.4	44.9
3. Family (husband, wife, and children)	(773)	56.5	20.3						
4. Marriage				(768)	46.2	17.8	(780)	70.6	12.9
5. Involvement in community affairs	(775)	9.5	32.8	(767)	6.0	13.2	(782)	6.0	38.4
6. Living with companion or partner				(749)	25.5	14.6	(724)	49.3	19.8
7. Involvement in leisure activities	(780)	33.3	44.7	(768)	41.5	37.6	(780)	22.4	56.5
8. Developing an independent lifestyle	(777)	37.6	31.0	(765)	40.7	29.8	(780)	29.1	40.5
9. Having enough money to live well							(785)	36.7	52.9
10. Your parents							(772)	68.9	24.7
11. Children							(777)	78.9	7.3
12. Health							(786)	70.0	25.8
13. Religion							(784)	18.4	24.4

relationship between SES and marital status. Those from medium-low and low SES backgrounds were somewhat more likely to report being married (10.1 per cent and 8.2 per cent respectively), compared to medium-high SES (4.4 per cent) and high SES (3.6 per cent) respondents.

One additional aspect of family life merits comment. Two respondents, one gay and one lesbian, reported in 1995 that when they were growing up, their families did not acknowledge their children's homosexuality. Alex attributed his difficulties in school to his fear of being 'discovered,' and Rebecca explained her truancy and drug addiction as partially related to her confusion with her gender identity. That Alex never told his surviving parent he was gay, and that Rebecca's mother seemed more willing to deal with and acknowledge her daughter's drug addiction than her lesbianism, underscored the particular challenges these individuals faced as they made the transition to adulthood.

In sum, family as a social institution held considerable importance for members of the Class of '73. Most reported being encouraged by their parents to pursue their life goals; and for some members of our cohort, parents' advice and counsel with regard to life goals played an important role even after high school. Financial dependence on one's parents was pervasive through the first three survey points of the project.

Leaving the Childhood Family: Developing Independence

By 1979 the vast majority of members of the Class of '73 had left their families of origin and were charting their own life courses. While patterns can certainly be detected in the paths their lives took, their actual trajectories were not entirely linear. Respondents experienced detours, backtracking, dead-ends, gaps, and leaps. In social and cultural terms, their lives featured both continuity with the previous generation, and significant change reflecting the tenor of the times.

By 1979, 40.9 per cent of respondents were married, 7.4 per cent were engaged, and another 4.9 per cent were living with a companion or partner (see Table 7.1). Another 1.6 per cent had been married but were now separated or divorced. Men had begun to close the marriage gap: one-third of the men reported being married, compared to almost half the women. Still, 45.2 per cent of respondents were single at the time of the 1979 follow-up survey. For many, marriage was still an important option for their future. When interviewed in 1979, Laura, who was employed as a secretary, did not plan to get married for another four or five years. She enjoyed being on her own and was 'not ready to settle down.' For her, being 'ready to get married' meant having a personally acceptable level of financial security, accepting responsibilities, and making certain that her prospective partner had a steady job. She stated, 'I don't want to get married yet ... maybe sometime. Everyone says I'd be a good mother. I'd only want a couple of children. My husband would at least have to have a job. I don't care what kind, just something steady' (Anisef, Paasche, and Turrittin, 1980: 302).

While not quite 50 per cent of respondents were married, almost half (46.2 per cent) reported that marriage was 'very important' to them (Table 7.2). In our 1979 survey we repeated (in a somewhat altered form) the personal values question we first employed in 1973, and the results were almost identical to those in 1973. Thus, in 1979, 54.9 per cent of respondents indicated 'developing friendships' was very important to them, and 39.0 per cent reported 'involvement in work or a career' as very important. Women in our 1979 cohort attached more importance to marriage than men, as was the case in 1973. We did not identify any differences in attitudes toward marriage that could be attributed to socio-economic status; however, a difference in attitudes toward marriage by region of origin was noted in 1979, with 54.0 per cent of small town and rural respondents indicating that marriage was very important to them compared to 38.6 per cent of respondents in Metro Toronto.

'Living with a companion' – a new personal-value item added in 1979 – was deemed 'very important' by 25.5 per cent of respondents, though as already noted, only about 5 per cent of our respondents indicated that they were living with a companion or partner in 1979.

Thus, independent living, marriage, or companionate relationships were reflected in either the realities or the plans of Class of '73 members by 1980. By age 23, virtually all respondents were no longer living with their parents. Yet fully one-quarter returned to the family home at some point. Most did so between 1975 and 1981. Indeed, 3 per cent were living with their parents in 1993. As recent studies have indicated, financial need is the most common factor behind such 'returns home,' and this in all likelihood was true of a certain portion of the Class of '73 (Mitchell and Gee, 1996). As reported in 1995, women, those with high-SES origins and those from Metropolitan Toronto were somewhat more likely to return home to live with parents.

Coming Full Circle: Marriage, Family, and Domestic Obligations

Table 7.1 shows the marital status of the Class of '73 members at successive points in time beginning with our Phase III survey in 1974. The 1979 data caught respondents at a point in life when most had completed their education. As mentioned earlier, 40.9 per cent of respondents were married, following the conventional path of women marrying at a somewhat earlier age than men. By 1987–88, the proportion married had topped out at 78 per cent. A few were divorced, separated, or widowed, and 16.1 per cent were single. By 1995, the proportion of married respondents had dropped slightly to 77.3 per cent; 6.3 per cent were living with companion or partner, and 8.1 per cent were single. A separate question, 'Who currently lives in your household?' shed some light on living arrangements by 1995. Nearly 7 per cent were living in an extended family (with a parent, sibling, or other relative), and 4 per cent were heading a single-parent family (with 20 of the 28 cases being female-headed). The number of divorced and separated combined stood at 7.9 per cent, and 7.5 per cent of respondents were in a second or third marriage. Those with more education were more likely than those with less education to remarry. Also, 9 in 10 respondents who were married had children, as did 4 in 10 who were living with a companion or who were divorced, and as did 6 in 10 of separated persons. In total, 71.2 per cent of respondents reported living with a spouse or partner and children.

Participants seemed to attach greater importance to marriage as an institution in 1995 than in 1979 (Table 7.2). While married people overwhelmingly rated marriage as important in their lives, one-third of persons living with a companion and one-quarter of single persons rated marriage as very or somewhat important. Also, marriage was still rated as very or somewhat important by 46 per cent of separated and divorced persons. No differences in the level of importance attached to marriage could be attributed to gender or SES. Parents, children, and health were also viewed as personally very important. Respondents whose residence of origin was a smaller city or small town or rural area were somewhat more likely to attach importance to having children. We return to the question of personal values at the end of the chapter.

Our study examined the issue of responsibility for carrying out household tasks, and found that women still bore the brunt of these duties, including looking after the children, cooking meals, cleaning up the kitchen, and shopping for groceries (Table 7.3). Women reported that they were usually more responsible than men for cleaning the house, grocery shopping and doing laundry, while men reported that they tended to do the small repairs around the house. Approximately equal numbers of male and female respondents (less than 30 per cent) reported that they shared equally the responsibility of looking after household finances, while proportionately more women (21.0 per cent) than men (11.0 per cent) reported that they were exclusively responsible. Consistent with this finding, 25.4 per cent of men told us that their wives were mainly responsible for household finances. In contrast, only 16.2 per cent of female respondents claimed that their spouses were mostly responsible.

There were significant gender differences with regard to child care and childrearing, as reported in Table 7.4. Women reported (and their spouses agreed) that they were mainly responsible for dealing with children when they got sick, for locating a babysitter, and for buying clothes for the kids. Discipline, supervision, education, and job planning were shared equally between spouses. While some men were involved in transporting children to activities, helping with homework, and talking about sexual matters, women tended to shoulder the major responsibility for these activities. A number of parents reported that providing education and job planning, talking about sexual matters, and helping with homework did not occur in their households.

There were some modest differences by SES in 1995 regarding responsibilities for household tasks and childrearing. Men in lower-SES categories tended to more often share cooking duties and grocery shopping with their spouses than did men in high-SES categories. Lower-SES women were likely to do their own shopping and house cleaning than high-SES women. More lower-SES women looked after their household finances than did high-SES women. There was more sharing of house cleaning and looking after finances as one moved up the SES ladder, and a tendency for men to increase their involvement in household finances as SES increased. A greater proportion of lower-

Table 7.3. Sharing household responsibilities between married persons or persons living with companions, 1995 (percentage)

Household Tasks

	Cooking meals		Cleaning up kitchen		Grocery shopping		House cleaning	
	Male (n = 318)	Female (n = 336)	Male (n = 318)	Female (n = 339)	Male (n = 319)	Female (n = 339)	Male (n = 319)	Female (n = 338)
Response category								
Only you	0.6	13.4	0.0	10.6	2.2	28.3	0.6	13.9
Mostly you	6.3	58.0	7.5	49.0	9.1	39.8	6.6	51.2
Shared equally	21.1	20.2	38.7	33.3	26.6	18.6	33.5	25.4
Mostly spouse	61.6	6.5	48.7	4.7	43.3	12.1	49.2	1.5
Only spouse	9.4	0.6	3.1	0.3	18.8	0.9	7.2	0.0
Mostly other	0.6	0.9	1.9	2.1	0.0	0.3	2.8	8.0
Total	100.0	100.0	100.0	100.0	100.0	100.0	100.0	100.0

Household Tasks

Response category	Laundry		Looking after household finances		Small repairs		Making important family decisions	
	Male (n = 317)	Female (n = 337)	Male (n = 319)	Female (n = 334)	Male (n = 320)	Female (n = 337)	Male (n = 319)	Female (n = 339)
Only you	0.9	40.7	11.0	21.0	32.2	1.8	0.9	0.3
Mostly you	2.5	37.1	25.7	27.2	56.3	6.2	6.3	4.1
Shared equally	20.8	18.7	29.2	26.9	9.1	15.1	91.5	93.2
Mostly spouse	48.3	1.8	25.4	16.2	1.6	55.2	0.9	2.1
Only spouse	26.2	0.0	8.8	8.4	0.3	18.7	0.3	0.3
Mostly other	1.3	1.8	0.0	0.3	0.6	2.7	0.0	0.0
Total	100.0	100.0	100.0	100.0	100.0	100.0	100.0	100.0

Question: Who usually does these household tasks? 1) Cooking meals; 2) Cleaning up kitchen; 3) Grocery shopping;
4) House cleaning; 5) Laundry; 6) Looking after household finances; 7) Small repairs; and 8) Making important family decisions.

Table 7.4. Division of responsibility for raising children for persons indicating that they are married or living with a companion/partner, with children present, 1995 (percentage)

Response category	Aspects of child-raising responsibility							
	Dealing with sickness		Finding a babysitter		Buying clothes		Transportation to activities	
	Male (n = 267)	Female (n = 287)	Male (n = 265)	Female (n = 288)	Male (n = 267)	Female (n = 289)	Male (n = 268)	Female (n = 289)
Only you	0.0	11.1	0.4	34.7	0.4	49.1	1.1	3.8
Mostly you	3.0	61.0	1.9	46.5	1.9	44.3	12.3	34.9
Shared equally	36.3	27.5	21.5	14.2	12.0	6.2	64.2	52.6
Mostly spouse	58.4	0.3	60.8	1.0	64.8	0.0	21.6	7.3
Only spouse	2.2	0.0	12.8	0.0	20.6	0.0	0.7	0.7
Mostly other	0.0	0.0	0.0	0.0	0.0	0.0	0.0	0.7
Does not occur	0.0	0.0	2.6	3.5	0.4	0.3	0.0	0.0
Total	100.0	100.0	100.0	100.0	100.0	100.0	100.0	100.0

Aspects of child-raising responsibility

Response category	Discipline		Supervision		Helping with homework		Education and job planning		Talking about sexual matters	
	Male ($n = 266$)	Female ($n = 289$)	Male ($n = 267$)	Female ($n = 288$)	Male ($n = 263$)	Female ($n = 288$)	Male ($n = 263$)	Female ($n = 287$)	Male ($n = 261$)	Female ($n = 286$)
Only you	0.0	1.4	0.0	1.7	0.4	6.9	0.4	3.5	0.0	10.1
Mostly you	13.5	22.8	3.4	34.7	9.5	37.5	3.8	20.6	5.0	34.6
Shared equally	80.5	73.7	74.3	61.8	50.2	46.9	68.8	60.6	51.7	42.3
Mostly spouse	6.0	1.7	22.0	1.4	30.8	4.5	14.1	1.0	23.8	3.5
Only spouse	0.0	0.0	0.0	0.0	0.4	0.0	0.4	0.3	2.7	0.3
Mostly other	0.0	0.0	0.4	0.3	0.8	0.0	0.4	0.7	1.1	0.3
Does not occur	0.0	0.3	0.0	0.0	8.0	4.5	12.2	13.2	15.7	8.7
Total	100.0	100.0	100.0	100.0	100.0	100.0	100.0	100.0	100.0	100.0

Question: In your household, who usually is/was responsible for the following child-raising issues? 1) Dealing with sickness; 2) Finding a babysitter or arranging child care if needed; 3) Buying clothing; 4) Discipline; 5) Supervision; 6) Providing transportation to activities; 7) Helping with homework; 8) Education and job planning; and 9) Talking about sexual matters.

SES men reported sharing responsibility for explaining sexuality to their children; high-SES men often reported that this subject did not arise in their household. Lower-SES women reported more often being solely or mostly responsible for dealing with sickness, and with the education and job planning of their children.

Interviews with respondents supported many of these findings. Laura had stated in 1979 that she was not ready for marriage. When we revisited her in 1995, we discovered that she was married and living in suburban Toronto, and the mother of three sons aged 9, 8, and 3. After her second child was born, Laura had switched to occasional relief work from the full-time secretarial position she held at a utility company. When her employer laid off its part-time staff, she was forced to register with a temporary employment agency. She found travelling to downtown Toronto and looking after three children very stressful and decided to stay home full-time. Laura was very involved in her children's school and sports activities. Although she found having primary responsibility for childrearing difficult at times, she also derived considerable satisfaction from it. She described herself as 'Ms Chauffeur,' telling us that 'it seems much busier now that they [her sons] are in activities. But I like it. I enjoy it.'

At the time of her interview, Angela was living in a small suburban community south of Vancouver and was the mother of two boys aged 4 and 6, and a girl age 10. Expressing views similar to Laura's, she told us she considered herself fortunate that she and her husband could afford for her to be at home while the children were young. She commented that 'not everyone has that luxury. I'm really excited to be there when they come home from school. They tell me about their day. I help out in school.' And even though she spent so much time chauffeuring her children to various activities, she claimed that 'I wouldn't have it any other way.' Gary, her husband, viewed their children as 'quite entertaining.' He added that 'it's been quite amusing. People say your life ends when you have kids and to a certain degree it may be true that you lose one end of your social life, but on the other end, it's entertaining as the dickens to go out and watch them do some of these activities.' Similarly, Nancy, a veterinarian who worked part-time, stated that she was 'the primary caregiver' in her family because her husband's job was sporadic and he didn't have the patience she had with children. Gary, Angela's husband, claimed to 'do whatever needs to be done around the house' except for cooking. He wanted to show his children that 'it doesn't matter who does what as long as it gets done by somebody.'

Grant described the division of labour around his household as 'kind of the old ways of the fifties and sixties, and it works for us. My wife likes to cook and sew. She likes to do those things. She's good at them. She doesn't like doing construction type things and I do.' Jennifer, a middle manager at a bank, shared household and childrearing responsibilities equally with her husband. She found it difficult to manage the time she and her husband had to do all the chores and activities demanded of them: getting her two daughters to sports activities, school, and daycare required considerable co-ordination.

The discussion of sharing household tasks reflects the high proportion of respondents in dual-income families (71.0 per cent of respondents with spouses or companions/partners reported that the spouse or partner worked full-time, and 15.1 per cent reported that the spouse or partner worked part-time). However, female respondents were the most likely to adapt their occupations to their family responsibilities, entering occupations that have long been associated with women, such as nursing, teaching, and clerical/secretarial work. And as we have already noted, the women of the Class of '73 were more likely to have married in their early twenties than the men. However, it is also true that many did not marry until their later twenties, and certainly most waited to have children until they had a number of years in the labour force under their belts. Finally, unlike their parents, very few had more than three children – most had two.

To what extent were these decisions responses by women to their commitment to work and career, and to what extent were they responses to the realities of their situation? With the birth of the second child, women typically made compromises with respect to the work setting and their place in it, even when they continued to work full-time. This of course must be taken in the larger context of women's situation in the labour market, particularly with respect to their earning capacity. Given these practical matters, family decisions to accommodate the careers of men before those of women could be seen as rational and of economic benefit to the household. It should be noted, however, that having no children – or at most one child – would have proved more beneficial from both a financial and career standpoint. Thus, the commitment of the Class of '73 women to have and raise children seems to have been motivated largely by nonfinancial motives.

Personal income data for 1994 revealed that the most frequently reported income categories were $40,000 to $49,999 and $50,000 to $59,999 (15.4 and 14.3 per cent respectively of the Class of '73). Some

9.5 per cent earned $80,000 or more, while 10.8 per cent earned below $10,000. Those with no income comprised 2.6 per cent of respondents. The growing incidence of double-income households was indicated by the level of respondents' family incomes. Less than 1 per cent of families had no income, and only 2.4 per cent garnered less than $10,000. Some 35.8 per cent had household incomes between $50,000 to $79,999, and 21.4 per cent reported household incomes of more than $100,000. Of those who reported not being employed in 1995 (80 out of 786 cases), 45 per cent attributed this situation to family obligations (these were all women except for one male), 18.8 per cent gave a health or disability reason for not being employed, and 25 per cent gave a reason related to the job market. Notably, women were three times more likely than men to be employed part-time (28 per cent versus 8 per cent).

Even when women worked full-time, it was difficult for them to earn as much as their husbands because they were so often restricted to lower-status and/or lower-paying positions (see Chapter 4). In general, the experience of the Class of '73 reflected that of the population as a whole: family life, conducted in more diverse forms than in the past, remained central to the respondents' existence. Women found more outlets than ever outside the home, but continued to shoulder the burden of household responsibilities whether they were employed or not. Men contributed more than ever to domestic duties, but scarcely on equal terms with women. And women, often in creative ways, and often with a deep sense of frustration, strove to manage and reconcile the competing demands of employment, childrearing, and other household tasks (Vistnes, 1997; Baker and Lero, 1996; Luxton, 1992). The poorest among them faced the most daunting challenges of all.

Children's Futures – Parents' Views

The expectations that Class of '73 members held for their children's academic achievement were much higher than the expectations their own parents held for them. Tables 7.5 and 7.6 compare respondents' educational expectations for their children with their own parents' educational expectations. In 1974, respondents were asked about the 'highest level of formal education your parents expect you to attain.' As Table 7.5 indicates, almost 28 per cent of respondents believed that their parents expected them to complete high school or less, 25 per cent expected them to complete community college, and 43 per cent expected a university degree or higher. While there were no gender

Table 7.5. Parental educational expectations for members of the Class of '73 by parental socio-economic status, 1974 (percentage)

	(n)	High school or less	Community college	BA	MA	PhD	Other	Total
			Highest educational level expected by parents					
Parental socio-economic status*								
High	166	7.2	13.9	63.9	5.4	4.2	5.4	100.0
Medium-high	153	26.1	26.8	37.3	4.6	0.0	5.2	100.0
Medium-low	146	37.7	28.8	26.7	2.1	0.7	4.1	100.0
Low	166	41.6	31.3	23.5	1.8	0.6	1.2	100.0
All respondents	631	27.9	25.0	38.2	3.5	1.4	4.0	100.0

* Respondents' parental socio-economic status as of 1973

differences in perceived parental educational expectations, there were marked differences with respect to parental socio-economic status.

In our 1995 survey we asked our study participants to reflect on the level of education they would most like their children to achieve, focusing on their oldest child. Parental aspirations were very high in 1995 (Table 7.6). Less than 2 per cent of respondents reported that they wanted their oldest child to complete high school only, and only 15 per cent wanted them to obtain a community college diploma, whereas 39 per cent emphasized a university degree or higher, and another 39 per cent mentioned a professional degree. For example, Angela indicated that she hoped her three children would go to university and that she would be disappointed if they elected not to go. However, she also stated that she would accept their decision not to attend university if they had a clear idea of what they wanted to do. Moreover, if any of her children turned out not to be 'academically minded,' she would encourage them to go to a community college.

We also found a strong commitment to postsecondary education among single-parent families. By way of illustration, Joan's husband left her when her son was born, and she was struggling to make ends meet, working for low pay as a bookkeeper in a strip club. Though beset with financial problems, she had started a scholarship fund for her son, age 4. She expected him to complete high school and claimed that 'it would be nice if he wanted to become a professional.' Joan wanted her son to attend college or university, but at the same time she wanted him to do whatever would make him happy. Debbie, a

Table 7.6. Respondents' educational aspirations and expectations in 1995 for their oldest child by socio-economic status (percentage)

Highest educational aspirations and expectations for oldest child

	(n)	High school or less	Technical diploma	Trade certificate	Community college	BA	MA	PhD	Professional degree	Total
Socio-economic status*										
High										
Aspiration	142	0.7	0.0	1.4	9.2	26.8	18.3	4.9	38.7	100.0
Expectation	142	2.8	0.7	2.1	13.4	40.8	15.5	1.4	23.2	100.0
Medium-high										
Aspiration	154	0.6	1.3	4.5	12.3	24.7	10.4	2.6	43.5	100.0
Expectation	153	9.9	2.0	4.6	23.5	38.6	5.9	0.7	15.0	100.0
Medium-low										
Aspiration	151	2.0	1.3	6.0	20.5	15.9	13.2	3.3	37.7	100.0
Expectation	151	12.6	2.6	4.0	25.8	33.1	6.6	2.0	13.2	100.0
Low										
Aspiration	166	2.4	1.2	4.8	17.5	23.5	11.4	1.8	37.3	100.0
Expectation	165	7.3	3.0	5.5	29.7	33.9	8.5	1.2	10.9	100.0
All respondents										
Aspiration	613	1.5	1.0	4.2	15.0	22.7	13.2	3.1	39.3	100.0
Expectation	611	8.2	2.1	4.1	23.4	36.5	9.0	1.3	15.4	100.0

* Respondents' socio-economic status as of 1995

single parent living in Ottawa, explained that her parents never encouraged her to go to college, so she didn't. 'But I'm not going to let that happen to my children. I know they're going to have to have a degree to get a decent job, and that's what I'm telling them.'

While there was a relatively strong correlation between respondents' aspirations for their children's education and what they realistically expected their children to attain, it was clear that expectations were somewhat lower than aspirations. Table 7.6 compares the educational aspirations that parents held in 1995 for their oldest child with their actual expectations. Whereas nearly 8 in 10 respondents wanted their children to achieve a university degree or higher, only 6 in 10 expected that their children would graduate with some type of university degree.

Few respondents expected their oldest child to earn only a high school diploma (8.2 per cent); 23.4 per cent expected their oldest child to obtain a community college certificate or diploma. Close to half of respondents (46.8 per cent) expected their oldest child to obtain a university degree or higher, and 15.4 per cent expected a professional degree. For example, Trevor, who left high school one credit short of obtaining his grade 13 diploma, was quite adamant that his son would eventually go to university. 'My son is two years old. And the best that I can tell you is I've got a nice little fund set aside and he's going to university. That's how I feel. He's got a long way to go, but I'm thinking ahead right now. He's going to go. He may not like it, but he's going to go.' Many respondents believed that in a poor employment market, a university education would provide their children with better opportunities. Julia stated, 'In all likelihood I'll pressure my kids to go to university because with the initials after their name, it might give them the edge and I don't want to take the chance that it won't.'

While there were no differences in educational expectations between Class of '73 mothers and fathers, there were significant differences relating to socio-economic status, using our 1995 measure of SES (see Table 7.6). The two lower-SES groups were more likely to expect their children to obtain a community college education (about one-third of these respondents); the two higher-SES groups were more likely to expect a university degree or a professional degree (over three-quarters of these respondents). However, some university-educated respondents believed that a community college education would serve their children better. For example, Rachel, an unemployed librarian with five children, claimed that she was no longer as positive about a university education, even though both she and her husband held university degrees. 'I don't think I'll push my kids to go to university,' she stated. 'I would rather encourage them to go to a community college and get some kind of practical education and then they can get a steady job, if there is such a thing in the future.' Kelly, on the other hand, felt that 'we encourage kids to go to school for too long. I don't see the point of so much education when there are no guarantees for jobs after it. College educated kids are working in factories. I think it's crazy.' Several respondents concurred with her.

Respondents' expectations for their children's education seemed to arise from their own educational experiences and attainment, their experience with and perceptions of the job market in 1995, and, most significantly, their satisfaction with the quality of education their children were receiving. Martin, a civil engineer living in a small town in midwestern Ontario, claimed that he was very pleased with the education his three boys (ages 11, 9, and 7) were receiving. His children enjoyed going to school, and he credited their teachers with motivating them to learn. Martin stated that he would like 'all doors to be left open to them' with respect to their education. As a university-educated engineer, he leaned toward his children pursuing a university education, but he also felt that opportunities for entering university were no longer the same: 'The standards are much higher and the pressure to achieve is enormous. There are Ontario scholars [students with graduating averages of at least 80 per cent] who can't get into university engineering programs and are going to community colleges.' Close to 7 out of 10 participants reported that they were at least somewhat satisfied with the quality of their children's education. However, we found no statistical relationship between what people expected their children to achieve educationally and their level of satisfaction with the education their children were presently receiving.

Several respondents expressed concern that the education system no longer offered the same benefits as they had enjoyed in the 1960s and early 1970s. One respondent made the following comment:

What the educational system offered us in the sixties, for better or worse, may not be available to future generations of children, or immigrants whose first language is not English. Increases in class sizes, combined with the disillusionment of teachers (not all), threaten the link students should have with their schools. My concern is that a lot of these young people will lose their love of learning from sheer frustration because the school system has changed since then. Some schools are run administratively better than others. Taking into account provincial budget cuts, student needs such as ESL, learning disabilities, students at risk from violent homes, and so on, where are the schools going?

Another respondent stated:

I think my generation has more and different fears for our children than our parents' generation had for us. I hope to see a greater emphasis placed on educational programs and elsewhere to build self-esteem and teach problem solving and conflict resolution. Any information needed at any time can be gained once good research skills are acquired, but effective and rewarding relationship-building skills need practice and support as well as specific instruction. Creative thinking and mutual respect need to be future cornerstones, in my view, for future directions in education.

Reflections on Life Satisfaction

Members of the Class of '73 were asked to reflect on a number of life issues. Clearly, many of the quality-of-life factors that provide meaning and satisfaction in contemporary times are different from the past (Michalos, 1980). With respect to personal values, in both 1979 and 1995 we asked respondents to indicate which value gave them the most satisfaction in life and which the least satisfaction. In 1979 (see Table 7.7), marriage, developing friendships, and work and career most often gave the most satisfaction. Involvement in community affairs was most often listed as providing the least satisfaction, followed by living with a companion or partner, and marriage. We suspect that the rejection of involvement in community affairs is the rejection of politics. Cross-tabulation found that those for whom marriage was least satisfying selected as giving most satisfaction developing friendships, or work and career, or an independent lifestyle. Also, those who found living with a companion or partner least satisfying selected developing friendships, or work and career, or marriage as giving the most satisfaction.

By 1995, children and marriage were overwhelmingly chosen as providing the most satisfaction with life, with work and career receiving only modest acknowledgement. Religion, involvement in commu-

Table 7.7. Personal values that give most satisfaction and least satisfaction, as reported in 1979 and 1995 (percentage)

Personal Values	1979: Phase IV		1995: Phase VI	
	Presently gives you most satisfaction ($n = 761$)	Presently gives you least satisfaction ($n = 745$)	Presently gives you most satisfaction ($n = 771$)	Presently gives you least satisfaction ($n = 768$)
1. Developing friendships	19.7	1.3	6.0	2.0
2. Involvement in work or a career	18.5	8.7	7.7	7.3
3. Marriage	29.2	12.9	25.0	5.2
4. Involvement in community affairs	0.7	46.6	0.3	21.5
5. Living with companion or partner	5.9	16.0	5.4	5.6
6. Involvement in leisure time activities	11.7	4.6	3.5	9.2
7. Developing an independent life style	10.6	9.5	3.2	7.9
8. Having enough money to live well			2.3	5.2
9. Your parents			1.6	1.8
10. Children			34.5	2.2
11. Health			1.7	2.0
12. Religion			3.8	30.1
13. Other	3.7	0.4		
14. Marriage and children (both #3 and #10 marked)			5.1	0.0

Note: To some degree, the reductions in percentages with respect to the personal value that gave respondents the greatest or least 'satisfaction in life' in 1995 (questionnaire items #2 and #3), compared to the similar question asked in 1979 (questionnaire item #D2), are the result of lengthening the list of value choices from seven in 1979 to twelve in 1995.

nity affairs, leisure time activities, and developing an independent lifestyle were seen as giving the least satisfaction. These data suggest that religion and politics 'lose out' in competition with marriage and children, likely because of people's time constraints, with work and career probably being considered an economic necessity. Indeed, religious services, which were attended once a week by 47 per cent of respondents when they were growing up, had diminished in importance dramatically by 1995, with only 12 per cent reporting that they attended religious services weekly.

Many members of the Class of '73 included additional comments when they completed the 1995 survey. Many of their remarks reflected personal value priorities, or were opinions on the changing importance of marriage, family, work, and education in their lives. The comments also provide insight on life satisfaction among members of the Class of '73. By way of illustration, one respondent wrote:

> Despite what you may gather from this survey, I'm very happy with the outcome of my life: marriage, children and work. At some time, many of us wish for a better life! But I'm not complaining, at this time, considering the economy as such. Remember, to be fairly successful in life, no matter how much education or how many diplomas you acquire, you have to chase the dream whether it be happiness or wealth or both. Mind you, a great education helps immensely, and having a good attitude towards life doesn't hurt either.

Another participant, commenting on his interests and plans for the future, added:

> I am presently continuing my interest in artwork. I've always been independent and self-reliant, able to deal with my problems without support from family or friends ... I feel my occupation (in government) has been a benefit but too stressful at times ... I would like to look at my job as a stepping stone. My interests are in art and other avenues, such as my own store or business, marriage and a house, in the future. A good relationship is important to me now and also to work towards other goals in life.

Finally, describing the values she shares with her husband, this respondent wrote:

> My parents believed that if you were willing to give 100 per cent to a job and try your best, you could succeed. This philosophy coupled with the opportunity of higher education, has made my life rewarding and fulfilled. I believe that much of my success stems from the values which my parents believed in and encouraged our family (five children) to 'live by.' My husband and I have the same values of hard work and dedication and are trying to show our children the benefits of these beliefs. Encour-

Table 7.8. Retrospective satisfaction with life areas as reported in 1995 (percentage)

Life areas

Level of satisfaction	Personal life Male (n = 378)	Personal life Female (n = 407)	Family life Male (n = 376)	Family life Female (n = 406)	Work or a career Male (n = 376)	Work or a career Female (n = 404)	Where you living Male (n = 378)	Where you living Female (n = 407)	Education Male (n = 377)	Education Female (n = 407)
1. Very satisfied	35.2	45.5	48.9	56.2	25.0	27.0	39.4	44.2	18.6	22.9
2. Satisfied	44.7	41.3	31.6	33.3	42.8	37.6	38.1	35.1	40.3	37.8
3. Neither satisfied nor dissatisfied	14.8	9.1	12.0	6.7	20.5	23.5	15.1	15.5	30.8	27.8
4. Dissatisfied	3.7	2.5	5.3	2.7	8.8	8.4	5.6	3.9	8.8	10.1
5. Very dissatisfied	1.6	1.7	2.1	1.2	2.9	3.5	1.9	1.2	1.6	1.5
Total	100.0	100.0	100.0	100.0	100.0	100.0	100.0	100.0	100.0	100.0

Question: Thinking back to when you were in high school and the kinds of hopes you had then, how satisfied are you now with the way things have turned out for you now in each of the following areas?

aging them to believe in themselves, to value hard work and dedication to their goals and to enjoy all of life's pleasures have been and continue to be our goals in child-rearing.

We also asked people who responded to our most recent survey to think back to when they were in high school and to try to recall the kinds of hopes they had then. We then asked them to assess how things had turned out in the areas of personal life, family, work or career, where they lived, and education (Table 7.8). Family life stood out as the area that gave respondents the greatest satisfaction. Women reported somewhat greater satisfaction with family and personal life. Commenting on her aspirations and how they eventually turned out for her, Kelly said:

> I remember in nursing, actually, we had to do this thing in psychology and we had to draw this picture, whatever you wanted to draw. And I remember the teacher analysing my picture. This is what I wanted in life ... a family and a picket fence. Actually, I'm getting my veranda in this new house. So my life is pretty boring, but I like it.

Only about one-quarter of respondents indicated that they were 'very satisfied' with their career, and with their education. Those who indicated that marriage and children were very important to them also, for the most part, indicated being satisfied or very satisfied with regard to how family life had turned out for them.

Conclusions

Interactions within families, and between families and the larger society, have changed over time. Life choices are determined by personal needs and dispositions and by social pressures, values, and circumstances. The Class of '73 came of age in an era when higher education was attracting both popular enthusiasm and a large share of public resources, and sons and daughters alike were encouraged by their parents to pursue postsecondary schooling. Furthermore, more affluent families were able and willing to provide significant financial aid to their university and college bound children. Notwithstanding their adolescent struggles for independence, most young people had close bonds with their families, and – especially in the case of women – had committed to the idea of family life.

They were also intent on forging vocations and careers, and many consciously delayed marriage and having children in order to pursue these ends. Once they married or were cohabitating – the latter being more socially acceptable by the late 1980s – family life, and especially raising children, was their chief source of life satisfaction. Family values endured in another significant way: women remained primarily responsible for household labour, whether or not they were employed outside the home. While decision making within the family was evidently more equitably shared than in the past, Class of '73 women, like those in society at large (and like their mothers before them), spent far more time than their spouses managing the house and raising their children.

Raising children provided respondents with enormous satisfaction, but it also impeded women's upward mobility in the workplace. Mothers described both the joys of home life and the challenges, sacrifices, and trade-offs they made in reconciling family responsibilities with their vocational goals and demands. Men were less conflicted because their jobs, which were normally more lucrative than those of their spouses, had higher priority within the family. Women customarily relocated to their husband's place of work; rarely vice versa. Still, many men were more involved in childrearing and domestic chores than their fathers had been. By the 1990s there was a greater diversity of family types, the structure of family life had been modified, and more women than ever were employed in the work force. But for the Class of '73, as for the larger society, gender-distinctive roles still dictated how family life was conducted.

Class of '73 members had very high hopes for their own children, and education was central to these aspirations. Among those who had offspring, we found a strong commitment to providing for the next generation's education. Many, including single parents, believed that postsecondary education was a minimum requirement for entering a secure and lucrative vocation. Unprecedented rates of college and university attendance suggest how pervasive this view was. Overall, respondents' aspirations for their own children were greater than the aspirations they perceived their parents had had for them. At the same time, partly in response to their own frustrations in an increasingly uncertain job market, some parents questioned the value of a higher education. Also, many respondents found it a challenge to maintain and enhance their existing lifestyles in order to facilitate their children's future. This was particularly true for single women, who struggle with everyday financial obligations and must contend with employment policies that have impeded their ability to balance their work with family obligations.

Overall, individual and family choices were shaped by a combination of personal concerns and social pressures. Structural factors, including gender, region, race, and social class, influenced but did not invariably determine the life courses of the Class of '73. Most of the people in the cohort were optimistic about their lives and hopeful for their children. However, we must be cautious, as future societal changes may shift a greater burden onto women with regard to work, the home, and childrearing. It is essential to find mechanisms that will enable women to balance the competing demands of the different areas of their lives, something that requires the full participation and commitment of men. The lives of the Class of '73 indicate that though traditional pathways were not always followed, traditional values relating to marriage, family, and children, while showing some signs of change, continued to receive strong support.

CHAPTER EIGHT

Constructing the Life Course: Five Biographies

To this point we have reviewed a range of issues within a framework that seeks to identify the interplay between structure and agency in the life courses of members of the Class of '73. We have explored educational pathways after high school; school-to-work transitions; intergenerational and career mobility; the special impact of having been raised by foreign-born rather than Canadian-born parents; and the family experiences of the Class of '73, both as children and subsequently as parents. Our analysis has addressed their status passages from adolescence to adulthood in terms of two fundamentally important themes: the relationship between social forces and personal agency; and the fluidity of values, beliefs, self-evaluation, and satisfaction. In addition, we have examined separate trajectories, including education, career, and marriage and childrearing. Elder (1991) defines a *trajectory* as a lifeline or pathway over an extended span of time that can vary in direction, degree, and rate of change. Each trajectory is marked by a series of specific life-event transitions such as entering and leaving a postsecondary institution, getting married or divorced, and entering or leaving a job. The interlinking of trajectories, transitions, and turning points is often of critical importance in understanding how the life course unfolds for individuals (Elder, 1985: 31). Furthermore, biographical construction is continually changed by new experiences, with individual decisions linking different life sequences (Hoerning and Alheit, 1995).

In this chapter, using the dynamic longitudinal data we have gathered over a long period of time (George, 1993), we take a biographical approach in examining the transitions and trajectories that have made up the life course for five members of the Class of '73. References have already been made to their experiences, and all five have been quoted at relevant points in our discussion. Here we present their stories more completely in order to demonstrate how they navigated their educational and occupational pathways in a society in which (as illustrated in earlier chapters) rapid social change provided alternative life options and risks to a degree unknown by previous generations (Heinz, 1991: 9).

When we first met the members of the Class of '73 in their late adolescence, they were in the process of entering a number of adult roles, including full or part-time postsecondary study, full-time or part-time employment, marriage, and parenthood. Yet the data show that the pathways taken by individuals varied with respect to dimensions of the life course (e.g., stage, position). In some cases trajectories were interdependent, while in others they were independent. For example, some followed a traditional lockstep approach, entering university full-time, completing a BA in three years without benefit of employment during study, and obtaining full-time employment after receiving a degree. After four or five years of employment, marriage and children may have followed. Others took time off after high school to travel, then entered community college or university on a part-time basis while working full-time. Some within this group elected to marry either before enrolling in postsecondary education or while enrolled. The trajectories of their spouses may then have influenced the directions they took. As members of the Class of '73 moved out of adolescence into early and then later stages of adulthood, the diversity of their life pathways increased significantly. According to Rindfuss (1991), their young adult years would have been the period during which the greatest number of changes occurred in the life course. During these years individuals experience multiple transitions – they are most likely to leave school, move, gain employment, and marry and become parents.

What we have observed, then, is the extent to which, as Heinz (1995) argues, 'uncertainty concerning the long-term consequences when deciding for one status passage against the other requires the individuals to design their biographies like a patchwork in time.' The variations in the pathways taken by members of the Class of '73, in terms of sequencing and the duration of transitions, are far too complex to summarize easily. For this reason it is important and instructive to examine their individual life biographies. As Heinz also notes, individual life histories inform us of people's coping strategies and negotiating processes as they contribute to the continuity and discontinuity of their own biographies. Individuals make choices within a structure of opportunities and constraints in which they feel that they are 'constructing their individual life courses.'

The examination of selected individual biographies allows us to explore life course pathways in ways that are not possible when we rely solely on survey data analysis techniques.[1] It also allows us to examine the timing and duration of life events, both scheduled and unanticipated (Schlossberg, 1984). Mayer and Tuma (1990) argue that single events or life phases cannot be adequately understood in isolation. Rather, life events and phases must be studied as part of life trajectories in which later outcomes are partly the consequences of earlier conditions, events, and experiences (also see Buchmann, 1989). Marini, Shin, and Raymond (1989) state that the age at which certain roles are entered is not as important as the timing and sequencing of these roles. In adopting a biographical approach, we are not determining the trajectories that will be explored. Rather, our assumption is that the trajectories and transitions that make up the life course of each individual can be more clearly identified through biographical analysis.[2] We are making no prior judgement as to what comprises a 'normal biography'; each person writes his or her own life script, and we are responsible for relating the narrative as accurately as possible. As Elder (1998: 9) notes: 'Life course theory and research alerts us to this real world, a world in which lives are lived and where people work out paths of development as best they can. It tells us how lives are socially organized in biological and historical time, and how the resulting social pattern affects the way we think, feel, and act.'

Navigating the Life Course: Five Members of the Class of '73

When we selected our five biographies, our concern was to reflect the richness and diversity of trajectories and transitions. First there is Anna, a woman who immigrated to Canada with her parents and siblings from Germany as a very young child and settled with them in a farm community in Niagara. Anna married in her early twenties and within ten years had three children. Soon after the arrival of her third child, Anna experienced a traumatic divorce and was forced to re-evaluate her life course and to make career decisions that would enhance her future and that of her children. Next is Paul, who grew up with a passion for travel. This desire significantly influenced his entry into the banking industry after practical training in chartered accountancy.

Paul married in his late twenties, joined a major bank, and spent the next few years transferring between numerous branches across Canada and the United States. Then he moved to Vancouver, where his priorities changed. No longer driven by the need to travel, he was content being a father and raising his two young children.

Sarah's biography provides significant contrasts. Though shy and somewhat introverted in her early adolescent years, Sarah's unique personality inspired her to explore several career options. A talented artist, she initially pursued a career in graphic arts, though firmly convinced that she had yet to discover her true vocation. Once she decided to become a minister, nothing distracted her from this goal – not marriage, and not even a diagnosis of multiple sclerosis. Dom, the fourth person featured, was the youngest child of Italian working-class immigrants. Unlike many of the children of foreign-born parents in our study, Dom had no strong desire to become upwardly mobile. He spent most of his twenties drifting from one low-paid job to another. It was only when he married and had children that he began to sort out his personal and work life.

And finally there is Rebecca. Rebecca had a turbulent adolescence consumed with drugs and a struggle over her sexual identity. She briefly dropped out of high school but returned to complete her studies. Eventually she went on to university, where she developed a strong interest in anthropology. Just short of completing her BA, she moved to Vancouver and found a job in the newspaper printing industry. At the time of the interview, major labour disputes in the printing industry had cost Rebecca her job and led her to re-evaluate her personal and career goals.

Anna

When Anna was two years old, her parents, who were of German Mennonite origin, immigrated to Canada. They settled on a farm in the Niagara region, but her father was unable to earn a living in farming and supplemented his income by working as a cabinet maker. Her mother occasionally cleaned homes in the area to earn extra money. Anna's mother did not want to see her five children have to do the kind of unskilled work she did, so she stressed to all of them the importance of education.

Anna developed an interest in nursing at an early age. She recalled that as a small girl, she applied bandages to the pets on her farm, and instead of feeding and bathing her dolls as her friends did, she would apply splints to their arms and legs. In grade 13, Anna applied to a three-year nursing program at the local community college but was not accepted because her science marks were too low. She was devastated by the realization that she would have to give up her dream of becoming a nurse. Discouraged by and bored with her studies, she dropped out of grade 13 and immediately found employment as a teller in a bank. She found this job tedious, and after tolerating it for two years, she quit.

While in her senior year in high school, Anna developed a strong interest in religion. She attended the local Mennonite church youth club, where she met a local young man whom she began to date. But she felt compelled to explore the world outside her immediate environment, and when her cousin invited her to move to Vancouver, Anna jumped at the opportunity. Vancouver in the mid-1970s attracted many young people who wanted to follow alternative lifestyles. Anna described the University of British Columbia campus, where her cousin attended school, as filled with a variety of 'hippie' groups. Anna enrolled in a bible college but 'hung around' with her cousin, a born-again Christian, and her cousin's friends at the UBC campus. This group of young people was part of Campus Crusades for Christ, which Anna described as a 'quasi-hippie religious movement' whose main mission was to attract other university students into the organization. Anna became involved in the Campus Crusades cause, attending seminars and retreats in British Columbia and California. She decided to remain in Vancouver and devote her life to the religious movement. But a year later, while attending a religious retreat in California, she experienced a strange phenomenon: while she was meditating, she heard a voice urging her to return home to Niagara because her boyfriend was waiting to marry her. The experience was 'so overwhelming and compelling' that she left the seminar, packed up her belongings in Vancouver, and returned home. At 22, Anna married her boyfriend, and they moved to a nearby farm, on which many of their activities centred around the Mennonite Church.

When Anna returned to Niagara, she wasn't sure whether to search for employment or return to school. Her focus had shifted to religion and marriage. With nursing no longer an option, she decided to combine her clerical experience with her interest in medicine by taking a medical stenography course. She subsequently found work in a dentist's office, where she remained for eight years. She enjoyed working as a dental secretary but did not find it particularly challenging. When her second child was born, she quit her job to stay home full-time and help on the farm.

Six years after marrying, at 28, Anna had her first child, but she continued to work on a part-time basis. A second child followed two years later. Three years later her third and last child, a son, was born. By this time, Anna was 33 and her marriage was in trouble. She described her husband as 'an overwhelming presence who seeks out submissive people, but then is bored by them.' During their marriage, Anna played a very submissive role, always trying to please and appease him. Her submissiveness infuriated her husband. He demanded that she become more assertive, yet he had to control every situation. When her youngest child was 2, Anna's husband requested a divorce. She claims he initiated the divorce because he found 'my submissiveness boring.' During the interview, Anna was reluctant to discuss her marriage, and it was clear that she was still upset by the circumstances of her divorce.

Anna and her husband shared joint custody of their children, two boys and a girl. During the week, her older son lived with her husband, while her daughter and younger son lived with her. She and her husband looked after all three children on alternate weekends.

The financial consequences of the divorce were also painful for Anna. She moved out of the large home she had shared with her husband and rented a smaller house, where she was still living at the time of the interview. Her divorce settlement required her to become financially independent within three years. According to Anna, the women's movement's campaign for women's autonomy in society had resulted in changes to the divorce law, so that divorced women were no longer able to rely on indefinite alimony payments from their husbands. She viewed the accomplishments of the women's movement as a mixed blessing. After having spent numerous years at home raising a family and relying on her husband for most of the family decisions and for financial support, she was suddenly faced with having to become completely self-sufficient. She was also forced to become more assertive, and called it 'the beginning of my standing up for myself.'

Anna realized that she would have to make some decisions with respect to her future employment. Once again she considered pursuing a career in her first area of interest – nursing. She hoped that the fact that she was applying as a mature student would improve her chances of being admitted to a school of nursing. She quickly realized, however, that because of her responsibilities to her children and her poor financial position, she could not commit herself to the three full years of study and training that a registered nursing program demanded. She enrolled instead in a one-year licensed practical nursing (LPN) program offered at the local college.

Anna acknowledged that she had become considerably more assertive since the break-up of her marriage. Taking care of herself and her children had given her a strong sense of independence. She described herself as 'stubborn.' She displayed her assertiveness when she was told she was not eligible for admission to the LPN program because the program was geared to people on social assistance. This so infuriated her that she threatened to go on social assistance if they did not accept her into the program. Shortly thereafter, she was admitted.

Unfortunately, Anna's completion of the LPN program in the early 1990s coincided with cutbacks in the Ontario hospital sector. She discovered on graduation that there were no permanent jobs available at any of the local hospitals. Determined to gain some experience in nursing, she repeatedly contacted the human resources department at the local hospital until they finally offered her part-time employment on their operating ward. Anna loved her job, but the work wasn't permanent and did not provide her with a sufficient income to support herself. Reluctantly, Anna recognized that she would either have to supplement her income with another part-time job or find more permanent, full-time employment. One of her neighbours was planning to open a treatment centre for brain-injured people, and she contacted him, offering her services. He hired her after a short interview.

In 1995, Anna was employed as the medical manager of the treatment facility, where she acted as a liaison among the staff, the doctors, and the patients and their families. She was somewhat awed by the responsibilities of her job, but she also enjoyed the opportunities for learning that her work offered, such as workshops and lectures. She made it clear, however, that she would gladly have traded her present position for a chance to work full-time as a hospital nurse.

During the interview, Anna appeared self-confident and at ease. She made passing reference to the women's movement as having inspired her to take control of her life, yet she also held many traditional views, particularly with respect to marriage and family. She stated emphatically that she still hadn't given up on her intention to practise nursing. After her children left home, she planned either to work with sick children in a Third World country or to return to British Columbia.

Paul

It's a long way from the trombonist's seat in a high school band in suburban Toronto to the executive office of a large corporate bank in Vancouver. But that is essentially the route that Paul followed on what he called 'this great adventure.' Paul felt that his high school music program, and particularly his music teacher, greatly influenced the course of his life. He described his music teacher as an adventurer who 'was very good at motivating his students to do their best in music.' When Paul was in grade 10, his music teacher organized a summer tour of Europe for the school band. The band performed all over Europe, including Moscow and Leningrad, and the experience was wonderfully exciting, particularly for a young, impressionable 16-year-old. This led Paul to develop a keen interest in exploring new places – an interest that would later influence his career aspirations.

When Paul left high school he was unclear about his career plans. It was assumed by everyone in the family that he would go to university, as both his parents were university educated. His father had graduated from the University of Toronto with a degree in engineering, and his mother had a degree in nutrition. He decided to go to the University of Toronto because most of his friends were heading there and also because his father had completed his engineering studies there. He enrolled in a general arts program that included courses in music, but found his course selection wasn't very focused. It became evident early on that a music career was not for him. Paul transferred to the Bachelor of Commerce program, where he continued his education, but still with no clear sense of direction. Most of the students in the program were focused on becoming chartered accountants, so Paul covered his options by making certain that the courses he selected had the credits required by the Institute of Chartered Accountants.

When his university studies ended, Paul joined the wave of students who applied for jobs with CA firms. He was still not certain that his future lay in chartered accounting. But as he explained it:

> It was relatively easy to get a job with a CA firm and for those of us who weren't 100 per cent certain of what we really wanted to do, we justified things by saying, 'Oh this will give us a chance to see this business and this business and maybe we'll find out what we really want to do.' But that program is extremely intense and so if you're going to make a run for the finish line, you have to really focus in on it and just get it done,

which is exactly what I did. But I never really went into it with a conscious effort that I wanted to become a chartered accountant so that this would happen.

Paul joined one of the largest public accounting firms in Toronto as an articling student, and remained there for three years. He disliked public accounting. He found auditing 'very mundane, hours of relentless unrewarding work. I couldn't understand for the life of me why I would get up every morning and go to this horrid job.' He had difficulty adjusting to a 9 to 5 job with only two weeks' holiday, and he disliked working in a confined environment. He did not want to attend the courses the firm offered to prepare articling students for the certification exam. However, his parents made him realize that he would fail the CA exams if he continued in this vein and that all of his work would have been wasted. He had to decide: quit now, or prepare for the exams. So he 'geared up and for the duration was completely focused on getting that done.' He became a chartered accountant, even as he realized that he would eventually do something else. What 'that something' was remained unclear.

In 1981, Paul joined one of the largest banks in Canada. During his interview with the bank, he mentioned that he enjoyed travelling and was interested in working in a variety of settings. He was told that he would be categorized as 'mobile.' The bank then offered him a position in Montreal. After ten months, he was transferred back to Toronto, where he remained for two years. While in Toronto, he met and married his wife, who worked for a rival bank in the human resources department. They moved to Calgary, where he worked in the bank's oil and gas division. Paul viewed this as the beginning of 'the great adventure' – a move away from Ontario into a 'nomadic, investigative lifestyle.' In 1986 the bank offered him a position in New York City, and he and his wife lived there for two-and-a-half-years, then Atlanta for two-and-a-half years, then the Vancouver area, and from there, finally, downtown Vancouver.

Although Paul saw himself as mobile, he had not anticipated making so many moves within the organization. He noted that other employees also considered themselves mobile, and yet they were not given the opportunity to work in so many places. Paul believed that part of the reason for so many moves was a conversation he had with the bank's corporate human resources manager, when he emphasized that he wanted a 'global outlook' and was prepared to work in different places to obtain it. He also attributed his career mobility to his good performance record at the bank and his expressed desire to learn new things.

Paul believed that all the jobs he had held made sense. He was always moving in the 'right direction,' and learning new things. 'The great adventure' continued, so he never refused any of the jobs that were offered to him. In describing the amount of deliberate planning that went into his career decisions, Paul made the following observations:

> As far as personal planning, I sound probably highly influenced by whatever happens to be going on, and I only ended up here by accident. Not entirely true. What I actually ended up doing is not something that I would have actually been able to forecast. I would never have been able to say, 'We're going to live in this place, and this place, and this place.' And I can't tell you where I'm going to live in the future ... and I can't tell you what job I'm going to do. But I am quite happy with what we're doing, where we are, and the challenges that we have.

Paul pointed out that he had been able to put his personal stamp on each job he'd held with the bank and to diversify his job experience. He often discussed career development with other staff and encouraged them 'not to look at the square lines around their job,' but to examine what they might do with their job to get the skills they need to distinguish them from other employees and to allow them to do what they want. As Paul explained:

> It has to do with attitude. Because I've never had a mandate working in this bank. Which is a shocking statement. Nobody's said to me 'This is what we want you to do.' It never worried me ... it was sort of a sink-or-swim type of approach. You get in and you make what you can out of it and find a way to do what you need to do.

Paul and his wife did have some concerns with respect to his job transfers. Some were financial, and some were environmental, but they 'always figured out how to make it happen.' For example, his wife could not obtain a green card when they moved to the United States, so she stopped working. They were challenged by the need to adjust to new places, and the experience strengthened their relationship.

If the bank asked him to move once again, Paul and his wife were prepared to do so. However, a nomadic existence no longer appealed to them. Their key priorities were their children. After considerable difficulties having children, Paul and his wife were finally able to have two – a son and a daughter, ages 5 and 2. He now viewed his mobility in 'blocks of time.' He surmised that once his children were old enough for school, he would probably have to 'opt out' of moving around until they completed high school. Much depended on his children's personalities and on their self-confidence. If as teenagers they were fairly self-confident, he would consider transferring to another city in the middle of their high school years. He had attempted to provide a solid environment for his children and would not be willing to sacrifice their stability for his career. He had started an education fund for them, although he hoped they would go to university, he would not be upset if they took another route, provided they obtained some form of postsecondary education that would prepare them for the world of work.

Paul and his wife had a vision of what they would like to do in the future. His wife hoped to return to work once the children were in high school. Since the children were very young, she did not have a strong desire to return to the work force. Paul and his wife liked Vancouver, and they hoped to return and retire there, if they were to move somewhere else in the near future. In discussing his own future opportunities, Paul commented:

> Banking has become a very difficult business. It's very hard. Every day it's becoming harder. It's a commodities business. It's oversupplied. The opportunities for growth and revenue are harder to come by. And there's cost and efficiency pressure. So it's a tough business. I can't imagine doing that until I'm 65. I wouldn't mind doing something a little different. Maybe later. I couldn't tell you what that is, but I just have this sense that it would be nice to do something different. And when would that happen? Well, I just turned forty. So, ten years from now, twelve, thirteen. I don't know.

While it was clear that Paul was happy with the direction of his career in banking, he pointed out that he would refuse to continue in his job if it became too mundane.

Providing for his family financially, physically, and emotionally was now Paul's central focus. But he was caught between the demands of his job, his long working hours, and his desire to spend more time at home. His children provided him with the balance and emotional fulfilment he needed. He described himself as a 'perfectionist and fairly driven,' but found that having 'little people put their arms around you' placed life in perspective. It made him perform better and helped him act on his philosophy of 'every day being a move toward a positive accomplishment.'

Paul believed that he and his wife must have had a very powerful subconscious drive to have children. At times, with all the difficulties they encountered, they considered abandoning the idea. He thought they still would have had 'a fine life' without children. His wife would have returned to work, and they would have spent more time travelling and doing other activities. But he was really glad that 'it worked out this way.'

Sarah

We arranged to meet Sarah for her interview in the offices of a suburban Toronto church. Sarah was one of three ministers at that church and the only woman. Given that the number of female ministers in Canada was still small, we were curious to find out what led her to choose a career as a minister.

Sarah grew up in a town near Hamilton, Ontario, the middle of three sisters. Although neither of her parents was university educated, Sarah described her father as 'a professional man who realized the importance of education.' Her father's entire career was spent at a large Ontario corporation working in various management positions. Her mother had worked in the early part of her marriage, but 'was of the generation that stayed at home.' Her parents' expectation was that 'you do as much as you can with what you have.' They never channelled her toward any specific vocation, but believed that 'you [should] do the best you can.' Her parents applauded anything that she and her sisters achieved.

When Sarah was in grade 12, she decided she wanted to work with children in a helping profession. She spoke extensively with a guidance counsellor at her high school, read brochures, took aptitude tests, and ultimately decided to enrol in a social work program at a community college. Her decision not to complete grade 13 was based in part on her fear that she couldn't handle the academic subjects. She was also influenced by the fact that most of her friends had elected to attend a community college rather than enter grade 13.

Sarah enrolled in the social work program at a community college in Toronto, but after one semester she decided to leave. She described the program as 'not my cup of tea.' She found the program highly alienating, and she had little in common with the other students in residence, who were all in nursing. She spent the remainder of the year working at odd jobs, and returned to complete her high school studies the following September. In a 'reserved sort of way,' Sarah's parents had supported her decision not to complete grade 13. She only discovered the extent of their disappointment when she returned to complete grade 13 and saw the look of relief on their faces.

When Sarah returned to grade 13, she was unclear about what she would do once she completed high school. She was still toying with the idea of working with children, and explored the possibility of taking social work at the university level. Several of her teachers and friends urged her to pursue a career in art. She had always been interested in art as a hobby, and as a child she was very artistic, often electing to sketch or paint instead of playing with friends. She took another battery of interest and aptitude tests and finally resolved to 'follow up this artwork thing until I decided what it was I wanted to do with my life.' Sarah enrolled in a three-year graphic arts program at a college and simultaneously began working part-time for the graphics department of a translation company. She was offered a permanent job on graduation, and she remained in that position for two years. She then found work as a graphic artist with a local board of education. Her job, which she enjoyed, involved working with students and teachers. Sarah spoke about her career as a graphic artist with great enthusiasm, but she explained that she somehow knew that this would not be her final job:

> I loved my career ... I was working with kids again and teachers and it was a wonderful job. But it was always something that in the back of my head I knew I was doing until I decided what it was I wanted to do with my life. It took me about seven years I guess to figure that out.

When she began work at the board, Sarah considered herself shy and introverted. She had a minimal social life. All of her friends had moved away, and she was content to focus on her artwork and to spend most of her time alone. To occupy her time in the evenings, she began attending functions at her family church. Over some seven years, she ran the youth group and became chairperson of the church committee. As her involvement in the church increased, something profound was happening to her. Her father had always been heavily involved with the church, which as teenagers 'drove us crazy.' But his connection to the church left its mark. 'There was something here,' and she wondered what it meant:

> My first inkling was that perhaps I would go into Christian education and still be involved with kids through Sunday school work, and I recognized at that point that wasn't quite enough, that there was something more and that eventually evolved into going into the ministry.

On the fifth anniversary of her employment, Sarah left her job as a graphic artist and started taking university courses. Even though she would have to commit to a minimum of six years of study to become a minister, Sarah was thrilled about returning to school. None of her family had ever gone to university. Some had attended community college, and that was the route she had initially decided to pursue; however, she needed to complete a BA in religious studies before she could enrol in a divinity school.

Two people especially influenced Sarah's decision to become a minister. One was a minister, eventually hired by her church, who captivated her with his passion and eloquence. Another was a woman who was the facilitator of a church study group in Christian education that Sarah attended. Sarah described her as friendly, outgoing, and deeply committed to her work and to the people with whom she worked. This woman eventually became a minister as well.

> I guess I saw in them not so much what they were doing, but how they were doing it, how they were relating to people. And this was something that I wanted to do – to be able to relate to people on the level that they were relating to them. I wanted to feel that strongly about people, just be able to reach out to them, and just be interested and involved in their lives ... I had a couple of friends who, once I started in that area, were very encouraging and they also influenced me.

Sarah's parents were 'dead set' against her becoming a minister because they were concerned about job security. She described her father as a 'one-company man all through his life' who believed that 'you don't leave a secure position with benefits to go off into the netherworld where you just don't know what's going to happen.' They were objecting not to her new vocational choice but to the fact that she was abandoning a job that she loved, and that supplied her with a steady income. They made their views clear, but she was unswayed. Later they became more supportive.

Sarah loved university. She completed her BA with a major in religious studies in two years by doubling up on courses. She did this partly for economic reasons but also because she was determined to enter divinity school as quickly as possible. She made the dean's honour list both years and found the courses exceptionally stimulating and challenging. She described community college as being like high school, whereas university 'had a life of its own and was quite fascinating.'

Sarah began her master's degree at the University of Toronto. However, she did not manage to 'barrel through' the master's program as she had through her BA. She was diagnosed with multiple sclerosis shortly after entering the master's program and as a result was forced to study on a part-time basis. It took her five years to complete the program, including its one-year internship. Because she was seeking part-time employment and wanted to live in Toronto, where she would have access to medical services that met her needs, Sarah had to wait another year before a suitable church was found for her. Sarah considered herself fortunate to have found her subsequent position. She claimed that she had always been lucky finding employment. She placed her name on a list for occasional preaching in Toronto and was approached by a Toronto church to work part-time as a replacement for another female minister, who had decided to return to school. She was given permission by her church to accept the position and subsequently had been working there for five years. She began working on a part-time basis, not as an ordained minister but as a pastoral care minister, ministering mainly to the elderly. After nine months she was ordained.

At the time of the interview, Sarah had been married for seven years. When she first arrived in Toronto to study for her MA, she responded to an ad in *Toronto Life* offering personalized guided walking tours throughout Toronto. The tour guide turned out to be the man she would marry. The day they returned from their honeymoon, Sarah received the news that she had multiple sclerosis.

When Sarah was first diagnosed with MS, she was concerned mostly about the impact of her illness on her role in her marriage. Her husband was also disabled. He had contracted a rare illness seventeen years earlier that had left him paralysed from the neck down for two years, although since then he had regained many of his motor skills. He walked with a cane, had some vision problems, and required assistance with some daily activities.

When she and her husband decided to get married, she defined herself as the caregiver, the 'doer' in the family. Because her husband was limited by his disabilities, she anticipated that she would be the person responsible for all the driving and the household chores and the one to assist him. When she learned she had MS, she worried about the course her disease would take and whether it would prevent her from doing what needed to be done. And although she was still concerned about the consequences of her illness on her marriage, she had not allowed the circumstances of her disease or her husband's disability to depress or discourage her:

> What is my role now in the marriage and how are we going to be able to manage when the two of us are no longer able to fill in each other's gaps? Up to that point if a small thing needed to be done, one of us was able to do it. So all those kinds of things have been put into question. We're really good at filling in each other's gaps and now there's some gaps left that neither one of us can fill as much as we used to be able to do. I've never been depressed about it or overwhelmed by it. I've had a reasonably good course of the disease so far. I'm still able to drive. The only thing I can't do right now is work full-time. I can't take the hours and I have to pace myself during the day. We've both gotten along with it quite well. We just have to accept it and look for ways to get things done that we can't naturally race out and do.

Her husband had a 19-year-old daughter who was living with her mother but spent many weekends with them. Sarah never had a strong desire to have children, and while she enjoyed spending time with her nieces, she welcomed the time she had to herself. So having children had never been an issue.

Sarah enjoyed her work environment and was not planning to accept another placement in the near future. She was part of a three-person team, which she described as a 'cohesive unit.' They rotated their activities at all times and therefore were always involved in new and challenging projects. When asked if she ever had any doubts about her decision to change careers, she responded with an emphatic 'no':

> I gave it a really thorough examination when I was diagnosed with MS in terms of doors closing. Because up to that point doors kept opening. All along the way it was a go – I got a great internship. And this seemed to be a closing down of some things. But after I looked at what I was still capable of doing and what I was interested in doing, I didn't give it another thought from then on – another thought, in terms of having any doubts. All along the way I've examined every move that I have made to make sure that it was the right one. And I still believe in it being the right one.

She knew it would be 'a long hard struggle' to complete her MA, but she was determined to return to school. Even so, she was exhausted when she graduated.

The fact that she was a female minister was not an issue that concerned her very much. She viewed herself as a 'person' rather than as a woman entering the ministry. No one ever objected to her officiating at any ceremonies because she was a woman. With respect to moving up the church hierarchy, Sarah acknowledged that there 'is discrimination out there.' There had been incidents of women being overlooked for senior ministers' positions, and she was aware that certain members of the congregation were not comfortable dealing with a female minister. However, given that she was only able to work part-time, it is unlikely that she would have the opportunity to apply for a senior minister's position, regardless of her gender.

Sarah hoped to stay in her present job for at least five years, but because of her disease she found it hard to make long-term plans: 'I don't know what course my illness will take. With the course of my disease, there are some days when I just can't get up. That's just the way things go.' She hadn't really looked at what lay ahead with respect to her work. Sarah's husband had recently lost his job as a graphic artist after sixteen years with the same company. She described him this way:

> A victim 'of the scourge of the nineties.' He's a victim of what everybody else is a victim of ... It just happened ... The company he worked for folded. Unfortunately, his business has been taken over by computers and he is just not computer literate. He doesn't have the manual dexter-

ity to manage a computer, and he's just not of that generation. So he realizes he's going to have to make a career change. He's looking into whole tours, special events, and hospitality tours kind of avenues.

Sarah hoped to devote some time to helping her husband develop his tour business, because he had been very supportive to her in her career.

Her parents had been stoically quiet about her disease. They rarely discussed her medical condition, but Sarah believed that for a time they had felt guilty that they may have done or given her something to precipitate her illness. She described them as white Anglo-Saxon Protestants who tried to instil a strong work ethic in their children. She had absorbed their values but had modified them somewhat since contracting MS:

I don't work myself to death. I know that there's a place for work and there's a place for play and I don't feel guilty about the play when I have to. If an evening meeting comes along that I just can't drag my backside to, I will phone and say, 'I just can't do it.' My dad on the other hand would be there. I've taken some of their family values, the importance of family, the honesty and charity and all that. I've taken a lot of those in myself but I've also rounded off some of the devotion to things, and the commitment to things and said, 'Okay, we don't have to' ... I guess I've levelled off some of the guilt.

Sarah credited her strong sense of spirituality with helping her get through some of the difficulties she had experienced. She conceded:

Probably, on some days, it's the only thing that gets me through that particular day. It's always something that's in the background, at the very least. It's how I start my day. It's how I end my day. It's something that feeds me. It's what makes me do what I do with the people I'm involved with. It's something that helps me set my calendar for the week. It follows me home as well, and still keeps me civilized at the end of the day.

She tended to see life as a series of opportunities, which one could take or disregard. She admitted that she had been provided with opportunities in the past that she had chosen to dismiss. However, she viewed her choices in the context of her parents' dictum, that 'you do the best with what you have.' If asked later in life why she didn't do more with 'this or that,' she hoped she would be able to respond that she had taken as many opportunities as had been afforded her and that she had chosen the positive ones in which she truly believed.

Dom

Dom grew up in Niagara Falls, the youngest of five children of an Italian working-class family. His parents came to Canada in the mid-1950s, and Dom was the only one of his family to be born in Canada. When Dom was in grade 11, his father died and his mother became responsible for keeping the family together. She obtained work in a laundry, and Dom's older brothers and sisters, who were working at that point, helped out financially. Dom played football in grade 12, but he was not particularly interested in school and dropped out shortly after starting grade 13. When his mother discovered that he had quit school, she refused to let him 'loaf around the house' and insisted that he find employment. He found a job with a surveying company as a surveying assistant, but he did not enjoy the work and left after almost two years. He then completed a Manpower retraining program in painting and decorating at Mohawk College in Hamilton, and worked for a painting contractor for several months. A dispute with his employer resulted in his quitting his job and collecting unemployment insurance. At that point, Dom was very unclear as to what he wanted to do. He was still living at home, and his life revolved around 'hanging out' with his friends and working intermittently at odd jobs in the laundry where his mother was employed. He described his life at the time in the following way:

> To say what I've done is really ... I really haven't done anything. I was on the pogey, on to work. I was taking it easy. I was still living at home with my mother, and as long as you gave her some money for rent and you just let her know what you were doing, you could stay there forever.

For several years, Dom alternated between working at the laundry and collecting unemployment insurance. He subsequently obtained employment as a labourer in a construction company and worked intermittently in the construction industry for four years.

Dom lived at home until he was 27, and left only because he had met his future wife and felt it was time to move out, to 'get off the fence.' He met his wife, who is from Niagara Falls, New York, at a bar owned by his uncle. At the time of the interview, they had two daughters age 8 and 10 and two sons age 12 and 14. His wife had an older son, age 19 who did not live with them because of a 'conflict of interest.'

Dom believed that meeting his wife was a turning point in his personal and work life. They lived together for several years and had two of their four children before getting married. He continued to alternate between working in the construction industry and helping his mother at the laundromat. But as his family and financial responsibilities grew, he found the insecurity of working in the construction industry increasingly stressful. He realized that he needed to find work in a more stable environment that offered a steady income and benefits. So in 1985 he applied for a job with a major utility company. With the help of an uncle who worked there, he was hired as a janitor. It was only after he began working there that he decided to buy a house and get married:

> I think I've just kinda floated around life until ten years ago, because I really didn't have anything as of ten years ago. I wasn't married, didn't have a house, and boom, you get a full-time job and all of a sudden everything kind of falls into place.

After three years at the utility company, he was reclassified as a handy person, which involved doing odd maintenance jobs in the organization. He was still working there in 1995.

At the time they married, Dom's wife was working as a nursing assistant in a retirement home, but she became a full-time homemaker after the children were born. As the children grew older, it became more expensive to feed and clothe them, and Dom encouraged his wife to return to work. They were beginning to 'financially lose it,' and he told his wife, 'One of us has got to go to work, and I'm already working, so ...' She found a part-time job at a pizzeria, and her added income helped pay for some of the extras their children wanted. He lamented how expensive it was to raise children and how as a child he neither expected nor received what children today demand:

> Kids are expensive. If it were just my wife and I, she wouldn't have to work. But at one point when there was five in here ... even four is still bad. Your kids want everything now. You can't just buy them 'adventure' running shoes. They want Adidas or Reeboks. That's the killer ...

My parents didn't have much. To me, what I wanted and what I got were two different things. I just saw a kid walk by with a $150 starter coat. My son's got one too [laughs] and I'm thinking when does it end? I think I would have been satisfied growing up, to have a decent coat, never mind a starter coat with a Montreal Canadiens logo. Sure, I'd like my kids to have better than what I had or at least better than what my parents could give me, but then we put a gun to our head by doing this ... When does it stop?

Dom also expressed concern about being laid off. Ten years earlier he had deliberately set out to find a stable job in a large organization that had a reputation for offering 'lifetime' employment; but he well knew that in the harsh realities of the 1990s, 'no job is secure.' He was fairly high up on the seniority list, but his company had recently laid off more than 5,000 workers, and he was worried that because of his low occupational status, he was vulnerable to losing his position to a more highly skilled employee. He was optimistic, however, that his union would be able to protect his job for a while. He saw himself as fairly fortunate. Compared to many of his friends and neighbours, he was secure financially, and he and his wife were one of the few couples in the neighbourhood who were still married. Dom voiced some regret that he hadn't married sooner:

I just wish I'd just done everything sooner because look at me now, I'm forty. I think everything just dragged 'til I was thirty. Cause I'm gonna be forty this year, forty ... forty even with my oldest son, like I'll be almost fifty before I can be possibly a grandparent. Now that's a long time. For most people everything happens sooner. Even now, I struck my shoulder the other day at volleyball and I'm dragging myself around. My son wants me to do something with him, like I'm forty now. I've been instilling this in my mind, I'm forty now. I'm over the hill already ... I've thought about a lot of things. Like why didn't I do things before. I know why I didn't do nothing [sic] before because I didn't really assert myself in anything, when I had something, I just kind of let it go for a year. I didn't really apply myself to anything. I didn't know what I wanted. I really don't know what I want today because I just got into a job that's full-time. I guess that's what I wanted – a full-time job.

Dom expressed some apprehension about his children's future. He hoped they would grow up 'without getting into trouble.' He mentioned that there was a lot of drug-related crime in Niagara Falls, and while he hoped that his children would not get involved in illegal activities, he wanted to see them past the stage of having to deal with drugs and peer pressure. He was more concerned about his eldest son, who was 14. His son attended one of the 'worst' high schools in the city, and Dom often worried that he would get hurt in school. He expected all his children to complete high school, but he feared that his eldest son, who was obsessed with sports, was not giving enough thought to his studies and his future. Dom was not as concerned about his younger son, whom he described as more focused and therefore more likely to be successful. He described his daughters as 'still playing with dolls.' While Dom felt very close to his three younger children, his relationship with his eldest son had changed recently. He attributed this in part to his son's need, as a teenager, to distance himself from the family.

The family usually vacationed each summer by camping for a week. In addition, Dom had allocated four days of his holiday time to spend with each child, and he also took days off for activities such as school plays and meetings with teachers. His employer offered a generous holiday package (twenty-nine days off a year), so he had ample time to spend on various activities. He enjoyed working around the house and was slowly renovating his home. Dom compared himself to his father, a municipal government employee, who spent most of his free time fixing up his house. He described his father as 'a sanitary engineer, a "G man" – a garbage man,' who also worked in the sewers. He expressed pride in being Italian, in the fact that his immigrant parents had worked hard to establish themselves. He believed that today's immigrants were being 'given the royal treatment. They don't do anything. They're white-collar workers who aren't the backbone of this country. They can get welfare and other help.' His children considered themselves Italian, although his wife is of Native-Canadian and French descent.

Dom believed that 'it's a different world from when I grew up.' He recalled that while his parents never had to worry when he played in the street as a child, he made certain that he was outside, keeping an eye on his daughters when they were outdoors with their friends. He and his wife had not planned to have four children, yet he had no regrets and could not envision his life without them. Despite the frequent shortage of money, and the difficulty of providing for four children, he would not change things.

Rebecca

Rebecca grew up in a small town in Northern Ontario. Her father was a machinist and her mother was employed as a medical secretary. She was the first child of very young parents, barely beyond adolescence themselves, who never provided her with sufficient guidance in childhood and early adolescence. While her parents supplied her with some emotional support, they spent much of their time in trying to get their marriage on an even keel. Rebecca described her high school years as 'tumultuous, full of raging hormones, a real crazy period.' She began experimenting with soft drugs at 14, and by 15 she was dabbling in acid, mescaline, and MDA. By grade 11 she was addicted. The summer before grade 11, Rebecca joined a group of friends on a trip to the West Coast. It was the tail end of the hippie era. They drove to Vancouver in a van one of her friends had purchased and stayed in Gastown, joining other transient youth. Rebecca was quite charmed by Vancouver. When they returned to Toronto, Rebecca got involved with a group of drug runners.

Rebecca described those years as 'pretty confusing.' Her confusion was intensified by her need to come to terms with being a lesbian. She had her first relationship when she was 16, and when it ended she was heartbroken. Once Rebecca acknowledged her sexual orientation, the stigma of being a lesbian never really bothered her. However, while she recalled that 'I was never that confused or that bothered about it,' she also acknowledged that 'I labelled myself bisexual for quite a few years, until I was about twenty-two or so.'

By the time she was 16, Rebecca was physically and mentally depleted. She dropped out of school between September and December of that year and became heavily involved in drug taking. She described herself as 'pretty messed up ... I was doing it [drugs] every day and was hardly able to string sentences together.' She finally realized that if she did not stop taking drugs she would end up in the same state as some of the people she 'hung out with who were in their thirties and total mental and physical wrecks.' She told her parents about her drug dependency after she had lost a considerable amount of weight and had become quite ill. Her mother was working for a doctor at the time, and he arranged for Rebecca to see a psychiatrist. She was then referred to a social worker, who was instrumental in getting her off drugs and helping her turn her life around.

Rebecca's parents were upset by her drug addiction, but her mother was supportive and became focused on making certain she received proper nutrition. Her mother spoke regularly with Rebecca's social worker and guidance counsellor and on several occasions emerged from those sessions crying. While they did not discuss what had occurred, Rebecca suspected that the subject of her sexuality had come up during those discussions. To this day she and her mother have never spoken openly about her sexual preference.

Rebecca returned to school and completed her year by writing make-up exams. She began to take her school work more seriously, and her marks improved considerably. In addition to her social worker, Rebecca credited her English teacher with restoring her self-esteem and helping her change her attitude toward school. She described their relationship as follows:

> My English teacher also was a good friend. I had a crush on her and I told her. She said 'thank you,' which was just about the best thing anyone could have said. She felt that due to what I had experienced, I had insight that I could pass on to some of the other students.

Rebecca began to participate in class discussions. Her confidence soared, and with it her interest in doing well in school.

When Rebecca completed grade 12, she decided to attend an arts program at a community college. Rebecca always believed that she would go to university. She saw community college as an alternative to taking grade 13 and as a place where she might discover what she wanted to do. She took a two-year program that included courses in film, photography, and anthropology, and won an academic award. Rebecca's mother worked as a secretary for an insurance company that provided bursaries to the children of employees who were enrolled in postsecondary education, and this helped pay for her college tuition. Rebecca noted that while her mother hated her job at the insurance company, she refused to look for other employment until after her daughter had received her college diploma. Rebecca then moved to London, Ontario, where she worked for a year in a variety of jobs, including tobacco picking and managing pop shops. The following autumn she enrolled at the University of Western Ontario as a part-time student. There, she took mainly social science courses – psychology, sociology, and anthropology. She described Western as a very conservative school, except for the anthropology department, which was 'a pretty crazy place.' Her experiences at university were basically positive. While she was too intimidated to speak out in her large introductory psychology and sociology courses, she was more outspoken in her smaller anthropology classes and developed good relationships with several of her professors. She majored in social and cultural anthropology and planned to work in a Third World country on graduation.

Rebecca could not afford to attend university full-time and found employment as an apprentice printer at a small, two-person company. She did not want to end up 'doing waitressing or secretarial work' to pay for her tuition. She sought a trade that would give her sufficient money to pay for university and that she could fall back on at any point. Printing involved some photography and darkroom work, and since this was an area she had been interested in since taking photography courses at college, it seemed like a logical choice. She began her apprenticeship by taking a nineteen-week printing course through her local Canada Employment Centre, and was offered a full-time job as a commercial offset printer by one of the people who came in to fix the presses at the training site.

In her fourth year at university, Rebecca took an interdisciplinary graduate course that focused on various overseas development projects. She became quite disillusioned when she discovered that many of the development projects produced more problems than solutions, and she couldn't see herself fitting into that environment. At that point, Rebecca had lived in London for eight years and was one-and-a-half credits short of completing an honours BA in anthropology. She and her partner, who was also a fourth-year student at Western, decided to temporarily abandon their studies and move to Vancouver. As both women were only one or two credits short of completing their degrees, they resolved to find employment and enrol as part-time students at a university in Vancouver. However, according to Rebecca, 'the focus changed after we moved out here. It was discovering a new place, discovering the city and the islands.' Rebecca found employment almost immediately as a printer; her partner, who had majored in English, had more difficulty finding work. She eventually found employment with the federal government, completed her undergraduate degree, and began teaching English at a community college while pursuing an MA on a part-time basis. Their relationship lasted for four-and-a-half years after the move to Vancouver.

Rebecca never returned to complete her university studies, but continued to work as a printer. At the time of her interview she had been working for six years for various newspapers, but her employment situation was extremely unsettled. Her employer was a major newspaper conglomerate confronted by considerable labour unrest, including strikes at several local papers. Following a dispute with both her employer and the union, which Rebecca believed failed to adequately represent her, she lost her job. Rebecca found the experience very frustrating and discouraging, but managed to maintain some sense of balance:

> I've always been very open, very direct and very honest. That's the thing that keeps me afloat, that keeps me fine. I see all of these webs being woven that are very disgusting around me and I feel untouched as long as I can focus on knowing what the truth is, telling the truth, and trying to make it clear.

Rebecca supported herself by managing the building she lived in, where she paid no rent and earned a small stipend. She also worked occasionally for a small suburban newspaper, but work had been sporadic.

Rebecca had found herself at a crossroads in her life and was trying to decide her future. She had contemplated several options, including returning to her home town. Her sister, a single parent with a 6-year-old son, still lived in Rebecca's home town and was encouraging her to move back, and Rebecca was very tempted to do so because of a strong need, at this point in her life, to be surrounded by family. On the other hand, her interest in anthropology had resurfaced strongly, and she wanted to complete her undergraduate degree and perhaps even pursue an MA in anthropology:

> The only thing I really have a passion for, is anthropology. If I could feasibly work in anthropology it would be quite wonderful. Aside from my birds, I don't have any dependants or attachments. If I was able to slot into something that would carry me to other countries, I could do it. So having travelled a little bit at this point in my life, I feel quite capable in that vein. However, I feel a need to jump into the milieu to discover what my choices are. I can't believe that all these years have gone by and I haven't continued to pursue it. I did come to a realization fairly recently that I will not be happy unless I do that.

In appraising the changes over time in her values and belief system, Rebecca contended that she now had less faith or trust in people: 'I feel slightly jaded and I think that's fairly normal.' She attributed much of her cynicism to her experiences in dealing with her union and the newspaper organization. In addition, the need to constantly upgrade her skills because of rapid technological changes in the printing and newspaper industries was making her question her commitment to the field. She described her work in printing as having been her career, but not necessarily her dream. Her main goal in the near future was to complete her university education, and she was optimistic that she would be able to pursue her studies.

> I can't believe that all these years have gone by and I haven't continued to pursue it [a university degree]. I did come to a realization fairly recently that I will not be happy unless I do that. Not even necessarily jumping in. It will have to be part-time again. I think if I was to latch on to something that could give me a job, I would go full-time and go all out for it. I'm not willing to give up earning a good dollar for that type of thing, but my situation [managing the building] is really ideal for doing this at this point in my life. And if I could find an evening class that would be ideal. Because I could work and I could accept the shifts that are offered to me, few as they are right now, but hopefully they'll pick up.

She insisted, 'I couldn't possibly live with myself if I didn't follow through with this dream.'

Discussion

This biographical examination of five members of the Class of '73 provides insights into their diverse life courses. When we visited them in 1995, all were working, but not necessarily at the occupations to which they originally aspired. Their stories demonstrate that while their experiences and situations had been structured by such things as schooling, employment, family, religion, and geography, it was their readings of the impact of these structures on them, their aspirations for themselves and their families, and their circumstances at the time that did most to influence the decisions they made with respect to their education, occupation, family life, and so forth. Some, like Paul and Sarah, were able to successfully negotiate the structures and attain their desired educational and career goals; others, like Anna and Rebecca, were still struggling to attain their dreams. Throughout their life courses, parents, friends, and specific events influenced their respective paths.

All of them except Anna indicated that they did not have firm career goals while in high school. Nevertheless, all seemed to realize that further schooling (i.e., beyond grade 13) and training would be necessary if they were to obtain employment. Interestingly, most of them left school after grade 12 but took additional training to qualify them for employment. For instance, Anna dropped out of school while in grade 13, but during the early part of her marriage took a medical stenography course. She later went to college to become a licensed practical nurse. Similarly, after dropping out of grade 13 and working in several jobs he disliked, Dom, who was still undecided about his career goals, enrolled in a manpower training program in painting and decorating. Sarah left school after grade 12, enrolled in a community college, dropped out after one semester, and then returned to compete grade 13. Having struggled with a number of social and emotional problems, Rebecca dropped out of high school. But then she returned to complete her grade 12, and went on from there to complete a two-year arts program at college, which she regarded as an alternative to grade 13.

A lack of clear career aspirations affected the paths to employment taken by Dom, Sarah, and Rebecca. Paul was also without a clear occupational direction, but he chose a more linear route. He followed in the footsteps of his friends and parents, even attending the same university as the latter. Parental expectations in his case were quite high. They were for Sarah as well, even though she chose a more circuitous career route. In both these cases, family life was relatively stable and financial and other forms of support were forthcoming. Relative to Dom, Paul and Sarah enjoyed an advantaged social position, and this enhanced their prospects for higher education.

Anna's modest social-class origins did not deter her from pursuing her schooling. Her immigrant parents conveyed the importance of education as an instrument of social mobility (see Chapter 5). Dom's parents were also immigrants, but for them, community and family links and ethnic identity were more important than mobility and extended education. Obtaining employment was important – the rewards came from supporting one's family, not from securing high occupational status. From childhood to adulthood, Dom expressed pride in his Italian heritage and perceived himself to be an important part of the 'backbone of this country.'

Besides parents, teachers and other adults significantly influenced the life courses of these respondents. Paul credits his music teacher with developing his keen interest in travelling and exploring new places. Sarah's teachers encouraged her to pursue a career in art. This she did, until later in life, when her church minister and the facilitator of her church group inspired her to become a minister. As Sarah explained, it was not the role these individuals occupied, so much as what they modelled: 'I saw in them not so much what they were doing, but how they were doing it, how they were relating to people.' Rebecca's social worker and English teacher inspired her to complete high school.

Peers also influenced the choices made by our interviewees. Paul attended university both because his parents expected him to and because his friends were also planning to attend. Sarah left high school to attend college with her friends, who supported her decision to pursue art-related work. Rebecca and her peers spent a good deal of their adolescence experimenting with drugs and travelling. As the social-psychological literature indicates, peer influence is especially strong in adolescence, but is rarely the determining force in the life course (Coleman and Hendry, 1990: Ch. 6). As can be seen from these cases, young people choose to associate with those who share their interests. They seek not direction but rather confirmation.

Trajectories related to partnership, marriage, and subsequent family circumstances influenced the pathways of all five interviewees. Anna married her hometown boyfriend when she was 22, had three children by the time she was 33, and abandoned her desire to become a nurse. Instead, she qualified as a stenographer and settled for work as a dental secretary. After her divorce, her need to become financially independent of her husband motivated her to rekindle her interest in nursing. However, the demands of parenting and her financial situation meant that she could only become a licensed practical nurse. However, marriage and family responsibilities did not prevent Paul and Sarah from realizing their occupational goals. Paul married someone who easily accepted his need to be mobile in his work. Increasingly, as family priorities took hold, travelling diminished in importance for him and his wife. Sarah and her spouse shared both interests and disabilities and conducted a marriage that complemented her work situation. Dom chose to marry only after he had a secure job, which he had sought for some time. Rebecca and her partner chose, perhaps impulsively, to leave university and move to Vancouver – a decision that may well have limited their career prospects. As a consequence, Rebecca struggled financially.

Gender also influenced the life course of these individuals. Though in different social classes, Paul and Dom consistently worked outside the home, gaining experience that would enhance their occupational prospects. Having taken time out of the work force, Anna found it difficult to obtain secure employment in nursing, a 'helping' profession dominated by women. Sarah encountered few direct gender-related obstacles in her theological training, but as a person with health issues, she had no intention of trying to climb in the church hierarchy, where she might well have encountered gender-based barriers. As she acknowledged, 'there is discrimination out there.'

All five interviewees identified particular unpredicted events as having dramatically affected their life course decisions: health concerns, same-sex orientation, spiritual awakenings, and divorce touched the lives of our subjects. Arguably, chance itself was a force in these individuals' lives. Paul's trip to Europe aroused his interest in travelling. Sarah found life in the church while simultaneously grappling with multiple sclerosis. The 'voice' that Anna heard at a religious retreat had important consequences for her career and marriage. She might well have agreed with Beck (1992: 135): 'Decisions ... no longer can be made, they must be made.' Only after he met his future wife did Dom leave his mother's house and pursue a stable job. Rebecca's same-sex relationship appeared to affect her educational and employment decisions. As we note in the conclusion, how these unique individuals responded to their environments and circumstances (predicted or not) determined the shape and direction of their lives.

Conclusions

Destinations are determined by a combination of external circumstances and personal choice. This is well illustrated by the biographies of these five members of the Class of '73. Both Sarah and Paul constructed scripts for achieving their life goals. Paul employed his training in chartered accountancy to access a career in the banking industry, with the expressed intention of living in different places. In addition, his career trajectory in banking was linear. Though Sarah's career trajectory was nonlinear, she also crafted and implemented a life script, taking advantage of opportunities as they presented themselves and forging ahead, in spite of numerous obstacles. She did not initially have a specific vocational goal. Her obvious talents as an artist and the encouragement of others to pursue a career in this area led her to find employment as a graphic artist – a career that would not fulfil her. Against her parents' advice, and through sheer resolve and determination, and despite poor health, she pursued a career as a minister. Unlike Anna and Rebecca, she was not distracted from her true vocational interest. Dom, on the other hand, had no clear image of his future as he made the transition from adolescence to adulthood. He had no particular conception of what he wanted to become, and was not motivated to succeed in school, and had little ambition to exceed his parents' working-class origins. As a consequence, he drifted throughout his adolescence and early adulthood, and it was only after he married, just short of 30, that he became serious about altering the direction of his life. Faced with mass layoffs at his place of work, he expressed some concern about the security of his job, yet he had not developed a clear plan of action should he be laid off.

Rebecca illustrated the important connection between self-identity and a sense of personal agency or control. By her own admission, her actions during adolescence were governed by 'raging hormones' and a troubled sexual identity. These factors, combined with heavy drug use and dropping out of high school, made it very difficult for Rebecca to even conceptualize a life script or a clear future. Though she returned to school, enrolled in university, and developed an interest in anthropology, Rebecca (like Anna) abandoned her studies to follow a different lifestyle. Both Anna and Rebecca were forced by external circumstances to re-evaluate their future and their priorities.

For members of the Class of '73, life had offered various opportunities and uncertainties, which were influenced by the historical context in which they grew up and by the social forces that either constrained or facilitated their life pathways. Opportunities for the Class of '73 were undoubtedly greater than those available to subsequent generations; yet as they made status passage changes in their late twenties and early thirties, they also encountered the vagaries of a worsening economy. Our analysis here and in earlier chapters underscores the significance of gender, class, region, and immigrant background in explaining educational and career pathways. At the same time, the use of personal biographies reveals the unique ways in which people manage social and cultural capital, and demonstrates the value of incorporating personal agency into analyses of their lives. Periods of adversity notwithstanding, most of the Class of '73 were able to gain a sense of satisfaction and accomplishment by the time they reached their middle years. How they will confront the challenges and continuing uncertainties of the future remains to be seen.

CHAPTER NINE

Conclusion

The preceding chapters charted the twists and bends in the life course pathways of the Class of '73 from grade 12 to the leading edge of middle age. The interplay between structure and agency, and between stability and change, was carefully examined as we followed the lives of this baby-boom cohort. We expected that our findings would provide benchmarks for comparing the Class of '73 with more recent generations. We contend that though transitions from schooling to employment are admittedly more complex, more uncertain, and more nonlinear for contemporary youth than for previous generations, the importance of gender, class, cultural background, and region on the construction of life scripts has not declined. Similarly, while these structural factors are useful for predicting youth's values and behaviours, they do not completely explain perceptions and choices. Individual circumstances and personal agency also require exploration, and for this reason the authors turned to life course theory. This perspective attempts to explain the dynamic relationship between the individual and the social order; it examines a cohort's collective experience without oversimplifying it, and is sensitive to individual differences without ignoring social context. Time, viewed from a multidisciplinary perspective, is a key feature of the life course approach. Thus, psychology stresses individual development; history highlights the impact of social historical changes; and sociology examines institutional and social structural changes.

By focusing on a panel of people who were quickly approaching mid-life, we sought to probe the substance of education as an integral and life-long process. We also identified the kinds of educational opportunities these people utilized in constructing their lives. Finally, we considered how they evaluated their preparedness for obtaining additional education and training, especially with respect to the needs of a changing society; and how they evaluated both the impact of education and its usefulness in terms of shaping and influencing their career mobility and their children's educational and occupational prospects.

We began our exploration of the Class of '73 with a social historical analysis of their roots. The children of this generation were raised in an era of relative prosperity, supported by a spirit of expectancy and optimism. The message of the time, reinforced by ample public funding, was that schooling would provide the transition to a good and productive life. The Class of '73 grew up in a time of rapid social change, during which critics charged that true individuality and social equality had yet to be achieved in Ontario and the rest of Canada. Young people growing up in the late 1960s adopted liberal modes of social interaction and stressed the merits of choice and autonomy – attitudes that extended into the 1970s. At the same time, young people, consistent with the expectations of their parents, pursued postsecondary education in unprecedented numbers, clearly anticipating useful and rewarding careers, despite the downturn in Ontario's economy in the 1970s.

Though historical forces shaped the environment in ways that individuals could not influence, the experiences of the Class of '73 were far from identical with respect to growing up and adopting particular life course pathways. Rural and working-class youth were less likely to obtain university education than their middle-class, urban counterparts; and young women, though able to access a wider range of educational and career options than their mothers, held tenaciously to the cultural notion of domestic 'responsibility.' Foreign-born young people and those from religious, ethnic, and racial minorities often perceived themselves as outside the social mainstream; they also encountered distinctive challenges at home, at school, in the peer group, and in the workplace.

We found that advanced education was important to the Class of '73. While respondents were reluctant to support the idea that everyone had the right to the kind of job for which their education and training had prepared them, those with advanced degrees were strongly inclined to believe it important that their jobs should be related to their field of study or specialization. Structural factors such as class, gender, and region clearly played a strong role in shaping educational choices developed during the high school years, notwithstanding that personal educational preferences also developed. Moreover, the organizational structures of high schools facilitated the educational sorting of students into lower and higher streams. These factors influenced subsequent educational decisions independently, particularly at critical points when members of the Class of '73 assumed career, marital, and parental responsibilities. Evidence that Canada was rapidly becoming an education-led society was revealed by this study. By 1979, when participants were in their mid-twenties, two-thirds of respondents had obtained at least some formal postsecondary education, and by 1994/95 nearly half the respondents had returned to pursue further formal education. For two-thirds of this latter group, further education did not constitute a significant upgrade in educational credentials. Investigation of further educational acquisition after 1979 revealed very complex transition patterns; this highlights that individual differences and agency were important factors as respondents moved through their life courses. The group that had no postsecondary education as of 1979 showed some openness to a life-long learning culture, in that a substantial number subsequently took further education, and about half completed community college certificates or diplomas.

These findings suggest that the school-to-work transitions for members of the Class of '73 were largely nonlinear and rather complex. This hunch is supported by the analysis provided in Chapter 4. Class origins strongly influenced the type and level of further formal education attained by 1979. Though the majority of respondents entered first jobs that were either unskilled or skilled, those with postsecondary qualifications were more likely to begin their careers as professionals, semiprofessionals, or mid-level/high-level managers. While class background was clearly a factor with respect to the transition to employment, its impact should not be overstated: merit, as reflected in educational attainment, was a very significant factor in the lives of the Class of '73. Thus, lower-class youth who attained higher education in the 1970s found success in the job market, and for upper-class youth, educational attainment had a greater impact than class background on career trajectories. Throughout the 1980s and 1990s, members of the Class of '73 traversed the world of employment – a world in which opportunity and uncertainty coexisted. Indeed, a significant minority of respondents reported being unemployed at some point between 1978 and 1994 and in 1994–95. Well over one-third of respondents claimed that their jobs were not related to the field of study of their most recent degree or diploma. In terms of employment experiences, 10 per cent reported that they worked part-time, and most of these 10 per cent were women who were seeking to fulfil their domestic obligations. An even greater proportion of those working in 1994–95 reported that they were self-employed (19.4 per cent), and of this group, the majority were men residing in rural areas and small towns.

Job training played an important role for many members of the Class of '73: two-thirds received such training at least once between 1989 and 1994. Over this time period, a greater proportion turned to job-related training for coping with economic changes in Ontario, such as corporate restructuring. As reasons for taking job-related training, many respondents mentioned changes in their work environment and the need to upgrade their skills. Consistent with other studies, our results indicated that higher levels of formal education and occupational prestige are correlated with participation in job-related training. Finally, participation in job-related training tended to result in positive job outcomes, including greater job satisfaction and job security.

In 1994–95, over two-thirds of respondents were satisfied with how things had turned out for them with respect to work and career, though a larger proportion expressed satisfaction with their family and personal life. Interviews with respondents indicated that while some expressed appreciation for the standard of living that their occupational incomes provided, others had sacrificed money for the sake of a desirable way of life, which might involve living in the country, spending more time with family, or being one's own boss in a small company rather than an employee in a large firm.

The occupational experiences of the members of the Class of '73 were further explored in terms of inter- and intra-generational mobility. The middle class was particularly vulnerable to the changes in Ontario's economy, with over 60 per cent moving either up or down the ladder of success relative to their parents. A minority of respondents from working-class origins took advantage of opportunities and moved into upper socio-economic positions. With respect to gender, we found greater occupational inheritance among men and a tendency for the gross mobility patterns of women to be quite distinct from those of their male counterparts. Residence and geographical mobility mattered insofar as living in a city favoured upward mobility, and moving away from home enhanced intergenerational mobility. Though our longitudinal information is insufficient to fully establish the links between migration and occupational success, a number of correlates were identified. For example, 'stayers' were more likely to be drawn from lower socio-economic origins; were less likely to assess positively their chances of graduating from university; and were less likely to evaluate themselves as effective, important, or interesting.

An analysis of career mobility over the life course revealed that fewer than one-third of respondents experienced no movement from first to current full-time occupation by 1994–95. Movement either up or down was incremental, with most respondents experiencing no more than three steps or shifts by 1994–95. Both men and women experienced upward career mobility, though this pattern was somewhat stronger for men. Socio-economic origin proved more influential over the long term, and favoured those with higher socio-economic origins. As was the case with intergenerational mobility, residence and migration were factors in career mobility. Thus, respondents with city backgrounds and 'movers' were more likely to have experienced intra-occupational mobility by 1994–95.

The study also considered how well members of the Class of '73 with foreign-born parents have done with respect to their educational and occupational attainments relative to peers with Canadian-born parents. The former respondents were more likely to come from a working-class family background, yet they tended to hold higher occupational aspirations and expectations. To achieve their ambitions, they needed to acquire high levels of education. That they were remarkably successful in accomplishing this can be attributed to 'immigrant drive' or 'minority determination.' Studies show that immigrant parents are more likely to place their faith in the power of education and to strongly encourage their children to actively pursue a postsecondary and particularly a university education. While this finding is validated in this study, we also found that sons were significantly more likely to receive this type of encouragement, and to be financially assisted by parents in their pursuit of higher education. Nevertheless, many female respondents of foreign-born parents were able to obtain a postsecondary education and to secure work that was commensurate with their education. Compared to female counterparts with Canadian-born parents, they were also less likely to be unemployed and twice as likely to be self-employed.

While the respondents of foreign-born parents experienced positive employment and career mobility outcomes associated with higher educational attainment, they were also less likely to be geographically mobile. Foreign-born parents and their children were more likely to live in urban communities, where they forged links with other members of their ethnic communities. Respondents with foreign-born parents utilized these familial and social connections to obtain job training and pursue occupational goals.

Whatever their residential origins, the Class of '73 attached great importance to family life, especially to the raising of children. They were uncertain about the quality of modern schools, yet they were determined to encourage their children to extend their education, and planned to help pay for it. Women, whether they worked outside the home or not, continued to bear the major responsibility for rearing children and performing household tasks. Balancing the demands of employment and family life was a major challenge for women, especially for financially burdened single mothers.

In the final chapter we conducted a micro life course analysis of five members of the Class of '73. Earlier chapters had examined separate trajectories or pathways pertaining to education, careers, marriage, and childrearing. While charting these separate trajectories is useful, linking trajectories, transitions, and turning points is of critical importance in grasping how the life course unfolds for individuals. Furthermore, while the Class of '73 grew up in a society in which status passages were governed by clear and explicit expectations, as they moved through their twenties and into their thirties they encountered times of greater risk and uncertainty. We made the assumption that there is no standard biography and that each person becomes responsible for writing his or her own life script. Thus, it was important to examine the types of individual solutions and decisions that respondents formulated at various transitions between schooling, work, marriage, and parenting.

Our examination of five personal biographies revealed a diversity of life course pathways, ranging from the strongly traditional (i.e., linear, school-to-work pathways) to those of a more chaotic and nonlinear nature. These pathways were sometimes influenced by traumatic events such as the breakdown of a marriage, a death in the family, or the emergence of a significant health problem. A closer examination of these biographies also revealed the important role played by personal agency. Some respondents articulated a clear vision of the future while still in adolescence, and vigorously pursued this beacon. Others drifted with relatively little focus through adolescence and early adulthood, giving little thought to the conscious pursuit of life goals. We concluded that a personal locus of control in planning life trajectories was related to the clarity with which respondents envisioned their future. The personal biographies we reviewed accentuated the various and unique ways in which people manage their social and cultural capital; in turn, this underscored the value of incorporating personal agency for appreciating how individuals define and act on the opportunities and uncertainties they encounter in moving from adolescence to adulthood.

This sums up the major findings of our study. We believe this book should prove useful to life course researchers who wish to compare the aspirations, expectations, and experiences of their cohorts with the Class of '73. Though we now live in an altered society, one in which young people are more subject to risk in the choices they make, the life course pathways and experiences of younger generations may not differ in substance and quality from those of the Class of '73. Indeed, the analysis presented in this book provides support for some general observations that may well apply to a range of generations. In adolescence, the participants in our study were generally optimistic about their future and convinced that a commitment to further formal education beyond the high school years would pay handsome career and lifestyle dividends. However, as they moved into their mid-twenties and early thirties and experienced the downturn in Ontario's economy, their optimism faded as they became more aware of the uncertainties in the larger environment and the changing world. A significant proportion experienced personal uncertainty, which manifested itself in the form of unemployment, underemployment, job insecurity, and downward social mobility. Yet many did not lose heart. They altered their life scripts to include more education, more job upgrading, and other forms of advanced learning. Note also that the experiences of this cohort varied, sometimes enormously, which lends credence to the notion that individual factors are important when it comes to adapting to the many transitions experienced in moving from adolescence to adulthood. And close biographical examination revealed a rich texture in the intersection of trajectories among those who experienced conventional and nonconventional school/work transitions.

Though we do not at this stage have similar analyses of other (younger) Ontario generations to compare with those for the Class of '73, we can turn to a similar study conducted in British Columbia (Andres, 1998). This longitudinal research project surveyed 10,000 members of the B.C. graduating grade 12 class of 1988. Two follow-up surveys were also conducted, one in 1993 and the last in 1998. Nearly

90 per cent of high school graduates aspired to earn a university degree, and over 60 per cent expected that they would acquire such credentials. By 1993, 55 per cent of the Class of '88 had earned a postsecondary credential.

When questioned about the relationship between education and work, most respondents expressed a firm belief that postsecondary participation would enhance future job prospects, increase their incomes, and allow greater access to a wider choice of jobs. This commitment to education as a means of enhancing future prospects appeared to be stronger among the Class of '88 than the Class of '73. However, in both cohorts the majority shared the view that 'compared with the past, higher levels of education are required today' (Andres, 1998: 6). Also, when surveyed in 1993, slightly more than one-quarter of the Class of '88 reported that they were married or in a marriagelike relationship, and only 6 per cent had children. These figures, significantly lower than those reported in Chapter 7, may indicate that young adults are either postponing marriage and children or committing to alternative lifestyles.

While there can be no doubt that education is an important determinant of one's position in society (a finding documented in Chapter 5), it is also true that educational mobility (i.e., the difference between the educational attainments of parents and their children) is now common in Canada, as indicated by the finding in 1994 that about half of Canadians age 26 to 35 reported having more education than their parents (de Broucker and Lavallee, 1998: 22). This upward trend would appear to auger well for labour market success, given the positive interrelationship between parents' formal education, provision of social and cultural capital, supportive home learning environments for children, and higher educational attainment levels. Yet a cautionary note should be introduced here, given the strong mediating influence of social class, particularly in the form of financial capital available within the family for supporting the development of intellectual capital in children (e.g., purchase of home computers), educational achievement in school, and successful school/work transitions. A study based on the U.S. Department of Education's National Education Longitudinal Study of 1988 found that even among students who scored well on standardized tests and took rigorous high school courses, those from low and middle income families were less likely than those from high income families to go to college. Many low and middle income students said that they couldn't afford college and had to support their families (*Academe Today*, 1998). While educational policy may be a powerful instrument for influencing human capital formation, de Broucker and Lavallee (1998: 28) indicate that 'other public policies that recognize the link between low education and low income also play an important role. Such programs could help young low-income parents to complete their higher education, find adequate day care facilities, obtain career counselling and integrate into the labour market.'

A final observation relates to the positive school-to-work and social mobility experiences of those opting to alter their geographical location (referred to as 'movers' in this study), and the similar experiences of children of foreign-born parents. Among both groups, complacency is challenged and people are called on to examine status passages and critically evaluate the direction of their lives (or in the case of foreign-born parents, the lives of their children). Canadians who opt to make significant changes in their lifestyle (e.g., move from rural areas to a city) confront the need to reflect on the past while preparing new scripts for the future. Practices that are taken for granted in one context may fail to operate in the new environment, so that new forms of reflexivity and consciousness must be developed. As a consequence, these people increase their capacity to adapt to new environments, which enhances life outcomes. Foreign-born parents often attain personal success not by improving their own social status, but, vicariously, through the efforts of their children. As newcomers, the foreign-born are compelled to question conventional strategies for achieving success, and may lack the social capital available to Canadians. Yet, as in the case of 'movers,' foreign-born parents are made more reflexive by their migration experiences, and aspire to do well in Canada by sponsoring their children. Canadian-born parents might well learn from the experiences of 'movers' and the foreign-born as a means to broaden the life experiences of their children and to prepare them for the twenty-first century.

Sample Attrition over the Six Phases of the Class of '73 Study

Longitudinal studies suffer sample attrition, or loss of cases, over the duration of the research project. The Class of '73 study is no exception. In this appendix we try to assess the extent and impact of sample attrition as it affects our research.

Members of the Class of '73 were studied at six different times. The initial in-school questionnaire survey was completed in June 1973. Because the name of the student and parents' name and address was obtained in this initial survey, two telephone follow-up surveys were possible, one in October 1973 (Phase II), and another in October 1974 (Phase III). Based on this same name and address information, members of the Class of '73 were tracked down in 1979, and a questionnaire was sent to the reduced sample in the summer of 1979 (Phase IV). Anticipating future surveys, the Phase IV questionnaire asked respondents to 'provide us [with] the names and addresses of two friends or relatives who will probably know of your location in five years and are not likely to have moved themselves.' Previous address information and this new name and address information was used during the summers of 1987 and 1988 to track as many of the Phase IV sample as we could at that time, updating our address information for the Class of '73. This information became the basis of our efforts to locate the Class of '73 again for the 1995 Phase VI survey.

Detailed consideration of previous sample attrition can be found in the appendices of two reports that have emanated from the Class of '73 study over the years, the reports associated with Phase III (Anisef, 1975) and with Phase IV (Anisef, Paasche, and Turrittin, 1980). Both of these appendices included case weights that permitted estimates of parameters for the whole of the population of Ontario grade 12 students in 1973. Due to significant sample attrition by 1995, however, we felt that it was no longer proper to weight our 1995 sample so as to represent the original 1973 Ontario grade 12 student population. We decided to let the Class of '73 as surveyed in 1995 stand on its own as a sample.

Table A.1 presents information on the attrition of our sample from survey to survey with respect to selected key variables. Table A.2 shows similar information giving distributions of characteristics for each of the sample surveys. As the top portion of Table A.1 shows, we were able to contact again almost all respondents six months and a year later after the original June 1973 survey. However, with the passage of five years from 1974 to 1979, we were only able to recover 60 per cent of the original sample in Phase IV. Roughly, we experienced a 70 per cent drop in relocating respondents between successive phases after 1974. In Phase VI (1995), only 31 per cent of the original sample group was retained.

While we reported retaining 31 per cent of the original sample, in fact we did somewhat better in terms of locating former respondents. After a diligent search, before undertaking our questionnaire mailing, we had names and addresses of 1,150 members of the Class of '73. In all, 788 questionnaires were returned after follow-up reminders. In addition, seven completed questionnaires were returned too late for entry into our data base.

While retaining only one-third of the original sample, we were surprised by how well our Phase VI sample still represented the original sample of students first studied in 1973. For example, as indicated in Table A.2, the gender ratio of respondents was practically constant across all phases of our longitudinal study. Using the same measure of socio-economic status based on 1973 respondent data, the socio-economic status distribution for the 1995 sample was nearly the same as in 1973. However, the attrition data in Table A.1 indicate that we retained slightly more respondents in the high socio-economic group compared to the medium-low and low socio-economic groups; however, the differences are not large (5 per cent at most).

Even with respect to educational attainment, sample attrition did not have a major impact. The bottom portion of Table A.2 shows the distribution of educational attainment in 1979. The distribution of 1979 educational attainment for our 1995 sample is remarkably similar to the 1979 distribution. The attrition data in the lower portion of Table

A.1 show, however, that we retained 5 per cent more university graduates than those without postsecondary education based on 1979 educational attainment by the time of the 1995 survey.

It should be noted that our sample is education oriented. That is to say, pursuing further formal education is a characteristic of the Class of '73, as shown by the far lower right-hand corner of Table A.2, which gives the distribution of educational attainment in 1995 in parentheses. A sizable minority of the Class of '73 went on to obtain college diplomas and certificates and complete university and professional degrees after 1979.

There were, however, two significant deformations of our samples over time, which had to do with region of origin in the province of Ontario and an interaction of region with socio-economic status. Region as a variable reflects the original sampling design that selected samples of high schools based on four sampling strata: Metropolitan Toronto, other large cities in Ontario, other cities including the suburban area around Metropolitan Toronto, and small towns and rural areas. As shown in Table A.2, the original sampling design tended to favour the latter two sampling strata. Locating former respondents proved to be more difficult for those individuals originating in Metro Toronto and the other larger cities of Ontario, and easiest for those individuals from small towns and rural areas. As the second panel of Table A.2 shows, the distribution of respondents by strata shifted so that by Phase VI, Metro Toronto respondents had dropped from 21 per cent to 16 per cent, and small town and rural area respondents had risen from 33 per cent to 41 per cent. The second panel of Table A.1 shows the differential pattern of attrition by region across the phases of the Class of '73 study. By Phase VI, only 24.1 per cent of Metro Toronto subjects were retained, compared to 38.3 per cent of subjects from small towns and rural areas.

The nature of the attrition experienced by the Class of '73 study is revealed in the third panel of Table A.1, where we have cross-tabulated socio-economic status by geographical region in examining attrition from Phase I to Phase VI. The table compares only the highest socio-economic group with the lowest for all four geographical regions. When this cross-tabulation was done for Class of '73 members with high socio-economic status background, the retention levels dropped to about one-third for all regions except for the small town and rural area region, which showed a 41 per cent retention through to the final phase of the research. However, for the low-SES group, roughly one-third from the small town and rural areas and other cities and one-fifth from other Ontario cities were retained until the final phase; the rate dropped to a very low one-in-ten for the Metro Toronto area. The dramatic loss of Metro Toronto low SES Class of '73 members does not show up in the SES distributions of Table A.2 because the loss of low-SES background persons from Metro Toronto was balanced by the retention of those with low-SES backgrounds from small towns and rural areas. In general, we believe that the pattern of losses indicated above is due to the greater difficulty we experienced in tracking individuals whose initial residence was in large Ontario cities. This leads to the question of whether there were any differences relevant to our findings between lower-SES persons of urban as opposed to rural origins – a question that our data cannot definitively answer due to the small number of Metro Toronto low socio-economic background persons retained to Phase VI (n = 10).

While we worked very hard at locating members of the Class of '73, we ultimately had only modest success at tracking respondents. It may therefore be useful to compare our retention rates with those found in other longitudinal research. An inventory of longitudinal studies, largely in the United States, was published in 1991 by Young, Savola, and Phelps. This inventory lists only a few studies that are comparable to the Class of '73 study in terms of modest to large sample sizes, a fairly long time span, and a focus on educational attainment and labour market entry. For example, the Wisconsin Longitudinal Study, begun in 1957 with 10,317 youth 18 years of age, retained 88.6 per cent through to 1975. The (U.S.) National Longitudinal Survey of Youth Labor Market Experience (NLSY), begun in 1979, retained 90.2 per cent of respondents through 1988. The high retention rates of these studies were likely due to the researchers having access to government records in helping them track respondents as in the Wisconsin study, or as in the NLSY study, an annual return to sample members. Still, the (U.S.) National Longitudinal Surveys of Labor Market Experience (NLS) initiated in 1965, which utilized an annual return to its sample members, had a retention rate of only 65.0 per cent for the young men's sample, which began in 1966 with 14 to 24 year old men and ended in 1981, and only a 68.0 per cent retention rate for the young women's sample, begun in 1968 with 14 to 24 year old women and ended in 1988. The (U.S.) National Longitudinal Study of the High School Class of 1972 began with a sample of 23,451 high school students aged 16 to 21, with restudies in 1973, 1974, 1976, and 1979, and had a retention rate of 45.2 per cent when completed in 1986. While Copeland, Savola, and Phelps provided a great deal of information about each longitudinal study, unfortunately the one piece of information lacking in their inventory was a commentary on the method of tracking over time, such as the availability of government or other records used to help find sample members. In terms of the Class of '73 longitudinal study, it is clear that our tracking was hampered by infrequent returns to sample members and a lack of access to any kind of government or other records (both strategies would have required extensive resources for implementation).

We have already noted that the Class of '73 appeared to be particularly successful in terms of levels of educational attainment. In turn, more education pays off in terms of higher-status occupations, and correspondingly higher individual personal incomes. To confirm this hunch about educational success, we draw on two comparative data sources. The first is the Census of Canada, 1991: Individual Public Use Microdata File, provided by Statistics Canada for public use.[1] The second source is the 1993 General Social Survey (GSS) Public Use Microdata File, based on a telephone survey conducted by Statistics Canada, a data file that is available for public use on personal computers.[2] Tables A.3 and A.4 compare Class of '73 data with data drawn from these two Statistics Canada surveys.

In Chapter 3 we noted that by sampling grade 12 Ontario high school students in 1973, we did not secure a true sample of Ontario youth aged 18 because of dropouts from the educational system prior to grade 12. We estimated a dropout rate of 20 percent by grade 12. In order that the Statistics Canada samples correspond to the original Class of '73 sample, we restricted the data from Statistics Canada to students with high school graduation or higher educational levels. We tried in other ways to ensure correspondence between the 1995 Class of '73 sample and the Statistics Canada data. In the Phase VI survey, members of the Class of '73 were typically 40 years of age.[3] Because of the large sample size of the 1991 census data, we were able to select out an equivalent age group who were 36 years of age in 1991. The 1993 GSS reported data in terms of two age categories that break at age 40. Thus, we report 1993 GSS data for two age groups, ages 35 to 39, and ages 40 to 44. Members of the Class of '73 were, of course, Ontario residents and largely Ontario born, but not exclusively since the sample included some youth whose families had moved to Ontario from other parts of Canada, and some foreign-born youth whose parents had immigrated to Canada. For the 1991 census data we reported two subsamples, one based on 1991 residence in Ontario, and the other based on birthplace in Ontario. For the 1993 GSS, the sample was restricted to Ontario residents who were also born in Ontario.

As Table A.3 indicates, compared with the other Ontario samples, Class of '73 members appear to excel in terms of the very high proportion with a university degree or higher by 1995, with women slightly ahead of men.[4] We regard the proportion of university graduates as a significant measure because it is the least ambiguous educational status of all the levels of the education variables. Interestingly, as column D in Table A.3 shows, the 1993 GSS age category 35–39 (the typical age of Class of '73 members in 1993 was 38) indicates that 32.7 per cent of men had university education or higher – a figure very close to the men of the Class of '73. While Class of '73 men appeared to have similar levels of university education to men in the 1993 GSS survey, this was not the case for women. Only 17.7 per cent of GSS women aged 35 to 39 had university education or higher – much lower than the 35.1 per cent figure for Class of '73 women.

We would argue that in general, higher levels of education (in time) translate into higher-status occupations and higher personal incomes. Thus, the education-oriented Class of '73 should also show success in the occupational and personal income realms, compared to the Statistics Canada survey groups. This generalization is born out by the middle and bottom panels of Table A.3, and by the personal income data by key variables shown in Table A.4. Some 54 per cent of Class of '73 men reported managerial and professional occupations by 1995, but the percentage of Class of '73 women in this occupational category was even higher, at 61.9 per cent. These proportions were much higher than those of that 1933 GSS survey group, aged 35–39, found in Column D of Table A.3. With respect to personal income, and in contrast to educational attainment, Class of '73 men outdid Class of '73 women. In addition, the men earned substantially more personal income than the men of any of the Statistics Canada surveys. In spite of their high levels of education and occupation, the Class of '73 women appeared to be similar to the other women reported in the Statistics Canada surveys, at least based on the categories shown in the bottom panel of Table A.3. However, as Table A.4 shows, when averages were computed by educational and occupational categories, average incomes for Class of '73 women were higher than for women in the Statistics

Canada surveys. Column E in Table A.4, which reports personal income data for the 40–44 year age group, compared to the data for the younger age group shown in column D, indicated the independent effect of age in producing higher incomes for men as men increased their seniority in the work place.

In conclusion, while we have argued that the Class of '73 as surveyed and studied in 1995 is strongly representative of the original Class of '73 as grade 12 students in Ontario, comparison with Statistics Canada cross-sectional surveys in 1991 and 1993 reveal that the Class of '73 experienced greater success, as of 1995, in terms of educational attainment, higher status occupations, and, for men in particular, substantially higher reported personal income compared to peers in other kinds of similar populations.

1 The number of cases on the unweighted individual file for 1991 is 809,654, of which the Ontario portion is 299,278, which, when weighted, becomes 9,975,923. All calculations based on the Ontario public use file are weighted data.

2 The topic of the 1993 General Social Survey was personal risk. Data is reported for 11,960 individuals which, when weighted, represents a total Canada population of 24,678,196. The Ontario sub-sample is 2,609 respondents representing a population sample of 9,231,654.

3 On the 1995 Phase VI survey, respondents reported the following years of birth (n = 777): 1951, 0.1 per cent; 1952, 1.2 per cent; 1953, 3.7 per cent; 1954, 12.9 per cent; 1955, 66.4 per cent; 1956, 15.2 per cent; and 1957, 0.5 per cent.

4 The recoding of Statistics Canada's educational categories proved difficult in terms of matching the four educational attainment groups used for the Class of '73. For the 1991 census data, we dropped the lowest three educational categories, retaining secondary school graduation as equivalent to our Class of '73 category of high school only. We included the category high school trade certificate as equivalent to the Class of '73 community college certificate; other non-university education with a trade certificate, and other non-university education with a non-university certificate were also included in the community college certificate category. The highest four categories beginning with a bachelor's or first professional degree were treated as equivalent to the Class of '73 category of university degree or higher. All the other categories were treated as indicating the Class of '73 category of some college or some university education (absence of a certificate or university graduation). With respect to the 1993 GSS, the excluded educational group was those individuals with some secondary education, elementary school, or no schooling; the secondary school graduate was retained as equivalent to the Class of '73 high school only category; the categories diploma/certificate-college and diploma/certificate-trade were treated as equivalent to the Class of '73 community college certificate category; the GSS category obtaining a bachelor's degree (including an LLB), or the category of higher post-secondary degrees was equated with the Class of '73 category of university graduate or higher; finally, all other educational categories coded for the GSS became equivalent Class of '73 category some college or some university.

With respect to the 1991 census data reviewed, dropping individuals with less than high school graduation removed 21.9 per cent of the weighted sample for Ontario residents, and removed 20.9 per cent of the weighted sample for the Ontario born. For the age group category of 35–39 in the 1993 GSS survey, 9.9 per cent of the weighted individual sample for Ontario residents born in Ontario had less than high school graduation, and for the age category 40–44 this proportion was 17.1 per cent.

Table A.1. Sample Attrition over Six Phases of the Class of '73 Study

Variable		1973 Phase I	1973 Phase II	1974 Phase III	1979 Phase IV	1987/88 Phase V	1995 Phase VI
Cases		2,555	2,156	2,163	1,522	1,129	788
% of original cases		100.0%	84.4	84.7	59.6	44.2	30.8
% of previous survey		100.0%	84.4	00.3	70.4	74.2	69.8
Region							
Metro Toronto	n = 535	100.0%	89.3	85.4	52.0	37.8	24.1
Other large cities	n = 564	100.0%	86.7	84.0	60.1	44.5	26.1
Other cities	n = 618	100.0%	84.8	83.5	60.4	41.9	30.9
Small towns and rural areas	n = 838	100.0%	79.4	85.4	63.5	49.8	38.3
Socio-economic status 1973							
High	n = 582	100.0%	90.9	87.1	64.1	46.7	33.2
Medium high	n = 538	100.0%	88.7	86.7	61.5	47.6	34.8
Medium low	n = 626	100.0%	81.5	83.1	56.7	41.4	28.6
Low	n = 529	100.0%	79.4	84.2	59.5	44.4	30.0
Missing cases SES		143	111	109	67	46	30
Socio-economic status 1973 High SES	Metro Toronto	n = 167	100.0%	92.8	89.8	63.5	41.9	32.3
	Other large cities	n = 150	100.0%	92.0	86.0	62.7	48.0	29.3
	Other cities	n = 150	100.0%	92.0	86.0	64.7	44.0	32.0
	Small town and rural areas	n = 115	100.0%	85.2	86.1	66.1	55.7	40.9
Low SES	Metro Toronto	n = 89	100.0%	94.4	92.1	47.2	33.7	11.2
	Other large cities	n = 109	100.0%	80.7	80.7	57.8	38.5	20.2
	Other cities	n = 150	100.0%	81.3	82.7	58.7	44.0	32.0
	Small town and rural areas	n = 318	100.0%	73.9	84.0	63.8	49.7	37.7

Table A.1. Sample Attrition over Six Phases of the Class of '73 Study *(continued)*

Variable		1973 Phase I	1973 Phase II	1974 Phase III	1979 Phase IV	1987/88 Phase V	1995 Phase VI
Educational attainment 1979	High school only	n = 571			100.0%		48.0
	Some college/university	n = 228			100.0%		46.5
	College diploma	n = 298			100.0%		58.1
	University degree	n = 425			100.0%		53.2

Table A.2. Background Variable Distributions over Six Phases of the Class of '73 Study

Variable		1973 Phase I	1973 Phase II	1974 Phase III	1979 Phase IV	1987/88 Phase V	1995 Phase VI
Gender	Cases	2,555	2,156	2,163	1,522	1,129	788
	Males	49.0%	48.7%	49.1%	48.0%	47.8%	48.4%
	Females	51.0	51.3	50.9	52.0	52.2	51.6
Region	Cases	2,555	2,156	2,163	1,522	1,129	788
	Metro Toronto	20.9%	22.2%	21.1%	18.3%	17.9%	16.4%
	Other large cities	22.1	22.7	21.9	22.3	22.2	18.7
	Other cities	24.2	24.3	23.9	24.5	22.9	24.2
	Small towns and rural areas	32.8	30.8	33.1	35.0	36.9	40.7
Socio-economic status	Cases	2,412	2,045	2,054	1,455	1,083	758
	High	24.1%	25.9%	24.7%	25.6%	25.1%	25.4%
	Medium high	22.3	23.3	22.7	22.7	23.6	24.6
	Medium low	26.0	24.9	25.3	24.4	23.9	23.6
	Low	27.6	25.9	27.3	27.2	27.3	26.4
Educational attainment 1979	Cases				1,531		788
	High school only				37.9%		35.9% (26.9%)*
	Some college/university				14.9		13.5 (10.0%)*
	College diploma				19.5		22.0 (39.3)*
	University degree				27.8		28.7 (33.8)*

* Educational attainment by 1995 of Class of '73 members surviving through to the 1995 Phase VI survey.

Table A.3. Class of '73 Compared with Ontario 1991 Census of Canada and Ontario 1993 General Social Survey

| Variable | A. Class of '73 Phase VI Survey (Typical age is 40) | | 1991 Census, Individual Public Use Microdata File (Sub-sample for age 36) | | | | 1993 Statistics Canada General Social Survey, Ontario Residents Born in Ontario | | | |
| | | | B. By residence in Ontario | | C. By birthplace in Ontario | | D. Age 35–39 | | E. Age 40–44 | |
	Male	Female	Male	Female	Male	Female	Male	Female	Male	Female
Education										
University	32.3%	35.1%	26.9%	22.5%	23.3%	22.8%	32.7%	17.7%	24.2%	16.8%
College	28.6	30.0	34.1	28.4	36.1	30.2	37.1	32.9	48.5	24.8
Some university/ some college	12.9	7.4	22.3	24.3	21.6	22.0	16.9	24.5	13.5	18.9
High school graduate	26.2	27.5	16.7	24.8	19.0	24.9	13.3	24.9	13.8	39.5
Number	381	407	65,033	69,000	44,767	48,633	264,638	221,091	221,743	173,163
Current occupation										
Managerial/professional	54.7%	61.9%	34.0%	39.3%	33.4%	43.2%	48.8%	50.0%	46.9%	40.4%
Clerical and sales	12.5	28.5	13.8	38.3	14.4	38.7	10.1	35.1	19.3	30.5
Other	32.8	9.6	52.2	22.3	52.1	18.1	41.1	14.9	33.8	29.1
Number	351	333	76,933	68,667	53,767	47,633	249,413	153,854	182,363	133,036
Personal annual income										
No income or loss	0.0%	0.9%	1.0%	2.1%	0.5%	1.7%	1.7%	0.0%	0.0%	0.0%
Less than $5,000	0.9	5.0	2.7	7.4	2.1	7.9	0.0	2.6	0.0	3.8
$5,000–9,999	0.6	5.0	3.3	9.2	3.2	9.2	0.0	5.3	0.0	7.1
$10,000–14,999	0.9	8.5	3.0	11.7	2.8	11.9	0.9	10.9	0.0	5.2
$15,000–19,999	0.9	7.6	5.3	11.7	5.3	11.4	8.2	11.2	6.1	9.4
$20,000–29,999	8.1	18.5	17.2	24.8	16.3	22.2	2.7	32.5	3.2	27.2

$30,000–39,999	12.9	18.2	23.6	17.3	24.9	19.1	28.4	13.3	23.1	30.5
$40,000–49,999	17.2	16.5	19.0	9.0	20.6	9.6	21.6	8.4	26.3	9.9
$50,000–59,999	22.6	9.1	12.2	4.0	12.5	4.4	21.7	12.7	18.3	4.1
$60,000–79,999	20.4	6.8	8.2	1.6	7.5	1.5	10.9	1.5	11.8	2.9
$80,000 or more	15.7	3.9	4.4	0.9	4.3	1.0	4.0	1.5	11.2	0.0
Number	349	340	76,933	68,667	53,767	47,633	237,475	126,733	166,543	128,203

Note: The education variable for all samples is based on high school graduation or higher, and all occupational and income data is reported only for those reporting that they were currently employed (full- or part-time or self-employed).

Table A.4. Personal Income Averages and Personal Income by Educational Attainment and Occupational Status, Class of '73 Compared with Ontario 1991 Census of Canada and Ontario 1993 General Social Survey

Average Personal Income by Indicated Variable	A. Class of '73 Phase VI Survey (Typical age is 40)		B. 1991 Census, Individual Public Use Microdata File (Sub-sample for age 36) By resdidence in Ontario		C. By residence in Ontario		D. 1993 Statistics Canada General Social Survey Ontario Residents Born in Ontario Age 35–39		E. Age 40–44	
Personal income	Male	Female	Male	Female	Male	Female	Male	Female	Male	Female
Overall average	$56,461	$34,603	$39,749	$24,514	$40,179	$24,907	$45,007	$29,765	$50,187	$29,111
Number	349	340	76,933	68,667	53,767	47,633	237,476	126,732	166,542	128,204
Education										
University	$66,949	$43,283	$52,122	$35,455	$53,473	$36,270	$53,892	$37,118	$54,056	$42,030
Number	118	115	16,833	13,133	10,167	9,433	76,531	29,864	53,724	25,521
College	$53,075	$33,113	$37,614	$23,417	$38,582	$23,281	$42,525	$35,301	$48,858	$28,325
Number	100	106	21,000	15,900	15,467	12,267	95,792	43,287	65,773	33,089
Some university/ some college	$57,444	$30,000	$38,305	$24,637	$39,035	$24,858	$39,302	$18,746	$53,170	$30,041
Number	45	24	13,400	12,933	8,900	8,467	38,967	26,320	18,524	19,622
High school graduate	$45,494	$26,921	$35,996	$20,503	$37,304	$20,972	$36,612	$23,557	$44,028	$22,669
Number	86	95	9,967	13,333	8,100	9,600	26,185	27,261	28,521	49,972

Occupation										
Managerial/ professional	$62,037	$39,650	$48,824	$30,951	$48,330	$31,292	$50,492	$31,331	$54,047	$36,079
Number	189	200	26,133	27,000	17,967	20,600	118,124	69,177	76,657	53,791
Clerical and sales	$54,360	$28,049	$37,482	$21,592	$35,279	$21,288	$49,379	$31,721	$62,873	$29,847
Number	43	91	10,633	26,333	7,767	18,433	24,239	38,788	33,752	35,730
Other	$48,157	$26,452	$34,444	$18,197	$36,312	$17,370	$37,081	$19,947	$37,289	$18,742
Number	114	31	40,167	15,333	28,033	8,600	95,112	18,767	56,133	38,682

Note: Personal income is based on income category data. Means calculated using the mid-point of the income category of each individual. The education variable for all samples is based on high school graduation or higher, and all occupational and income data are reported only for those who reported that they were currently employed (full- or part-time or self-employed).

Class of '73 Project

An Ongoing Study of
Post Secondary Education
and Occupation

January 1994

Information Now...
Means Better Choices for the Future

For centuries, writers throughout the world have been fascinated by the role of personal decisions and actions in determining what happens to us in the course of our lives. This is one of the most common themes in literature: the proverbial crossroads; the door not opened; the road not travelled. To what extent can we control our future, influence our destiny, through decisions made at these crucial moments of truth? Are there things we can do, or not do, which might affect the eventual outcome of our lives and help ensure for us the quality of life and values we want? Don't circumstances beyond our control sometimes make our decisions seem useless, as if a predetermined path or destiny just seems to take over?

"Wait! Wait!
Listen to me!...
we don't have to
be just sheep!"

Our "Class of '73" study is very much about these same ideas. By following the students in our original class, we've gained insight into how decisions about post secondary education have affected their careers and personal lives. Likewise, factors such as gender, geographic location, the nature of that first job, children and family, and subsequent courses and training are being looked at and evaluated. As our file of information and data about the "Class of '73" grows, we've seen trends develop and drawn conclusions that will add to the body of wisdom related to educational choices and career paths.

It would take a book to relate all of our findings drawn so far from our "Class of '73" project. In fact, once our 1994 research update is completed, we're hoping to roll our 20 years of fact finding into exactly that: a published study that draws together the connecting chords related to the many of pieces of information we've gathered about education, occupation and other little twists of life that find our "Class of '73" students where they are in 1994. It's been interesting and fun to trace our Class along and to weigh the importance of personal decisions and circumstances on their lives. Take Kathryn[1], for example. Kathryn grew up in a northern Ontario pulp and paper community. The middle of three children, Kathryn graduated from a Grade 12 commercial course in 1973 and evaluated carefully what her next step might be. Our research indicates that high school students from small towns and rural communities are less likely to pursue post secondary education, and Kathryn followed this pattern. Less than a year after high school graduation, Kathryn married a former classmate. As her husband operated heavy equipment and could find ready work in the area, they decided to stay in the community. As of

---

[1] Names have been altered to protect confidentiality

➤

Our *Class of '73* Project:
A Snapshot Review

We've been through a lot together since 1973 when the study team first put our province-wide class together. Let's go back in time and review the major steps taken so far, as we prepare to work together here in 1994.

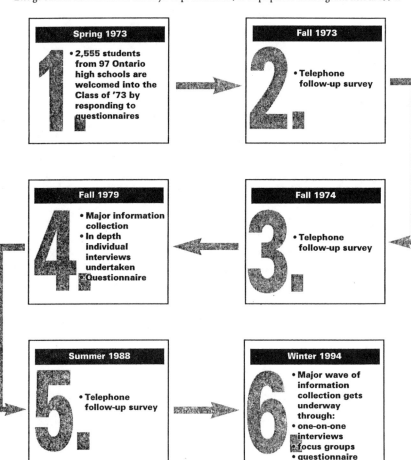

Spring 1973

1. • 2,555 students from 97 Ontario high schools are welcomed into the Class of '73 by responding to questionnaires

Fall 1973

2. • Telephone follow-up survey

Fall 1979

4. • Major information collection
• In depth individual interviews undertaken
• Questionnaire

Fall 1974

3. • Telephone follow-up survey

Summer 1988

5. • Telephone follow-up survey

Winter 1994

6. • Major wave of information collection gets underway through:
• one-on-one interviews
• focus groups
• questionnaire

Information Now... Means Better Choices for the Future (continued)

1988, Kathryn and her husband have three children, and as the family grows up and advances through school, Kathryn now works full-time as a secretary in a small real estate office.

Kathryn and her husband are happy with their lives and what they've accomplished. But how about their children? Opportunities are limited in the north. Ontario's manufacturing and resource industries are in the decline. Will we see a growing trend in the '90's for kids like these, perhaps by necessity, to be more inclined to seek higher education and the job opportunities that may result?

1988

Highlights of 1988 Findings

- Approximately 32.5 years old
- 2/3 were married
- About 69% had at least one child
- Almost 2/3 had attained at least some post-secondary education
- More men (96%) than women (68%) were working full-time
- Only 18% of women reported they were housewives

Linda, another "Class of '73" member, grew up in southwestern Ontario in the town of Huron Park, not far from Stratford. While her parents were not farmers, Linda was drawn to the farming life and left home after Grade 13 to study agriculture at the University of Guelph. While there she met Bob, a fellow agriculture student. They soon married and, after graduation, purchased a farm they were managing jointly when we last spoke to them in 1988. As well, our telephone survey at that time was interrupted more than once by the cries of their first child, born one year earlier in 1987. How are Bob and Linda making out during the cost-price squeeze that's hit Ontario's farmers in recent years? Do they see their son continuing with the family farm, or do they see him doing something different?

By contrast to Linda and Kathryn, Peter moved to Canada as a child and grew up in Toronto. His parents immigrated from Portugal with him and his two sisters in 1964. Life was tough for the young Peter, growing up in a large, strange city where both language and cultural differences posed constant barriers. Peter struggled through high school, viewing other students as superior and his teachers as insensitive to his continuing problems to adjust. Peter graduated from Grade 13, registered in a community college graphic arts program, but could not put behind him his feelings of uncertainty and lack of confidence.

After one year, Peter dropped out and took a job in the stock room at Eaton's. He was soon promoted to inventory clerk but an economic down-turn cost him his job. He then found a well-paying, blue collar job working for auto giant GM of Canada, where we found him in 1988. At that time, Peter was married, had two young children, and had decided to try community college once again through registration in an evening electronics technology course. Peter's children will now be aged nine and twelve. Will their educational experiences, as second generation Canadians with no language or first-hand cultural barriers, be different than their father's? Has Peter been able to upgrade his skills through adult community college education? How has a new college certificate affected his career?

Occupational attainment as at 1987/88

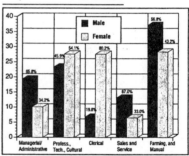

You see what we mean about choice and destiny: the dividing line really does become blurred as you review the files and case histories that make up our "Class of '73". As of 1988, we had more than 1,200 Peters and Kathryns and Lindas still active in the study, still giving us information about themselves in hope that it may be of benefit to others.

Your continued participation in the "Class of '73" study is important to us and to the generation that follows. Please stay with us and your classmates during our 1994 research. The information you provide might help to bring about the right decision, the right choices, to help ensure the best possible future for your children and theirs after them. ■

Educational attainment as at 1988

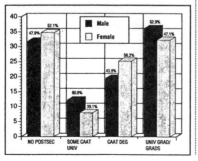

How You Can Help Us in 1994

As you can see from our "Snapshot Review" we're going to need you again in 1994. As with our research in 1979, we're going to use a combination of one-on-one interviews, focus group meetings and a mailed questionnaire to compile our updated data and information. We're going to be interested in finding out more about any additional education you've received, your recent employment experiences, how family obligations have linked with further education and employment, educational plans for your children, and related questions. The interviews and focus groups will be conducted on a selective basis throughout Ontario, beginning during January/February 1994. This information will be summarized in report form by June 1994 and will help us decide what issues we might want to follow up on in a questionnaire. The questionnaire will be mailed to all respondents in the sample group during Fall 1994. You can help us proceed more quickly with our work in 1994 by indicating an interest in our one-on-one interviews or focus groups by filling out the form below. We'll make every effort to ensure your involvement in these pre-questionnaire activities.

Meet Your "Class of '73" Research Team

The "Class of '73" research project, or "The Critical Juncture" study as it was known originally, was started by Prof. Paul Anisef of the Department of Sociology in the Arts Faculty of York University. In 1979 Prof. Anisef was joined on the project by two colleagues, Profs. Tony Turittin and Gottfried Paasche. These three researchers continue on the "Class of '73" project, along with three new additions to the team: historian Prof. Paul Axelrod, and specialists on education and work Drs. Fred Ashbury and Carl James. The research team encourages you to contact them at any time if you have questions or suggestions regarding the "Class of '73" study.

To leave a message, please call collect (416) 736-5995 anytime, 7-days-a-week, and a project member will return your call.

 Our Pledge of Confidentiality

As with all information received from previous stages of the "Class of '73" project, information gathered as part of our 1994 research will be held in strictest confidence. Reports will be based on group responses, such that no individual can be identified.

YES, I would like you to contact me regarding a one-on-one interview or to participate in a focus group

Name: _____

Address: _____

_____ Phone: _____

Return to: The "Class of '73" Research Team *(Please return in the enclosed self-addressed envelope.)*

All other mail enquiries should be sent to: Prof. Paul Anisef
Dept. of Sociology
226 Bethune College
York University
4700 Keele Street
North York, Ontario
M3J 1P3

Thank You once again for your continuing co-operation and support.

Notes

Introducing the Class of '73

1 This study of the Class of '73 has become the longest panel or longitudinal study of its kind in Canada, though it was not designed at its inception to be long-term.
2 While by Phase IV there had not been much migration out of Ontario, by Phase VI a significant number of participants had moved to other provinces in Canada, to the United States, or to other parts of the world. Most in-depth interviews were conducted in different parts of Ontario and, whenever possible, in other regions of Canada.

1. Navigating the Life Course

1 The idea of a *normal biography* is a recent phenomenon based on the demographic shifts witnessed in the last few decades, which made it possible to conceive of a 'structured, predictable life path' (Hagestad, 1991: 24).

2. Setting the Stage

1 Some 24.5 per cent of mothers and 25.4 per cent of fathers were born outside Canada. With respect to non-English languages spoken at home, for mothers 3.6 per cent spoke French, 3.1 per cent Italian, 1.9 per cent German, and 1.3 per cent Dutch. For fathers, 3.2 per cent spoke French, 2.8 per cent Italian, 1.8 per cent German, 0.8 per cent Polish, and 0.8 per cent Dutch.

2 Spending on education as a percentage of provincial and local expenditures declined from 23.5 per cent in 1970 to 18.7 per cent in 1975. See Manzer, 1994: 122; also Gerard, 1973: 7.

3 The Ontario Secondary School Teachers' Federation published a survey, *At What Cost? A Study of the Role of the Secondary School in Ontario* (OSSTF, 1976), which reported that the morale of teachers had reached an all-time low.

4 By 1989, 'this pattern had shifted so that more parents preferred and expected their daughters than their sons to attend university' (Looker, 1994: 173).

5 The American literature on the student movement and political change in the 1960s is voluminous. Useful Canadian sources include: Owram, 1996; McGuigan, 1968; Daly, 1970; Quarter, 1973; Levitt, 1984; Jasen, 1989; and Kostash, 1986. On the student movement in Ontario, see Axelrod, 1973.

6 Examples of childrearing advice: *Toronto Star*, 1973d; and the 'family' column of Helen Worthington, 1973. See also the regular advice column by Ann Landers.

7 *Maclean's* (1975) published a feature section titled, 'Getting On with the Seventies,' where these trends are discussed. See also Whitehurst, 1984; Elkin, 1975.

8 In Ontario, for men 15 to 19, the unemployment rate in 1977 was 15.8 per cent, and for those 20 to 24 it was 11.1 per cent. For women the numbers were 15.4 per cent and 11.3 per cent respectively. The comparable unemployment rates in 1976 for each of these groups were significantly lower. See Denton et al. (1981: 20), and A. Leslie Robb and Byron G. Spencer, *Unemployment and Labour Force Behaviour of Young People: Evidence from Canada and Ontario* (Toronto: Ontario Economic Council and University of Toronto Press, 1981: 20).

9 Anisef (1980: 33) reported that as of 1979, 36.2 per cent of the Class of '73 had no postsecondary education. Some 49 per cent had a university degree, a college diploma, or both, and 14.7 per cent had university or college experience but had not graduated.

3. Educational Pathways

1 The Critical Juncture project produced three publications (Anisef, 1973, 1974, and 1975a). The discussion in the paragraphs to follow centres on the last main report, *The Critical Juncture: Realization of the Educational and Career Intentions of Grade 12 Students in Ontario*. The data discussed in this

section of Chapter 3 are derived from Phases I and III of the Class of '73 longitudinal study. The sample size in Phase I was 2,555 respondents, and in Phase III was 2,163.

2 The research by Crysdale (Crysdale, 1991; Crysdale and MacKay, 1994; Crysdale, King, and Mandell, 1999) and Tanner, Krahn, and Hartnagel (1995) helps us understand this path.

3 In the Critical Juncture study there was much evidence of the workings of these factors – evidence on which we can touch only briefly here. The Critical Juncture report (1975a, Chapter 3) showed a correlation between father's education and fall of 1974 activity, with fathers of university enrollees tending to have more education (secondary education and higher) than fathers of young people in other activity outcome categories. Women were enrolled in community colleges more frequently than men (roughly a 60–40 percentage split). In Phase I, men's occupational aspirations and expectations were very similar, and many young men were willing to enter a wide range of blue-collar occupations for which there were literally no takers among the young women. Young women aspired frequently to medicine and health occupations (Statistics Canada occupational categories were used here), to teaching, and to artistic, literary, recreational, and related occupations. But while 18.8 per cent aspired to clerical and related occupations, 34.5 per cent expected to end up in such jobs (1975: 65–6). Ethnicity was also a factor in educational choice, but no details were presented in the 1975a report (see Anisef, 1975b). (Chapter 6 takes up the topic of immigration status and the Class of '73.)

4 In 1979 we were successful in reaching 1,522 respondents of the original 2,555 Critical Juncture study students. Focusing here on the 788 class members that were followed up in 1995 would, of course, result in somewhat different numbers than reporting 1979 data based on 1,522 respondents. However, the differences in using the Phase VI sample of 788 compared to the 1979 sample are quite minimal. We chose continuity of our sample across our chapters rather confusing readers by changing the sample size from time period to time period.

5 Based on the cross-tabulation of fall of 1974 activity by 1979 educational attainment, the fall of 1974 activity groups for the 788 Class of '73 members is 36.6 per cent working full-time in the fall of 1974, 15.7 per cent attending community college, 34.8 per cent attending university, 1 per cent doing part-time study, and 11.9 per cent engaged in other activities ($N = 732$).

6 Twenty-eight per cent of high-SES respondents were drawn from Metro Toronto, and 24.4 per cent from small towns and rural areas – fairly similar

proportions. However, only 5.0 per cent of Metro Toronto respondents were in the lowest SES category, but 60.0 per cent of small town and rural area dwellers fell into this category.

7 A descriptive account of the high school and postsecondary years can be found in the report on the 1979 Phase IV data published under the title *Is the Die Cast?* (Anisef, Paasche, and Turrittin, 1980). The data reported here differ from the data in this earlier report: the findings reported here are based only on those Class of '73 members surveyed in the 1995 Phase VI follow-up study.

8 If one takes the plans indicated by grade 12 students in the spring of 1973 as predictions, and then compares these plans, individual by individual, with what was reported as their fall 1974 activity, the predictions were correct 55 per cent of the time. Predictions were especially accurate for those who predicted for themselves going to work full-time – 80 per cent. Many of these students were indeed only weeks away from entering the labour market permanently when the Phase I survey was done. The predictions of the university-bound students were 69 per cent accurate, also quite high. Predictions were a low 43 per cent for those headed for community college. Predictions were especially poor for those who indicated part-time studies or some other activity. The presence of these latter two groups, which were very volatile with respect to their actual fall 1974 behaviour, significantly brought down the overall accuracy of predictions for the whole sample. The use of multiple factors in explaining educational outcomes using our longitudinal data base is explored in MacKinnon and Anisef (1979), and Turrittin, Anisef, and MacKinnon (1983).

9 Socio-economic status, for example, is strongly related to level of educational expectations (LEE). Taking the three levels of LEE as *expect to go to work, expect to attend community college,* and *expect to attend university,* then, of Class of '73 members with low-SES background, 40.4 per cent expected to work, 37.3 per cent expected to attend college, and 22.4 per cent expected to attend university ($N = 161$) as reported in the Phase I survey of 1973. Of those with medium-low SES background, the respective percentages of expectations were 28.6 per cent, 37.4 per cent, and 34.0 per cent ($N = 147$); of those with medium-high SES background, the respective percentages of expectations were 22.9 per cent, 31.4 per cent, and 45.8 per cent ($N = 153$). In contrast, of those Class of '73 members with high-SES background, 8.7 per cent expected to go to work, and 20.7 per cent expected to attend college, but 70.7 per cent expected to attend university ($N = 150$) based on the survey of 1973.

4. The World of Employment

1 In all of our surveys, respondents' occupations were coded using the four-digit numbers of the Canadian Classification and Dictionary of Occupations (CCDO). In turn these CCDO codes were used to place respondents' occupations in an occupational classification scheme developed by Pineo, Porter, and McRoberts. This scheme was subsequently revised by Creese, Guppy, and Meissner (1991: 34), who took into account changes in the labour force, the nature of gender segregation in occupations, and other factors, and reduced the 16 categories to 10. Occupational data throughout this study utilize this ten-category system.

2 All occupational information obtained in our surveys mentioned previously was categorized according to the ten revised occupational categories (see endnote 1). The occupations of fathers and mothers as reported in 1973 on the Phase I questionnaire were also categorized in this way. The use of CCDO coding permitted us to attach Blishen scores to reported occupations, Blishen scores being a two-digit index representing the social status of an occupation. Blishen scores are created based on the average educational and income levels of holders of an occupation for each of the approximately 500 occupational groups utilized by Statistics Canada (Blishen, Carroll, and Moore, 1987). While the occupational information from the six phases of our study provides information to track career mobility, the occupations of father in 1973 and the occupations of fathers when they were age 55 as reported in our 1995 survey provide the basis for making intergenerational occupational comparisons.

3 The top panel of Table 4.1 represents a single point in time. Of the Class of '73 members reporting attending a university or college in the fall of 1974, 27.9 per cent reported also working full- or part-time. In the bottom panel of the table, where a first full-time job could have been taken up at any time between 1974 and 1979, first full-time job could have preceded, coincided, or followed educational attainment.

4 It should be noted that general occupational categories proved insensitive to gender differences; we will return to this issue later in the chapter.

5 The data for education by occupational category cross-classifications are not shown for each of these four points in time. However, these detailed data do appear in Table 4.4 for the years 1979 and 1995.

6 Between 1975 and 1994, the part-time employment rate for young women (15 to 24) more than doubled, from 22 per cent to 48 per cent. The equivalent trend for young men was from 17 per cent to 38 per cent. By 1994, 54 per cent of young employed women were in nonstandard jobs (part-

time and/or temporary positions), along with 45 per cent of young employed men (Krahn: 1996: 16).

7 Respondents were asked, 'Given your education, training, and experience, do you feel that you are now earning ... More than you deserve? About the right amount? Less than you deserve?'

8 Respondents were asked to indicate how true a series of statements were with respect to their current (or last) job. The response alternatives were: 'very true,' 'true,' 'somewhat true,' 'not very true,' or 'not at all true,' or 'doesn't apply to me.'

5. Social, Career, and Geographic Mobility

1 We have focused exclusively on father's occupation for the intergenerational comparison because there was occupational information for 85.2 per cent of fathers in the Phase VI survey, whereas there was similar information for only 37.8 per cent of mothers. In the Phase VI survey, respondents were asked to indicate their father's job at age 55 if employed and their mother's job at age 55 if employed.

2 As used in earlier chapters, the 1973 socio-economic status of family of origin is a continuous variable produced by a factor analysis of five kinds of information, including father's education, mother's education, parents' total income, father's occupation (Blishen score), and mother's occupation (Blishen score). We developed a similar variable for Class of '73 members in 1995 using five similar kinds of information, in particular respondent's completed level of education by 1995, spouse's completed level of education, household income, respondent's occupation (Blishen score), and spouse's occupation (Blishen score). To simplify for the purposes of comparison, the 1973 and 1995 SES scores were divided into three equally sized SES levels. While the factor analyses used to develop the 1973 and 1995 socio-economic status measures each employed the five variables outlined in the text above, in some cases the full range of information on all five variables was not available for each subject. In these cases, an SES score was still calculated but was based on the information that was given. In the twenty-nine cases where missing data did not allow a calculation of the continuous SES score, a category assignment was made by the researchers based on a review of the information available for the case. In this way all Class of '73 members were provided with SES categories for both 1973 and 1995 socio-economic status measures. The most obvious situation of missing information regarding SES was the group of Class of '73 members who were not married at the time of the 1995 survey; thus there was no

information on spouse's education or occupation. In these cases, personal income was used in the SES assessments in place of household income. For information on the Blishen score, consult Blishen, Carroll, and Moore (1987).

3 Of the Class of '73 members who reported in 1973 that their mothers were working full-time or part-time, half of these mothers held clerical or sales occupations. In contrast, in 1995, of all Class of '73 employed women, 30.1 per cent of those without children reported being in clerical and sales jobs, with 33.6 per cent of women with children reporting such occupations. Thus, it is clear that employed Class of '73 women in 1995 held a more diverse range of occupations than their employed mothers in 1973 – an indication that job ghettoes for women have been disappearing in the last several decades.

4 In the first phase of the Class of '73 project, 30.3 per cent of grade 12 students indicated that they did not know their parent's income. We assume that those students who replied were aware of their parent's total income in a rough way sufficient to realistically select an income category from the response categories offered in the relevant questionnaire item.

5 In Phase I, respondents reported that 18.2 per cent of mothers were employed part-time, and 24.5 per cent were employed full-time, for a total of 42.7 per cent employed; in Phase VI, 84.9 per cent of respondents reported on the employment status of a spouse or partner, and of these spouses or partners, 71.2 per cent were employed full-time and 15.1 per cent were employed part-time, for a total of 86.3 per cent employed. We have argued that the income improvement of Class of '73 members relative to their parents is due to the high levels of education that lead to intergenerational occupational mobility, and their having employed spouses. Citing data derived from Statistics Canada, Krahn and Lowe (1998: 138) report that individual earnings for the age cohort 35 to 44 years old in 1993, which includes the Class of '73, declined 11.1 per cent for men from 1981 to 1993, though individual earnings for women in that cohort rose 11.9 per cent over the same period of time.

6 Both intergenerational and intragenerational occupational mobility require a measure of occupational status. This is conventionally done by grouping occupational titles. Respondents' occupations in all of our surveys were coded using the four-digit numbers of the Canadian Classification and Dictionary of Occupations (CCDO). In turn these CCDO codes were used to place a respondent's occupation in an occupational status classification scheme developed by Pineo, Porter, and McRoberts. This classification is a 16-category scale, a rank ordering of occupations from the highest (self-

employed professionals) to the lowest (farm labourers) in terms of years of schooling and income. The Porter-Pineo-McRoberts scale was subsequently revised by Creese, Guppy, and Meissner (1991: 34), who took into account changes in the labour force, the nature of sex segregation in occupations, and patterns of inconsistency, and reduced the 16 categories to 10 (1991: 36). Occupational mobility itself is shown by comparing the father's occupation with the occupational attainment of the son or daughter. In the 1995 Phase VI survey we asked respondents to give their current occupation if employed, and to report the occupations of their parents when their parents were 55 years of age if employed. The Porter-Pineo-McRoberts scale is more effective for discerning gender differences than a measure derived from factor analysis, and so we employ it in this section. For the tables in this chapter we reduced the 10-category Creese-Guppy-Meissner occupational scale to either 9 or 5 categories. The agricultural category always combines farmers and farm labourers.

7 In the Phase VI survey we asked respondents to tell us about their current full-time occupation or, if not currently working full-time, their most recent full-time occupation. Data from this question refer almost entirely to current employment (on a previous question, only 23 our of 381 men reported that they were not currently employed or self-employed). Thus, in our occupational mobility data for men, the 1995 occupation is indeed their current occupation. For women the situation is somewhat different; some women reported on occupations that they did not hold by the time of the Phase VI survey in 1995. On the current employment status question in the Phase VI survey, 54 out of 407 women reported not being currently employed or self-employed. Thirty of these women ended their last full-time employment in the same year they started working. Of this group, 7 ended their last full-time employment in the period 1979–84, 17 ended their last full-time employment in the period 1985–90, and 6 ended employment in the period 1991–95. Thus, the label of 1995 occupation is accurate for approximately 87 per cent of women in the Class of '73; for the other 13 per cent, the occupational data provided and listed as 1995 occupation are actually for an earlier occupation; however, an estimated three-quarters of these occupations were between 1985 and 1995.

8 The results shown in Table 5.3 indicate that women compared to men were less likely to have fathers employed in lower-prestige occupations (e.g., blue-collar) (40.2 per cent versus 46.7 per cent for men), and more likely to have fathers employed in the high management/professional group (20.7 per cent versus 15.4 per cent). We attribute these relatively small differences to sample

attrition (more women than men with high occupational status fathers remained through to the Phase VI survey). The higher proportion of women with higher occupational status fathers leaves our Class of '73 women more vulnerable than men to downward mobility.

9 In Table 5.3, occupational inheritance is represented by the diagonal cells in the table – that is to say, the cells where son's or daughter's occupational category in 1995 is the same as father's occupational category at age 55. The cells to the right of the diagonal cells reflect downward occupational mobility, where the son's or daughter's occupational category in 1995 is lower in the hierarchy of occupational categories than the father's occupational category at age 55. Similarly, the cells to the left of the diagonal cells reflect upward occupational mobility. The mobility patterns of Table 5.3 are similar to results from the 1986 General Social Survey as reported by Creese, Guppy, and Meissner (1991). Comparison of the Class of '73 to this study, however, is made difficult because summary data are available in the text for only the nonagricultural portion of the 1986 sample.

10 Upper-status occupations include high-level management, professional, middle management, and semiprofessional and technical occupational categories. Lower-status occupations include upper and lower white-collar and upper and lower blue-collar occupational categories.

11 For recent international comparisons employing state-of-the-art methodology, see R. Erikson and John H. Goldthorpe (1992). An overview of comparative stratification research is contained in Ganzeboom, Treiman, and Ultee (1991). Recent data on social fluidity are contained in a paper by Michel de Sève (1998). After reviewing studies on social mobility, Krahn and Lowe write: 'Studies using more recent data (from the 1970s and 1980s) and a larger number of occupational categories suggest few differences between mobility patterns and trends in Canada and the United States. However, they do indicate that Canada may have a somewhat more "open" stratification system than Sweden, the United Kingdom, France, and the Netherlands' (1998: 119). On mobility in Canada, see Turrittin (1974).

12 The statistical test is the t-test for means drawn from independent samples, and the grouping variable is the stayer/mover variable. While the comparisons of means in Table 5.8 generally do not yield statistical significance, for the bottom panel of data regarding current occupation, for the small town and rural area Class of '73 members, the stayer/mover comparison is statistically significant for both the high and low (though not the medium) parental origin SES groups.

6. The Experiences of First-Generation Canadians

1 Country of birth of parents was reported in the initial survey of 1973.
   Altogether, 33.1 per cent had at least one parent who was born outside
   Canada (11.8 per cent with one parent born outside Canada, and 21.3 per
   cent with both parents born outside Canada). For this discussion we focus
   on those respondents with two foreign-born parents. Our particular
   representation of respondents with first-generation status in Canada is a
   product of our initial sampling process and the difficulties of follow-up
   in longitudinal studies. The lower racial minority representation in our
   initial 1973 survey likely reflects the fact that it was only in the early 1970s
   that significant numbers of racial minorities immigrated to Canada; hence
   few were in their graduating high school classes in 1973. Furthermore,
   immigrants as a whole have tended to settle in Canada's three major
   cities: Montreal, Toronto, and Vancouver. Our initial 1973 survey was
   province-wide and covered cities, towns, and rural areas, thus diluting
   the data related to immigrant segments present in Ontario's major urban
   centres.
2 According to Richmond and Kalbach (1980: 38) 'the proportion of immigrants coming from Britain, Northern, Western, Central and Eastern
   Europe declined from 69.1% in the period 1946–60 to 41.6% in the decade
   1961–71. At the same time, the proportion of immigrants from Southern
   Europe increased from 17.4% to 24.2%. There was an even more dramatic
   increase in the numbers from other parts of the world, from 13.5% to
   34.2%. The consequence was a substantial diversification in the ethnic
   composition of immigrants.' The 1971 census shows that the ethnic groups
   that immigrated in significant numbers post-1946 through to 1971 were
   Italian, Chinese/Japanese, Hungarian, and Dutch, among others (Richmond and Kalbach, 1980: 155).
3 Of the 48 respondents born outside of Canada who provided information
   on their age of arrival (two respondents of the original 50 did not give
   age of arrival), 73 per cent arrived in Canada at age 5 or earlier, and the
   remainder were scattered evenly between arrival at ages 6 to 16. Exploring respondents' experiences as children of foreign-born parents was not
   an original intent of our investigation. However, as we talked with
   respondents in our qualitative interviews and focus group sessions and
   examined the survey data, we noted that while there were many similarities among respondents of foreign- and Canadian-born parents, there
   were also notable differences that deserved to be identified and discussed.
   Furthermore, we know that the age at which individuals immigrate has a

significant influence on their acculturation and of the subsequent cultural values by which they live and that they pass on to their children. Since we did not ask respondents the age at which their parents moved to Canada, we can only speculate on the influence that such a move might have had on the experiences of these respondents. It should be noted that 18 respondents with foreign-born parents either were interviewed individually, or participated in the focus group discussions. James (1995) makes the point that ethnic and in particular racial minority Canadians tend to be viewed as immigrants. This construction interacts with race, language, and ethnicity to influence their experiences and opportunities in Canada.

4 We maintain that structural inequality in Canada is in part based on cultural differences due to ethnicity, language, race, and degree of acculturation and assimilation.

5 In his seminal work, Porter (1965: 63–64) explained that new immigrant groups to Canada were assigned 'entrance status,' which generally meant that they tended to hold lower-level occupational positions compared to the native-born.

6 It should be noted that success is related to the cultural values of the immigrant group. For instance, as Vallee and Shulman (1969) argue, unless it is characteristic of the particular immigrant group to place a special emphasis on educational and vocational achievement, this may not be featured in their notion of success.

7 Parents who immigrate with children often claim that they do so in the interest of their children, that is, to provide them with the educational and thus the career opportunities that they 'did not have' and neither would the children have had in their homeland. One consequence of this is that the children grow up with the feeling of obligation to fulfil their parents' wishes and expectations (James, 1990).

8 In the immediate postwar period up to 1961, there was a steady and significant increase in the number of immigrants who came and worked as clerks, professionals, and managers, compared to earlier periods, when most immigrants entering Canada worked in farming and other primary occupations. And as a result of the point system, immigrants who arrived between 1961 and 1971 were generally better educated and more highly qualified than earlier cohorts. However, 'immigrants from Southern Europe and others in the nominated streams continued to be recruited mainly for the construction and service industries' (Richmond and Kalbach, 1980: 39). And according to the 1971 census, Europeans from Eastern Europe and the Netherlands tended to be overrepresented in farming (Richmond and Kalbach, 1980).

9 Ashworth (1975), in analysing issues faced by immigrant students (South Asian, Greek, Italian, Portuguese, and Caribbean), reported that, coupled with limited access to school facilities, immigrant students had teachers who were not sufficiently aware of their culture and often lacked the sensitivity to the problems the immigrant students faced in adjusting to a new environment. Also, many first-generation immigrant students were likely to be in vocational programs at school because they tended to settle in areas where schools offered vocational programs (Masemann, 1975; Costa and DiSanto, 1972).

10 It should be noted that Jason took English as a second language (ESL) classes until grade 11.

11 Roughly twice as many youth in 1973 aspired to managerial and profes- sional occupations as had entered these occupations by 1979. But 1979 was still early in the careers of many respondents. The data on occupation in 1979 caught respondents at different stages of their occupational trajecto- ries. Those who left high school after grade 12 or 13 for the working world had some six or seven years in the work force, with about two or three years less for those who went on for community college diplomas and certificates. Most university graduates were in the labour force at least one year by 1979. About 18.5 per cent of the Class of '73 were still attending an educational institution in 1979, 15.0 per cent on a full-time basis. Regard- less of birthplace of parents, women disproportionately enter clerical occupations, compared to men (84 per cent of the 29 per cent in clerical occupations in 1979 were women).

12 For a description of the kinds of jobs in the skilled and unskilled catego- ries, as well as occupations typical of the other job categories, see Chapter 5.

13 This is not taking other characteristics into consideration (e.g., race, language). In fact, racial minorities were only a very small proportion of our sample.

14 To determine region of residence in 1995, the address of each respondent was classified according to the same categories used in 1973, namely, Metropolitan Toronto, other large cities, smaller cities, and small towns and rural areas. An individual living in Calgary in 1995 would be placed in the 'other large cities' category, and someone living in rural Alberta in 1995 would be coded as 'small towns and rural areas.' As of 1995, 89.4 per cent of respondents still lived in Ontario, 7.0 per cent elsewhere in Canada, 2.8 per cent in the United States, and 0.8 per cent elsewhere other than Canada or the United States. The 1973 data underestimate the Toronto region population. In 1973 the suburban fringe of Metropolitan

Toronto was included in region 3, the region including smaller Ontario cities. By 1995, Metropolitan Toronto had been superseded in the public mind by the Greater Toronto Region, which incorporated the suburban fringe. Thus in 1973 Class of '73 members attending a high school in Mississauga were designated as belonging to the region 3 category, whereas in the 1995 count, respondents now living in Mississauga were considered as residing in the Greater Toronto Area.

15 The modal personal income categories were $40,000 to $49,999 for children of Canadian-born parents, and $50,000 to $59,999 for children of foreign-born parents. The median is the middle point of any distribution, and the mode is the most frequent category. Household income was significantly higher for the children of foreign-born parents (median of $70,000 to $79,999) compared with peers of Canadian-born parents (median of $60,000 to $69,999). With respect to household income, the most frequently reported income category for both groups was $100,000 or more; 19.8 per cent of children of Canadian-born parents were in this category, but 28.3 per cent of children of foreign-born parents.

16 Socio-economic status is a composite measure based on occupation, education, and income. The table does not show the strides in socio-economic status made by the respondents with Canadian-born parents because the socio-economic categories for individuals with Canadian-born parents shown in Table 6.6 (rows one and three) are equal by virtue of dividing socio-economic scores into four equal parts for the whole sample (individuals with Canadian-born parents comprise 81.1 per cent of our Phase VI sample).

17 We used fathers' occupations as a reference, since in most cases mothers were listed as homemakers.

8. Constructing the Life Course: Five Biographies

1 As George (1993) notes, current research does not adequately link micro and macro evidence about the origin and consequences of transitions. An integration of micro and macro life course information is vitally important for depicting and explaining the dynamics of change at the social and personal levels and for better identifying how social and historical contexts shape lives and human development (Elder, 1998).

2 Earlier notions of life course borrowed heavily from biology, focusing on maturation and growth, followed by decline and regression. The idea of lifelong development was a minor topic of concern. While this has changed, with the study of human lives becoming more elaborate, socio-

logical treatments of the life course have been segmented into a number of specialities, such as the sociology of youth, the sociology of education, and family studies (Setterstein and Mayer, 1997: 233). The challenge now rests in moving away from such fragmentation toward a more integrative study of the life course.

References

Aboud, Frances E. 1981. 'Ethnic Self-Identity.' In *A Canadian Social Psychology of Ethnic Relations*, edited by R. Gardner and R. Kalid. Toronto: Methuen.

Academe Today. 1998. 'Money, More Than Brains, Governs Whether Students Will Attend College.' 10 August.

Adams, Michael. 1998. *Sex in the Snow: Canadian Social Values at the End of the Millennium*. Toronto: Penguin.

Adams, O., and N. Dhruva. 1989. 'Marrying and Divorcing: A Status Report for Canada.' *Canadian Social Trends* 13(Summer): 24–7.

Akoodie, Mohammed Ally. 1984. 'Identity and Self-Concept in Immigrant Children.' In *Multiculturalism in Canada: Social and Educational Perspectives*, edited by R.J. Samuda, J.W. Berry, and M. Laferrière. Toronto: Allyn & Bacon.

Andres, Lesley. 1998. 'Paths on Life's Way: Class of '88 Ten Years after High School.' A report to the University of British Columbia.

Anisef, E., F.D. Ashbury, C.E. James, and J.G. Paasche. 1994. *Life Transitions: Twenty Years Later*. Paper prepared for Annual Meeting of the Canadian Sociology and Anthropology Association, June 1994. Calgary.

Anisef, Paul. 1973. *The Critical Juncture: Preliminary Survey. Educational and Vocational Intentions of Grade 12 Students in Ontario*. Toronto: Ontario Ministry of Colleges and Universities.

– 1974. *The Critical Juncture. Follow-up Survey. Educational and Vocational Intentions of Grade 12 Students in Ontario*. Toronto: Ontario Ministry of Colleges and Universities.

– 1975a. *The Critical Juncture: Realization of the Educational and Career Intentions of Grade 12 Students in Ontario*. Toronto: Ontario Ministry of Colleges and Universities.

– 1975b. 'Consequences of Ethnicity for Educational Plans among Grade 12 students.' In *Education of Immigrant Students: Issues and Answers*, edited by Aaron Wolfgang, 122–36. Toronto: Ontario Institute for Studies in Education.

– 1980. 'A Study of Women's Accessibility to Higher Education.' *University and College Placement Association Journal* 14(2): 9–12.

– 1998. 'Transitions from Schooling to Employment in Canada and Student Retention: Literature Review, Successful Interventions and Policy Recommendations.' In *Determinants of Health, Children and Youth*. Papers commissioned by the National Health Forum Canada Health Action. Toronto: Editions Multi Mondes.

Anisef, Paul, et al. 1994. 'The Causes and Consequences of Underemployment among University Graduates in Ontario – a Longitudinal Study of a Baby Boom Cohort.' Unpublished.

Anisef, P., and P. Axelrod. eds. 1993a. *Transitions: Schooling and Employment in Canada*. Toronto: Thompson Educational Publishing.

Anisef, Paul, and Paul Axelrod. 1993. 'Universities, Graduates and the Marketplace: Canadian Patterns and Prospects.' In *Transitions: Schooling and Employment in Canada*, edited by P. Anisef and P. Axelrod, 103–14. Toronto: Thompson Educational Publishers.

Anisef, P., F. Ashbury, K. Bischoping, and Z. Lin. 1996. 'Post-Secondary Education and Unemployment in a Longitudinal Study of Ontario Baby Boomers.' *Higher Education Policy* 9(2): 159–74.

Anisef, P., F.D. Ashbury, and A.H. Turrittin. 1992. 'Differential Effects of University and Community College Education on Occupational Status Attainment in Ontario.' *Canadian Journal of Sociology* 17(1): 69–84.

Anisef, P., U. Hortian, M.A. Bertrand, and C. James. 1985. *Accessibility to Postsecondary Education in Canada*. Ottawa: Education Support Branch, Department of the Secretary of State.

Anisef, P., Z. Lin, F.D. Ashbury, and A.H. Turrittin. 1995. *Skills Learning and Occupational Mobility in the Life Course*. Paper prepared for Learned Societies Meeting, 5 June. Université du Québec à Montréal.

Anisef, P. and N. Okihiro. 1982. *Losers and Winners: The Pursuit of Equality and Social Justice in Higher Education*. Toronto: Butterworths.

Anisef, Paul, J. Gottfried Paasche, and Anton H. Turrittin. 1980. *Is the Die Cast? Educational Achievements and Work Destinations of Ontario Youth. A Six-Year Follow-up of the Critical Juncture High School Students*. Toronto: Ministry of Colleges and Universities.

Armstrong, Pat, and Hugh Armstrong. 1984. *The Double Ghetto: Canadian Women and Their Segregated Work*. Toronto: McClelland & Stewart.

Arnup, Katherine. 1994. *Education for Motherhood: Advice for Mothers in Twentieth-Century Canada*. Toronto: University of Toronto Press.

Ashworth, Mary. 1975. *Immigrant Children and Canadian Schools*. Toronto: McClelland & Stewart.

Axelrod, Paul. 1973. 'Patterns of Student Politics.' *University Affairs*. October.

– 1982. *Scholars and Dollars: Politics, Economics and the Universities of Ontario, 1945–1980*. Toronto: University of Toronto Press.

Axelrod, Paul, and Paul Anisef. 1996. 'Transitions, the Life Course, and the Class of '73.' In *Youth in Transition: Perspectives on Research and Policy*, edited by B. Galaway and J. Hudson, 144–51. Toronto: Thompson Educational Publishers.

Aylward, Sandra. 1983. 'The Status of Women in the Canadian Union of Educational Workers,' A report to the research and communications committee of the Canadian Union of Educational Workers. September.

Baker, Maureen. 1989. *Canadian Youth in a Changing World*. Ottawa: Research Branch, Political and Social Affairs Division, Library of Parliament.

– 1996. 'Introduction to Family Studies: Cultural Variations and Family Trends.' In *Families: Changing Trends in Canada*, edited by Maureen Baker, 3–34. Toronto: McGraw-Hill Ryerson.

Baker, Maureen, and Donna Lero. 1996. 'Division of Labour: Paid Work and Family Structure.' In *Families: Changing Trends in Canada*, edited by Maureen Baker, 78–103. Toronto: McGraw-Hill Ryerson.

Baltes, P.B. 1987. 'Theoretical Propositions of Life-Span Developmental Psychology: On the Dynamics Between Growth and Decline.' *Developmental Psychology* 23(5): 611–26.

Baron, James N., and William T. Bielby. 1980. 'Bringing the Firms Back In: Stratification, Segmentation, and the Organization of Work.' *American Sociological Review* 45(5): 737–65.

Beck, Ulrich. 1992. *Risk Society: Towards a New Modernity*. London: Sage.

Bell, Daniel. 1973. *The Coming of Post-Industrial Society*. New York: Basic Books.

Bellamy-Andres, Lesley. 1993. 'Life Trajectories, Action, and Negotiating the Transition from High School.' *Transitions: Schooling and Employment in Canada*, edited by P. Anisef and P. Axelrod, 137–58. Toronto: Thompson Educational Publishing.

– 1994. 'Capital, Habitus, Field and Practice: An Introduction to the Work of Pierre Bourdieu.' In *Sociology of Education in Canada: Critical Perspectives on Theory, Research and Practice*, edited by Lorna Irwin and David McLellan, 120–36. Toronto: Copp, Clark, Longman.

Berg, Ivar. 1970. *Education and Jobs: The Great Training Robbery*. London: Penguin.

Berry, John W., Rudolf Kalin, and Donald M. Taylor. 1977. *Multiculturalism and Ethnic Attitudes in Canada*. Ottawa: Ministry of Supply and Services Canada.

Best, Pamela. 1995. 'Women, Men and Work.' *Canadian Social Trends*, 36(Spring): 30–3.

Biggs, B., and R. Bollman. 1994. 'Urbanization in Canada.' In *Canadian Social Trends*, edited by Craig McKie and Keith Thompson, 67–72. Toronto: Thompson Educational Publishing.

Billingsley, Brenda, and Leon Muszynski. 1985. *No Discrimination Here? Toronto Employers and the Multi-Racial Workforce*. Toronto: Social Planning Council of Metropolitan Toronto.

Blau, Peter M., and O.D. Duncan. 1967. *The American Occupational Structure*. New York: John Wiley & Sons.

Blishen, Bernard R. 1967. 'A Socio-Economic Index for Occupations in Canada.' *Canadian Review of Sociology and Anthropology* 1(4): 41–52.

Blishen, B.R., W.K. Carroll, and C. Moore. 1987. 'The 1981 Socioeconomic Index for Occupations in Canada.' *Canadian Review of Sociology and Anthropology* 24(4): 465–88.

Bourdieu, P. 1984. *Distinction*. Cambridge: Harvard University Press.

Bowles, Samuel, and Herbert Gintis. 1976. *Schooling in Capitalist America: Educational Reform and the Contradictions of Economic Life*. New York: Basic Books.

Boyd, Monica, John Goyder, Frank E. Jones, Hugh McRoberts, Peter C. Pineo, and John Porter. 1985. *Ascription and Achievement: Studies in Mobility and Status Attainment in Canada*. Ottawa: Carleton University Press.

Brathwaite, Keren. 1989. 'Black Student and the School: A Canadian Dilemma.' In *African Continuities/L'Heritage Africain*, edited by S.W. Chilungu and S. Niang. Toronto: Terebi.

Breton, Raymond. 1970. 'Academic Stratification in Secondary Schools and Educational Plans of Students.' *Canadian Review of Sociology and Anthropology* 7(1): 17–34.

– 1972. *Social and Economic Factors in the Career Decisions of Canadian Youth*. Ottawa: Queen's Printer.

– 1995. *Ethnicity and Race in Social Organization: Recent Developments in Canadian Society*. Unpublished paper, University of Toronto.

Brice, Janet. 1982. 'West Indian Families.' In *Ethnicity and Family Therapy*, edited by Monica McGoldrich, John K. Peace, and Joseph Giordana. New York: Guildford Press.

Buchmann, Marlis. 1989. *The Script of Life in Modern Society: Entry into Adulthood in a Changing World*. Chicago: University of Chicago Press.

Burnstein, M., N. Tienhaara, P. Hewson, and B. Warrander. 1975. *Canadian Work Values: Findings of a Work Ethnic Survey and a Job Satisfaction Survey.* Ottawa: Manpower and Immigration.

Bush, E. Diane, Robert G. Simmons, Bruce Hutchinson, and Dale A. Blythe. 1977/8. 'Adolescent Perception of Sex Roles in 1968 and 1975.' *Public Opinion Quarterly* 41(4): 459–74.

Calliste, A. 1982. 'Educational and Occupational Expectations of High School Students.' *Multiculturalism* 5(3): 14–19.

Canadian Youth Foundation. 1995a. *Youth Unemployment: Canada's Rite of Passage.* Ottawa: Canadian Youth Foundation.

– 1995b. *Youth Unemployment: Canada's Hidden Deficit.* Ottawa: Canadian Youth Foundation.

Carey, Elaine. 1998. 'They're Smart, Ambitious but Just Don't Do the Math.' *Toronto Star*, 19 April: A3.

Carrier, S. 1995. 'Family Status and Career Situation for Professional Women.' *Work, Employment and Society* 9(2): 343–58.

Cebotarev, E.A. 1995. 'Domesticity to the public Sphere: Farm Women, 1945–86.' In *A Diversity of Women: Ontario 1945–1980*, edited by Joy Parr, 200–31. Toronto: University of Toronto Press.

Cheng, Maisy, Maria Yau, and Suzanne Ziegler. 1993. *The 1991 Every Secondary Student Survey, Part II: Detailed Profiles of Toronto's Secondary School Students.* Toronto: Research Services, Toronto Board of Education.

Chimbos, Peter D. 1980. 'The Greek Canadian Family: Tradition and Change.' In *Canadian Families: Ethnic Variations*, edited by K. Ishwaran. Toronto: McGraw-Hill Ryerson.

Chisholm, Lynne. 1999. 'From Systems to Networks: The Reconstruction of Youth Transitions in Europe.' In *From Education to Work: Cross National Perspectives*, edited by Walter R. Heinz, 298–310. Cambridge: Cambridge University Press.

Chisholm, Lynne, and Manuela Du Bois-Raymond. 1993. 'Youth Transitions, Gender and Social Change.' *Sociology* 27(2): 259–79.

Clark, W., and Z. Zsigmond. 1981. *Job Market Reality for Post-secondary Graduates: Employment Outcome by 1978, Two Years after Graduation.* Ottawa: Government of Canada.

Cohen, Marjorie Griffin. 1995. 'Paid Work.' In *Canadian Women's Issues, Volume II: Bold Visions*, edited by Ruth Roach Pierson and Marjorie Griffin Cohen. Toronto: Lorimer.

Coleman, James S. 1984. 'The Transitions from School to Work.' *Research in Social Stratification and Mobility* 3(1): 27–59.

Coleman, John C., and Leo Hendry. 1990. *The Nature of Adolescence.* London: Routledge.

Coles, Bob. 1995. *Youth and Social Policy: Youth Citizenship and Young Careers.* London: UCL Press.

Corak, Miles R. 1993. *The Duration of Unemployment during Boom and Bust.* Ottawa: Analytical Studies Branch, Statistics Canada.

Cornell, Bonnie. 1973. 'Woman Engineers Get Good Jobs.' *Toronto Star,* 30 October: E3.

Coser, Rose Laub. 1974. *The Family: Its Structure and Functions.* New York: St. Martin's Press.

Costa, Elio, and Odoardo Di Santo. 1972. 'The Italian-Canadian Child, His Family and the Canadian School System.' In *Must Schools Fail?,* edited by Niall Bryne and Jack Quarter. Toronto: McClelland & Stewart Ltd.

Coté, James E., and Anton L. Allahar. 1994. *Generation on Hold: Coming of Age in the Late Twentieth Century.* Toronto: Stoddart Publishing.

Country Report: Canada. 1991. *The Flow of Graduates from Higher Education and Their Entry into Working Life: A Contribution to the OECD Study on Higher Education and Employment.* Ottawa: ECD.

Creese, G., N. Guppy, and N. Meissner. 1991. 'Ups and Downs on the Ladder of Success: Social Mobility in Canada.' General Social Survey Series 5. Statistics Canada.

Creighton, Judy. 1973. 'Toronto's Male-Dominated Bay Street Is Meeting Its Match.' *Toronto Star,* 11 August: E3.

Crouter, Ann C. 1984. 'Spillover from Family to Work: The Neglected Side of Work/Family Interface.' *Human Relations* 378(6): 425–42.

Crysdale, Stewart. 1991. *Families under Stress: Community, Work and Change.* Toronto: Thompson Educational Publishing.

Crysdale, Stewart, and Harry MacKay. 1994. *Youth's Passage through School to Work: A Comparative, Longitudinal Study.* Toronto: Thompson Educational Publishing.

Crysdale, Stewart, Allan J.C. King, and Nancy Mandell. 1998. *On Their Own: Launching Youth from Home and School to Work.* Montreal and Kingston: McGill Queen's University Press.

– 1999. *On Their Own: Making the Transition from School to Work in the Information Age.* Montreal and Kingston: McGill-Queen's University Press.

Curtis, Bruce, D.W. Livingstone, and Harry Smaller. 1992. *Stacking the Deck: The Streaming of Working-Class Kids in Ontario Schools.* Toronto: Our Schools/Our Selves.

Daly, Margaret. 1970. *The Revolution Game.* Toronto: New Press.

Danziger, Kurt. 1978. 'Differences in Acculturation and Patterns of Socialization among Italian Immigrant Families.' In *Socialization and Social Values in*

Canadian Society, edited by E. Zureik and R.M. Pike. Toronto: McClelland & Stewart.

Davies, Scott. 1994. 'In Search of Resistance and Rebellion among High School Dropouts.' *Canadian Journal of Sociology* 19(3): 331–50.

de Broucker, Patrice, and Lavalle Lavallée. 1998. 'Getting Ahead in Life: Does Your Parents Education Count?' *Education Quarterly Review* 5(1): 22–8.

Dei, George J.S., L. Holmes, J. Mazzuca, E. McIsaac, and R. Campbell. 1995. *Drop Out or Push Out? The Dynamics of Black Students' Disengagement from School.* Toronto: Department of Sociology in Education, Ontario Institute for Studies in Education.

Demers, Linda. 1986. *Young People and the Family: Some Demographic Aspects.* Ottawa: Secretary of State.

Denton, Frank T., L. Robb, and B.G. Spencer. 1981. *Unemployment and Labour Force Behaviour of Young People: Evidence from Canada and Ontario.* Toronto: Ontario Economic Council and University Press.

Deosaran, Romesh A. 1976. *The 1975 Every Student Survey: Program Placement Related to Selected Countries of Birth and Selected Languages.* Toronto: Board of Education for the City of Toronto.

Deosaran, R., E.N. Wright, and T. Kane. 1976. *The 1975 Every Student Survey: Student's Background and Its Relationship to Program Placement.* Toronto: Board of Education for the City of Toronto.

Department of Secretary of State, Canada. 1978, 1984, and 1988. National graduate surveys. Ottawa: Secretary of State.

de Sève, Michel. 1998. *The Erikson and Goldthorpe Core Model of Social Fluidity Revisited: A Comparison of Canada with England and France and with the United States and Australia.* Paper prepared for Meetings of Research Committee 28 of the International Sociological Association, 14th World Congress of Sociology, 26 July–1 August, 1998, Montreal.

Dodge, David. 1972. *Returns to Investment in University Training: The Case of Canadian Accountants, Engineers, and Scientists.* Kingston: Queen's University Press.

Douvan, E., and J. Adelson. 1966. *The Adolescent Experience.* New York: John Wiley.

D'Oyley, V., and H. Silverman. Eds. 1976. *Black Students in Urban Canada.* Toronto: Ministry of Culture and Recreation.

Driedger, Leo. 1996. *Multi-Ethnic Canada: Identities and Inequalities.* Toronto: Oxford University Press.

Driver, M.J. 1985. 'Demographic and Societal Factors Affecting the Linear Career Crisis.' *Canadian Journal of Administrative Studies* 2(2): 245–64.

Eichler, M. 1983. *Families in Canada Today: Recent Changes and Their Policy Consequences.* Toronto: Gage.

Elder, Glen H. 1974. *Children of the Depression: Social Change in Life Experiences.* Chicago: University of Chicago Press.

– 1978. 'Family History and the Life Course.' In *Transitions: The Family and the Life Course in Historical Perspective,* edited by Tamara K. Hareven, 17–64. New York: Academic Press.

– 1985. 'Perspectives on the Life Course.' In *Life Course Dynamics, Trajectories and Transitions, 1968–1980,* edited by Glen H. Elder, Jr. Ithaca: Cornell University Press.

– 1987. 'Families and Lives: Some Development in Life-course Studies.' *Journal of Family History* 12(1–3): 179–99.

– 1991. 'Lives and Social Change.' In *Theoretical Advances in Life Course Research,* edited by W.R. Heinz. Weinhem: Deutscher Studien Verlag.

– 1998. 'The Life Course as Development Theory.' *Child Development* 69(1): 1–12.

Elkin, Frederick. 1975. 'Life Styles of Canadian Families.' In *Marriage, Family and Society: Canadian Perspectives,* edited by S. Parvez Wakil. Toronto: Butterworths.

Ellis, D., and N. Stuckless. 1996. *Mediating and Negotiating Marital Conflicts.* Thousand Oaks: Sage Publications.

Empson-Warner, Susan, and Harvey Krahn. 1992. 'Unemployment and Occupational Aspirations: A Panel Study of High School Graduates.' *Canadian Review of Sociology and Anthropology* 29(1): 38–54.

Erickson, Robert, and John H. Goldthorpe. 1992. *The Constant Flux: A Study in Class Mobility in Industrial Societies.* Oxford: Clarendon Press.

Evans, Karen, and Walter R Heinz. 1994. 'Transitions in progress.' In *Becoming Adults in England and Germany,* edited by Karen Evans and Walter R. Heinz, 1–16. London: Anglo-German Foundation.

Felmlee, Dianne H. 1988. 'Returning to School and Women's Occupational Attainment.' *Sociology of Education* 61(1): 29–41.

Ferguson, B. 1988. 'Studying the Family in Canada.' In *Social Issues: Sociological Views of Canada,* edited by D. Forcese and S. Richer. Scarborough: Prentice-Hall.

Ferri, Elsa. Ed. 1993. *Life at 33: The Fifth Follow-up of the National Child Development Study.* London: National Children's Bureau.

Feuer, Louis. 1969. *The Conflict of Generations: The Character and Significance of Student Movements.* New York: Basic Books.

Finnie, R. 1993. 'Women, Men, and the Economic Consequences of Divorce: Evidence from Canadian Longitudinal Data.' *Canadian Review of Sociology and Anthropology* 30(2): 205–41.

Flacks, R. 1979. 'Growing Up Confused.' In *Socialization and the Life Cycle*, edited by Peter I. Rose. New York: St. Martin's Press.

Fleming, W.G. Ed. 1971. *Schools, Pupils and Teachers*. Toronto: University of Toronto Press.

Friendly, Martha, Saul V. Levine, and Linda Hagarty. 1979. 'Adolescents in the Urban Social Context.' In *The Child in the City: Change and Challenges*, edited by W. Michelson, S. Levine, A.R. Spina, et al. Toronto: University of Toronto Press.

Fuller, Tony. 1998. 'Rural Society, English Canada.' In CD-ROM. *The Canadian Encyclopedia Plus*. Torono: McClelland & Stewart.

Furlong, A., and F. Cartmel. 1997. *Young People and Social Change: Individualization and Risk in Late Modernity*. Buckingham: Open University Press.

Gallagher, Paul. 1995. *Changing Course: An Agenda for Real Reform of Canadian Education*. Toronto: OISE Press.

Gallaway, Burt, and Joe Hudson. 1996. 'Introduction.' In *Youth in Transition: Perspectives on Research and Policy*, edited by Burt Gallaway and Joe Hudson, 2–13. Toronto: Thompson Educational Publishing.

Gambetta, Diego. 1987. *Were They Pushed or Did They Jump? Individual Decision Mechanisms in Education*. Cambridge: Cambridge University Press.

Ganzeboom, H.B.G., D.J. Teiman, and W.C. Ultee. 1991. 'Comparative Intergenerational Stratification Research: Three Generations and Beyond.' *Annual Review of Sociology* 1991(17): 227–302.

Gaskell, Jane, Arlene McLaren, and Myra Novogrodsky. 1989. *Claiming an Education: Feminism and Canadian Schools*. Toronto: Our Schools/Our Selves and Garamond.

George, Linda K. 1993. 'Sociological Perspectives on Life Transition.' *Annual Review of Sociology* 1993(19): 353–74.

Gerard, Warren. 1973. 'The School Budget Crisis: Who Is to Blame.' *Toronto Star*, 31 May: 9.

Gerson, Kathleen. 1985. *Hard Choices: How Women Decide about Work, Career and Motherhood*. Berkeley: University of California Press.

Gidney, R.D. 1999. *From Hope to Harris: Ontario Education since 1945*. Toronto: University of Toronto Press.

Gilbert, Sid, L. Barr, W. Clark, M. Blue, and D. Sunter. 1993. *Leaving School: Results from a National Survey Comparing School Leavers and High School Graduates 18 to 20 Years of Age*. Ottawa: Ministry of Supply and Services.

Gilbert, Sid, and Hugh McRoberts. 1977. 'Academic Stratification and Educational Plans: A Reassessment.' *Canadian Review of Sociology and Anthropology* 14(1): 34–46.

Gilligan, Carol. 1982. *In a Different Voice: Psychological Theory and Women's Development*. Cambridge: Harvard University Press.

Gollub, James O. 1991. *The Decade Matrix: Why the Decade You Were Born into Made You What You Are Today*. New York: Addison Wesley.

Gower, David. 1987. *Trends in Government Employment, 1976–1986*. Ottawa: Labour and Household Survey Analysis Division, Statistics Canada.

Granatstein, J.L., and Peter Neary. Eds. 1995. *The Good Fight: Canadians and World War II*. Toronto: Copp Clark.

Gray, John. 1973. 'Job Outlook Gloomy for Young: Andras.' *Toronto Star*, 12 November: A11.

Green, A.L., and Susan M. Wheatley. 1992. 'I've Got a Lot to Do and I Don't Think I'll Have the Time: Gender Differences in Late Adolescents' Narratives of the Future.' *Journal of Youth and Adolescence* 21(6): 667–86.

Greene, A.L. 1990. 'Great Expectations: Constructions of the Life Course during Adolescence.' *Journal of Youth and Adolescence* 19(4): 289–306.

Greenglass, Esther. 1973. 'Issues Affecting Women's Rights Get Low Government Priority.' *Toronto Star*. 17 July: 55.

Gwyn, Richard. 1973. 'Study Sees 1 Job for Every 2 Graduates.' *Toronto Star*. 10 November: B4.

Haas, Jack, and William Shaffir. 1978. *Shaping Identity in Canadian Society*. Scarborough: Prentice-Hall.

Hagan, John, and Blair Wheaton. 1993. 'The Search for Adolescent Role Exits and the Transition to Adulthood.' *Social Forces* 71(4): 955–80.

Hagestad, G. 1991. 'Dilemmas in Life Course Research.' In *Theoretical Advances in Life Course Research*, edited by W.R. Heinz. Weinheim: Deutscher Studien Verlag.

Hartmann, H. 1981. 'The Family as the Locus of Class, Gender and Political Struggle: The Example of Housework.' *Signs* 6(3): 366–94.

Harven, T. 1974. 'The Family as Process: The Historical Study of the Family Life Cycle.' *Journal of Social History* 7(3): 322–29.

Head, Wilson. 1975. *The Black Presence in the Canadian Mosaic*. Toronto: Ontario Human Rights Commission.

– 1984. 'Historical, Social, and Cultural Factors in the Adaptation of Nonwhite Students in Metropolitan Toronto Schools.' In *Multiculturalism in Canada: Social and Educational Perspectives*, edited by Ronald J. Samuda, John W. Berry, and Michel Laferrire, 266–79. Toronto: Allyn and Bacon.

Heinz, Walter R. 1987. 'The Transition from School to Work in Crisis: Coping with Threatening Unemployment.' *Journal of Adolescent Research* 2(2): 127–41.

- 1991. 'Status Passages, Social Risks and the Life Course: A Conceptual Framework.' In *Theoretical Advances in Life Course Research*, edited by Walter R. Heinz, 51–65. Weinheim: Deutscher Studien Verlag.
- 1995. 'Status Passages as Micro-Macro Linkages in Life Course.' In *Society and Biography: Interrelationships between Social Structure, Institutions and the Life Course*, edited by A. Weimann and W.R. Heinz. Weinheim: Deutscher Studiem Verlag.
- 1996a. *Transition from Education to Employment in a Comparative Perspective*. Toronto: Centre for International Studies, University of Toronto.
- 1996b. 'Youth Transition in Cross-Cultural Perspective: School-to-Work in Germany.' In *Youth in Transition: Perspectives on Research and Policy*, edited by Burt Gallaway and Joe Hudson, 2–13. Toronto: Thomson Educational Publishing.
- Ed. 1999. *From Education to Work: Cross-National Perspectives*. New York: Cambridge University Press.

Helmes-Hayes, Richard C., and Anton H. Turrittin. 1995. *Class Inequality, Social Justice and English-Language Canadian Sociology, 1945–1970: John Porter as an Exemplar*. Paper prepared for meetings of the Association for Canadian Studies in the United States, Seattle, Washington, 15–19 November.

Henry, Frances, and Effie Ginzberg. 1985. *Who Gets the Work: A Test of Racial Discrimination in Employment*. Toronto: Social Planning Council.

Henry, F., C. Mattis Tator, and T. Rees. 1995. *The Colour of Democracy: Racism in Canadian Society*. Toronto: Harcourt Brace & Company.

Herberg, Edward. 1982. 'Ethnic Family Characteristics and Educational Attainment.' *Multiculturalism* 5(3): 20–3.

Hessing, M. 1993. 'Mothers' Management of Their Combined Workloads: Clerical Work and Household Needs.' *Canadian Review of Sociology and Anthropology* 30(1): 37–63.

Hilliard, Marion. 1957. *A Woman Doctor Looks at Love and Life*. Garden City: Doubleday.

Hobart, Charles W. 1972. 'Orientations to Marriage among Young Canadians.' *Journal of Comparative Family Studies* 3(2): 171–93.
- 1974. 'The Social Context of Morality among Anglophone Canadian Students.' *Journal of Comparative Family Studies* 5(1): 26–40.
- 1979. 'The Courtship Process: Premarital Sexual Attitudes and Behaviour.' In *Courtship, Marriage and the Family in Canada*, edited by G.N. Ramu. Toronto: Macmillan.
- 1996. 'Intimacy and Family Life: Sexuality, Cohabitation, and Marriage.' In *Families: Changing Trends in Canada*, edited by Maureen Baker, 143–73. Toronto: McGraw-Hill Ryerson.

Hochschild, A.R. 1990. *The Second Shift*. New York: Avon Books.

Hoerning, Erika M., and Peter Alheit. 1995. 'Biographical Socialization.' *Current Sociology* 43(2–3): 14.

Hogan, Dennis P. 1981. *Transitions and Social Change: The Early Lives of American Men*. New York: Academic Press.

Hogan, Dennis P., and Nan Marie Astone. 1986. 'The Transition to Adulthood.' *Annual Review of Sociology* 1986(12): 109–30.

Hughes, Karen D. 1998. *Restructuring Work, Restructuring Gender: Women's Movement into Non-Traditional Occupations in Canada*. Paper prepared for Restructuring Work and the Life Course: An International Symposium, 7–9 May (Session C-2). University of Toronto, Canada.

Hughes, Karen D., and Graham S. Lowe. 1993. 'Unequal Returns: Gender Differences in Initial Employment among University Graduates.' *Canadian Journal of Higher Education* 23(1): 37–55.

Human Resources Development Canada. 1994. *Profile of Post-Secondary Education in Canada*. Ottawa: Education Support Branch, Human Resources Development Canada.

– 1995. 'Youth Face Tough Times.' *Internet*: http://hrdc-drhc.gc.ca

– 1996a. 'Youth Employment: Some Explanations and Future Prospects.' *Applied Research Bulletin* 2(2): 3–5.

– 1996b. 'Labour Market Polarization ... What's Going On.' *Applied Research Bulletin* 2(2): 5–7.

Iacovetta, Franca. 1995. 'Remaking Their Lives: Women Immigrants, Survivors, and Refugees.' In *A Diversity of Women: Ontario 1945–1980*, edited by Joy Parr, 135–67. Toronto: University of Toronto Press.

Ishwaran, K. 1976. *The Canadian Family*. Toronto: Holt, Rinehart and Winston.

– 1979a. 'Childhood and Adolescence in Canada: An Overview of Theory and Research.' In *Childhood and Adolescence in Canada*, ed. K. Ishawaran. Toronto: McGraw-Hill.

Ishwaran, K., and Kwok Chan. 1979b. 'The Socialization of Rural Adolescents.' In *Childhood and Adolescence in Canada*, edited by K. Ishawaran, 97–118. Toronto: McGraw-Hill Ryerson.

Jackson, R.W.B. 1977. 'A Statement of Conditions, Causes, and Issues: Interim Report.' A report to the Commission on Declining School Enrolments in Ontario, Ministry of Education.

Jacobs, Sheila C. 1995. 'Changing Patterns of Sex Segregated Occupations throughout the Life Course.' *European Sociological Review* 11(2): 157–71.

James, Carl E. 1990. *Making It: Black Youth, Racism and Career Aspirations in a Big City*. Oakville: Mosaic Press.

– 1993. 'Getting There and Staying There: Blacks' Employment Experience.' In *Transitions: Schooling and Employment in Canada*, ed. Paul Anisef and Paul Axelrod, 3–20. Toronto: Thompson Educational Publishing.

– 1995. *Seeing Ourselves: Exploring Race, Ethnicity and Culture*. Toronto: Thompson Educational Publishing.

– 1995a. 'Multicultural and Anti-Racism Education in Canada.' *Race, Gender & Class* 2(3): 31–48.

Jansen, Clifford 1981. *Education and Social Mobility of Immigrants: A Pilot Study Focussing on Italians in Vancouver*. Toronto York University: Institute for Behavioural Research.

Jasen, Patricia. 1989. 'In Pursuit of Human Values (or "Laugh When You Say That"): The Student Critique of the Arts Curriculum in the 1960s.' In *Youth, University and Canadian Society: Essays in the Social History of Higher Education*, edited by Paul Axelrod and John G. Reid, 247–71. Montreal and Kingston: McGill-Queen's University Press.

Johnson, Laura C., and Jeffrey G. Reitz. 1981. *Youth Unemployment in Metropolitan Toronto*. Toronto: Social Planning Council of Metropolitan Toronto.

Jones, Alan. 1994. 'Native Youth.' In *Learning and Sociological Profiles of Canadian High School Students: An Overview of 15 to 18 Year Olds and Educational Policy Implications for Dropouts, Exceptional Students, Employed Students, Immigrant Students, and Native Youth*, edited by Paul Anisef, 105–20. Queenston: Edwin Mellen Press.

Jones, Gill, and Claire Wallace. 1992. *Youth, Family and Citizenship*. Buckingham: Open University Press.

Jones, Gill. 1995. *Leaving Home*. Buckingham: Open University Press.

Kalbach, W.E., and W.W. McVey. 1979. *Demographic Bases of Canadian Society*. Toronto: McGraw-Hill.

Kalin, Rudolf. 1981. 'Ethnic Attitudes.' In *Canadian Social Psychology of Ethnic Relations*, edited by Robert C. Gardner and Rudolf Kalin. Toronto: Methuen.

Kallen, Evelyn, and Merrijoy Kelner. 1976. 'Parents and Peers: Who Influences Student Values.' In *The Canadian Family*, edited by K. Ishwaran, 213–26. Toronto: Holt-Rinehart and Winston.

Karp, David A., Gregory P. Stone, and Yoels C. William. 1991. *Being Urban: A Sociology of City Life*. New York: Praeger.

Kerckhoff, Alan C. 1995. 'Institutional Arrangements and Stratification Processes in Industrial Societies.' *Annual Review of Sociology* 1995(21): 323–48.

King, V., and G.H. Elder. 1995. 'American Children View Their Grandparents: Linked Lives across Three Rural Generations.' *Journal of Marriage and the Family* 57(1): 165–78.

Kostash, Myrna. 1986. *Long Way from Home: The Story of the Sixties Generation in Canada.* Toronto: Lorimer.

Krahn, Harvey. 1996. *School-Work Transition: Changing Patterns and Research Needs.* Consultation paper. Ottawa: Applied Research Branch, Human Resources Development Canada.

Krahn, Harvey, and Graham Lowe. 1991. 'Transitions to Work: Findings from a Longitudinal Study of High School and University Graduates in Three Canadian Cities.' In *Making Their Way: Education Training and the Labour Market in Canada and Britain,* edited by David Ashton and Graham Lowe, 130–70. Toronto: University of Toronto Press.

– 1993. *Work, Industry, and Canadian Society.* Scarborough, Ontario: Nelson Canada.

– 1998. *Work, Industry, and Canadian Society.* 3rd edition. Toronto: ITP Nelson.

– 1999. 'School-Work Transitions and Post-Modern Values: What's Changing in Canada?' In *From Education to Work: Cross-National Perspectives,* edited by W.R. Heinz, 260–83. Cambridge: Cambridge University Press.

Kruger, Helga. 1998. *Social Change in Two Generations, Employment Patterns and Their Costs for Family Life.* Paper prepared for International Conference on Restructuring Work and the Life Course. 7–9 May. Toronto.

Lam, Larry. 1994. 'Immigrant Students.' In *Learning and Sociological Profiles of Canadian High School Students: An Overview of 15 to 18 Year Olds and Educational Policy Implications for Dropouts, Exceptional Students, Employed Students, Immigrant Students, and Native Youth,* edited by Paul Anisef, 121–30. Queenston: Edwin Mellen Press.

La Novara, P. 1993. *A Portrait of Families in Canada.* Statistics Canada, Housing, Family and Social Statistics Division, Target Groups Project. Ottawa: Statistics Canada.

Larter, S., M. Cheng, S. Capps, and M. Lee. 1982. *Post Secondary Plans of Grade Eight Students and Related Variables.* Toronto: Board of Education for the City of Toronto.

LeBlanc, S., and V.W. Marshall. 1995. *Combining Work and Family: The Influence of Organizational Structure on Women's Work-Related Choices and Experiences.* Paper prepared for the Annual Conference of the Canadian Sociology and Anthropology Association, June. Quebec City.

LeDain, Gerald. 1973. 'Final Report of the Commission of Inquiry into the Non-Medical Use of Drugs.' Report to Information Canada.

Lennards, Jos. 1986. 'Education.' In *Sociology,* edited by Robert Hagedorn, 451–86. Toronto: Holt, Rinehart and Winston of Canada.

Lenton, R. 1992. 'Home versus Career: Attitudes Towards Women's Work among Canadian Women and Men, 1988.' *Canadian Journal of Sociology* 17(1): 89–98.

Leslie, G.E., and S.K. Korman. 1985. *The Family in Social Context*. New York: Oxford University Press.

Levesque, Jean-Marc. 1987. *Growth of a Part-time Work Force in a Changing Industrial Environment*. Ottawa: Statistics Canada.

Levin, Benjamin. 1995. 'How Can Schools Respond to Changes in Work?' *Canadian Vocational Journal* 30(3): 8–20.

Levine, Daniel U., and Rayna F. Levine. 1996. *Society and Education*. Boston: Allyn & Bacon.

Levitt, Cyril. 1984. *Children of Privilege: Student Revolt in the Sixties*. Toronto: University of Toronto Press.

Looker, E. Dianne. 1993. 'Interconnected Transitions and Their Costs; Gender and Urban/Rural Differences in the Transitions to Work.' In *Transitions: Schooling and Employment in Canada*, edited by Paul Anisef and Paul Axelrod, 43–64. Toronto: Thompson Educational Publishing.

– 1994. 'Active Capital: The Impact of Parents on Youths' Educational Performance and Plans.' In *Sociology of Education in Canada: Critical Perspectives in Theory, Research and Practice*, edited by Lorna Erwin and David MacLennan, 164–87. Toronto: Copp Clark Longman.

– 1995. 'Transitions to Adult Life.' Unpublished paper presented to the Youth 2000 Conference, July. Middlesbrough, England.

Looker, E. Dianne, and Peter C. Pineo. 1983. 'Social Psychological Variables and Their Relevance to the Status Attainment of Teenagers.' *American Journal of Sociology* 88(6): 1195–1219.

Lowe, Graham S., and Harvey Krahn. 1995. 'Destructuring or Restructuring of School-Work Transitions.' Paper prepared for the Sociology of Education Joint CSAA-CSSE Session, 4 June, Montreal.

Luxton, Meg. 1992. 'Two Hands for the Clock: Changing Patterns in the Gendered Division of Labour in the Home.' In *Canadian Family History*, edited by Bettina Bradbury, 304–18. Toronto: Copp Clark.

– 1996. 'Conceptualizing "Families": Theoretical Frameworks and Family Research.' In *Families: Changing Trends in Canada*, edited by Maureen Baker, 35–52. Toronto: McGraw-Hill Ryerson.

MacKinnon, Neil J., and Paul Anisef. 1979. 'Self-Assessment in the Early Educational Attainment Process.' *Canadian Review of Sociology and Anthropology* 16(3): 305–19.

Maclean's. 1975. 'Getting with the Seventies.' 21 January.

Macmillan, Ross. 1995. 'Changes in the Structure of Life Courses and the Decline of Social Capital in Canadian Society: A Time Series Analysis of Property Crime Rates.' *Canadian Journal of Sociology* 20(1): 51–79.

Makabe, T. 1980. 'Provincial Variations in Divorce Rates: A Canadian Case.' *Journal of Marriage and the Family* 42(1): 171–6.

Mandell, Nancy, and Stewart Crysdale. 1993. 'Gender Tracks: Male-Female Perceptions of Home-School-Work Transitions.' In *Transitions: Schooling and Employment in Canada*, edited by Paul Anisef and Paul Axelrod, 21–41. Toronto: Thompson Educational Publishing.

Mandell, Nancy, and Ann Duffy. Eds. 1988. *Reconstructing the Canadian Family: Feminist Perspectives*. Toronto: Butterworths.

Manzer, Ronald. 1994. *Public Schools and Political Ideas: Canadian Educational Policy in Historical Perspective*. Toronto: University of Toronto Press.

Mare, Robert D., and Christopher Winship. 1985. 'School Enrollment, Military Enlistment, and the Transition to Work: Implications for the Age Pattern of Employment.' In *Longitudinal Analysis of Labor Market Data*, edited by James J. Heckman and Burton Singer. New York: Cambridge University Press.

Marginson, Simon. 1995. 'The Decline in the Standing of Educational Credentials in Australia.' *Australian Journal of Education* 39(1): 67–76.

Marini, Margaret Mooney, Hee-Choon Shin, and Jennie Raymond. 1989. 'Socio-Economic Consequences of the Process of Transition to Adulthood.' *Social Science Research* 18(2): 89–135.

Marks, Gary N. 1992. 'Ascription Versus Achievement in Australia: Changes over Time 1965–1990.' *Australian and New Zealand Journal of Sociology* 28(3): 330–350.

Marquardt, Richard. 1998. *Enter at Your Own Risk: Canadian Youth and the Labour Market*. Toronto: Between the Lines.

Marsden, Lorna R., and Lorne J. Tepperman. 1985. 'The Migrant Wife: The Worst of All Worlds.' *Journal of Business Ethics* 4(3): 205–13.

Masemann, Vandra. 1975. 'Immigrant Students' Perceptions of Occupational Programs.' In *Education of Immigrant Students*, edited by Aaron Wolfgang, 107–21. Toronto: Ontario Institute for Studies in Education.

Matras, Judah. 1984. *Social Inequality, Stratification and Mobility*. Englewood Cliffs: Prentice Hall.

Mayer, Karl Ulrich, and Nancy Brandon Tuma. 1990. 'Life Course Research and Event History Analysis: An Overview.' In *Event History Analysis and Life Course Research*, edited by Karl Ulrich Mayer and Nancy Brandon Tuma, 3–22. Madison: University of Wisconsin.

McCalman, Janet. 1993. *Journeyings: The Biography of a Middle-Class Generation, 1920–1990*. Melbourne: Melbourne University Press.

McGuigan, G.F. Ed. 1968. *Student Protest*. Toronto: Metheun.

McGuire, W.J., C.W. Child, and T. Fujioka. 1978. 'Salience of Ethnicity in the Spontaneous Self-Concept as a Function of One's Ethnic Distinctiveness in the Social Environment.' *Journal of Personality and Social Psychology* 36(5): 511–20.

McRoberts, Hugh A. 1985. 'Mobility and Attainment in Canada: The Effects of Origin.' In *Ascription and Achievement: Studies in Mobility and Status Attainment in Canada,* edited by Boyd et al., 67–100. Ottawa: Carleton University Press.

Michalos, Alex C. 1980. 'Satisfaction and Happiness.' *Social Indicators Research* 8(4): 385–422.

Mitchell, Barbara A., and Ellen M. Gee. 1996. 'Young Adults Returning Home: Implications for Social Policy.' In *Youth in Transition: Perspectives on Research and Policy,* edited by Burt Galaway and Joe Hudson. Toronto: Thompson Educational Publishing.

Moen, P. 1992. *Women's Two Roles: A Contemporary Dilemma.* Westport: Auburn House.

Moloney, Joanne. 1986. *Recent Industry Trends in Employment.* Ottawa: Statistics Canada, Labour and Household Surveys Analysis Division.

Moon, Sueng Gyu. 1979. 'Courtship Process: Dating and Mate-Selection.' In *Courtship, Marriage, and the Family in Canada,* edited by G.N. Ramu. Toronto: MacMillan.

Morgan, D.H.J. 1985. *The Family, Politics and Social Theory.* London: Routledge and Kegan Paul.

Mortimer, J., and M.K. Johnson. 1999. 'Adolescent Part-time Work and Post-Secondary Transition Pathways: A Longitudinal Study of Work in St. Paul, Minnesota (U.S.).' In *From Education to Work: Cross-National Perspectives,* edited by W.R. Heinz, 111–48. Cambridge: Cambridge University Press.

Neatby, Hilda M. 1953. *So Little for the Mind.* Toronto: Clarke, Irwin.

Nett, Emily. 1986. *Canadian Families: Past and Present.* Toronto: Butterworths.

Neugarten, Bernice L. 1979. 'Time, Age and the Life Cycle.' *American Journal of Psychiatry,* 136(7): 887–94.

O'Neill, Jeff. 1994. 'Changing Occupational Structure.' In *Canadian Social Trends, A Canadian Studies Reader,* edited by Craig McKie and Keith Thompson, 259–64. Toronto: Thompson Educational Publishing.

O'Rand, Angela M., and Margaret L. Krecker. 1990. 'Concepts of the Life Cycle: Their History, Meanings, and Uses in the Social Sciences.' *Annual Review of Sociology and Anthropology* 1990(16): 241–62.

Ontario Legislative Assembly. 1965. 'Debates.'

Ontario Secondary School Teachers' Federation. 1976. *At What Cost? A Study of the Role of the Secondary School in Ontario.* Toronto: OSSTF.

Orenstein, Peggy. 1994. *School Girls: Young Women, Self-Esteem, and the Confidence Gap.* New York: Bantam Doubleday Dell.

Ostry, Sylvia. 1972. 'Quoted in *The Financial Post,* 23 February.'

Owram, Doug. 1992. *Coming Home: Family Expectations and Readjustments after the War, 1945–1950.* Paper prepared for Canadian Historical Association, Charlottetown, P.E.I.

– 1996. *Born at the Right Time: A History of the Baby-Boom Generation.* Toronto: University of Toronto Press.

Pavalko, Ronald, and David Bishop. Eds. 1968. *Peer Influence on the College Plans of Canadian High School Students.* Itasca: F.E. Peacock.

Peters, John. 1984. 'Cultural Variations in Family Structure.' In *The Family: Changing Trends in Canada,* edited by Maureen Baker, 63–84. Toronto: McGraw-Hill Ryerson.

Phillips, Myfanwy. 1975. 'Lives of Girls and Women, Interviews and Photographs.' *Maclean's,* 22–5 February.

Picot, W. Garnett, and Ted Wannell. 1987. *Job Loss and Labour Market: Adjustment in the Canadian Economy.* Ottawa: Social and Economic Studies Division, Statistics Canada.

Pierson, Ruth Roach. 1995. 'Education and Training.' In *Canadian Women's Issues, Volume II: Bold Visions,* edited by Ruth Roach Pierson and Marjorie Griffin Cohen. Toronto: Lorimer.

Pike, Robert M. 1970. *Who Doesn't Get to University – and Why.* Ottawa: Association of Universities and Colleges of Canada.

– 1975. 'Legal Access and the Incidence of Divorce in Canada: A Sociohistorical Analysis.' *Canadian Review of Sociology and Anthropology,* 12(2): 115–33.

Porter, James N. 1974. 'Race, Socialization and Mobility in Educational and Occupational Attainment.' *American Sociological Review* 39(3): 303–16.

Porter, John. 1965. *The Vertical Mosaic: An Analysis of Social Class and Power in Canada.* Toronto: University of Toronto Press.

Porter, John, et al. 1971. *Towards 2000: The Future of Post-Secondary Education in Ontario.* Toronto: McClelland & Stewart.

Porter, John, Marion R. Porter, and Bernard R. Blishen. 1973. *Does Money Matter? Prospects for Higher Education in Ontario.* Toronto: Macmillan.

Porter, J. 1987. *The Measure of Canadian Society: Education, Equality and Opportunity.* Ottawa: Carleton University Press.

Porter, J., M. Porter, and B. Blishen. 1982. *Stations and Callings: Making It through the School System.* Toronto: Methuen.

Prentice, Alison, et al. 1988. *Canadian Women: A History.* Toronto: Harcourt Brace Jovanovich.

Pringle, M.L.K. 1974. *The Needs of Children.* London: Hutchinson.

Quarter, Jack. 1973. *The Student Movement of the 1960s.* Toronto: OISE Press.

Rajulton, Fernando, and Zenaida R. Ravanera. 1995. 'The Family Life Course in Twentieth-Century Canada: Changes, Trends, and Interrelationships.'

In *Family over the Life Course,* edited by Roderic Beaujot, Ellen M. Gee, Fernando Rajulton and Zenaida R. Ravanera, 115–50. Ottawa: Statistics Canada.

Ramcharan, Subhas. 1975. 'Special Problems of Immigrant Children in the Toronto School System.' In *Education of Immigrant Students,* edited by Aaron Wolfgang. Toronto: Ontario Institute for Studies in Education.

Ramu, G.N. 1979. 'Courtship, Marriage and the Family in Canada: An Overview.' In *Courtship, Marriage and the Family,* edited by G.N. Ramu. Toronto: MacMillan.

Rea, K.J. 1985. *The Prosperous Years: The Economic History of Ontario, 1939–1975.* Toronto: University of Toronto Press.

Redpath, Lindsay. 1994. 'Education-Job Mismatch among Canadian University Graduates: Implications for Employers and Educators.' *Canadian Journal of Higher Education,* 24(2): 89–114.

Rich, John. 1971. 'Watching All the Liberated Girls Go By.' *Chatelaine.* April, 34.

Richmond, Anthony H., and Warren E. Kalbach. 1980. 'Factors in the Adjustment of Immigrants and Their Descendants.' Census Analytical Study, Cat. 99 –761. Ottawa: Statistics Canada.

Rindfuss, Ronald R. 1991. 'The Young Adult Years: Diversity, Structural Change, and Fertility.' *Demography* 28(4): 493–512.

Rindfuss, Ronald R., C. Gary Swicegood, and Rachel A. Rosenfeld. 1987. 'Disorder in the Life Course: How Common and Does It Matter?' *American Sociological Review* 52(6): 785–801.

Robb, A. Leslie, and Byron G. Spencer. 1981. *Unemployment and Labour Force Behaviour of Young People: Evidence from Ontario and Canada.* Toronto: Ontario Economic Council and University of Toronto Press.

Roberts, K., S.C. Clark, and Claire Wallace. 1994. 'Flexibility and Individualization: A Comparison of Transitions into Unemployment in England and Germany.' *Sociology* 28(1): 31–54.

Rockett, Eve. 1971. 'The Under 21s: What Are They Thinking?' *Chatelaine.* December, 40.

Rosenbaum, J. 1999. 'Institutional Networks and Informal Strategies for Improving Work-Entry for Disadvantaged Youth: New Directions for Research and Policy.' In *From Education to Work: Cross-National Perspectives,* edited by W.R. Heinz, 235–59. Cambridge: Cambridge University Press.

Rosenbaum, James E., and Takehiko Kariya. 1987. 'Japan Offers Way to Link School, Job.' *Forum for Applied Research and Public Policy* 4(4): 63–70.

Rosenbaum, James Ekariya, Rick Takehiko Settersten, and Tony Maier. 1990. 'Market and Network Theories of the Transition from High School to

Work: Their Application to Industrialized Societies.' *Annual Review of Sociology* 1990(16): 263–99.

Rothman, Robert A. 1987. *Working, Sociological Perspectives.* Englewood Cliffs: Prentice Hall.

Royal Commission on Learning. 1994. *For the Love of Learning: Report of the Royal Commission on Learning.* Toronto: The Royal Commission on Learning.

Rudd, P. and K. Evans. 1998. 'Structure and Agency in Youth Transitions: Student Experiences of Vocational Further Education.' *Journal of Youth Studies* 1(1): 39–62.

Sangster, Joan. 1995. 'Doing Two Jobs: The Wage Earning Mother, 1945–70.' In *A Diversity of Women: Ontario 1945–1980,* edited by Joy Parr, 98–134. Toronto: University of Toronto Press.

Schlossberg, Nancy K. 1984. *Counselling Adults in Transition.* New York: Springer.

Schneider, Barbara. 1994. 'Thinking about an Occupation: A New Developmental and Contextual Perspective.' In *Research in Sociology of Education and Socialization,* edited by Aaron Pallas, 239–59. Greenwich: American Sociological Association.

Setterstein, Richard A., Jr., and Karl U. Mayer. 1997. 'The Measurement of Age, Age Structuring, and the Life Course.' *Annual Review of Sociology* 1997(23): 233–62.

Sewell, John. 1993. *The Shape of the City: Toronto Struggles with Modern Planning.* Toronto: University of Toronto Press.

Shavit, Y., and H.P. Blossfeld. 1993. *Persistent Inequality.* Boulder: Westview.

Shilling, Chris. 1988. 'School to Work Programs and the Production of Alienation.' *British Journal of Sociology of Education* 9(2): 181–98.

Shulman, Norman, and Robert E. Drass. 1979. 'Motives and Modes of Internal Migration: Relocation in a Canadian City.' *Canadian Review of Sociology and Anthropology* 16(3): 333–42.

Simmons, Alan B., and Jean E. Turner. 1976. 'The Socialization of Sex-Roles and Fertility Ideas: A Study of Two Generations in Toronto.' *Journal of Comparative Family Studies* 7(2): 255–71.

Smart, Reginald G., and Dianne Fejer. 1974. *Changes in Drug Use in Toronto High Schools between 1972 and 1974.* Toronto: Addiction Research Foundation.

Special Committee on Visible Minorities in Canadian Society. 1984. *Equality Now: Participation of Visible Minorities in Canadian Society.* Ottawa: Ministry of Supply and Services.

Spring, Joel. 1976. *The Sorting Machine.* New York: David McKay.

Stamp, Robert. 1982. *The Schools of Ontario, 1876–1976*. Toronto: University of Toronto Press.

Statistics Canada. 1978. *Historical Compendium of Education Statistics, from Confederation to 1975*. Ottawa: Government of Canada.

– 1978b. *Out of School – Into the Labour Force: Trends and Prospects for Enrolment, School Leavers, and the Labour Force in Canada, the 1960s through the 1980s*. Ottawa: Ministry of Industry, Trade and Commerce.

– 1980. *Canada's Female Labour Force*. Ottawa: Statistics Canada.

– 1995. *The Labour Force Survey*. Ottawa: Statistics Canada.

Stephenson, Stanley P., Jr. 1979. 'From School to Work: A Transition with Job Search Implications.' *Youth & Society* 11(1): 114–32.

Stevenson, Hugh A. 1970. 'Developing Education in Post-War Canada to 1960.' In *Canadian Education: A History*, edited by J.D. Wilson, R.M. Stamp, and W.P. Audet. Scarborough: Prentice Hall.

Steward, Hartley. 1973. 'Thousands of Metro Youth Ready to Hit the Road.' *Toronto Star*, 26 May, 1.

Strong-Boag, Veronica. 1991. '"Home Dreams": Women and the Suburban Experiment in Canada, 1945–60.' *Canadian Historical Review* 72(4): 471–504.

– 1995. '"Their Side of the Story": Women's Voices from Ontario Suburbs, 1945–60.' In *A Diversity of Women: Ontario 1945–1980*, edited by Joy Parr, 46–74. Toronto: University of Toronto Press.

Sturino, Frank. 1980. 'Family and Kin Cohesion Among Southern Italian Immigrants in Toronto.' In *Canadian Families: Ethnic Variations*, edited by K. Ishwaran. Toronto: McGraw-Hill Ryerson.

Survey Research Centre. 1979. *Project: Ethnic Pluralism in an Urban Setting, 1978–79*. Toronto: Institute for Social Research, York University.

Tanner, Julian, Harvey Krahn, and Timothy F. Hartnagel. 1995. *Fractured Transitions from School to Work: Revisiting the Dropout Problem*. Toronto: Oxford University Press.

Thomas, Alan M. 1993. 'Transitions: From School to Work and Back: A New Paradigm.' In *Transitions: Schooling and Employment in Canada*, edited by Paul Anisef and Paul Axelrod, 117–27. Toronto: Thompson Educational Publishing.

Thompson, Nora K. 1971. 'Women's Rights: Two Perspectives.' *Canada and the World* 37(November): 7.

Tilly, L.A., and J.W. Scott. 1978. *Women, Work and Family*. New York: Holt, Rinehart and Winston.

Toronto Star. 1973a. 'Aimless Schools Hit "Bottom" with Lax Rules: Commissioner.' 7 May, 1.

- 1973b. 'High Schools' Meaningless Diploma.' Editorial. 30 March, 6.
- 1973c. 'Job Outlook Gloomy for Young Andras.' 12 November.
- 1973d. 'Parents Told How to Help Teens.' 9 May, 86.
- 1973e. 'Survey Shows Teachers Fear "Pick-Your-Own-Course" Harmful.' 12 June, 83.
- 1973f. 'Thousands of Metro Youth Ready to Hit the Road.' 26 May.
- 1973g. 'Toronto's Male-Dominated Bay Street Is Meeting Its Match.' 11 August.

Townson, M. 1995. *Women's Financial Futures: Mid-Life Prospects for a Secure Retirement.* Ottawa: Canadian Advisory Council on the Status of Women.

Treiman, Donald J. 1985. 'The Work Histories of Women and Men: What We Know and What We Need to Find Out.' In *Gender and the Life Course,* edited by Alice S. Rossi, 213–31. New York: Aldine.

Trottier, C., R. Cloutier, and L. Laforce. 1996. 'Vocational Integration of University Graduates: Typology and Multivariate Analysis.' *International Sociology* 11(1): 91–108.

Turritin, Anton H. 1974. 'Social Mobility in Canada: A Comparison of Three Provincial Studies and Some Methodological Questions.' *Canadian Review of Sociology and Anthropology* 1974 (special issue): 163–86.

Turrittin, Anton H., Paul Anisef, and Neil J. MacKinnon. 1983. 'Gender Differences in Educational Achievement: A Study of Social Inequality.' *Canadian Journal of Sociology* 8(4): 395–419.

Tyler, Elaine May. 1988. *Homeward Bound: American Families in the Cold War Era.* New York: Basic Books.

Vallee, Frank. 1981. 'The Sociology of John Porter: Ethnicity as Anachronism.' *Canadian Review of Sociology and Anthropology* 18(5): 639–50.

Vallee, Frank G., and Norman Shulman, 1969. 'The Viability of French Groupings Outside Quebec.' In *Regionalism in the Canadian Community, 1867–1967,* edited by Mason Wade, 83–99. Toronto: University of Toronto Press.

Venne, Rosemary A. 1996. 'Demographic and Career Issues Relating to Youth in Transition to Adulthood.' In *Youth in Transition, Perspectives on Research and Policy,* edited by B. Galaway and J. Hudson, 46–52. Toronto: Thompson Educational Publishing.

Vistnes, Jessica Primoff. 1997. 'Gender Differences in Days Lost from Work Due to Illness.' *Industrial and Labor Relations Review* 50(2) Jan: 304–23.

Wallace, Ruth A., and Alison Wolf. 1995. *Contemporary Sociological Theory, Continuing the Classical Tradition.* Englewood Cliffs: Prentice Hall.

Wand, Barbara. 1977. 'Sex Differences in Educational Aspirations and Academic Performance.' *High School Students Atlantis* 3(1, Autumn): 98–111.

Weir, Ramar, and Ronald J. Burke. 1979. 'Two People, Two Careers, and One Relationship! Making It Work.' *Business Quarterly* 44(1): 47–52.

Whitehurst, Bob. 1984. 'The Future of Marriage and the Nuclear Family.' In *The Family: Changing Trends in Canada,* edited by Maureen Baker. Toronto: McGraw Hill Ryerson.

Williams, Trevor H. 1972. 'Educational Aspirations: Longitudinal Evidence on Their Development in Canadian Youth.' *Sociology of Education* 45(2): 107–32.

Willis, Paul. 1977. *Learning to Labour: How Working Class Kids Get Working Class Jobs.* New York: Columbia University Press.

Willits, Fern K. 1988. 'Adolescent Behavior and Adult Success and Well-Being: A 37-Year Panel Study.' *Youth & Society* 20(1): 68–87.

Wilson, A. 1985. *Family.* London: Tavistock.

Wilson, J.D. 1982. 'From the Swinging Sixties to the Sobering Seventies.' In *Education in Canada: An Interpretation,* edited by E. Brian Titley and Peter J. Miller. Calgary: Detselig.

Wilson, Susannah J. 1990. 'Alternatives to Traditional Marriage.' In *Families: Changing Trends in Canada,* edited by Maureen Baker, 93–114. Toronto: McGraw-Hill Ryerson.

– 1991. *Women, Families and Work.* Toronto: McGraw-Hill Ryerson.

Wortherspoon, Terry. 1998. *Sociology of Education in Canada: Critical Perspectives.* Toronto: Oxford University Press.

Worthington, Helen. 1973. 'Parents Advised to "Hang Loose" When Children Shock Them.' *Toronto Star.* 19 October, E1.

Wright, E.N. 1970. 'Student's Background and Its Relationship to Class and Program in School [The Every Student Survey].' A Report to the Toronto Board of Education.

Wright, E.N. 1971. 'Program Placement Related to Selected Countries of Birth and Selected Languages.' A report to the Toronto Board of Education.

Wyn, Johanna. 1996. 'Youth in Transition to Adulthood in Australia: Review of Research and Policy Issues.' In *Youth in Transition: Perspectives on Research and Policy,* edited by Burt Gallaway and Joe Hudson, 14–22. Toronto: Thompson Educational Publishing.

Young, Copeland H., Kristen L. Savola, and Erin Phelps. 1991. *Inventory of Longitudinal Studies in the Social Sciences.* Newbury Park, California: Sage Publications.

Young, M., and P. Willmott. 1975. *The Symmetrical Family.* Middlesex: Penguin.

Index